Derrick Cargle's

Yee-da-dee
I Am that I Am
Yee-da-dee

HEBREW IN THE CHURCH

The Foundations of Jewish-Christian Dialogue

by

Pinchas E. Lapide

Translated by Erroll F. Rhodes

GRAND RAPIDS, MICHIGAN
WILLIAM B. EERDMANS PUBLISHING COMPANY

255 Jefferson Ave. S.E., Grand Rapids, Mich. 49505

Printed in the United States of America

Translated from Hebräisch in den Kirchen, *Forschungen zum jüdisch-christlichen Dialog 1, © Neukirchener Verlag, Neukirchen-Vluyn, 1976.*

Library of Congress Cataloging in Publication Data

Lapide, Phinn E., 1922-
Hebrew in the church.

Translation of: Hebräisch in den Kirchen.
Bibliography: p. 229
Includes index.
1. Hebrew language — Study and teaching — History.
2. Liturgical language — Hebrew. 3. Bible. N.T. Hebrew — Versions. 4. Christians — Israel. 5. Hebrew language — Religious aspects — Christianity. I. Title.
PJ4536.L313 1985 492.4'09 84-26044

ISBN 0-8028-3615-1

CONTENTS

FOREWORD

For anyone interested in Jewish-Christian relations in any aspect, this work opens up new vistas by providing a fund of information that is unique and has until now been largely inaccessible. The title certainly gives the impression that this book is concerned with a history of the use made of Hebrew on the part of Christian theology. But it is in fact, to the best of my knowledge, the only comprehensive attempt made thus far to survey all the efforts made among Christians and Jews from New Testament times for whatever reason to translate the New Testament and also the Christian liturgy into Hebrew, whether with the intent to convert Jews or to equip them with the tools necessary for discussing religion with Christians. Whatever the particular motive, the very fact of conversation serves a perennial human function in overcoming divisions. The demonstration of this fact is one of the virtues of this work.

Another virtue is the author's intimate knowledge of not only Biblical, but also of Mishnaic and Modern Hebrew, which has enabled him to appreciate the various translation efforts with an acute sensitivity. As a result, this work is virtually a catalogue of successes and failures in mutual understanding, exhibiting the full range of misunderstandings that have proceeded from the misconceptions of each other developed on either side.

And so, under the guise of a history of translations, this work provides far more than the mere data of history. For those who appreciate the significance of language, it is a most penetrating contribution to the entire history of Jewish-Christian relations, not only in its historical aspect, but also in its contemporary aspect with reference to the State of Israel, both of which are interesting and well deserving of attention. By reviewing the often shocking history of the relations between Christians and Jews from the perspective of their linguistic efforts to understand each other, not only is a fresh light brought to bear on the history itself, but important implications are also suggested, especially for anyone concerned with the exegesis of the New Testament.

This book is unprecedented. The mass of information assembled here is simply astounding. It should receive the serious attention not only of specialists but of all on both sides who work for a new encounter between Jews and Christians.

HELMUT GOLLWITZER
Free University of Berlin

Translator's Preface

Pinchas E. Lapide's survey of historic attempts by Christians and Jews to render parts or all of the New Testament into Hebrew was published in 1976 as the inaugural volume of *Forschungen zum jüdisch-christlichen Dialog,* a series of studies in Jewish-Christian dialogue under the editorship of Yehuda Aschkenasy and Heinz Kremers. It is a pioneering work, bringing together conveniently a wide range of information about Jewish-Christian encounters on the linguistic level in the medieval and modern periods, replete with documentary examples and references.

The works cited by Lapide have been quoted here from their published English translations whenever possible. Since the original work was written in the mid-1970s, the author has now added a supplementary chapter to update this American edition with further developments and publications since then. Some of these I have also mentioned in footnotes.

The translator owes a debt of gratitude to Professor Lapide, to the directors of Neukirchener Verlag, and to Mr. Allen Myers of Wm. B. Eerdmans Publishing Co. for their encouragement and kind assistance in making the present translation possible, to Prof. Oded Borowski of Emory University for counsel on medieval technicalities, and also to Harriet Rhodes for her patience and skill in producing a printable typescript from heavily corrected manuscript.

Erroll F. Rhodes

The Hebrew language is the best language of all, with the richest vocabulary. . . . If I were younger I would want to learn this language, because no one can really understand the Scriptures without it. For although the New Testament is written in Greek, it is full of hebraisms and Hebrew expressions. It has therefore been aptly said that the Hebrews drink from the spring, the Greeks from the stream that flows from it, and the Latins from a down-stream pool.

—MARTIN LUTHER, *Tischreden*

I

Hebrew: Lingua Sacra?

The New Testament has been translated, either completely or in part, into nearly eighteen hundred languages,[1] but among these the Hebrew language presents the best claim to central significance for the whole Bible. In the days of Jesus the common language of most Palestinian Jews was Aramaic, a language which was closely akin to Hebrew and was the source of most of the semiticisms found in the New Testament. But Hebrew remained the language of worship, of the Bible, and of religious discourse; in a word, it remained the sacred language (*lšwn hqdwš*) well into the period of the early Church. Otherwise it would be impossible to account for the great number of hebraisms in the New Testament, whose very frequency witnesses to their antiquity in the tradition as elements which resisted successfully all efforts at translation into Greek or into the Latin of the later Vulgate. The survival of original hebraic forms to the present in nearly all the languages of Europe demonstrates, in the words of François Mauriac, that Hebrew is the mother tongue of all the biblical religions.

It is difficult to imagine the New Testament without such key words or concepts as Sabbath,[2] Passover,[3] Messiah,[4] rabbi,[5] Israel,[6] hosanna,[7] hallelujah,[8] and amen, the last of which occurs thirty-one times in Matthew alone. Nor could the New Testament be imagined without its numerous Old Testament quotations or its key Hebrew concepts such as the kingdom of heaven, redeemer, the Passover meal, covenant with God, the end time, atonement, eternal life, election, love of neighbor, the grace of God, or words such as salvation, worship, the fall of man, or such names as Jacob, Judah (Jehuda), Simon, Joseph, John (Yoḥanan), Mary (Miriam), and Elizabeth (Elisheva) borne by eighteen of Jesus' companions.

Paul was proud of being a Jew (2 Cor. 11:22), a Hebrew of Hebrew ancestry (Phil. 3:5); the voice which he heard from heaven called to him in Hebrew (Acts 26:14); the last words of Jesus on the cross (Matt. 27:46; Mark 15:34) were quoted from a Hebrew psalm (Ps. 22:2)[9]—all these facts only reinforce the conviction that the theological structure of the Christian and Jewish scriptures alike are rooted in Hebrew soil.

The discovery of the Dead Sea Scrolls has laid to rest all literary and philological doubt that Aramaic had displaced Hebrew as the common language in the time of Jesus, yet it has clearly demonstrated that at least until the destruction of the Second Temple Jews considered the use of Hebrew normal for religious discourse. Not only do the Qumran texts illuminate many obscure passages in the New Testament,[10] they also reveal a close verbal similarity between the Hebrew writings of the Qumran sect and the thought world of the Synoptic Gospels.[11] This similarity has most probably contributed also to the persistence of the theory that the first Gospel was originally written in Hebrew. According to a tradition cited by Bishop Papias in the mid-second century C.E., the Jew Levi, who later became the apostle Matthew, compiled the "Logia" or sayings of Jesus and edited them "in the Hebrew language." Eusebius reports that "everyone translated them as best he could."[12] Eusebius also cites the church father Irenaeus as saying: "Matthew published a Gospel for the Hebrews in their own language."[13] And also Jerome, when studying in Antioch about 380, compared the Greek and Latin versions of the Gospels with the Hebrew text which he had found among the Ebionites of Aleppo.[14]

Epiphanius writes that the "Nazoraioi," the second Jewish-Christian sect, "carefully cherished the Hebrew language" in which they read both the Old Testament and the Gospel of Matthew.[15] Eusebius relates that Pantaenus found the Hebrew Matthew in use among the people of India,[16] and Franz Delitzsch believes that Trypho in Justin's *Dialogue* (mid-second century) refers to the Sermon on the Mount in this Gospel where he says: "The requirements stated in what you call your Gospel are so amazing and demanding that they seem to me impossible to observe."[17]

A tenth-century polemic in Arabic, based partly on a fifth-century Aramaic document, also seems to allude to this lost earliest Gospel. The manuscript, excerpts of which were recently published by Shlomo Pines,[18] contains a fairly accurate account of the teachings of the early Jerusalem church shortly after the death of Jesus. It is explicit in its praise of the Hebrew language, "the language of Christ and the prophets," in which "the true Gospel" had also been written,[19] and it censures the (non-Jewish) Christians for their apostasy from this language,[20] forsaking it for "other languages not spoken by Jesus and his disciples."[21] Further, in the fifth century Pope Nicholas V offered a considerable reward to anyone who could find a copy of the original Hebrew text of the Gospel of Matthew. Although the reward was never claimed, the search it instigated led to the beginnings of the present collection of Hebraica in the Vatican.[22]

At the time of the Reformation the claim is echoed even by such opponents of Hebrew studies as the scholar Johann Eck: "Hebrew is not a sacred language for the Christian church, for the Gospels were not written in it, with the exception of the Letter to the Hebrews and the Gospel of Matthew. . . ."[23] Delitzsch summarized: "An early tradition reports that the Christian scriptures began with Matthew writing his Gospel for the Hebrews in Hebrew. As early as the Middle Ages and also during the Reformation period attempts were made to translate it back into its original form."[24]

This hebraic character may be detected in the other Synoptic Gospels as well, according to Robert L. Lindsey, one of the leading New Testament translators in Israel today: "Rather to my surprise the preliminary study of the Greek text of Mark turned up the conclusion that the Greek word order and idiom was more like Hebrew than literary Greek. This gave me the frightening feeling that I was as much in the process of 'restoring' an original Hebrew work as in that of creating a new one."[25] A few pages later he remarks further: "It looked as if Luke had universally copied more faithfully whatever Greek sources he had and that those had been translated earlier from a Hebrew source or sources, or at least from some Semitic document or documents as much like Hebrew that in retranslation it was impossible to tell the difference."[26]

The rarity of Hebrew scholarship in Christendom during the millennium from Jerome to Johann Reuchlin is all the more astonishing. The Christian Middle Ages certainly acknowledged a (platonic) respect for Hebrew, but when the Latin Vulgate was recognized as the official standard text of the Bible, interest in the original Hebrew and Greek texts naturally waned. Further, even before Jerome the "language of the Jews" had come to be regarded increasingly by theologians as a symbol of the alien, the sinister, and the hostile. This was only a short step beyond the New Testament progression beginning with accusations of the Jews: "You are of your father the devil" (John 8:44), proceeding through the description of them as "those who say that they are Jews and are not, but are a synagogue of Satan" (Rev. 2:9; cf. 3:9), and ending in accusations of the collective guilt of deicide and impenitence, resulting in the Jewish people's rejection, their apostasy, their ostracism, and their condemnation—to cite only a few of the more salient clichés found in polemical caricatures of Judaism.[27] And further, from the time of Jerome and Augustine the parable of the barren fig tree (Matt. 21:18–22; Mark 11:12–14, 20–23; cf. Luke 13:6–9) was applied to the Jewish people. This alleged unfaithfulness of "Judaism, withered to the roots but still standing, attests by its very sterility to the divine curse which has struck it" is typical of dozens of pronouncements found in the writings of the Church Fathers from the fourth century on.[28] A student of the history of magic from antiquity to the medieval period has pointed out that "it was not at all rare to find hebraic equated with satanic."[29] Who could possibly have been interested in learning the language of a people so morally depraved, theologically condemned, and intellectually sterile!

And yet Hebrew remained a "lingua sacra"—and not just because of the trilingual inscription over the cross, as Augustine and other Fathers asserted[30]—preserving the Hebrew truth, as Jerome stressed and demonstrated.[31] This frequently produced an inconsistent view of the Jews, who were not only esteemed as the "people of the Book" and of the "Old Covenant," but also castigated as the "enemies of God" and "murderers of the Lord." Their language inherited a similar love-hate tension.

Typical of the ambivalence of the medieval Christian scholar's attitude toward the Hebrew language were the attitudes of Dante Alighieri, the greatest poet of the period, and of Desiderius Erasmus, the humanist of Rotterdam. Dante expressed a deep respect for the Hebrew language, but he never made any effort to learn it. It is true that in his native city of Florence there were few if any Jews,[32] yet from the thirteenth century there were Jewish communities in other cities of Tuscany, such as Pisa and Siena; and the Dominican Giordano da Rivolta, who preached in Florence from the beginning of the fourteenth century—to mention only one of Dante's contemporaries—often praised the Jewish teacher who had taught him Hebrew.[33]

Dante's familiarity with the books of the Hebrew Bible[34] is apparent not only in his frequent quotations and his numerous allusions to a variety of Old Testament persons, peoples, and places, but also in his use of Hebrew words which are left untranslated in the Septuagint (e.g., "Hosanna," "Lord Sabaoth," and "Malachoth" in *Purg.* xi.11; *Par.* viii.29; xxviii.118, etc.). It is also evident in his prose composition *De Vulgari Eloquentia* i.4, where Hebrew is described as the first language of mankind, the language of Adam, and where the first human word is identified as the Hebrew *El,* the word for God.[35] Dante continues: "This form of speech was inherited by the sons of Heber, and called Hebrew after him. It remained their peculiar possession after the confusion (of the Tower of Babel), so that our Savior, who was their descendant in his humanity, might use a language of grace and not of confusion. The Hebrew language, then, was formed by the lips of those who were the first to speak."[36]

Finally, it should also be noted with regard to this ambivalence that the two great Christian hebraists who stand at the beginning and end of the medieval period not only devoted decades of their lives to the study of Hebrew, but each found it necessary to make an apology to his contemporaries. In the preface to his translation of the books of Chronicles, Jerome stresses that the purpose of his work was the achievement of a reliable text "against the Jews"; and in the preface of his translation of Isaiah the author of the Vulgate writes:

> Qui scit me ob hoc in peregrinae linguae eruditione sudasse, ne Iudaei de falsitate scripturarum ecclesiis eius diutius insultarent. (He [i.e., the Christ] knows that it is for this purpose I have so labored in the study of a foreign language, that the Jews may no longer accuse his Church of perverting the scriptures.)

Reuchlin, the spiritual father of all modern Christian hebraists, wrote in his old age, some eleven hundred years later:

> Nulla me fames auri adegit ad Hebraica mysteria discenda, nulla inanis gloria sitis, ea enim studia tum celenda vulgo erant, ut quae in tanta dignitate constituto viderentur indecentia.[37] (It was not greed for gold that drove me to learn the mysteries of Hebrew, nor was it a desire for mere reputation. Rather, these studies had to be pursued in secret, because they were considered unworthy of a man of position.)

The medieval church was notoriously lacking in scientific method, and although great value was assigned to the interpretation of each word of holy scripture, very rarely if ever was there any consultation with the Jewish scholarship in any of the larger cities.[38] Yet there was a small number of Christian scholars who achieved a greater or lesser proficiency with Hebrew, not to mention an even greater number who made claims to it. Peter Browe, S.J., concedes that "ignorance of the Hebrew language" was one of the principal causes "for the small success of the Jewish mission" in the medieval period,[39] and he adds that when early medieval theologians such as "Hebraeus Maurus, Paschasius Radbertus, and Florus of Lyons wished to determine the precise meaning of a Hebrew expression, they had to consult with a rabbi."[40]

The study of Hebrew often brought "undesirable" results, as the following examples show:

—A Cistercian was disciplined in the Catalan monastery of Poblet in 1198 because he studied Hebrew with a Jew.[41]

—The Franciscan preacher Robert de Reddinge, who studied Hebrew with Jews in England about 1270, created no small sensation there when he converted to Judaism a year later.[42]

—In 1477 King John of Aragon in Sicily annulled a legacy which had been created by a Jew in Girgenti for the establishment of a chair in Hebrew studies, "because many Jews would receive training in Hebrew and the Talmud there, and be able to write against our faith."[43]

Since the area of Hebrew studies among Christians lies beyond the compass of the present work, we will only suggest some bibliography[44] and offer a few conclusions. Whenever a Christian achieved any extensive acquaintance with the biblical language, it was due to his association with a Jewish teacher. This fact is attested by such examples as Origen, Jerome, Raymundus Martini, Roger Bacon, and Reuchlin. Even enemies of the Jews such as Bishop Agobard of Lyons (779–840), the author of the libelous epistle *De insolentia Judaeorum,*[45] had to consult with Jews ''almost daily'' on matters of biblical exegesis.[46]

The number of Christian hebraists and their actual familiarity with the language, like so many other matters in this area, is still a matter of dispute. Charles Singer[47] recognizes only four western Christians who attained to anything like real Hebrew scholarship (and of these, he says, certainly one—Paul of Burgos—and perhaps also a second—Nicholas of Lyra—were converted Jews), while Geddes MacGregor[48] can count nine such scholars, and Jehuda M. Rosenthal mentions no less than seventy-two before the close of the fifteenth century.[49]

The circumstances in the late medieval period may be inferred from the example of the converted Jew Paulus de Bona Fide, the only teacher of Hebrew at the University of Paris from 1394 to 1420. His salary was inadequate for his needs, and he left Paris for Bezançon in 1420. His letter of commendation from the University of Paris described him as ''the only scholar in all France with a command of the Hebrew and Chaldee languages.''[50]

The fact that some free spirits succeeded in learning Hebrew despite the numerous edicts forbidding any association between Christians and Jews, and the concern among Jews, which was not wholly unjustified, about sharing a knowledge of the holy language (*lšwn hqdš*) with the gentiles,[51] demonstrates that no obstacles can deter a genuine desire for knowledge.

The motivation for nearly all Christian hebraists until well into the modern period was either the evangelization of the Jews[52] or the correction of the Vulgate, which had suffered transcriptional ''improvement'' in the medieval scriptoria, sometimes to the point of unintelligibility.

Only a few of these early hebraists bequeathed to us any substantive writings—apart from incomplete grammars, some letters, and some collections of quotations from the Bible or the Talmud—so that most of the early Christian Hebraica of the medieval period is anonymous.

II

MEDIEVAL CHRISTIAN HEBRAICA

Apart from a few scant references in the patristic literature to a "Hebrew Gospel" and/or a Hebrew original of the (first) Gospel, next to nothing is known about the Hebrew beginnings of early Christian literature. In the Arabic East the Gospels may have been known to many Jews in Arabic translations[1] as well as in the Syriac Peshitta version,[2] but in the early medieval West the number of Jews who read the New Testament in the Latin Vulgate version was probably no greater than the number of Christian hebraists of the time.[3]

The first steps toward translating Christian literature into Hebrew are shrouded in the mists of the early Carolingian period. Samuel Krauss attempts to prove that a Hebrew version of the New Testament already existed in the mid-ninth century, in the time of Bishop Amulo of Lyons (841–851).[4] Amulo, who is called by Cecil Roth one of "the fathers of medieval antisemitism,"[5] writes in his polemic work *Liber contra Judaeos*[6] that "by a malicious change in spelling, they call the Gospel 'The Wicked Scroll,'" but this polemic pun was cited even earlier in the Talmud,[7] and the enterprising bishop, who knew some Hebrew and would frequently trade insults with Jewish converts, never gives the slightest hint that he himself has seen a copy of Hebrew translation of the New Testament.

1. *The First Auinu Sebassamaim*

Indirect evidence of translated portions of the New Testament from this period is found in two different versions of the Pater Noster which both seem to have originated in the Carolingian Renaissance.

The earlier text[8] comprises fourteen groups of words in roman letters which transcribe the three verses of Matt. 6:9–11 in a defective form of Mishnaic Hebrew. The text comes from the mid-ninth century.

1 *Auinu . sebassamaim .*

2 *cudessatehe . semah .*

3 *tauo . Bemalchuthah .*
4 *tehe . rokonagkauassa .*
5 *amaim . uba . arez .*
6 *Lah . hemehenu . thamia .*
7 *tenlanu . haggeon .*

From this brief text all that can be determined with confidence is that it is an overly literal rendering of the Latin Vulgate, that the scribe was not familiar with Hebrew, and that unlike most later Hebrew renderings of the New Testament there is lacking any missionary purpose, because not a trace of Christian theology is to be found in these lines. The contrary is far more likely, for three words in the first three lines seem to be derived from the Kaddish, a Jewish (Aramaic) prayer most closely related to the Pater Noster and one of the oldest in use in the synagogue: the words *cudessa* (*qwdš'*), *semah* (*šmyh*), and *bemalchuthah* (*bmlkwtyh*). The textual affinity is obvious.

Pater Noster:	Hallowed be thy Name. Thy Kingdom come.
Kaddish:	Hallowed be his (great) Name. May he establish his Kingdom.

The words "his Name" and "his Kingdom" have apparently been changed to the second person singular masculine forms (*šmk, mlkwtk*). *Tmyd* "daily" (probably intended by *thamia*) is apparently found here in an adverbial sense probably derived from the Lucan form of the Vulgate text, "panem nostrum quotidianum" ("our daily bread"), a reading found also in the *Christiana Elementa Trilingua* of Petrus Artopoeus, published in Basel in 1545. The collocation of *lḥm* "bread" with *tmyd* (adverbial) is found in the Old Testament in a similar sense three times: 2 Sam. 9:7, 10; Jer. 52:33. Further, *lḥm tmyd*, or continual bread, is used in Num. 4:7 as a synonym for the Showbread (*lḥm hpnym*), which was replaced fresh every Sabbath in the Temple and was consumed by the priests as "sacrosanct."[9]

This attempted back-translation of the Lord's Prayer could well have originated about 835 C.E., in the Lyons of Bishop Agobard—an era not only when Jews and Christians mingled together as friends, but when many Christians were in frequent attendance at the synagogue and said that "the Jews preach better than do our own priests"—as Bishop Agobard complained with a touch of bitterness.[10] Or it could perhaps be related to the missal of the court chaplain of Louis I the Pious, the aristocratic Aleman Bodo, who began to learn Hebrew at precisely this time before converting to Judaism in 839.

The "Sephardic" pronunciation (of the Arabian diaspora) is noticeable, with its stressed gutturals which the scribe heard quite distinctly and took pains to reproduce explicitly (even to excess, e.g., *lah . hemehenu*).

2. *The Abinu Sebacamaim of Cusa*

This text consists of twenty-eight word groups in Latin transcription (litteris majusculis) and is found on folio 64 (recto) of the so-called *Psalterium Triplex Cusanum.*[11] It derives from the late ninth or the early tenth century, and translates the entire Pater Noster in the Matthean form without the doxology. The manuscript of sixty-six folios contains Pss. 109–150 in the Greek of the Septuagint text, a Latin transcription of the Greek, and the Latin of the Gallican Psalter. Following the Hebrew Pater Noster are given also the Hebrew, Greek, and Latin alphabets, apparently to fill out or ornament the final pages.

The text as edited by Karl Ludwig Friedrich Hamann reads as follows:[12]

1 *Abinu . Sebacamaim . acadec . at simak . ibua*
2 *malcothak . vihi . hephzhak . kabassamain*
3 *vba ares; lehem silanv . tamid tenlanv*
4 *hic iom . vahanna hlanv . hobotinv*
5 *kamoseanv manihim . hobotinv . vaalto*
6 *likaotanv . benitselom vaatsilinv*
7 *mi re*

Despite certain superficial similarities, this translation does not seem to be derived from the one discussed above, but rather from a scribe familiar with Mishnaic Hebrew and Aramaic. This is evident inter alia from *acadec at simak* in line 1, which is apparently derived from the Targum version of Ezek. 36:23, and also from the correct imperative in line 4 (*hanna*) and in line 6 (*atsilinv*), which is a slip but reflects the proper Hebrew forms. Less elegant, however, are *silanv* and *kamoseanv*.

As a translation it is less literal and consequently better than the previous one, but the scribe's nearly complete ignorance of the Hebrew language is evident from the errors in word division (e.g., *vahanna hlanv* and *vaalto likaotanv*), slips (e.g., *ibua* for *tbw'*), and errors of hearing (*benitsilom* for *bnsywn*).

In line 5 the word *lbʿly* has evidently been omitted before *hobotinv*, but even more surprising is the omission of the Hebrew Amen at the end of the last verse. The recurrence of *tamid* to translate "supersubstantialem" can hardly be coincidental, particularly as it appears also in Latin versions. Did some medieval forms of the Vulgate read "quotidianum"[13] or even "sempiternum"? Or did the Christian hebraist translate the difficult Greek "epioúsion" in this simplified way for his Jewish mentor? *Tmyd* seems to be used here adverbially—an irregular use, but found also in Jer. 52:33 and 2 Sam. 9:7. In 2 Kgs. 25:29 *lḥm tmyd* is used in the same sense as in the Pater Noster and in the following verse is explained more explicitly as *'rḥt tmyd* "continual allowance."

Since it also occurs as a synonym for the Showbread in Num. 4:7, as noted above, "continual bread (offering)" can be regarded as an Old Testament expression.

The pronunciation of the Jewish translator, who apparently dictated, was characteristic of pre-Ashkenazi Sephardic Hebrew, in which Chaim Rabin has demonstrated that *heth* (ח) was pronounced as *he* (ה) until the twelfth century in the German and French diaspora.[14]

3. *The German Abinu Aschär Baschamaim*

This version is from a collection of the Pater Noster as translated into twenty-eight languages and preserved in three manuscripts. First compiled by Jacques Cellier and François Merlin in 1583[15] it was further edited in 1593[16] and 1597.[17] The text with its trivial variants was edited recently by Jean Carmignac.[18] The Rheims manuscript reads as follows:

1 *Abinu aschär basschamaim:*
2 *iikkadesch schimcha. Thabo ma-*
3 *cutcha: Thieiäch rethzoncha,*
4 *chemo basschamaim chem be-*
5 *arätz: Lahhemenu thamid ti-*
6 *than lanu haiiom: vatthissa la-*
7 *nu mascheotheinu chemo, anah-*
8 *henu nose ini lehhobeinu: velo*
9 *thebienu leniassaion: Æla hatz-*
10 *zilenu min hara. Amen.*

The Germanic origin of the scribe, if not of the translator, is clearly indicated by two orthographical traits: (a) the Hebrew seghol is transcribed three times with the umlaut ä (*aschär, thieiäch, bearätz*), and once in capital letters as *Æ* (*Æla*); (b) the Hebrew *shin* (שׁ) is rendered *sch* six times (*aschär, basschamaim* twice, *iikkadesch, schimcha, maschiotheinu*). Both these transcriptions would be inconceivable from a Spanish, Italian, French, or Slavic background, and they also indicate a *terminus ad quem* (fifteenth-sixteenth century) for the transcription, if not for the version. The Hebrew is not only without error (such slight slips as *macutcha* and *nose ini* are doubtless due to the scribe), but even classically biblical in its vocabulary and syntax. The biblical *ʾšr* "which" should be noted, in contrast to the talmudic *še* of the two earlier versions. In the fourth petition of the Pater Noster the *thamid* is of interest for its phonetically precise rendering of *tau* (ת) as *th,* as well as for its translation of the Vulgate "supersubstantialem."

The translation of the verb "dimittere" ("dismiss," lit. "let down") and its object "debita" ("debts") in the fifth petition by the closely corresponding Hebrew words *nšʾ* and *mšʾh* (in the biblical sense of "pardon" and "debt") is peculiar here. Carmignac's suggestion[19] that the play on words is continued alliteratively in the next petition by *nsywn* "temptation," which must surely be intended by *leniassaion,* is open to question. The fact that the translation is not only literal in all ten lines, but even follows the word order of the Latin Vulgate, suggests that *thissa–mascheotheinu–nose ini–niassaion* is an attempt to provide a Hebrew parallel to the alliteration of the key words in Latin: "dimittere–debita–dimittimus–debitores."

On folio 28 of this same Ms. 1111 of the St. Genevieve Library, Paris, there is a rhymed version of the Pater Noster in Old High German taken from the heroic poem *Krist* [*Christian*] composed by Otfrid von Weissenburg in 860 C.E. While this fact alone is hardly sufficient to justify Carmignac's sanguine proposal that the *Abinu* comes from the same period, yet it is not altogether impossible, for others of the twenty-eight versions of the Pater Noster (such as the Icelandic, Arabic, and Armenian) appear to be from the eleventh and twelfth centuries.

4. The Credo and Magnificat from Kaisheim

The twelfth-century manuscript Clm 7955 in the Cistercian monastery at Kaisheim contains on folio 154 (verso) a Latin transcription of the Apostles' Creed in Hebrew and of the Magnificat (Luke 1:46–55). Despite numerous scribal errors which mar whole sentences, it is possible to decipher both texts from the context. As might be expected in early texts of this kind, the translation is so literally dependent on the Vulgate that the Hebrew is intelligible only in the light of the Latin text.

In the Apostles' Creed the following may be noted specifically.

(a) *Tigga bez* for "crucifixus." Only the *bez,* which undoubtedly represents *bʿṣ* "on a tree," is clear, although it seems that the translator follows the Jewish understanding of "tree" in the sense of "cross," found also in Acts 10:39. Yet instead of citing Deut. 21:22 (*wtlyt ʾtw ʿl-ʿṣ* "and you hang him on a tree"), he seems to refer to Gen. 3:3 (*wmpry hʿṣ . . . wlʾ tgʿw bw* "and of the fruit of the tree . . . neither shall you touch it"). Theology was naturally more important than philological accuracy to the translator, and when he thought of the implications of "crucifixus etiam pro nobis" ("crucified even for us"), associations would easily suggest the fall of man in the garden of Eden (he was doubtless also familiar with the medieval contrast between the first Adam who sinned and Christ the second Adam who atoned for sin), and it would have been only a short step to *wlʾ tgʿ* (*bʿṣ*) "and do not touch (the tree)." The well-known curse on a hanged man (*ky-qllt h″*[20] *tlwy* "for a hanged man is cursed by God") in Deut. 21:23 could have given pause to a translator familiar with the Pentateuch.

(b) *Liminauif* for "ad dexteram Patris" ("at the right hand of the Father") with the addition of "his" Father could reflect either familiarity with Jewish liturgical usage (*'b* "father" always has a personal suffix in the synagogue prayers) or the intention of the translator to stress the divine Sonship of Jesus.

(c) The interpolation *el auif col iacol* coming after the words "ad dexteram Patris" could also be theologically significant, for it places an emphasis on monotheism in a way that would be particularly pleasing to Jews.

(d) *Bazar hegiaz vheie ed* is a rare anacolouthon for "carnis resurrectio" ("resurrection of the body") which brings together significantly the "end of all flesh" (Gen. 6:13) with "eternal life."

(e) *Kadoz edad byiehet kadosim svtafin* should represent "sanctam ecclesiam catholicam sanctorum communionem" ("the holy catholic church, the communion of saints"). If *edad byiehet* here can be construed as "the whole church," then the "holy fellowship" reflects "apostoli."[21]

The version of the Magnificat in the same manuscript is awkward at times to the point of the ridiculous. "Magnificat" ("magnifies"), for example, is rendered *kadol esza,* and "fecit potentiam" ("he has shown strength") is *eza hezaka*. But elsewhere, especially in quotations from the Old Testament, the version is splendid, e.g.:

Luke 1:50 "et misericordia eius a progenie in progenies timentibus eum"
verechmaf midor lador lireaf

1:52 "deposuit potentes de sede et exaltavit humiles"
mazbil moslim michizozzam anauim

1:55 The final verse is typical of the Old Testament, both in vocabulary and thought: "sicut locutus est ad patres nostros Abraham et semini eius in saecula"
Kazer amar lavozzenv leabraham visareo ed olam

Such expressions as *'l-yr'yw* "upon those who fear him" (Ps. 103:17), *'ny 'mtw* "the affliction of his maidservant" (1 Sam. 1:11), *mšpyl mwšlym* "he brings low those who have dominion" (2:7), *ks' kbd* "seat of honor" (v. 8), *r'bym ml'-ṭwb* "the hungry he fills with good things" (Ps. 107:9), *ky 'šrwny* "for they will call me happy" (Gen. 30:13), etc., are easily recognized as derived from the Old Testament.

The transcription here is imprecise (e.g., *sama* for *nšmh* "breath, spirit," *dolot* for *gdwlwt* "great things"), and inconsistent, as it is in so many manuscripts.

—*Shin* (שׁ) is often represented by *z* (*zelli* for *šly* "my"), often by *sz* (*iszi* for *yš'y*), but also by *s* (*smo* for *šmw* "his name").

—*Heth* (ח) is usually *ch* (*lachen, samyech, zachar*), but also occasionally *h* (*mispahoz, hezaka iannihum*).

—*Tau* (ת) is frequently *z* (*ge doloz, daaz, amozv*), but also *zz* (*lavozzenv*).

Because of its numerous scribal errors, it is quite questionable to what extent this text may be useful in determining the pronunciation of (Ashkenazi) Hebrew in the twelfth century.

The great difference in the quality of the Hebrew justifies the hypothesis that the first two verses of this version of the Magnificat were not derived from the same pen as the remainder of the prayer. The first part is the work of a novice, while the last is at times masterful.

5. The New Testament Passages in the Pugio Fidei

A religious debate was held publicly in Barcelona in 1263 before King James I of Aragon between Rabbi Moses ben Nachman (Nachmanides) and the convert Pablo Christiani, in which the victory was achieved by Pablo according to Latin sources but by Nachmanides according to the Hebrew accounts. One of its results was a papal bull against the Talmud which Pablo compiled at Rome in 1264 and brought with him to Spain. James I implemented it by ordering the confiscation of all Hebrew books belonging to Jews within his realm, which included parts of southern Provence, and their examination for blasphemous passages by an ecclesiastical committee of five members, which would deal with them appropriately.[22] Of the five the only qualified hebraist was the Dominican Raymundus Martini,[23] a monk who had studied Hebrew, Arabic, and Aramaic for several years in the school of Raymundus de Peñaforte, and later occupied the chair of Hebrew studies at Barcelona until 1282.[24] It seems certain that he was responsible for reading most if not all of the confiscated writings. Thirteen years later (1278) Martini published his *Pugio Fidei adversus Mauros et Judaeos*, an eight-hundred-page work containing extensive quotations from the Babylonian and Jerusalem Talmuds, the *Midrash Rabbah, Sipra, Sipre,* the *Mekilta,* the works on biblical exegesis by Redaq (David Kimḥi), Nachmanides, and Abraham ibn Ezra, as well as from the *Mishneh Torah* and the *Moreh Nebuḥim* [*Guide for the Perplexed*] of Maimonides. Among the sources cited in Martini's monumental work, which was to become the vade mecum of all Christian religious polemicists, were also some quotations from the New Testament in Hebrew. In the Carpzov edition (Leipzig: 1687) these included only Matt. 2:1–12 (page 772); Matt. 3:13–15; and Mark 16:15–16 (both on page 818); the editio princeps (Paris apud Ioannem Henault: 1651) also included Matt. 4:17; 19:29; Luke 6:20; and Rom. 14:17 (all on page 606).

The greater part of Martini's *Pugio Fidei* is directed against the "Saracens and Infidels," and in his arguments Martini exhibits a remarkable knowledge of Arabic literature, so that the scarcity of New Testament quotations is understandable. He evidently made use of many others, probably the most important ones, in his lost second work, *Capistrum Judaeorum*, an attempt to confute and convert the Jews which is alluded to in the *Pugio Fidei* (page 290 of the Leipzig edition) as a general resource against the Jews.

Not only Alexander Marx[25] but Jehuda M. Rosenthal[26] and Adolf Neubauer[27] as well are confident that the Hebrew New Testament quotations in the *Pugio Fidei*, along with the hundreds of other Hebrew quotations, were taken from the confiscated Hebrew books in the library at Aragon. Marx draws the inference that "a Hebrew translation of the Gospels existed in Spain in the thirteenth century."[28]

A closer examination of the New Testament Hebraica in the *Pugio Fidei* permits the hypothesis that Martini himself was the translator of the Gospel passages he cites. That he was competent is attested not only by the hundreds of passages he translated correctly into Latin from biblical, rabbinic, and exegetical Hebrew sources, but also by the praise of such renowned hebraists as Leopold Zunz,[29] Heinrich Hirsch Graetz (who goes so far as to claim that Martini had a better command of Hebrew than did Jerome),[30] and Neubauer.[31] And there is even less doubt as to his motivation. His writings and his biography richly attest that his zeal to convert the Jews was the principal reason for his decades of devotion to the study of the Hebrew language and its theological literature. And yet his knowledge of the Hebrew language and of Jewish thought was not sufficient to exempt him from certain mistranslations and errors.[32]

It still remains to be proved that the few New Testament passages which have survived are from his hand, and not from the Jews of Aragon. The following comparison with translations of the New Testament by Jewish authors strengthens the case for Martini's authorship.

(a) Only Christians and converts such as Giovanni Battista Jona translate "Jesus" as *yšwʿ*, which appears five times in the *Pugio Fidei*. Jakob ben Reuben (twelfth century) and Shemtob ibn Shaprut (fourteenth century) consistently use *yšw* in order to avoid the soteriological meaning of the name (cf. Matt. 1:21).

(b) The "Magi" of Matt. 2:1 are referred to by Ibn Shaprut correctly though pejoratively as *ḥwzym bkwkbym* "those who gaze on the stars," and by Bishop Jean Du Tillet (1555) as *mkšpym* "sorcerers." But only a Christian apologist can translate this exegetically as *mlkym ḥkmym bkwkbym* "kings wise in the stars" as does Martini.

(c) And again, a Jewish pen would rightly balk at translating literally "principes sacerdotum" (Matt. 2:4), because there actually never existed any *r'šy hkhnym* "heads of the priests," just as "scribae populi'' (''scribes of the people'') in the same verse were never known in Israel. Only a Christian hebraist could translate the Vulgate literally as *r'šy hkhnym wswpry h'm* ''heads of the priests and scribes of the people,'' while Ibn Shaprut, for example, translates the meaning less literally as *gdwly hḥkmym whswprym* ''great ones of the wise men and the scribes.''

(d) Christian as well as Jewish translators (Sebastian Münster, Du Tillet, Ibn Shaprut, and Battista Jona) translate ''per prophetam'' (Matt. 2:5) simply as *'l yd hnby'* (lit. ''by the hand of the prophet'') or *mpy hnby'* ''from the mouth of the prophet.'' But this does not satisfy Martini the missionary, who supplements the Vulgate with *'l yd hnby' mykh* ''by the hand of the prophet Micah,'' to indicate precisely the Old Testament reference for the birthplace of Jesus.

(e) No Jewish or Jewish-Christian translator of Matthew has ever taken the liberty Martini permitted himself in the story of Jesus' birth: he simply omits both verses of Matt. 2:7–8, evidently because they are irrelevant to his purpose of demonstrating the biblically-determined manner of Jesus' birth. He compensates for the omission by arbitrarily changing the words ''qui cum audissent regem'' (''and when they heard the king,'' v. 9) to ''cum reges audissent,'' i.e., *wk'šr šm'w hmlkym* ''and when the kings heard.'' He also omits completely, evidently as irrelevant, the words ''apertis thesauris suis'' (''opening their treasures'') at the end of v. 11.

(f) While Jewish translators are all content with rendering ''adoraverunt eum'' as *wyšthww lw* ''and worshipped him'' (Matt. 2:11), only a Christian exegete would exaggerate this adoration to *wyšthwn lw 'pyym 'rṣh* ''and worshipped him with their faces to the earth.''

(g) The Jewish translations by Ben Reuben and Ibn Shaprut both render ''ut baptizaretur ab eo'' (Matt. 3:13) correctly as *lhṭbl mmnw* ''to be baptized by him.'' The passive form which appears in the next verse as ''baptizari'' is rendered by both Jews with the niphal form. Only Martini insists on the incorrect active form *lṭbwl* in both verses.

(h) The meaning of John the Baptist's unidiomatic Hebrew expression (Matt. 3:14) is given correctly by Ben Reuben (*'ny r'wy lhywt nṭbl mmk w'th b' 'ly* ''I need to be baptized by you and you come to me'' as well as by Ibn Shaprut (*ṣryk 'ny lṭbwl 'l ydk w'th tbw' 'ly* ''I need to be baptized by your hand but you come to me.'' Martini did not lack for Hebrew vocabulary, but his insensitivity to nuances transformed the Baptist's protest into *ṣryk 'ny lṭbwl 'l ydk w'th tbw' 'ly* ''I need to baptize by your hand and you come to me.''

(i) Latinisms, which are not only alien to Hebrew, but which also reveal a greater familiarity with the Vulgate than could be expected among medieval Jews, are frequent in Martini's work.

(i) In Matt. 19:29 he translates ''centuplum'' literally as *m'h pʿmym* "a hundred times," while Ibn Shaprut translates with the more biblically correct *m'h šʿrym* "a hundred measures." Admittedly *m'h šʿrym* occurs only once in Gen. 26:12, yet it is a frequent formula of blessing in the synagogue liturgy—in analogy with the "hundredfold" blessing Isaac received.

(ii) Martini translates "regnum Dei" in the first Lucan Beatitude (Luke 6:20) with *mlkwt 'lhym* "Kingdom of Elohim (God)," an expression completely literal and un-Jewish, found in no Jewish translator prior to the nineteenth century.

In conclusion, it may be stated that while the individual examples cited above could well be attributed to chance or to scribal error, their cumulative weight makes it almost certain that the author of the *Pugio Fidei* is probably the first Christian hebraist known to us by name to have translated any substantial part of the New Testament into Hebrew.

6. Petrus Negri's Eight Prayers

One of the first hebraists among the German humanists was Petrus Negri (1435–1483), who entered the Dominican order about 1460 at Salamanca in Spain, and "was instructed in Hebrew by Jewish teachers along with Jewish children."[33] The Hebrew prayer he composed for the foreword of his missionary essay *Tractatus contra perfidos Judaeos de conditionibus veri Messiae* (published at Esslingen in 1475) is linguistically interesting. Because it is the first work of its kind, it is reproduced here in his own transcription and Latin translation.

"Messia fili altissimi / confirma tu dicta mea"
Messchia ben helion tamoch attah debarai
"Jhesu nazarene / miserere mei festina domine"
Jeschuah hanozri huenneni maher adonai
"custodi me a peccato o petra mea et fortitudo mea"
Schomreni mi hauon anna zalhi ve zurai
"satan ne superbus rapiat / animam vite mee"
Schatan pen sadon iitrof lenefes haiai
"recipe me de inferno pone in terram robustissimi i.e. dei"
Qah oti mischol siti be erez schadai Amen.

If one overlooks the generous poetic liberty Negri indulges here at the expense of both Hebrew grammar and syntax, we can appreciate in this the first attempt to compose a Hebrew-Christian prayer. The elements of both rhythm and meter reveal the author's interest in psalmody, although it is unknown whether this prayer was intended to be said or sung.

The other seven hebraized prayers and liturgical selections (Nunc Dimittis, Magnificat, Pater Noster, Ave Maria, Credo in Deum, Gloria

Patri, Angelus) suffer from numerous scribal errors, inconsistencies, confusions of Biblical, Mishnaic, and Modern Hebrew, and poorly translated latinisms.

It is interesting to compare the text of the Credo with its twelfth-century antecedents, and of the Pater Noster with its ninth- and tenth-century antecedents.

Credo in Deum (twelfth century)	**Petrus Negri**
"Animaemin beel avi	*Maamin ani baJhuh haab*
col iacol bore samaym varez	*kol ischol bore schamaim vaarez*
vui iesv messias	*vbaJeschuah hamaschiah*
bno ehet	*beno ehad*
adonay lanv hara	*adonenu hanolid*
rvha kadoz	*meruah haqqodesch*
Nolat me Maria alma	*iulad mimirJam hahalma*
Saual bi poncia pilato	*azur tahat ponze pilat*
tigga bez vmez venicbar	*talui met veniqbar*
viarad lege hinnam	*Jarad el scheol*
vuerum [!] hazlizi kam	*vbaschlischi iom iaqam*
min hamiza	*mim hammetim*
vela lazamaym	*halah el hasschamaim*
viozef liminauif el	*iaschaf lemin adonai*
auif col iacol	*ab kol iachol*
Eherehim ezzit	*mischam labo*
lispot eheyim vahamezim.	*ladun hahaiim vehametim.*
Animaemin ruha kadoz	*Maamin ani beruah haqqodesch*
kadoz edad byiehet kadosim	*qedoschah haqqahal ioschrim*
svtafin kaparaz es amos	*qedoschim zod kaper hauonot*
bazar hegiaz vheie ed	*besar iequmot hai holamim.*
Amen."	*Amen.*

(a) "In Deum." Only a non-Jew could have used the Tetragram here (*baJhuh*); the twelfth-century Jew would normally translate *ʾl* "God."

(b) "Crucifixus." The non-Jew felt no compunctions with regard to *tlwy* in Deut. 21:23. On the contrary, although it means "hanged," it appeared to him simply as the equivalent of "crucified," and therefore he omitted *ʿl ʿṣ* "on a tree."

(c) "Jeschuah." Since the fifteenth century all translators have followed in Negri's footsteps, returning to the original etymological meaning of the biblical name. The fact that this twelfth-century Jew wrote "iesv" (*yšw*) shows that the pronunciation without the final guttural (found also in the second column of Origen's *Hexapla*) lacked any pejorative nuance.

(d) "Mischam labo." a latinism from "inde venturus est" ("thenceforth he has come") just as "sanctam ecclesiam catholicam sanctorum communionem" ("holy catholic church, communion of saints") becomes *qedoschah haqqahal ioschrim qedoschim zod.* If "catholicus" is intended by *yšr,* Negri evidently had in mind formulas such as *qhl hyšrym hqdwš* "congregation of the holy community" and *swd hqdwšym* (lit. "holy counsel"), with *swd* understood as "fellowship" in the sense of Ps. 111:1 and Jer. 6:11.

(e) "Carnis resurrectionem." Negri has *besar iequmot,* perhaps a corruption of *tqwmh* "arising," and standing in sequence with *hauonot,* perhaps also an example of homoioteleuton.

The Pater Noster exhibits several new expressions.[34]

Tefillah le Meschiah ben helJon.
Abinu asscher baschamaim
niqdasch schimcha kische iabo
malchutcha ihJeh rezoncha ken
baschamaim ken baarez.
Lahamenu iom iom ten lanu haJom
vmho lanu hafonotenu kaascher
anu mohalim onauotenu (margin:
uel hazbechenu) ve lo tabinu
lemazzah ki im tinzerennu
mi rah. Amen.

(a) *Niqdasch* is an improvement over *cudessa* and *acadec* in the earliest versions, but it is still more primitive than *iikkadesch* in the Rheims version of the sixteenth century. Negri's bold attempt to combine both petitions of Matt. 6:10 in a single conditional construction is interesting theologically as well as grammatically. Is it possible that this recognized theologian and scholastic of the University at Ingolstadt misunderstood these simple sentences in the Vulgate? Or could he have thought that a simple mistranslation into Hebrew would in some way promote his missionary purposes among the Jews?

(b) *Iom iom* is postbiblical, and as a translation of Gk. "epioúsion" appears to be an exegetical novelty. In this context it can only be taken as adverbial, but the threefold use of *iom* in a single line is only one of a large number of stylistic gaucheries.

(c) *Onauotenu* is impossible as a translation of "debitoribus nostris" ("our debts"). Negri himself sensed this and added in the margin *uel hazbechenu*. Apparently intended was *msbykynw* "those who would ensnare or confound us."

(d) *Massă* for "tentatio" ("trial") is proper Biblical Hebrew.

This is surprising here because the same petition is found nearly verbatim in the daily morning prayer of the synagogue, but as *w'l tby'nw . . . lydy nsywn* "and do not bring us . . . to the hands of temptation" with the postbiblical *nsywn* for "temptation"—as it also appears in the earlier translations of the Pater Noster.[35]

III

Medieval Jewish New Testament Hebraica

The Christian Church, daughter of the Synagogue, proclaimed herself as the sole fulfilment of Israel. This alone was sufficient to produce friction and rivalry. But from the days of Paul, as the new faith added non-Jewish elements[1] to its Jewish heritage, the seed of conflict was sown. The divisive strains were painful, and despite many conciliatory voices on either side, the introduction of gentile elements in the early Church easily gave occasion to anti-Jewish incidents.

Bitter echoes of this schismatic sibling quarreling may be found in the Talmud,[2] in the (now blunted) insertion in the twelfth petition of the Shemoneh ʿEsreh prayer,[3] in some three dozen New Testament passages,[4] and especially in the numerous references to "the Jews" in the Fourth Gospel. The position of the early Church was not easy. Struggling with its own Jewish Christians and Judaizers on the one hand, and against the anti-Jewish extremists such as the heresiarch Marcion on the other, it faced the task of proving to the pagan world of late antiquity that it, and it alone, was the "true Israel," and that Judaism was merely an illegitimate pretender to the title of a kingdom it had founded and which still carried its name—and this all had to be demonstrated from Jewish sources. Christian rulers since the fourth century have denied to Judaism—a defeated cult, without a temple, and in exile—any participation in the contemporary scene. Theologians deprived it of any eschatological future—the Messiah had already come—and by laying claim to the whole of the Hebrew scriptures the Church Fathers robbed the synagogue of even its own past.

The Jewish canon of Holy Scripture comprising the Law, the Prophets, and the Writings (*Torah, Nebiim, Ketubim*) was first demoted to the status of an "Old Testament"—still sacred, but obsolete—then exploited by means of innumerable subtle mistranslations as a quarry for some 160 christological allusions, and finally used to belabor the Jews with all the sins, slanders, and imprecations of their own prophets.

The heroes of the scriptures were interpreted ex post facto as Christians, or reinterpreted by a prefigurative typology in a Christocentric universe.

> From the Jewish standpoint, this most incredible plundering of history converted the Old Testament to the service of the Church. The experience of a thousand years of Jewish prophets, priests, sages, sons and fathers, expressed in prayer, sacrifice, liturgy, poetry, and proclamation—the fruit of unspeakable suffering and grief long before and long after the Babylonian Captivity—all of this fell as spoils to the "New Israel," the church, as its own unquestionable heritage.

This statement by a Catholic religious historian[5] aptly formulates the feelings of the Tannaim and the later Amoraim with regard to the *ecclesia triumphans,* most eloquently expressed in their systematic attempt to ignore it completely. By ignoring all heresies—especially Christianity, which was regarded as a Jewish heresy—the intent was to consign them to oblivion. Furthermore, after the *privilegia odiosa* of the Theodosian Code and the even more offensive Justinian Code, the Jews, as the result of external pressures, also experienced the paradoxical fear of holding negative attitudes towards the Nazarenes yet of not permitting them expression even in ostensibly free religious discussions.

Despite this doubly grounded silence, Jewish reactions to Jesus and his church found expression in the talmudic Ben-Pandera legend cycle and in the later *Toledot Yeshu,*[6] a Jewish anti-Gospel which Heinrich H. Graetz called "a parody of the Gospels."[7] Although this "piece of folklore," as Joseph Klausner more generously described it,[8] contains numerous paraphrases of the New Testament in Hebrew and a few almost verbal citations, most religious historians do not credit it with any real historical value.

This stands in contrast with the apologetic literature of Christianity from the second century, which required the presence of Jewish partners in presenting real or imaginary dialogues proving the messianic role of Jesus, the abrogation of the Torah, and the mission of the Church—in short, the truth of Christianity on the grounds of the "falsity" of Judaism! The Jason-Papiscus Dispute, the Timothy-Aquila Discussion, and the Trypho–Justin Martyr Dialogue,[9] to mention only the most important, represent from the second century the prototypical contrast of the Christian protagonist triumphant and the nervous Jew on the defensive.

In the course of several centuries this unequal contrast produced a threefold reaction within European Judaism, which was no longer content to accept the passive role ascribed to it by the Christian intelligentsia. The first reaction was to assemble Old Testament citations in a kind of theological antitestimonia proving that God had not rejected his people, that the Messiah had not yet come, and that Jesus could not be the Redeemer foretold by the prophets.[10] A second reaction sought to repay Christian attacks in like coin by citing the Old Testament with particular constructions and nuances, but with a non-Christian tendency. Such passages, which may be traced to Rabbi Eliezer (late second century) in the Mishnah, include Num. 23:19 (Balaam); Deut. 13:6–9; Isa. 44:6–8; and Prov. 24:21.[11] A third reaction was a counteroffensive which sought to transfer the battlefield to the New Testament. For this purpose the Christian scriptures had to be studied, and that in the original text if possible.

1. *Three Early Fragments*

The noted hebraist Adolf Neubauer stated: "It is remarkable that Jews in every age read the New Testament, some from curiosity, and others for controversy. We shall see that they even made a Hebrew translation of it."[12] The sources concede to him at least a partial justification.

(a) The earliest quotation from the New Testament (perhaps from the lost Aramaic [Matthaean?] stage of the tradition) is found in the Babylonian Talmud, in an episode which cites Rabbi Gamaliel and Rabbi Meir (before the end of the second century), where the following paraphrase of Matt. 5:17 also appears:

> "I have not come to detract from the Law of Moses,
> Nor have I come to add to the Law of Moses." (*Šabb.* 116a)

In the same passage "the Law of the *ʿwwn glywn*" (literally, "the sin of the scroll") is indicated as a source, so that there is no doubt that the New Testament is intended, even though Jesus is not mentioned explicitly.

(b) A fragment from the Cairo Geniza apparently from the mid-ninth century[13] which inveighs in Hebrew against Christianity, Islam, the Karaites, and the Samaritans, contains an allusion to Matt. 27:34 together with a brief citation of Isa. 44:20.

> They gave him lime (?) in vinegar, and God will not save him . . . in the presence of those who persecute him.

The trinitarian formula appears in Aramaic a few sentences later:

> Therefore they called Jesus, the son of Panderas, Father and Son and Holy Spirit . . .

as well as the terms "New Israel" and "New Covenant":

> For the Christians came only to appropriate for themselves the heritage of Israel, and their erring teachers deceived them, telling

them: "You are the sons of the New Israel, and you will be given a new teaching, a new heart, a new covenant, and a new heaven and a new earth . . . and this is the Messiah, the son of David."

(c) Also to be noted here is the work *Hobot ha-Lebabot* [*Duties of the Heart*] by Baḥya ibn Paquda (*ca.* 1050–1120), which was translated from Arabic into Hebrew by Jehuda ibn Tibbon. The critical edition[14] includes a paraphrase of Matt. 5:33–37 which describes a *ḥasid* teaching his "disciples".

And one of the pious said to his disciples: "The Law permits us to swear to the truth in the name of the Creator. But I tell you not to swear by Him, whether truly or falsely. Say yes or no . . ."

2. *The Book of Nestor Hakkomer*

This document, "which can be called the first serious attempt in Hebrew to compose a critique of the New Testament,"[15] belongs to the early apocryphal period of polemic. Its author, place, and date are still in dispute. The document comprises some fifteen folios and is attributed to a monk by the name of Nestor, who wrote to a brother in his order when on the brink of conversion to Judaism. In it he presents thirty-five theological arguments to convince the brother of the truth of Judaism. The unknown author refers to himself simply as "Nestor Hakkomer" at both the beginning and the end of the manuscript.

The oldest manuscripts are written in good Biblical Hebrew, and may be dated by palaeographic, stylistic, and linguistic criteria, as well as by several historical references in the text itself, to the period between the sixth and ninth centuries. The provenance is certainly to be sought in the Middle East.

The document is preserved with a great number of textual changes and variants in many manuscripts, including two late medieval manuscripts in the Vatican;[16] it served as a pattern for nearly all subsequent anti-Christian tracts. It is even cited specifically in certain Jewish polemic writings which acknowledge their indebtedness to its arguments with gratitude, such as the *Milḥamot ha-Shem* [*Wars of the Lord*] of Jakob ben Reuben,[17] the *ʿEzer ha-Dat* [*Defense of the Religion*] of Isaac ben Joseph Pulgar, and the *Magen we-Romaḥ* [*Shield and Spear*] of Ḥayyim ibn Musa.[18] It is duly noted in Johann Christoph Wolf, *Bibliotheca Hebraea*,[19] in Giovanni Bernardo de Rossi, *Bibliotheca Judaica Antichristiana*,[20] as well as in Umberto Cassuto's Vatican catalogue,[21] and in Jehuda M. Rosenthal's bibliography of Jewish anti-Christian polemics.[22]

A single reference to the author, which should be weighed with the greatest caution, is found in a brief note about a certain "Nestor" appended in several manuscripts of the *Toledot Yeshu* [*The Generations of Jesus*], e.g., in the nineteenth chapter of the Jellinck manuscript:[23]

> Afterward (i.e., after Paul) the kingdom of Persia came again to power. At that time there lived a Christian called Nestor. . . . He said, "You (i.e., the Catholics) are heretical because you claim that Jesus was God, although he was born of a woman (*ylwd-'šh*) and was therefore a son of man (*bn-'dm*). The Holy Spirit was uon him, as upon one of the prophets. . . ." This Nestor was the first to engage in controversy with the *nwṣrym* ["Christians"] . . . . Nestor then came to *'rṣ-yśr'l* ["the land of Israel"], where he said: "Paul deceives you when he says you should not be circumcised. On the contrary, *mylh* ["circumcision"] is necessary, because *yšw* ["Jesus"] was himself circumcised."[24]

Since all the above arguments are found in the Nestor text, the author of the *Toledot* must have been familiar with at least its contents, if not with the identity of its author.

It should be noted incidentally that the Patriarch Nestorius was taunted with being "a Jew" at the Council of Chalcedon (451 C.E.) because of his Old Testament interests. Several of his disciples in the East were frequently called similar names or worse by other Christian dignitaries.[25] Later all Nestorians in the Eastern churches were slandered as "Jews" because of their literal and historical exegesis.

The text was first edited by Abraham Berliner in 1875. The title page of this edition promises the reader a preface discussing the biographical and bibliographical details of the work in German (*bśpt 'šknz* "in the German language"), but the fifteen-page work contains neither a foreword nor an epilogue.[26] The Berliner edition was reprinted with minor revisions and corrections by Judah David Eisenstein in his *Anthology*.[27] A critical analysis of the text is still needed.

The document reveals not only a thorough knowledge of both Testaments but also a certain familiarity with Greek philosophy, and is free of the bitterness and sharp irony of later polemic works. Brevity, objectivity, and rhetorical skill characterize its contents, which include twenty-five rather extensive quotations from the New Testament, a greater number of paraphrases, and several quotations from Christian apocrypha (which I have not been able to identify). Several of the New Testament quotations differ from the canonical text, especially in four passages which are cited in Hebrew transliterations of the Greek text. The languge is Biblical Hebrew with a small admixture of mishnaic expressions and some obvious hellenisms.[28]

Of linguistic interest are the Hebrew translations of such theological terms as "incarnatio" (*h'lh 'lyw bśr* "he caused flesh to come upon him"; *hbn htlbš bśr* "the son clothed himself with flesh"), "apotheosis" (*l'śwtw 'lwqh* "to make him God"), "homoousios" (*yšw hyh bšwh ʿm 'byw* "his being is equivalent with his father"), and "dyophysitism" (*ht'ḥd bw h'lwqwt wh'nwšwt* "unification in him of divinity and humanity").

Circumlocutions for hypostasis, Trinity, and the problems of Arianism and Monotheletism are also found in Nestor. He stresses the loyalty of Jesus (*yšw*) to the Torah, and is even prepared to concede prophetic powers to him, but refuses to accept the birth stories (*l' bšwm nwld wl' b'šr ywld* "neither in establishing descent nor in confirming birth"), the unbiblical idolatry of his contemporaries ("the Holy Cross found by Queen Helena"), prayer to relics, and celibacy—"none of these is to be found in the Gospel."[29]

The translation of Matt. 5:17 should also be mentioned, for Nestor adds to it the first word of the next verse ("Amen") but translates it as *'mt* ("truth"): "I have not come to oppose or to diminish the Law and the Prophets, but rather to fulfil it with words of truth."

3. *Jakob ben Reuben's Wars of the Lord*

About 1170 the rabbinic scholar Jakob ben Reuben[30] composed a book which he called *Sepher ha-Mekaḥed weha-Meyaḥed* [*Book of the Denier and the Affirmer*],[31] but which was copied and circulated later under a number of titles,[32] one of the most popular of which was *Sepher Milḥamot ha-Shem* [*Book of the Wars of the Lord*]. In the prefatory remarks the author states that in his native[33] Gascoigne, from which he was now in exile,[34] he had known a noble and scholarly priest who once asked him: "How long will you and your brothers insist on being blind to the truth of Christianity? Are you not diminishing daily in numbers and prestige, while we are growing? . . . I want to ask you just one question, and hope you will answer me in all frankness."[35] And Ben Reuben continues: "Whereupon he took the books . . . first of Jerome, then of Augustine, and then of Paul (Pablos) . . . those pillars of error . . . and of Gregory (Grigorî)[36] who made music from their books (sic!). . . . After listening to his questions I gave him the answers I now offer here in my book."[37]

The book is divided into twelve chapters, "just as our father Jacob had twelve sons,"[38] in which (except for the last two chapters) the Denier begins the dialogue with an attack, to which the Affirmer (i.e., the author) responds pointedly, sometimes sarcastically. This is probably not only the most aggressive, but also the most liberal example of a religious debate in the medieval period, because both disputants maintain a high spiritual level, and both speak frankly and freely. The author insists that his friend the priest challenged him to speak openly and fearlessly, which witnesses to a spirit of tolerance rare in the twelfth century outside Provence and Gascoigne.[39] The twelve chapters treat in sequence:

(a) The Trinity, the Virgin Birth, and the Incarnation of Jesus
(b) Christological implications in the Pentateuch
(c) Christology in the Psalms
(d) Christology in Jeremiah
(e) Christology in Isaiah
(f) Christology in Ezekiel
(g) Christology in the Latter Prophets
(h) Christology in the Book of Daniel
(i) Christology in the Book of Job
(j) Christology in the Proverbs
(k) The first systematic critique of the Gospels, especially of Matthew, against which Ben Reuben raises sixteen objections
(l) Proofs from the scriptures that the Messiah has not come, derived from the writings of Saadia Gaon,[40] Ibn Ezra, Abraham bar Ḥiyya, and other scholars of the Torah.

The work is written in fluent Mishnaic Hebrew (except, of course, for the many Old Testament quotations in the original Biblical Hebrew) and contains many citations from patristic literature, e.g., Isidor of Seville, Jerome, Eusebius, Novatian, Justin Martyr, Tertullian, and even Marcion, as well as dozens of theological expressions which Ben Reuben himself coined in Hebrew or hebraized, e.g.,

"Trinitas"	*šlwš* "three"	"trinity"
"Triunitas"	*šlwš š'ynw ywṣ' mkll mḥwd* (lit.) "three persons, each different"	"trinity"
"Salvatio"	*lhwšyʿ nbr'ym* "to deliver creation"	"salvation"
"Incarnatio"	*hnbr' btbn't bśr* "the creature made of flesh"	"incarnation"
"Theologia"	*ḥkmt dywynyt'd* "wisdom of divinity"	"theology"
"Beata passio"	*nṣlb bʿd yṣwryw* "crucifixion on behalf of his creatures"	"atonement"
"Substantia"	*yšwt* "being"	"entity"
"Peccatum originale"	*ḥṭ' qdmwn* "ancient sin"	"original sin"
"Evangelium"	*'wngylywš, 'wnglyws,* also *sprm* "their book," *dbry ʿdwtm* "their witness"	"gospel"
"Persona"	*prṣwp,* derived in Mishnaic Hebrew from the Greek "prósōpon"; hebraized by Ben Reuben (*pyrswn'*), who cites Tertullian in Romance Latin transliterated in Hebrew: "persona distintas realmente, tres in persona et una in substantia" ("distinct persons in reality, three in person and one in substance")	"person"

''Spiritus sanctus qui ex patre filioque procedit''	*whrwḥ ywṣ' mbyn šnyhm hw' h'b whw' hbn* ''and the spirit proceeding from the two of them, the one who is the father and the one who is the son''	''the Holy Spirit who proceeds from the Father and the Son''

Ben Reuben protests vigorously against Jerome's christological translations. For example:

Isa. 16:1	''Emitte agnum'' for *šilḥû-ḵar* ''they have sent lambs''
45:8	''Salvatorem'' for *yešaʿ* ''Savior''
51:5	''Salvator meus'' (''my Savior'') for *yāṣāʾ yišʿî* ''my salvation has gone forth''
62:11	''Ecce salvator tuus venit'' for *hinnēh yišʿēḵ bā* ''Behold your savior comes''
Lam. 4:20	''Christus dominus captus est in peccatis nostris'' (''Christ the Lord . . .'') for *m^{e}šîaḥ h'' nilkaḏ bišḥîṯôṯām* ''the Lord's anointed was taken in their traps''
Hab. 3:13	''In salutem cum christo tuo'' (''. . . your Christ'') for *l^{e}yēšaʿ eṯ-m^{e}šîḥeḵā* ''for the salvation of thy anointed''
3:18	''In Deo Iesu meo'' (lit. ''in the God of my Jesus'') for *ʾagîlâ bēlōhê yišʿî* ''I will rejoice in the God of my salvation.''

He protests particularly that secular rulers such as Saul (1 Sam. 24:6) and Cyrus (Isa. 45:1), who are admittedly designated *māšîaḥ* (i.e., ''anointed'') in the Old Testament, are called ''Christ'' in the Vulgate.

Similarly *ʿalmâ* in Isa. 7:14 should not be ''virgo,'' but ''a young woman,'' and *ʿaḏ kî-yāḇōʾ šîlōh* in Gen. 49:10 is not ''donec veniat qui mittendus est'' (''until the one who was sent comes'') but ''until Shiloh comes.''

Besides fourteen quotations and paraphrases scattered through the first ten chapters of the book, there are nineteen extensive quotations from Matthew in the eleventh chapter introduced by the rubric ''His questions are over, and now I interrogate him on the Gospel.'' The passages are arranged in the following order:

Matt. 1:1–16	12:1–8	21:19
3:3–17	8:1–4	28:16–19
4:1–11	9:13	16:21–25
5:33–39	10:32	18:11–13
5:39–40	26:36–39	13:10–13
5:43–44	26:41	12:30–32
11:25–27		

Some quotations and interpolations not in the canonical New Testament text are also found in Ben Reuben, e.g., John 5:30 "What I have said is not from myself but from God who himself sent me and who places words on men's lips,"[41] which is followed by the sentence: "And Jesus said further about himself, 'I am a servant and a prophet, and a messenger from God' ";[42] "And Jesus said again in the book of Simon Cephas: 'Behold, the Devil purposes to kill me, but I will ask God to shorten my days and not deliver me into the hands of Satan' ";[43] "And another time he (Jesus) said: 'Serve God, my Lord and your Lord.' "[44]

In contrast to the dialogue in the first ten chapters, the eleventh chapter begins with a brief preface in which Ben Reuben expresses his hesitation and reluctance to write down the arguments that follow, but "my friend persuaded me to say something about them . . . so I have noted briefly only a few of the errors in their book . . ."[45] And then the Affirmer (i.e., the author) cites passages from the New Testament, following each citation with a refutation which may be derived at times from Nestor Hakkomer, or from the works of Saadia Gaon,[46] but more frequently seem to be of his own composition.

A polemic interest is also reflected in Ben Reuben's translation. In the very first verse (Matt. 1:1) he translates *spr twldwt yšw qrysṭw* and explains the last word with the marginal note: "i.e., Messiah"; in v. 16 the transliteration *qrysṭws* occurs, again untranslated. "Jesus" is generally rendered as *yšw* or *yš″*w. The latter form, with the double stroke like that used for abbreviations in Hebrew (commonly in the names of well-known people, such as Rambam and Rashi), could have the following meanings according to rabbinical usage.

(a) *ymḥ šmw yzkrw* "May his name and his memory be blotted out" (cf. Ps. 109:13–14; Deut. 9:14).

(b) *yšmrnw wyṣylnw* "May he protect and save us" (a common liturgical formula).

(c) *yb' šylh wlw* "Shiloh will come, and him (will the nations obey)." This obscure passage in Gen. 49:10 is construed messianically in both Jewish and Christian tradition.[47]

The end of Matt. 1:16 appears in nearly all manuscripts as a literal translation of the Latin Vulgate: "de qua natus est Iesus" (*ywsp 'yš mrym) hw' 'šr nwld mmnh yšw,* lit. "(Joseph the husband of Mary) the one who was born of her, Jesus"; the Oxford manuscript 2192, however, reads: *hw' 'šr nwld mmnw yšw* ". . . who was born of him . . . ," which is a patent reference to the fatherhood of Joseph, such as is found also in an Old Syriac manuscript of the New Testament[48] as well as in the whole manuscript tradition of the *Toledot Yeshu.*[49]

In the pericope Matt. 5:33–44 on the "intensification of the Law" the thrice-repeated "ergo autem dico vobis" ("but I say to you") is attenuated in a less aggressive *w'ny 'wmr lkm*. Perhaps to locate Jesus' roots in the morality of the Old Testament, "non resistere malo" in v. 39 is translated by Ps. 37:1 "Be not angry at those who do evil," while the later verse on "loving enemies" (v. 43) is attenuated by interpretation and hebraized to "hating enemies"; "diliges . . . tuum" now becomes "love your neighbor as yourself" (as in Lev. 19:18), "which commands only the love of neighbors (i.e., friends), and permits hating enemies." Ben Reuben was well aware that Jewish literature nowhere contains a commandment to hate enemies,[50] so that this gloss was objective rather than tendentious.

It is difficult to know whether the softening of the verb "vellere" in Matt. 12:1 (which means "to pluck" as does the corresponding Greek verb "tíllein"—an activity forbidden on the Sabbath) to the Hebrew *lqṭ* "to glean" (an act permitted on the Sabbath according to some Pharisaic authorities) reflects an apologetic interest. In any event, it seems to represent Jesus in a kindlier light and the Pharisees as more harsh and legalistic.

Clearer examples are the strengthening of "quidam autem dubitaverunt" ("some of them doubted") in Matt. 28:17 to the Hebrew "and some of them did not believe," and the shortening of the trinitarian formula following in v. 19 to "in the name of the Father, the Son, and the Spirit." Ben Reuben's translation of the immediately preceding words "docete . . . eos" as "teach all the nations (*gwym*) baptism" is evidently due to his own misunderstanding. This suggestion gains in credibility on reviewing some of the translation errors traceable to his faulty knowledge of Latin. For example:

—"Pinnaculum templi" (4:5) as *pnt hmqdš* "the corner of the temple."

—"Parvulus" (11:25) as *lqṭnym* "the little ones, children."

—"Quid vobis videtur" (18:12) as *mh r'wy lkm?* "What can you see?"

—"Mane autem . . ." (21:18) as "And it was at evening . . ."—possibly through association with the phrase "and it was evening" repeated six times in Gen. 1.

—In "oves quae perierunt domus Israhel" (15:24) Ben Reuben evidently did not recognize the genitive case of "domus" ("house"), for he translated it literally *ṣ'n 'bdwt byt 'śr'l* "the lost sheep, the house of Israel" (following Jer. 50:6), omitting the necessary preposition *l(byt)*.

—The translation error in 15:23, "dimitte eam" as *šlḥ n' 'lyk* "send to you," is interesting, suggesting that Ben Reuben may have had the legal formula "dimissus" in mind, which is frequently reproduced in the Talmud as *dymûs* (or *dymôs*)[51] and translated as *pṭwr 'th* "remove her"—unless he confused "dimitte" ("send down") with "remitte" ("send back")!

—"Decapoli" in 4:25 is translated overliterally as "ten villages."

—"Si cadens adoraveris me" (v. 9) is similarly translated: "if you fall and pray to me"—avoiding both the terms "prostration" and "worship."

And yet the following examples show greater conformity to the biblical source than to the text of the Vulgate.

—"Antiquis" ("of old"; 5:33) as *qdmwnym*.

—"In montem excelsum valde" ("onto a very high mountain"; 4:8) as *bhr gbh wtlwl* "On a mountain high and lofty."

—"Et sine crimine sunt" ("and are without reproach"; 12:5) as *wl*' '*šm* '*lyhm* (lit. "and they have no guilt").

—"Calix iste" ("this cup"; 26:39) as *kws hmwt* "cup of death," probably based on such phrases as *kûs ḥ*ᵃ*māṯô* "cup of his wrath" or *kûs hattar*'*ēlâ* "cup of staggering" (Isa. 51:17).

—"Omnis potestas in caelo et in terra" ("all authority in heaven and on earth"; 28:18) as *mlkwt šmym w*'*rṣ* "dominion of heaven and earth."

In his essay on religious controversy in the medieval period Isidore Loeb summarizes: "This is the earliest example of the polemic genre extant in Hebrew literature. It served as a pattern and example for many Jewish polemists in Spain in the following centuries."[52] One of these "heirs" was the renowned Shemtob ibn Shaprut (fourteenth century), who erroneously attributes this work to Rabbi Joseph ben Isaac Kimḥi[53] but expresses his gratitude and his debt to the author of *Milḥamot ha-Shem* [*Wars of the Lord*] three times in his magnum opus '*Eben Boḥan* [*The Touchstone*].[54]

Two further facts attest the success of this book. Nicolas of Lyra devoted a trenchant rebuttal to it entitled *Contra quendam Iudaeum impugnatorem evangelii secundum Matthaeum,*[55] in which he refers to Jakob ben Reuben only as "iste Iudaeus" ("that Jew"), but takes pains to analyze his arguments carefully and to "refute" them.[56]

The convert Alphonso of Valladolid (alias Abner of Burgos) paid Ben Reuben the compliment of stealing his title for an anti-Jewish book in Hebrew which he later translated into Spanish in 1321 under the title *Libro de las batallas de Dios.*[57] Rosenthal, the editor of the critical edition of *Milḥamot ha-Shem,* emphasizes that Ben Reuben's work remains "the first Jewish book devoted to the criticism of the New Testament."[58]

4. *The Book of Joseph the Zealous*

From the thirteenth century onward the number of Jewish-Christian controversies increased. They were invariably initiated from the Christian side—frequently with threats of coercion—with the Jewish response usually coming only after lengthy hesitation and with great apprehension, although there was no lack of eagerness to join in debate where genuine tolerance prevailed.

In Italy, Moses of Salerno was apparently the first to speak freely of his faith and express his opinions to his Christian rulers. Later Salomon ben Jekuthiel and Abraham Farissol followed his lead.[59]

In northern France there was the Official family,[60] from which five rabbis engaged in public debates not only with Dominican and Franciscan scholars, the bishops of Angoulême, Anjou, St. Malo, Mans, Poitiers, Senlis, and Sens, and the court chaplain of King Louis IX the Holy (St. Louis), but also with Popes Gregory IX and Gregory X. The principal Jewish participants in these controversies were Nathan ben Meshullam (in the twelfth century), his son Joseph ben Nathan, his uncle Nathan ben Joseph Official, and his uncle's son Joseph ben Nathan, who was called "the Zealous" (*ha-Meqanne*').[61] The latter immortalized the controversies of his family, and of some other French rabbis, in a work which he called *Teshubot ha-Minim* [*Answers for Heretics*], but which was entitled simply *Sepher Yoseph ha-Meqanne*' [*Book of Joseph the Zealous*] by later copyists. Compiled in the year 1274,[62] the book was devoted to a refutation of the christological and allegorical interpretation of the Old Testament. In its final chapter it mounts a counterattack with an analysis of the New Testament text, revealing its inner conflicts and contradictions and subjecting such doctrines as the divinity of Jesus, the virgin birth, the Trinity, and the sacraments of the eucharist, baptism, etc., to sharp and sarcastic criticism.

The Paris manuscript of the book[63] presents an extensive criticism of the New Testament in its last eight pages. It contains forty Hebrew quotations from the New Testament, of one to eight verses each, and eleven quotations from the Latin Vulgate in Hebrew transliteration, of which nine are from the New Testament, one (unidentified) quotation is apparently from a patristic source, and one is an abbreviated and simplified phrase from the Athanasian Creed.

While quotations from Matthew represent the majority (twenty-five in all) and are generally the best translated, five of the remaining fifteen quotations are merely paraphrases of New Testament passages (Mark 9:14–27; John 4:7–8; 5:25–30; 12:49; and 1 Cor. 15:21–22). Only two passages in Matthew (8:1–4; 28:16–19) are cited by both the *Milḥamot ha-Shem* of Jakob ben Reuben and the Paris manuscript of Joseph the Zealous, but the differences between them make it quite clear that the latter had no knowledge of the earlier. Passages translated in the Paris manuscript include the following:[64]

Matt. 23:37	8:18–20	9:14–27
12:31–32	9:6	Luke 12:22–24
9:12	8:23–26	23:34
13:37	28:16–19	John 4:7–8
15:17	28:20	14:14
20:23	10:1	15:22
1:16–18	10:9–10	8:26
1:21	19:16–21	12:49
9:13	6:25–26	4:5
1:16	26:39	4:6–8
2:13–14	27:46	2:1–5
8:1–4	12:31–32	1:29
9:2–6	Mark 1:5	5:25–30

The Latin quotations in Hebrew transliteration are: Matt. 11:19; v. 11; 26:38; 8:20; 26:39; 20:22; 1:25; John 2:4; Rom. 12:5; an unidentified and somewhat garbled sentence saying "per potentiam non per naturam creatoris fecit Creator"; and the following phrase from the Athanasian Creed (which is identified by its first words "Quicunque vult" ["whoever intends," *qqwnqylt*]): "Pater ingenitus, filius genitus, spiritus sanctus ab utroque procedit" ("Unbegotten father, begotten Son, Holy Spirit procedes from both").[65] The Latin is frequently distorted in the Hebrew transliteration, which represents phonetically a (northern French?) dialect pronunciation. Errors in word division (e.g., *prw ṣdns* for "procedens"), a number of homoioteleuta, and other corruptions point to the author's (or perhaps the scribe's) inadequate knowledge of Latin.

The text also includes seventeen French glosses which the author was evidently either unwilling or unable to translate, such as "sacrament" (*śqrmnt*), "hostie" (*hwsdyʾ*), "penitence" (*pnytnsʾ*), "baptême" (*btymʾ*), "confession" (*qwnpyʾwn*), and "apostle" (*ʾpwsṭl*).

Interesting mistranslations include:

—"Architriclinus" ("steward of the feast"; John 2:9)—promoted to *mlk ʾrtqlyn* (the one responsible for the triclinium).

—"Trans fretum" ("the other side"; Matt. 8:18)—the sea is demoted to the Euphrates river: *mʿbr nhr prt* "from across the River Euphrates."

Polemical sallies are not lacking:

—"Evangelium" ("gospel") is consistently *ʿwn glywn* "the wicked scroll."

—The passion of Jesus is a play on the word *psywn* "plague."[66]

—The Latin word "sicut" ("just as") becomes *šyqqwṣ* in transliteration.[67]

—The Trinity in Matt. 28:19 is *bšm h'b whbn wrwḥ hṭwm'h* "in the name of the Father and the Son and the unclean spirit," and on similar grounds "Jacob" in 1:16 is distorted to *yqwpy'* (from *qp'* "curdle").

The *Spr Hwkwḥ* "Book of Reproof" of Ms. no. 53 of the National Library in Rome, which is ascribed to the early fifteenth century on the basis of its colophon, the character of its paper, and its palaeography,[68] contains among other things several portions of the *Book of Joseph the Zealous*. This later edition of the work[69] contains two chapters[70] devoted entirely to a critique of the New Testament. In the second chapter are found twenty-five passages in Hebrew from Matthew, two from Mark, six from Luke, five from John, and one from Acts[71]—a total of thirty-nine passages ranging from one to nine verses in length. The passages translated are the following:

Matt.	3:5–6		13:1–17		9:36–40
	3:16–17		8:21–22	Luke	2:22–24
	3:13		8:23–25		1:31–33
	9:6–7		2:13–14		2:42–48
	9:8		15:21–28		9:46–49
	9:1–7		8:1–4		23:34
	8:18–20		5:19		16:19–24
	27:45–46		5:18	John	4:3–9
	21:17–19		5:43–44		2:12
	5:44		5:33–35		5:28–32
	18:2, 5		27:46		4:7
	13:54–56		5:17		8:24–25
	12:47	Mark	2:10	Acts	10:11–15 (paraphrased)

The lengthier passages are mostly paraphrases, with verses irrelevant to the discussion either condensed or completely omitted. Especially in the translations from Matthew the dependence of the Roman writer on the Paris manuscript is striking, although very few of the Hebrew translations of the New Testament passages are completely identical in both manuscripts.

In the Latin text transliterated in Hebrew, besides quotations from a baptismal liturgy ("exorcizo te, immunde spiritus . . ." ["I exorcize you, unclean spirit . . ."]), there is a sentence conflating the Vulgate texts of Matt. 12:30–32; Mark 3:28; and Luke 12:10, as well as the Vulgate version of Gen. 17:14 and Isa. 66:17 from the Old Testament.

The text contains three mistranslations of linguistic interest.

(a) The wedding at Cana of Galilee (John 2:1) is celebrated at *kn'n bglyl* "Canaan in Galilee."

(b) The "racha" ("fool") of the Vulgate at Matt. 5:22[72] is translated as "evil": "qui autem dixerit fratri suo, Racha," rendered *wmy šy'mr l'ḥyw rʿh* "and whoever says to his brother, 'Evil One.' "

(c) "Judas" is abbreviated to *ywd,* while "Jew" is *ywdy,* and "Jews" is *ywdym.*

The beginning of the chapter contains an allusion to the Anabaptist controversy.[73]

The sixth chapter of the Roman manuscript contains the following fifty-nine New Testament passages in Hebrew:

Matt.	1:17		15:1–14		14:22–24
	1:18		18:11–13	Luke	2:17–18
	1:23		19:16–17		2:22–24
	2:13–18		19:19–20		2:41–48
	3:5–6		20:28		3:23–38
	4:1–11		21:18–19		12:22–24
	5:17–19		24:29–34		16:19–31
	5:21–22		26:36–46		23:34
	5:29		27:45–46		23:39–43
	5:38–40		28:16–19	John	1:45–48
	5:44	Mark	2:10		2:1–4
	8:18–20		4:21–41		2:12
	8:23–26		7:1–15		4:3–9
	9:6–7		8:22–42		4:20–22
	11:25–30		9:14–27		5:30
	12:1–7		10:7–9		5:28–30
	12:10–12		10:31–44		7:1–10
	12:47		11:11–14		10:30
	13:13–51		13:24–34		14:28
	13:53–58				
	14:17–21				

The following mistranslations are significant:

—In Matt. 4:6 "si Filius Dei es mitte te deorsum" becomes *'m 'lqym 'th npwl l'ḥwryk* "if you are God, fall behind yourself."

—In Matt. 13:54 the translator adds the name "Capharnaum" to "in patriam suam" ("in his own country"), perhaps with 9:1 in mind (e.g., *lʿyrw lkpr nḥwm* "to his city, to Capernaum").

—In Matt. 11:28 the "heavy-laden 'onerati' ('laborers')" whom Jesus invites are confused with "honorati" (*b'w 'ly kl hyʿpym whtkbdw* "Come unto me all the tired and the honored"), and he does not offer them "rest" but "refreshment": "ego reficiam vos" ("I will restore you") becomes *'šbyᶜkm* "I will satisfy you," suggesting that the translator had "refectorium" in mind.

—The pericope of the healing of the lame man in 9:2–7 is placed on the Sabbath, although the text does not suggest it in the least. This may be due to association with the healing of the man with the withered hand in 12:10.

—In Matt. 28:16 the "undecim discipuli" ("eleven disciples") are still "twelve," because the unhappy fate of Judas was evidently forgotten, whether by chance or intentionally.

—In Luke 23:42 "in regnum tuum" ("in your kingdom") is interpreted as *lšmym* "to heaven," yet "in paradiso" in the following verse is translated *bmḥyṣty* "in my portion."

Three German words ("Krippe" [*kryp'* "manger"], "Taufe" [*twp* "baptism"], and "Seelmesse" [*zylmyś'* "Mass"]) compare with the seventeen French glosses in the Paris manuscript in providing evidence that the provenance of this late manuscript was in a Germanic region.

Names occur in the following abbreviated and variant forms.

Jesus: *yšw; yš"w; qryśṭwś; htlwy* "the Crucified"; *hmmzr* "bastard"

Matthew: *mty; mty'wš; mtywš*

John: *ywḥnn; ywḥn; ywhns*

Paul: *pwlws; pwylś*

Peter: *pṭr ḥmwr* "the firstling of an ass"; cf. Exod. 34:20

James (in Matt. 10:2, etc.): *yᶜqwr* "he is uprooted"

In verse Matt. 5:17 becomes here: "Do not think that I have come to destroy the Law . . . , but to confirm (*lqym*) and fulfil it."

In Matt. 26:39 "calix iste" ("that cup") becomes Isaiah's *kûs hattarᶜēlâ* "bowl of staggering" (Isa. 51:17, RSV).

In this chapter also occur some one dozen Latin sentences from the Vulgate and various Christian liturgical sources used as further proofs in the arsenal for Jewish disputants for whom this book was written. In defense of Graetz, who called the Official family "the freest debaters of their time,"[74] the following three examples are typical of the sarcastic answers which appear so frequently in the book of Joseph the Zealous.

(a) When asked by a bishop why the phrase "it was good" is lacking only for the second day of creation, Rabbi Official the Elder answered: "The Holy One, praised be his Name, who foresaw the future, knew what misfortunes and evils would be caused in the world by water (baptism), and because water was created on the second day, he did not pronounce it 'good.' "

(b) When asked why God appeared in a brier bush instead of some other kind of tree, Rabbi Joseph answered that this was the only kind of tree from which idols and (sacred) images could not be made.

(c) When a bishop explained to him that dividing the waters of the Red Sea so that the children of Israel could cross over with dry feet was a type prefiguring baptism, Rabbi Nathan immediately agreed, also noting that the only ones saved were those untouched by the water, and that all who entered the water perished.

5. Excerpts from the New Testament in Hebrew Polemic Works

Knowledge of the New Testament and other Christian literature appears in Jewish literature as early as the ninth century, and from then to the twelfth century a friendly exchange of views between Jewish and Christian scholars seems to have been the rule rather than the exception. For example, Hai Gaon consulted with Catholics as early as 1030 about the exegesis of a difficult biblical passage,[75] and the Karaites ascribed to Jesus a high degree of rabbinic authority.[76] Saadia Gaon,[77] Judah Halevy,[78] and Moses Maimonides[79] show an intimate knowledge of the New Testament, although they rarely cite it explicitly.

In Narbonne in the ninth century Rabbi Moses ha-Darshan ("the Preacher") compiled, so far as we can determine today, a rare midrash in which among other things he made use of Aramaic apocryphal literature from Syrian Christian sources.[80] This work was still available in fifteenth-century Salonika,[81] but unfortunately it is lost today. Neubauer thinks it likely that "ideas of the scholarly Christian priests with whom Rabbi Moses associated may have found their way into the book.[82] It is the consensus today, however, that Rabbi Moses was strongly influenced by esoteric Jewish materials.

It would be impossible within the space of a single volume to attempt a complete listing of all the polemical works containing paraphrases or allusions to New Testament passages in Hebrew,[83] but at least the principal such works should be briefly mentioned here.

About 1170 at Narbonne Rabbi Joseph ben Isaac Kimḥi (1090–ca. 1170) compiled a religious dialogue *Sepher ha-Berit* [*Book of the Bond*], which is known today only from fragments quoted in other books by himself or in works by his son Rabbi David Kimḥi or by other rabbis.[84] In it are some thirty-five verses of the New Testament quoted (either in Hebrew translation or in transliterated Latin) from Matthew (*mty*), whose book is called *spr twldwt yšw* "Book of the Generations of Jesus" (from the genealogy in the first chapter?), Mark (*mrqws hqdwš* "St. Mark"), and John (*yw'n*). Joseph Kimḥi was the first Jew to take up the charge of falsifying the scriptures, a charge made by Christians since Justin Martyr,[85] and turn it with ample documentation against the Christians themselves.[86]

The quotations and translations of the Pater Noster (*p'tyr nwśṭry*) in

Matt. 6:10, recorded in transliterated Latin, are of interest linguistically. "Fiat voluntas tua sicut in caelo et . . ." is followed by the translation: "this means: Do your will on earth immediately, as it is done in heaven."

The parable of the mustard seed in Matt. 17:20 is rendered by Kimḥi: "Jesus said, 'Amen, Amen, I tell you, whoever has in his heart faith, which is called "fide," as large as a mustard seed, can say to a large mountain: "Go from here to there . . ."' "

The key passage in John 1:29 is cited by Kimḥi as "Ecce agnus Dei tollit peccata mundi [*sic*]" ("Behold the Lamb of God who takes away the *sins* of the world"), and then translated correctly (following Isa. 53:7) and with some embellishments: "In the Gospel it is written that *yw'n* [John] said, 'This is the Lamb of God who takes (away) and forgives all your sins.' "

Finally we should note the division of world history into three parts, as Kimḥi finds it in Christian sources. This is a variation of the "Eternal Gospel" of Joachim of Flora (*ca.* 1172–1202), although a similar three-part division is also known from a late Tannaitic Baraita in *Sanh.* 97 a-b: "From Adam to Moses the Law of Nature ruled the world—in the foreign language *lyzy n'ṭwrh* ("lege naturae"). When Moses came, God gave the written Torah—in the foreign language *lyzy 'yl'y sqryṭh* ("lege illa[?] scripta"). When Jesus came he gave the doctrine of grace—in the foreign language *lyzy 'bngylyq'* ("lege evangelica")."[87]

His son Rabbi David Kimḥi, the famous Redaq, refers in his exegesis of the Prophets[88] to French proselytes who were apparently converted to Judaism (*grym ṣrptym ḥsydym ḥkmym* "intelligent, pious French proselytes") by the "contradictions in the Gospels," a collection of New Testament passages shown together with their related Old Testament passages to demonstrate the "error" of the evangelists' claim of their fulfilment of Old Testament types and allegories. The following are examples of the christological pairs cited and disproved by David Kimḥi, mostly on the grounds of linguistic usage and textual criticism.

Mark	8:17–18	—	Isa. 6:9–10
Matt.	15:8	—	Isa. 29:13
	21:5	—	Zech. 9:9
	21:16	—	Ps. 8:2 (Eng. v. 1)
	26:14	—	Exod. 21:32; Zech. 11:12 (ascribed erroneously by Matthew to Jeremiah)
John	3:14	—	Num. 21:9

Among the near literal quotations from the Vulgate is John 5:31, which David Kimḥi gives as follows in his usual Hebrew transliteration:

"Ego dico testimonium de me testimonium meum non est verum," and which he then translates into Hebrew: "If I speak of myself, my witness is not (a valid) witness"—an allusion to the juridical dictum of the Talmud: "the baker is not a fair witness for his own dough."

David Kimḥi is also familiar with the Quartodeciman controversy, and he includes the discrepancy between John and the Synoptics on the time of the crucifixion among his contradictions.

> It is written there that Jesus ate the Passover meal on the eve of his crucifixion. This would mean that Passover fell that year on a Friday, and that he was crucified on the first day of Passover, but this is a blatant impossibility, for no one could be executed on a holy day. . . . I have even discussed this question with a Christian scholar, who told me that he did not understand it.[89]

In his *Commentary on the Psalms* David Kimḥi further demonstrates his method of ascertaining the simple meaning of a word by combining Hebrew philology with history and common sense. He shows a knowledge of the Christian interpretation of many New Testament passages and also a familiarity with the thinking of Christian exegetes, particularly in his exegesis of such passages as Ps. 2:7; 19:10, and the whole of Pss. 21, 45, 72, and 110. His arguments also often contain paraphrases of the Church Fathers, such as Jerome and Augustine, whom he had apparently read in the original.

About 1245 Meir ben Shimeon of Narbonne wrote his work *Milḥamot Miṣwah* [lit., *The Decreed War,* in the sense of "Holy War"], which contains a précis of a religious dialogue held before the archbishop of their city. The second part of this five-part work presents a refutation of the heresies of the Christians in 120 paragraphs, in the course of which about forty passages from the New Testament are cited or paraphrased.

Abner of Burgos, who was baptized about 1330, under the name Alphonso of Valladolid not only compiled in Spanish several tracts against Judaism[90] and a response to Jakob ben Reuben's *Milḥamot ha-Shem* [*Wars of the Lord*] but also wrote several works in Hebrew about 1336. These include *Teshubot Meshubot* [*Responses*], a dogmatic work entitled *Moreh Ṣedeq* [*The Teacher of Righteousness*], most of which has been lost, and also three polemic letters to Spanish rabbis,[91] which contain some New Testament quotations.

He was in turn answered not only by Isaac ben Joseph ibn Pulgar about 1340 in his *ʿEzer ha-Dat* [*Defense of the Religion*], which makes use of several quotations from the New Testament to deny the messiahship of Jesus, but also by Rabbi Moses Kohen from Tordesillas in *ʿEzer ha-Emunah* [*The Defense of the Faith*], which he wrote about 1375 to oppose the christological exegesis of the Old Testament. Like many other polemicists Kohen also relied heavily on the book *Milḥamot ha-Shem* by Jakob ben Reuben for arguments and quotations.

An anonymous work bearing the often used title *Teshuboth ha-Minim* [*Answers for Heretics*][92] was recently published in a critical edition by Jehuda M. Rosenthal.[93] Compiled partly about 1240 and further expanded by a fourteenth-century hand, this brief manuscript[94] makes reference to six New Testament verses which it intends to refute.

The story of the next two writings would frankly be incredible if it were not so fully attested by authentic documentation. Profiat Duran (Isaac ben Moses Halevi, also called Efodi [Ephodi] because of his magnum opus *Maʿaseh Ephod* [*Deeds of the Ephod*], and therefore known by Christians as Efodaeus), the Jewish grammarian and philosopher, and his friend David Bonet (Bongiorno) were forcibly baptized in the Spanish pogrom of 1391. Both decided to emigrate to Palestine to escape the persecution in Spain, and they agreed to embark from a port in Catalan. When Profiat arrived at the port there he found a letter from his friend saying that Paul of Burgos[95] had convinced him "of the truth of Christianity." He was therefore remaining a Christian, and was writing to advise his friend to do the same. Profiat's answer, written about 1396—the main part of which began with the words *ʾl thy kʾbwtyk* "Do not be like your fathers," appears on the surface to be a pro-Christian apology in which he encourages his friend "in contrast to his fathers" to accept the doctrines of the incarnation, original sin, the Eucharist, and the abrogation of the Torah. The letter is written with such subtle irony and theological skill that it was at first generally regarded as a defense of baptism and the superiority of Christianity. Efodi writes:

> Do not be like your fathers, who believed in the One God, never associating with him any element of pluralism (*rbwt*) or partnership (*štwp*); they erred in understanding the words 'Hear, O Israel . . .' to describe the oneness (*ʾḥd*) of God as an absolute singularity, instead of a unity of kind, of class, or of relationship (*yḥs*), or subject to modification . . . . You should be different, acknowledge rather that the One is three, and that the three are one in an inward and essential unity . . . which the mouth cannot express nor the ear grasp. . . . Forget that you must avoid any physical representation (*htgšmwt*) of Him; acknowledge rather that He, i.e., one of his three persons (*prṣwpym*), assumed flesh (*lbš bśr*), so that his blood was shed as an atonement for his people (*kʾšr nšpk dmw lpdwt ʿmw*). . . . Thank Him for suffering death in order to save you, His wisdom had found no other way of salvation. . . . Hold fast to this faith which leads you to eternal life, and God will be with you, for you eat the Bread, your God. . . . Your fathers have eaten the bread of hardship (*lḥmʾ ʿnyʾ*) and were often hungry

> and thirsty. But you have saved your soul; eat and be satisfied by your Savior within you. . . .[96]

For years this letter was cited, translated, and commented on by Church apologists. It enjoyed such popularity that Christian apologists who did not understand its Hebrew title (i.e., its first words), christened it *Alteca Boteca*. About 1420, when it was demonstrated that the letter was actually a satirizing attack on the faith of the Church, all available copies were burned publicly.

Profiat Duran's more important work was written the following year (1397) at the request of his student and patron, Ḥasdai Crescas. The book entitled *Kelimat ha-Goyim* [*The Shame of the Gentiles*] comprises twelve chapters, corresponding to the twelve tribes of Israel, of which the first nine contain a systematic critique of Christian doctrine. Profiat cites more than 180 verses from the New Testament to refute the doctrines of the divinity of Jesus, the Trinity, the incarnation, the redemption, and the abrogation of the Torah. Further, on the basis of New Testament sources he asserts that transubstantiation, baptism, and the papacy have no claim to biblical roots. Mark and Luke, whom he quotes constantly, do not give eyewitness accounts, and their Gospels suffer (Profiat claims) not only from inconsistencies but also from an inadequate knowledge of the Old Testament.

It is also of interest that Efodi distinguishes consistently between Jesus, his disciples, and the leaders of the Church. He regarded Jesus as a "naive (or perfect) saint" (*ḥsyd tm*), his disciples as misguided (*ṭwʿym*), and the church leaders as misguided leaders who deceive others (*ṭwʿym hmṭʿym ʾḥrym*). Efodi begins with the claim of Jesus' divinity and says: "In order to demonstrate that it was not the intention of the imagined messiah (*mšyḥ mdwmh*) or of his disciples (*tlmydyw*) to lay claim to divinity as imagined by those who came afterward . . . Nowhere in the Gospels (*ʾwngylywnym*) and the Letters (*ʾgrwt*) do we find it written that they called him God. . . ." He then cites John 10:30 and 14:9, and says that these passages indicate an intimacy with God (*qrbh lh"*) but not divinity (*ʾlwqwt*). From Jesus' cry for help (Matt. 27:46; Mark 15:34) the same inference is drawn. Similarly he discusses here the Trinity, the incarnation (*htbśrwt!*) of God in Jesus, original sin, and the abrogation of the Torah "which Jesus never thought to oppose."

The last three chapters charge Jerome, Origen, Augustine, Eusebius, and other Church Fathers with christological eisegesis in their allegorization of the Old Testament, and an inadequate knowledge of Hebrew and Aramaic.

The book marks the first time that New Testament passages are cited with specific references, and that technical theological terms are both translated and explained. For example:

(a) "Eucharistia" is transliterated, translated literally (*ḥn ṭwb* "good grace"), and then explained: "they (the Christians) hold and believe that by means of this devotional service (*ʿbwdh*) they attain to eternal life."

(b) "Transubstantiatio" remains untranslated, but it is explained: "they hold that their offerings of bread and wine divest themselves of their forms in order to become instead the Body and Blood of Jesus—in the same form in which he was crucified."

(c) "Dyophysitismus" is apparently defined following the *Definitio de duobus naturis Christi* of the Council of Chalcedon (451) and the *De Incarnatione* of the Council of Ephesus (431) in the following way: "The Messiah was not a composite of these two natures, but rather they both came to perfect union (vera unione coeuntes) in him."

(d) The sacraments are the focal points or dogmas of the Christian religion (*hʿqrym bdt hnwṣrym* "the principles of the religion of the Christians"), and the following interesting enumeration of them is given with explanations.

> In their religion there are seven things which are like covenants between them and their God, and are called *šʾqrmynṭwš:*
> —Baptisma *hṭbylh* ["the immersion"]
> —Eucharistia *dbr hlḥm whyyn* ["the matter of the Bread and the Wine"; cf. the definition given above]
> —Matrimonium *hzwwg* [lit. "the pairing"]
> Congregatio *hqhylh hkwllt hmwn hʾwmh šl hmʾmynym* ["the assembling of the whole multitude of the people who believe"]
> —Ordinatio *htglḥwt* [lit. "shaving oneself," i.e., tonsure]
> —Poenitentia *htšwbh* ["turning oneself back"]
> —Unctio extrema *hmšyḥh hʾḥrwnh qdm hmyth* ["the last anointing before death"]

Also of interest are the following translations from the New Testament.

(a) Acts 20:28 "regere ecclesiam Dei quam adquisivit sanguine suo" *lhnhyg ʿdtw ʾšr qnh bdmw* "to lead the congregation which he obtained by his blood."

(b) Col. 2:8–9 "non secundum Christum . . . quia in ipso inhabitat plenitudo divinitatis corporaliter" *lʾlpy hmšyḥ . . . ky bw yškwn mlʾ hʾlwqwt bgšmywt* "not according to the Messiah . . . for in him dwells the full divinity in corporeality."

(c) Matt. 5:17 "Do not think that I have come to destroy (*lhtyr*) but to fulfil it (*lhšlymh*)"—where the final *h* of the last verb clearly points to the Torah.[97]

Profiat Duran's book soon created a school among Jewish scholars. His student Ḥasdai ben Abraham Crescas wrote a similar book in

Spanish *ca.* 1410, entitled *Tratado,* which Joseph ibn Shemtob translated into Hebrew in 1451 as *Biṭṭul ʿIqqari ha-Noṣerim* (*Refutation of the Principal Dogmas of the Christian Religion*). Of special interest in this polemic work are the following translations.

—"Conceptio immaculata" *hrywn blʾ mwm wblʾ ṣbʿ* "conception without blemish and without stain."

—"Peccatum originale" *ḥṭʾ hʾdm hrʾšwn* "sin of the first man."

—"Redemptio" *hgʾwlh wpdwt mhghnwm* "the redemption and ransom from Gehenna."

—"Incarnatio" *hlbšt yšw bbśr* "the clothing of Jesus with flesh."

—"Corporalitas" *gwpnywt* "embodiment."

—"Eucharistia" *qrbnwt lḥm wyyn* "sacrifices of bread and wine."

—"Parousia" *hwpʿt yšw pʿm šnyh* "the appearance of Jesus a second time."

—"Trinitas" is explained thus: divinity is mutually common and threefold, comprised of three distinct individualities which are called "personas" in their language but which they regard as a single being.

One hundred twenty-six verses of the New Testament are here translated into Hebrew. One of the means used to refute the divinity of Jesus is a count of how many times he is referred to as "Son of Man" (*bn ʾdm*): "thirty times in Matthew, twenty-seven times in Luke, fourteen times in Mark, eleven times in John, and once in Acts."

About 1428 Rabbi Joseph Albo, the last of the great medieval Jewish philosophers of religion, wrote his magnum opus, the *Sepher ha-ʿlqqarim* [*Book of Religious Fundamentals*], in which he rejects the anti-Jewish charges of the Church in a pretended dialogue with a Christian scholar (bk. III, ch. 25), and then proceeds to trace the eternal truths of Judaism to their basic principles: the existence of God, rewards and punishments, and the prophetic mission of Moses. After a penetrating debate in which twenty-six New Testament passages are quoted and analyzed, the author refers to "contradictions" in the genealogy of Jesus at Matt. 1:1–17 and Luke 3:23–38, "errors" at Acts 7:14–16 and 13:21, as well as "false" christological interpretations of Gen. 49:10; Isa. 7:14; and Jer. 31:15. In summary, Albo concludes that the apostles were not sufficiently familiar with "their Jewish Bible," and that the Law of Jesus (*twrt yšw*) was a human and not a divine revelation. He ends with the acclamation (from Ps. 19:8): "The Law of the Lord is perfect!"[98]

About 1450 Ḥayyim ibn Musa of Béjar wrote *Magen we-Romaḥ* [*Shield and Spear*] as a rebuttal to Raymundus Martini's *Pugio Fidei.* He cites only four passages from the New Testament with the aim of demonstrating the untrustworthiness of its witness to Jesus. He emphatically counsels all his coreligionists who are forced into controversy to accept only a literal exegesis of the scriptures and reject all allegories, to consent to neither Aramaic nor Greek texts as a basis for discussion, and to deny any authority a priori to the Haggadah.

About 1423 Simon ben Zemach Duran (Rashbatz) wrote *Magen Aboth* [*Shield of the Fathers*] as a defense of the Torah against its "two daughters," the Church and Islam. He evidently translated his nineteen New Testament quotations from the Latin Vulgate, with only a few minor errors.

Don Isaac Abrabanel, whose book *Yeshuʿot Meshiḥo* [*The Salvation of His Anointed*] marks the last stage of medieval polemics (about 1494), offers not only a dozen quotations from the New Testament apparently translated from the Spanish, but also two interesting comments. At Gen. 50:20 the author mentions that Joseph forgave his brothers their "sins," for "you intended to do me harm, but God has turned it to good," and then proceeds to draw an analogy with the trial and crucifixion of Jesus which in a similar way led to the fulfilment of a divine plan of salvation. The apologetic implication is obvious.

With regard to the Messiah "whom we await," Abrabanel imagines an "impersonal" savior in obvious contrast to Jesus, suggesting an anonymous and modern spiritual approach.

Before proceeding to a consideration of the first Jewish translation of a complete Gospel, we should notice a triad of comprehensive medieval Jewish polemical works whose authors, all things considered, showed an amazing knowledge not only of the New Testament, but also of the Church's teachings, customs, and interpretation of the scriptures.

6. *Three Books of Rebuttal*

"*Niṣṣāḥôn,* which means 'victory,' is such a common name among Jews for anti-Christian books that works of this genre needed some further word in their title to distinguish them."[99] With these words Johann Christoph Wagenseil begins the introduction to his edition of the book *Sepher Niṣṣaḥon, Yashan Noshan* [*The Old Book of Victory*], which he published with six other anti-Christiana in his bilingual (Latin-Hebrew) anthology *Tela ignea Satanae* at Altdorf in 1681.[100]

The earliest of these polemical manuals, later called the *Sepher Niṣṣaḥon Yashan Noshan* [*The Primal Victory*] was evidently compiled by the thirteenth century, and incorporated extensive elements from Jakob ben Reuben's *Milḥamot ha-Shem* [*Wars of the Lord*] and Nestor Hakkomer, as well as from *Sepher Yoseph ha-Miqenna*' [*Book of Joseph the Zealous*]. It contains several poorly translated pericopes from the New Testament which were probably based on oral translations from the Vulgate. Its successor was a more thorough and systematic work, the *Sepher Niṣṣaḥon* written by Rabbi Yomtob ben Solomon Lipmann of Mühlhausen shortly after the Prague pogrom of 1399, in the course of a debate forced upon him by the proselyte Peter (alias Päsach). The latter claimed that the Jewish liturgy contained slanders against Jesus and the Church.[101] Lipmann's Jewish *Summa Contra Gentiles* was written, according to its author, for Jewish intellectuals who had difficulty reconciling their learning with their faith, for "heretics" and Karaites, for faithful (non-intellectual) Jews unaware of the depth of their own religion, and for Christians—the four classes which Lipmann symbolized in the four sons of the Passover Seder liturgy.

Beginning with the first verse of Genesis, every controversial biblical word is scrutinized to rebut farfetched non-Jewish allegorical interpretations. The book is divided into 354 sections to remind Jews that a portion of the Bible should be studied on each day of the (lunar) year. Lipmann's knowledge of Latin and of the Vulgate is especially impressive in the second part of the book, where he cites the New Testament most astutely to prove that (a) Jesus never intended to promulgate a new teaching (*twrh ḥdšh*), (b) he could not be the Messiah because neither was he of Davidic lineage nor did he intend to bring peace but rather "a sword" (Matt. 10:34), and (c) the prophetic promise of "the latter days" (*b'ḥrym hymym*) was still unfulfilled.

Lipmann's *Niṣṣaḥon* achieved a profound and lasting impression. Beginning with the polemical tractate *Adversus Iudaeos*[102] by Stephan Bodeker, Bishop of Brandenburg (1459), there was a veritable flood of anti-Lipmann literature produced by such authors as Theodor Hackspan, Christian Schotan, and Wagenseil, among others.[103] Lipmann's book was also one of the only two singled out[104] by Johann Reuchlin during the book controversy of 1510 as especially deserving to be confiscated and destroyed.[105]

The third, if not also the latest, work of the triad[106] also is called *Sepher Niṣṣaḥon Yashan,*[107] and extends to more than 260 pages. It deals with practically all the christological passages of the Old Testament, first explaining the allegorical interpretation given them by the *mînîm* (i.e., the heretics, or Christians), and then refuting them by subtle arguments. Much of its reasoning is derived from the *Sepher Yoseph ha-Miqenna*ʿ and other Jewish polemicists.[108] The tone of controversy often becomes unpleasantly sarcastic, although within the range of acceptable usage for the fifteenth and sixteenth centuries. For example, when an opponent sees evidence for divine sonship in the plural form of the verb at Gen. 1:26 ("Let us make man"), the author answers with a derisive reference to the singular form in the following verse ("and God made man"), and suggests that "the Son was disobedient, leaving the Father to do the work by himself." Then in turn the Father "deserted the Son when he cried out on the cross" *ēlî 'ēlî lāmâ ʿazabtānî!* (Ps. 22:1). While some statements of this kind may be attributed to the heat of impassioned debate, this can hardly account for the opportunistic exegesis of the scriptures characteristic of some counterattacks, such as when Lipmann relates to Christian bell ringers the words of Isaiah, "Woe to those who draw iniquity with cords of falsehood" (Isa. 5:18).[109]

It is also interesting that Lipmann, in contrast to the nearly unanimous Jewish denial of responsibility for the death of Jesus, declares explicitly that Jesus was condemned in accordance with the Jewish law on blasphemy (cf. Mishnah *Sanh.* 4), and that the judgment "of our fathers" in this can only be applauded.[110] The tone frequently degenerates to coarse insults ("confounded idiots!" "ass, son of asses!"), and to downright crudity when speaking of clerical celibacy and the virgin birth of Jesus. One part of the New Testament translation seems to have been copied out verbatim from *Milḥamot ha-Shem,* preserving even its translational errors. Gen. 6:6; Isa. 45:17; Matt. 1:24; 26:45; the words "virgo" ("virgin") and "puella" ("young woman")—in the controversy over Isa. 7:14; and many other terms such as "foederunt" ("they have pierced" or "defiled")—in the controversy over Ps. 22:17, "ratio" ("account"), "dominus" ("lord"), and "recursus" ("return") are cited in Hebrew transliteration from the Latin Vulgate, which is called *lšwn ṭwm'h* ("defiled language") and *lšwn glḥym* ("language of [Roman Catholic] priests [lit., "shaved ones"]"). There are also two Latin passages from the Athanasian Creed as well as five passages from the Liturgy of the Mass. Two different translations of Matt. 5:17–19 are quite interesting.

(a) "I did not come to do away with the Law of Moses and the words of the Prophets, but to bring them to completion (*lhšlymm*). . . . Heaven and earth will pass away, but nothing will fail from the Law of Moses. . . . Anyone who removes a word from the Law of Moses will be called defective (*ḥsr*) in the Kingdom of Heaven."[111]

Then a few chapters later:

(b) "(Jesus himself said) that he did not come to destroy (*lʿqwr*) the Law of Moses and the words of the Prophets . . . and so long as heaven and earth remain, not a single letter, not even a punctuation mark (of the Law and the Prophets), will be destroyed or lost."[112]

The occurrence of fourteen words in New High German and the German Creed is also significant for locating the composition of the book with fair assurance in a German-speaking area about the early sixteenth century. These words include:

—"Christenheit" *qryśṭnhyṭ*

—"Menschheit" *mnšhyṭ*

—"Krippe" *qryp'*
—"Klocken" [*sic!*] *qlwqn*
—"Altarstein" *'lṭršṭyn*
—"Kloster" *qlwśṭr*
—"Kreuz" *hqryṣ* and *qrwṣ*
—"Taufe" *ṭwyp* and *ṭwp'*
—"Bezeugnisse" *bṣygnyś'*
—"Sonntag" *zwnṭ'g*
—"Laien" *lyn*—which is defined as the *š'ryt ʿm šl yšw* ("the remainder of the people of Jesus") and then translated into Latin as "barbari" ("foreign").
—"Latein" *lṭyn*

The Apostles' Creed is given in triglot, with the first lines of each section quoted in Latin and followed by a Hebrew translation of the whole, which may be back-translated in roughly the following form:

> I believe in God the Father Almighty, Creator (or, He created) heaven and earth, and in his son *Yšw*. He suffered martyrdom under Pontius Pilate. On the third day he arose from death. He sits at the right hand of God Almighty.[113]

In summary, it may be concluded that just as no genuine religious dialogue occurred in the medieval period, but only double monologues without a common ground, neither were there any objective translations of the New Testament into Hebrew. Christians made translations in order to bring out the christological "concordia" of the two Testaments and to convert the Jews. Jews translated passages from the New Testament and Christian doctrinal statements, selectively and tendentiously, to defend themselves in the face of the Church's doctrinal tradition of denying any validity to their older faith. A worthy exception to this general rule is the first (and best, prior to the modern period) translation of a complete Gospel into Hebrew made by a Spanish Jew in the fourteenth century.

7. *The Touchstone from Spain*

The first—and still apparently the only—translation of a complete Gospel into Hebrew prepared by a rabbi came from the pen of Rabbi Shemtob ben Isaak ibn Shaprut,[114] a Spanish scholar from Tudela, whose familiarity with both Testaments is best attested by the fact that he was chosen by the Jews of Castille and Navarre to represent them in a public debate arranged under ecclesiastical pressure and held at Pamplona on December 26, 1375. On that occasion he disputed—evidently with considerable success—the doctrines of original sin, the messiahship of Jesus, and the question of "salvation" against Cardinal Pedro de Luna, who became Benedict XIII in 1394 by election to the counterpapacy. The arguments and counterarguments he was able to assemble in this as well as in other religious debates, along with syllogisms found in the literature of controversy, he edited in a book which he called *'Eben Boḥan* [*The Touchstone*] (after Isa. 28:16), "for it should serve to tell the true from the false," as he stated in the preface.

In the words of Heinrich H. Graetz:

> To enable the Jews to use weapons out of the Christian armory, Shemtob ben Shaprut translated into Hebrew extracts from the four Gospels, with incisive comments. . . . He published (1380) a comprehensive work (*'Eben Boḥan*) unmasking the speciousness of the arguments adduced by Christian controversialists from the Bible and Talmud.[115]

The Touchstone, which first appeared in 1380 in Tarazona (on the border between Castille and Aragon), was copied in successively expanded forms in 1385, 1395, 1400, and again about 1402.[116] The circumstances and motives which led to its compilation are related in the book itself.

> The translator said: . . . When I observed the troubles of our time and the events of this age, how through our own fault many of our religion had deserted us and furthermore tormented us to ingratiate themselves with the Christian rulers . . . involving us in controversies, raising questions about the Bible and the Haggadot to make us look ridiculous and slander us. . . . Since many Christian scholars also wished to debate with us, and because of our sins, being exhausted by the cares of simple survival and the support of our families . . . , we were sinking deeper and the Torah was falling into oblivion in Israel, leaving us incapable of answering as we should, I presumed to act and compile a book about the Christians' questions and the answers we should give them. I also found it necessary to translate their books of the Gospels, so that we could make use of them in our answers. And then I was surprised to find an excellent book on this matter called *The Book of the Wars of the Lord,* attributed to Rabbi Joseph Kimchi. . . .[117] He frequently goes out of his way to attack his opponents harshly, in a way that would be injudicious today. . . . I believe that above all we must explain the Bible in its simple, literal sense (*pšṭ*), appropriately to the truth of our own religion, and go no further than refuting the attacks of our opponents. . . . This is why I have written in a gentle tone, as a servant speaks to his master. . . . *The Book of the Wars of the Lord* has been for me a useful resource.

The author is generally true to his word. While all his predecessors, including his model, Jakob ben Reuben, intruded their personal polemical attitudes into their translations of the New Testament, Ibn Shaprut translated with almost scholarly objectivity, limiting his rebuttals to fifty-three inserted paragraphs distributed among the 116 pericopes into which he divided the Gospel of Matthew.

Space does not permit an adequate treatment of *The Touchstone* in this book. It deserves fuller consideration elsewhere.

8. *Translations under Duress*

Among the half-dozen translations of parts of the New Testament into Hebrew known to us from the late medieval period,[118] the Hebrew manuscript Vat. Ebr. no. 100 of the Vatican Library[119] is perhaps the most interesting. This translation of the four Gospels was in all probability made under duress by a Jewish scholar, for only a degree of moral (or stronger) constraint can explain the great contrast between the comprehensive range of rabbinical knowledge and familiarity with the Hebrew language shown on the one hand, and the numerous errors on the other hand which sabotage the work, undoubtedly with the intent to misrepresent the meaning of the text.

The manuscript lacks both title page and colophon, giving no clue to the identity of the work's translator, its date, or its provenance. On paleographical grounds the copy seems to derive from Italy in the fifteenth century,[120] but like *The Touchstone* it could well have been based on an earlier Hispano-Jewish work which made its way to Italy and was transcribed there. This was the route followed by many Sephardic scholars as pogroms became more frequent in the late fifteenth century, especially after the expulsion of Jews from Spain in 1492 when the last Jewish cultural centers of the Iberian peninsula were forced to emigrate to France, Holland, and Italy. Such an odyssey would account for the mixture of Spanish and Italian influences discussed below.

The caviling nature of the errors which make the text either ridiculous or incomprehensible for Jewish readers, due to an excessively literal rendering of a Latin, Spanish, or Italian source, shows that this translation was either controlled or censored by a Christian with some knowledge of Hebrew—almost always the practice in Italy and Spain during the fourteenth and fifteenth centuries. There are three passages at the beginning and end of the work which clearly attest the reluctance of the translator, but which could very easily have escaped the notice of a Christian hebraist.

(a) The first words, preceding even the introduction, are *bs"r 'tḥyl,* which can be translated as "I am beginning under duress."[121]

(b) In the next line the name of the first Evangelist appears in illuminated letters in the usual Italian and Spanish form of St. Matthew, with the "San" written as *s″y*. This innocent abbreviation,[122] which was later used also for the three other Evangelists, was undoubtedly approved by the ecclesiastical censors, while by Jewish readers it was recognized as the familiar sign for "anti-Jewish" (*swn' ysr'l,* lit. "enemy of Israel").

(c) The final phrase on the last page of the manuscript is not one of the usual quotations from the Old Testament or a concluding prayer such as Moritz Steinschneider cites as typical in this context,[123] but simply the two words *brwk šptrny* "Blessed be he who sets me free," an expression still used by pious Jews today after they have completed a difficult and usually an unpleasant duty.

The missionary purpose of this book is indicated by the introduction, which contains the usual explanation of the doctrine of the Trinity and the medieval symbolism of the four Evangelists: ". . . Matthew has the face of a man . . . Mark of a lion . . . John of an eagle." But the symbol for Luke here is not the usual sacrificial bull, but "a calf" (*ʿgl*), taken as suggesting "the priesthood of Jesus,"and this office is translated as *glḥwt,* the term commonly used for the Christian clergy during the medieval period and derived from the word for tonsure (*glḥt*). The fact is probably not without its significance that of the twelve Old Testament instances where the word "calf" (*ʿēgel*) occurs, no fewer than five refer to the "golden calf,"[124] the embodiment of idolatry.

A Latin source is indicated by only two passages.

(a) Mark 15:39 "Centurio" *hsynṭwryw*

(b) John 1:9 "Lux vera" *'mytwt nr* [*sic*]

Passages suggesting an Italian or Spanish source are more numerous and convincing.

(a) Matt. 27:55 "Jesum a Galilaea" *ysws dglyly'h,* where not only the nominative suffix of "Jesus" but also the preposition "de" appears to point to a Romance source.

(b) "Holy Spirit" is always rendered as *qdš rwḥ, hqdwš rwḥ,* or *qdwš rwḥ,* following the Romance word order of "santo spirito" instead of the Latin "spiritus sanctus."

(c) "Herod" is called *'rwdyś* here. The unaspirated "H" betrays a Romance pronunciation.

(d) "Judaea" is rendered as *gwdy'h* or *dšwdy'h,* corresponding to the Romance pronunciation of the fourteenth and fifteenth centuries.

(e) Luke 24:52 "Cum gaudio magno" ("with great joy") *bgwdl šmḥh.* This is not only poor Hebrew, but also follows the Romance rather than the Latin word order.

(f) John 1:19 "Sacerdotes et Levitas ("priests and Levites") *khnym wdy'qś.* The second term is probably a corruption of the Romance "diaconos," for a Latin source would undoubtedly have become *lwym.*

(g) Luke 1:32 "Sedem patris" ("throne of his father") *qtdr'* (lit., "a professor's chair"). The Vulgate text could only have produced *ks* or *ks'* here, even if distortion were intended, while a Romance term ("siede"? "seggia"? "sede"?) would at least lend plausibility to the rabbinic Greek expression.

(h) Similar examples reflecting a Romance word order and idiom are quite frequent.

(i) While the name of John appears only in its Spanish form as Juan (*gw'n*), not only James but also James the Less (Mark 15:40) is exclusively the Italian Giacomo (*y'qwmw*). Peter appears as both Italian Pietro (*pytrw*) and the Spanish Pedro (*pdrw*), as well as in the abbreviated forms *pyrw* (Pierrot?) and *pydw.*

(ii) The first day of the week in Matt. 28:1 is explained in two languages, in Spanish as "domingo" (*dwmyngw*) and in Italian in a marginal note as "domenica" (*dwmynyg'*). A mistranslation found in Luke 3:1, where the "tetrarch" is christened a "patriarch" (*pṭry'q* [*sic!*]), is of psychological interest.

(iii) Typical examples of debiblicizing Hebrew names and ideas are found in the first four generations of Jesus' genealogy in Matt. 1:1–2, where the names are consistently rendered with the phonetic values of their latinized forms. Accordingly, David becomes *dwyṭ,* Abraham becomes *'br'm,* Isaac is *yšʿq,* Jacob *yqwp,* and Judas *ywd'.* Jesus remains either *yśwś* or *yśw'ś,* Mary is called *mry'h,* Joseph is *ywśp,* and Nazareth is *n'zryṭ.*

In some instances Romance literalisms verge on the ridiculous. For example:

—"The kingdom of heaven" *mlkwt šmymy*

—"Filius primogenitus" *bn r'šwn*

—Matt. 3:7 "Brood of vipers" *mšpḥt wybryš* (the Romance "vipers")

—Luke 3:4 "The book of the words of Isaiah the Prophet" *spr dbry yšʿyhw hnby'*

—Luke 1:72 "His holy covenant" *qdwšt ṣw'tw.* Here the word "testamenti" was undoubtedly translated in a nonreligious sense.

Nearly all the quotations from the Old Testament are similarly distorted by excessively literal back-translation. Thus Isa. 40:3 is cited in Matt. 3:3 as *qwl h" yqr' bmdbr yšrw hdrkym lpny whthpkw* [*sic!*] *'lyw* "the voice of the Lord crying in the wilderness: 'Make straight the ways before and turn round and round(!) before him,' " while the same passage is cited in Mark 1:3 as *'ḥt qwl tgdl bmdbr št'mr hkynw drk h'dwn yšrwt tʿśw drky h'dwn* "one voice becomes great in the wilderness which says: 'Prepare the way of the Lord, make straight the way of the Lord.'" Similarly, Jer. 31:15 is cited in Matt. 2:18 as *gd-wlym . . . qwlwt mbky wṣʿqh hyth nšmʿt brmh* (lit. "loud . . . voices weeping and crying out, you were heard in Ramah").

Typical of countless further arbitrary mistranslations is the sentence "Who taught you that you could escape from the coming wrath?" which is translated in Matt. 3:7 as *my lmd lkm lbrwḥ l'p h"* "who taught you to flee the wrath of the Lord." But in Luke 3:7 it becomes *my ylmd lkm brwḥ m'pynw hʿtydh lb'*. Here *brwḥ* (*brôḥ*? *brûḥ*?) is ambiguous, literally capable of representing either the infinitive form "to flee" or the phrase "in the spirit" with the meaning "Who will teach you in the spirit of our coming wrath?" But the words may equally well be translated "the breath of our nose," so that a literal translation here may provide for John the Baptist a new Hebrew nose just as Jerome endowed Moses with Latin horns.[125] The words addressed to those coming to John for baptism in Luke 3:8 are no less mocking: "Produce, then, fruit corresponding to your repentance" becomes *lkn ʿśw pyrwt hgwnym mṭbylh* "Reap, then, the appropriate fruit of your baptism." Similarly, the ending of Mark 1:34 becomes *wmgrš šdym ky hm mkyrym 'wtw* "He cast the demons out, because they were his kin."

In all these and many other distortions of the text, the translator's familiarity with proper Hebrew usage is no less evident than his intention to pervert or ridicule the text as much as possible within the limits of what could be represented to the Church's censors as the Gospel "ipsissimis verbis."

It is possible that this anonymous translation, exemplifying magnificently the principle "traduttore-traditore," was the work found in Rome in 1553 by Jean Du Tillet, the bishop of Saint-Brieuc, and on which he based his 1555 edition of the Gospel of Matthew in Hebrew, correcting it thoroughly.[126]

This may also have been the manuscript which underlay the version of the New Testament which Giovanni Battista Jona (alias Rabbi Jonas of Safed) found "by chance in a bookstore in Rome," whose style he found stiff and inept, so that "I wondered as I read it whether the translator was unfamiliar with the holy language, or whether the Jews had translated it so poorly intending to degrade the Gospel in the eyes of the reader."[127]

Richard Simon tells of a similar Hebrew manuscript in his possession with the note in Hebrew on its title page (lacking in our manuscript): "This is the book of Jesus. It is called the Evangelium which Matthew wrote about Jesus of Nazareth. It should not be trusted, because it is a worthless fraud and falsehood."[128] He adds further that from the Italian words "Matteo" (*mṭy'w*) and "evangelio" (*'wnglyw*)—forms which appear also in Vat. Ebr. no. 100—it may be inferred that both the writer and his exemplar were from Italy.

IV
Modern Christian Hebraica

1. *The Hebrew Gospel of Matthew by Sebastian Münster*

Among the Christian students of Elias Levita, the author of *Massoreth ha-Massoreth* [*Tradition of the Masorah*] (a still authoritative grammar of Biblical Hebrew), Sebastian Münster (1489–1552) was probably the most famous hebraist of his age. Münster is credited with the Latin translation of Levita's grammar; the first textbook on the Aramaic language (with title page woodcuts designed by Hans Holbein the Younger)[1]; a new edition of Johann Reuchlin's *De Rudimentis Hebraicis*[2]: a trilingual dictionary giving most of the biblical vocabulary in Latin, Greek, and Hebrew in an alphabetical arrangement[3]; and also a *Grammatica Hebraica Absolutissima* [*Sepher ha-Diqduq*], based principally on Rabbi David Kimḥi's *Miklol* [*Completeness*] and Levita's *Ha-baḥur* [*The Youth*].[4]

His love for "that holy and truly divine language," as he called it,[5] is attested not only by his coat of arms in the University register at Basel—encircled by Hebrew sayings and dated with an Old Testament phrase[6]—but also by the Hebrew tombstone and the Hebrew obituary he dedicated to his friend Johann Œcolampadius,[7] the fact that he wrote a long preface for his edition of the Bible, and also a book of his own which he wrote in Hebrew for Heinrich Petri, his printer at Basel. The inscription on his tomb at Basel describes him correctly as "Germanorum Esdras et Strabo," for like Ezra he was "a scribe skilled in the law of Moses" (Ezra 7:6), and like the German theologian Walafrid Strabo he was a master of allegorical exegesis.

Although Martin Luther seconded Johann Eck's judgment of the "Rabi Munsterus" that "there was hardly anyone in Germany so familiar with the Hebrew language as he"[8] and that his knowledge of the language even surpassed that of the translator of the Septuagint,[9] yet Luther charged Münster with "judaizing."[10] He made this accusation of Münster the philologist, in contrast to Münster the theologian who would often cite rabbinic conjectures in his edition of the Bible, just as he also frequently made use of rabbinic commentaries in his works without any hesitation. Luther wished to distinguish between the Hebrew language and Hebrew grammar, admitting that the grammar had to be learned from the Jews and yet insisting that the language itself had changed so drastically since the days of the Old Testament precisely because of the violence done to biblical words by the rabbis.[11] Münster, however, was frank in acknowledging the scholarly value of Jewish religious literature, defending it against the attacks of such scholars as Philipp Melanchthon, who refused to find in it any philosophical value at all.[12]

Münster's attitude toward the Jewish religion was in direct contrast, for although as an intelligent reformer he tolerated it, this was only because he was firmly convinced of "the delusion and blindness of the Jews."[13] Further, he tried to debate with the Jewish scholars whom he frequently consulted on matters of grammar and translation, discussing with them exegetical and hermeneutical problems, even disputing on a biblical basis the Jewish polemics against Jesus "the magician." As early as 1520, while he was still a Franciscan monk and before his alienation from the Catholic church, he translated the Pater Noster, the Ave Maria, the Benedictus, the Apostles' Creed, the Magnificat, and several other passages of the New Testament into Hebrew in order to convince his debating colleagues, with whom he agreed on the inerrancy of the Old Testament, of the biblical character of the New Testament as well.[14] Nor did he hesitate to make minor changes in the Latin text which he printed beside the Hebrew translation, as at Luke 1:42 which concludes as follows: "et benedictus fructus ventris tui Ieschua meschia, amen" *wmbwrk pry bṭnk yšwʿh* [*sic*] *mšyḥ ʾmn* ("and blessed is the fruit of your womb Jesus the Messiah, amen").

In 1537 Münster published his Hebrew version of the Gospel of Matthew at Basel, the first printed edition of the New Testament in the so-called "mother tongue of the evangelist," as he states in his preface ("Matthaei Evangelium, in nativa sua hoc est Hebraica lingua"). Although the title *Torat ha-Mashiaḥ* [*The Teaching of the Messiah*] makes the missionary motive clear, Münster held little hope of its converting the Jews, who "cum oculos haberent nihil videbant, etiam si oculatissimis sese arbitrarentur" ("with the eye have seen nothing, although they imagine themselves conspicuous"), as he said in the letter to King Henry VIII of England, to whom he dedicated the book. He had found the Hebrew version "among the Jews but in a defective state, with many omissions," and in his edition he made the necessary supplements.[15] This remark seems to have led Richard Simon[16] later to identify Münster's unknown source with Shemtob ibn Shaprut's *Eben Boḥan* [*The Touchstone*], an hypothesis which was to be adopted by many biblical scholars[17] and provide Adolf Herbst with a Ph.D. dissertation at Göttingen in 1879. In this dissertation on "Shemtob ben Shaprut's Hebrew Translation of the Gospel of Matthew, according to the editions by Sebastian Münster and Jean Du Tillet-Mercier" Herbst also asserts that Ibn Shaprut's chief purpose in his *'Eben Boḥan* was the polemical translation of the text of Matthew, to which "he then added fourteen appendices." The twelfth appendix (i.e., the translation of Matthew) contains a "refutation of the doctrine of the Trinity . . . from the paraphrase of Onkelos." This "Onkelos," however, is derived from Bartolocci's misreading of the word *'wngylywš* ("gospel") as *'wnqlws* ("onkelos"), which was repeated by Johann Christoph Wolf but corrected by Antonio Maria Biscioni in 1757 and Giovanni Bernardo de Rossi in 1800. Herbst cites both the latter scholars, but on the same page of the dissertation[18] he repeats Giulio Bartolocci's error and concedes that he has never examined a manuscript of *'Eben Boḥan*—although he lists eight copies of it. He states, nevertheless, as "a firm conclusion," that it was Ibn Shaprut who wrote this translation of Matthew.[19] And yet with even the most superficial comparison of the two works the radical differences between their vocabulary, style, and diction would have demonstrated the impossibility of a common origin.

Münster's edition begins with a lengthy Latin preface lamenting the "hate borne by the Jews against Christ" and their secret anti-Christian propaganda, of which he gives a three-page citation in the original Hebrew. This polemic, which includes antichristological interpretations of such Old Testament passages as Num. 24:23; Deut. 13:7; Isa. 44:6; and Jer. 17:5, is taken from the work *Sepher Niṣṣaḥôn Yashan* [*The Old Book of Victory*], a copy of which was in Münster's possession.[20]

Following this is a Hebrew-Latin tractate on the superiority of the Christian religion, entitled *Z't 'mwnt hmšyḥyym hqdwšh wnkwnh šlmh wbly spq* [*This is the belief of the Christians, completely holy and true without doubt*], then a derogatory outline of the Jewish religion, and finally on p. 45 the beginning of *Torat ha-Mashiaḥ* [*The Teaching of the Messiah*]—*Lex Dei novae quae est doctrina et vita Christi*, subtitled *Evangelium domini nostri Jesu Christi secundum Mattheum—Twrh ḥdšh why' bśwrt h'dnynw yšwʿ hmšyḥ kpy mty hmbśr* [*A new Torah, which is the tidings of our Lord Jesus the Messiah according to Matthew the messenger*]. These words introduce a fully-pointed Hebrew version of the Gospel of Matthew, to which Münster has added his Latin translation and several detailed polemical notes.

The comments of several prominent biblical scholars and hebraists on the quality of the Hebrew text of this first edition are interesting.

Lodewijk de Dieu, in his commentary on Matthew,[21] censures Münster's edition as "incorrect and ungrammatical," as evidenced by the first three words of Matt. 1:1: *spr htwldwt yšwʿ* ("book of the generations of Jesus"). Besides the erroneous use of the article, the frequent occurrence of the negative particle *ʾyn* instead of *lʾ* is a patent solecism which can hardly be attributed to a Jewish scholar but must be "a christiano quodam hebraizante" ("by some Christian writing in Hebrew").

On the other hand, Jacques Le Long[22] regards the edition by Johannes Quinquarboreus, a literal version which appeared in Paris in 1551, as "the true and authentic Gospel of Matthew," and only regrets that Münster did not identify his additions to it with an asterisk.

Richard Simon's view is that "Münster's edition is written in poor Hebrew, teeming with solecisms and barbarisms . . ." which could be due either to the original translator or to Münster's revision.[23]

Pierre Daniel Huet[24] thinks Münster should be criticized severely for supplementing the omissions in the manuscript himself, and finds the style of the edition both "heavy and awkward."

Finally, in 1964 Josef Prijs states:[25] "According to data in Oswald Schreckenfuchs' funeral oration for Münster (1552) . . . Münster came by chance into the possession of a Hebrew version of Matthew, which he proceeded to translate into Latin. The Hebrew text so violates proper grammatical usage that it must have been the work of a convert."

Actually the Hebrew text is often not only awkwardly phrased and replete with impossible latinisms (which can only derive from the Vulgate), but it is also characterized by solecisms and faulty vowel pointings. Examples of semantic, grammatical, and syntactic latinisms include the following.

1:19 "Cum esset iustum" *kšhwʾ ṣdyq*

1:20 "Quod enim in ea natum est" *mh šywld btwkh*

1:25 "Donec peperit filium suum" *ʿd yldh bnh*

16:12 "Doctrina" *tlmwd*

16:14 "Eliam" *ʾlyh*

16:15 "Vos autem quem me esse dicitis" *wʾtm ʾwty my tʾmrw hywt*

16:16 "Filius Dei vivi" *bn ʾlqym ḥy*

16:17 "Beatus es" *ʾšry ʾth*

16:18 "Porta inferi" *šʿry htḥtywt*

16:20 "Ut nemini dicerent quia ipse esset Jesus Christus" *šlʾ lʾyš yʾmrw šhwʾ hyh yšwʿ hmšyḥ*

16:21 "Coepit Jesus ostendere . . . quia opportet eum ire" *wmʾz htḥyl . . . yšwʿ lhwdyʿ . . . šhṣṭrk llkt*

26:3 "Qui dicebatur Caiaphas" *šnʾmr qʾypʾ*

26:8 "Quid perditio haec!" *ʿl mh zʾt hʾbydh*

26:14 "Qui dicebatur iudas iscariotes" *šnʾmr mr yhwdh ʾyśkrywty*

26:15 "Triginta argentos" *šlšym kspym*

26:17 "Prima die azymorum" *bywm r'šwn hmṣwt*

26:18 "Magister dicit" *hmlmd 'wmr*

26:29 "Cum illud bibam vobiscum novum *šbw 'šthw 'tkm ḥdš*

26:50 "Amice, ad quid venisti? *'l mh b't?* [*sic*] *r'h* (*r'h* may be a formal conflation of *r'* and *r'h* "see!")

26:56 "Ut adimplerentur scripturae" *'yk ytqymw mktbym*

26:74 "Et gallus cantavit" *wšr htrngwl*

28:15 "Fecerunt sicut erant edocti" *wy'św k'šr hm lwmdw*

While these and many similar latinisms point to a Christian hand, the following un-Jewish errors add support to the hypothesis that neither a Jew familiar with the Torah, nor even an ex-Jew, could have been responsible either for the translation of this text or for its intentional distortion.

—*'yn* is almost always used for *l'*, e.g., 16:17 "caro et sanguis non revelavit tibi" *bśr wdm 'yn glh lk;* v. 18 "non praevalebunt" *'yn ygbrw;* v. 22 "non erit tibi hoc" *'yn thyh lk z't;* 26:5 "non in die festo" *'yn bywm hḥg;* v. 29 "non bibam amodo" *'yn 'šth m'th.*

—"Domine" as the disciples' form of address for Jesus is always translated *'dny.*

—26:44 "Eundem orationem dicens" *wy'mr tplh h'wth.*

—26:13 "Hoc evangelium" *bśwrh hy't ṭwbh.*

—1:21 "Pariet autem filium" *why' tld 't bn.*

—1:22 "Hoc autem totum factum est" *wkl hz't hyth.*

—16:18 "Ecclesiam meam" *mqhly.* This hapax legomenon is derived from Ps. 26:12 *b*ᵉ*maqhēlîm* ("in the assemblies"), which Jerome translated "in ecclesiis." Evidently the translator considered the word *qhl,* so often rendered as "ecclesia" by Jerome, as too simple for this crucial passage.

—16:21 "Multa pati a senioribus et scribis" *lsbwl šm rbwt m't zqnym wswprym.* The omission of the article (unavailable in Latin) makes a critical difference in the meaning of the sentence; in this form it places the guilt for the crucifixion of Jesus on only a few unspecified "elders and scribes."

—26:20 "Discumbebat cum. . . ." *yšb 'l hšlḥn.*

—The construct state is represented by *šl* and paraphrased, e.g., 14:1 "famam Jesu" *šm'w šl yšw';* 23:33 "a iudicio gehennae" *mmšpṭw šl gyhnwm.*

—28:11 "Omnia quae facta fuerant" *kl šnhyw.*

—"Filius hominis" is consistently translated as *bn 'dm.*

—"The kingdom of heaven" is frequently called *hmlkwt hšmym.*

—"Synagogue" is called *knst* (pl. *knsywt*).

Despite the fact that almost no verse is completely free of errors, there are still some passages, such as the Pater Noster and the Sermon on the Mount, which achieve a degree of fluency and even of eloquence. It is impossible to determine whether this is due to the purportedly Jewish(?) author, or to his reviser, Sebastian Münster. But the kinds of errors and their frequency, as well as the correction to the New Testament of all the Old Testament quotations (nearly seventy), point to the hand of an assiduous Christian hebraist such as Münster himself.

Apart from insignificant variations of word order and trivial changes (such as "porro" ["and so on"] for "autem" ["also"], "sed" ["but"] for "enim" ["for"], "impregnata" ["pregnant"] for "in utro habens" ["having in the womb"], "verbum" ["word"] for "quod dictum est" ["that which was said"], "evigilans" ["awakening"] for "exsurgens" ["rising up"]), back-translations into Latin are in general agreement with the Vulgate, as are also the back-translations of Old Testament names in the genealogy of Matt. 1:2–16 (e.g., Iehuda, Hezron, Boaz, Iisai, Uzijahu, Hizkijahu, Aelijakim, etc.). Münster appears to have been satisfied with his work, for his second diglot edition of Matthew in 1557 is an unaltered reprint of the first edition, but with the Epistle to the Hebrews added, the Hebrew text and Latin back-translation(?) of which show all the above-mentioned characteristics of Münster's work. A third edition, issued posthumously in 1582 and edited by Münster's printer, Heinrich Petri, contains the identical text.

In summary, it may be concluded that Sebastian Münster, the first Christian translator of the Gospel into Hebrew, holds an ambiguous position. His scholarly interest in the field of Jewish studies, which was still in its infancy, frequently came into open conflict with his Christian religious convictions. In his New Testament translations he is both a faithful disciple of medieval scholasticism with its anti-Jewish eristic and the father of the later evangelical Jewish mission.

2. *The Besorath Mattay of the Bishop of Saint-Brieuc*

In 1553 Jean Du Tillet, the bishop of Saint-Brieuc, travelled to Rome where he was able to obtain, by circumstances which he has unfortunately not described, "the Gospel of Matthew in Hebrew, which I would not presume to suggest Matthew wrote by divine inspiration in his own language . . . but yet I can affirm is clearly not in the rabbinic style, and is written in a pure form of the language that in no way resembles the writings of post-Christian Judaism." In the preface to his Hebrew-Latin edition of Matthew published in Paris in 1554, the Bishop follows these introductory words with this remark: "It is completely different from the (Gospel) foisted upon us by Münster ("nobis . . . obtrusit"), which is full of barbarisms and errors. This is neater ("nitidius"), and furthermore its Hebrew diction is in many instances much clearer."

The bishop sent the Hebrew manuscript, of whose origins nothing more has yet been learned than that it was "rescued from the Jews in Rome,"[26] to his friend and mentor Jean Mercier with the request that he provide it with a Latin translation, present the work to Cardinal Charles de Lorraine, and then publish it. This was done in Paris in 1555 under the pregnant title *Bśwrt Mty ʿd hywm hzh kmwsh ʿm hyhwdym wnḥbʾh bmʿr wtm wʿth bʾḥrwnh mtwk ḥdryhm wmhwšk mwṣʾt lʾwr šnt hn"k* ["Gospel of Matthew until this day hidden with the Jews and concealed in caves and now brought out by the latter from within the chambers and darkness to light again"]—"Evangelium Hebraicum Matthaei, recens e Judaeorum penetralibus erutum, cum interpretatione Latina, ad vulgatam, quoad fieri potuit, accommodata" ["Hebrew Gospel of Matthew, newly brought forth from the hiding places of the Jews, with Latin interpretation, accommodated to the common language so far as could be done"]. (*Hn"k* in the Hebrew title has the gematric value of seventy-five, the equivalent of 1315 C.E., but it may also be *hnk,* the first word of the quotation from Isa. 7:14 which follows immediately in a slightly adapted form: *hnk hrh wywldt bn* [*lprṭ qṭwn*] *mgʾwltnw ph bpʾrys hʾm bṣrpt* "Behold . . . has conceived and will bear a son [for small detail] redeeming us here in Paris, France.")

In his own preface Mercier emphasizes with scholarly discretion that, although the Hebrew text often departs from the Vulgate, it can scarcely be considered the authentic work of the evangelist, nor yet as the Gospel of the Nazarenes mentioned by Jerome, especially as the latter "is regarded by most as having been written in Aramaic." Although the text is written in a "rather pure Hebrew" which may be described as "not far removed from the style of the Old Testament," the Franciscan hebraist warns the reader that nevertheless "a number of rabbinisms" appear frequently.

In the edition published at Paris in 1555 by Martin the Younger ("apud Martinum Iuvenem"), after the bishop's preface and the introduction to his (back-)translation follows the sixty-nine-page text of Matthew in unpointed Hebrew, followed in turn by twenty-three "Jewish objections to the Gospel," Mercier's Latin (back-)translation, and finally, at the end, the royal sanction for publication written in French. It should be noted that the sanction is dated January 29, 1552, about a year before the bishop's journey to Rome during which, according to his preface, he "obtained" the manuscript of Matthew.

Of no less interest are the linguistic evaluations of the Tillet-Mercier edition given by acknowledged biblical scholars and hebraists.

De Dieu, who criticized Münster's edition sharply[27] and considered it the work of a Christian hebraist, finds the style and diction here "considerably purer." But he still cannot accept it as the work of a *homo hebraicus*, especially in the face of Matt. 16:17, where the words "my father who is in heaven" are rendered as un-Jewishly as *'by šhw' bšmym.*[28]

Bartolocci is convinced that this is Ibn Shaprut's *'Eben Boḥan*, which he describes as "coarse and filthy," and as a kind of "anti-Gospel" which had already appeared in several other editions and was now printed in Paris in 1555 "in the same inept Hebrew."[29]

Hugo Grotius says only that Matthew was undoubtedly not the author of the text Du Tillet published.[30]

Matthaeus Polus demonstrates[31] that neither Münster's nor Du Tillet's edition contains "any genuine elements." Further, the stylistic peculiarities as well as the differences between the texts are sufficient to prove that they were translated "from the Greek or the Latin" by Jews who shared a common perspective and were anti-Christian, but were also from different backgrounds.

Richard Simon, for whom the Münster edition is "teeming with barbarisms,"[32] comes to the conclusion that "however much Bishop du Tillet might praise his own edition, it cannot be old. The Jew who wrote this Gospel in Hebrew did not use the rabbinic language, but the usage of the Old Testament."[33] As an example he cites the first words of Matt. 1:1 (*'lh twldwt yšw* "these are the generations of Jesus") "which are patterned after the Old Testament."[34]

Moritz Steinschneider catalogues both the Münster and the Du Tillet editions under Ibn Shaprut's *'Eben Boḥan*,[35] and expresses the suspicion that they both derived "from the same source."

Franz Delitzsch reports that Du Tillet's edition "gave many people the feeling that they were holding the apostle's original writing in their hands."[36]

The Bible catalogue of the British and Foreign Bible Society states with reserve that this work was edited "from a manuscript found in Rome."[37]

And last but not least, Herbst is convinced that "Shem Tob Shaprut was the one who translated the Gospel of Matthew published by Tilius."[38] Herbst also shows in the title of his dissertation that he believed Münster had used the same source: "Des Schemtob ben Schaphrut hebraeische Übersetzung des Evangelium Matthaei nach den Drucken des S. Münster und J. du Tillet-Mercier neu herausgegeben von Dr. Adolf Herbst, Göttingen, 1879."[39] He gave preference, however, to Du Tillet's edition as his primary text, entering Münster's variants only as footnotes.

The fact that Münster's text has almost nothing in common with the *'Eben Boḥan* has been proved by the example of Matt. 2:1–10,[40] and the same is true for Du Tillet's. Yet it is clear that the professor from Basel as well as the bishop of Saint-Brieuc both relied on the same document—of which each could very well have obtained copies in Rome in their different ways—not only from their literal identity in many verses, but also from a whole series of errors they have in common. For example:

5:37 "Est est, non non" *kn kn; 'yn 'yn* (Ibn Shaprut has *hn hn; l' l'*)

5:7 "Ipsi misericordiam consequentur" *ky lhm yrwḥm* (Ibn Shaprut has *ky hm yrwḥmw*)

5:13 "Vos estis sal terrae" *'tm ḥm mlḥ b'rṣ* (Ibn Shaprut has *mlḥ 'tm bʿwlm*)

5:22 "Reus erit iudicio" *hw' hyh lmšpṭ* (Ibn Shaprut has *ḥyb hw' mšpṭ mwt*)

5:18 "A lege" *m't htwrh* (Ibn Shaprut has *mhtwrh*)

5:43 "Diliges proximum tuum" *t'hb lrʿk* (Ibn Shaprut has *w'hbt lrʿḥ*)

7:6 "Sanctum" *dbr qdš* (Ibn Shaprut has *bśr qdš*)

16:14 "Elias" *'lyh* (Ibn Shaprut has *'lyhw*)

16:18 "Ecclesiam meam" *mqhly* (Ibn Shaprut has *byt tpylty*)

26:18 "Magister" *hmlmd* (Ibn Shaprut has *hrb*)

26:20 "Discumbebat" *yšb ʿl hšlḥn* (Ibn Shaprut has *hw' ywšb lšlḥn*)

26:56 "Scripturae prophetarum" *mktby hnby'ym* (Ibn Shaprut has *hktwbym mhnby'ym*)

There are at least one hundred further similar examples of identical mistranslations shared by these two sixteenth-century editions.

The major differences between Münster and Du Tillet are that the latter consistently translates "Jesus" as *yšw* except at Matt. 1:21, where the play on words demands *yšwʿ*, and in most instances not only evinces a better command of Hebrew idiom, but also frequently indulges in asides for the sake of clarity. The following passages are typical of more than 160 instances of the latter difference.

	Vulgate	**Münster**	**Du Tillet**
26:3	"principis sacerdotum"	*śry hkhnym* "chiefs of the priests"	*hkhnym* "his priests"
26:4	"et occiderent"	*wlhrwg* "and to kill"	*wlhrgw* "and to kill him"
26:5	"non in die festo"	*'yn bywm hḥg* "not on the day of the feast"	*l' nʿśh zh bywm hḥg* "let us not do this on the day of the feast"
26:9	"multo" (i.e., money)	*tḥt rb* "in return for much"	*bmmwn rb* "much in money"
26:12	"haec unguentum"	*hšmn hz't* "this oil"	*hšmn hzh* "this oil"

26:13	"hoc evangelium"	*bśwrh hz't ṭwbh* "this good news"	*hbśwrh hṭwbh hz't* "these good tidings"
26:13	"in memoriam eius"	*lzkrwnh* "to her memory"	*ʿl šmh wlzkrwnh* "to her name and to her memory"
26:14	"qui dicebatur"	*šn'mr* "who is called"	*whw' 'šr nqr'* "and he who is called"
26:26	"cenantibus autem eis"	*wyhy kšhm hyw 'wklym* "and it happened as they were eating"	*wyhy k'šr yšbw l'kl* "and it happened as they sat to eat"
26:48	"ipse est"	*hzh hw'* "this is he"	*hw' hw'* "that is he"
26:58	"ut videret finem"	*lr'wt hqṣ* "to see the end"	*lr'wt mh yhyh hqṣ* "to see what will be the end"
26:72	"non novi hominem"	*'yn ydʿty h'dm* "I do not know the man"	*'ny l' ydʿty 'wtw* "I do not know him!" [emphatic]

Here Du Tillet also shows a better acquaintance with Jewish customs, for Jesus' table companions could hardly have already begun to eat before their master "took bread, blessed, and broke it."[41] Yet in many instances Du Tillet's attempts at correction are not improvements. For example:

	Vulgate	**Münster**	**Du Tillet**
16:17	"Simon Bar Iona"	*śmʿwn br ywnh*	*śmʿwn bn ywnh*
26:6	"In Bethania"	*bbyt ʿnyh*	*bbyt ʿnyh 'ḥt*
26:22	"Et contristati valde"	*wyz ʿpw*	*wyḥr 'pm m'd*
26:26	"Hoc est corpus meum"	*zh hw' gwpy*	*zh šhw' gwpy*

Here the second and last passages arouse the suspicion that Du Tillet attempted to correct the Münster text, or whatever he had before him, more or less mechanically by means of simple additions or deletions. Examples include *mlkwt šmym* "kingdom of heaven" (Münster has *mlkwt hšmym* and *hmlkwt hšmym* [with definite article]), the correction of *'yn* to *l'* (Münster's idiosyncratic use of *'yn* has already been mentioned), and the proper use of the preposition *'t* "with" which Münster often used indiscriminately.

The Vulgate origins of Du Tillet and Münster's common source is apparent in the number of latinisms. For example:

5:11 "Omne malum" *kl rʿ* "all evil."

5:20 "Nisi abundaverit iustitia vestra" *lwl' twtr ṣdqtkm* "unless your righteousness exceeds." (This is apparently by analogy with Ruth 2:14 *wattōṯar,* although there the Vulgate translates "tulit reliquias" ("bears a remnant"). But "abundaverit" in the sense of "be left over, be more than enough" could have been a variant.)

5:26 "Novissimum quadrantem" *rbwʿ ʾḥrwn* "last quadrans."[42]

16:23 "Scandalum es mihi" *ʾth hwʾ ly mkšwl* "you are a stumbling block to me"

26:14 "Iudas Iscariotes" *yhwdh ʾyśqrywṭy* "Judas the Iscariot."

26:60 "Duo falsi testes" *šnym ʿdy šqr* "two witnesses of falsehood"

It seems certain that the common source document could not have been written by a Jew, for any medieval Jew with a comparable command of Hebrew vocabulary would have understood enough Aramaic from studying the Talmud to recognize that:

(a) Peter (*kyph,* instead of *kypʾ*) is not a Hebrew word. Matt. 16:18 here begins *ʾth kyph* (*kph?*) *wʿl kyph* (*kph*) *zʾt* . . . ("You are *kyph* [*kph?*] and on this *kyph* [*kph*] . . .), to translate "Peter" in the sequel consistently as *kyph* (*kph*), which can mean either "stone" or "vault."

(b) *Raca* is to be understood in 5:22 as *ryqʾ*[43] "good for nothing," and should not be mistranslated as *rʿh* "evil one."

(c) The town of Bethany should not be construed as "the house of a poor woman," especially when it is forthwith identified as the house of Simon the Leper.

(d) *Śmʿwn br ywnh* "Simon Bar-Jona" (16:17) should not be translated *śmʿwn bn ywnh* "Simon ben Jonah."

The following "un-Jewish" errors argue for the hypothesis that a Christian prepared the source document, although perhaps with the (oral?) assistance of a Jew.

5:16 "Patrem . . . qui in caelis est" *ʾbykm šhwʾ bšmym* "your Father, the one who is in heaven"

5:18 "Unus apex" *ʿqṣ ʾḥd* "one point" (Ibn Shaprut: *nqwdh ʾḥt* "one dot")

5:19 "De mandatis istis minimis" *mhmṣwwt hʾlw qṭnwt* "from these commandments of small things" (Ibn Shaprut: *mhmṣwwt hqlwt bywtr* "from the commandments the especially unimportant")

26:30 "Et hymno dicto" *wkšʾmrw ʾt hthlh* "and when they had sung the psalm" (Ibn Shaprut: *wyšbḥw* "and they praised")

26:59 "Et omne concilium" *wkl hknst* "and all the assembly"

26:74 "Et continuo gallus cantavit" *wmyd šr htrngwl* "and immediately the cock sang"

Mercier's back-translation into Latin departs from the Vulgate more widely than Münster's, because Du Tillet's Hebrew text characteristically shows a greater degree of freedom with the canonical text.

In conclusion, it should be reiterated that the "twenty-three Jewish objections to the Gospel" which Du Tillet appends to his Hebrew text are in no way to be identified with the fifty-three objections inserted among the pericopes of the Gospel of Matthew by Ibn Shaprut, although four of them have a similar content. All twenty-three are taken almost verbatim from the *Sepher Niṣṣaḥon Yashan*.

3. The Four Revealed Stones of Rabbi Jonas

"The sixteenth century witnessed a spate of translations of selected passages from the New Testament, all with the scholarly intention of showing how the prophetic and apostolic writings are mutually illuminating, just as the Old and New Testaments are mutually related." So wrote Franz Delitzsch in surveying the various factors contributing to the history of Hebrew translations of the New Testament up through the nineteenth century.[44]

The beginning of this surge of hebraeophile interest—which unfortunately was restricted to linguistic matters—is associated with Emmanuel Tremellius (1510–1580), a Jew who had converted and been baptized. His achievements include a new Latin translation of the Bible, a Hebrew grammar, and commentaries on the Thirty-nine Articles as well as the Anglican *Book of Common Prayer*. Tremellius devoted himself to the latter as Regius Professor of Old Testament at Cambridge, a position he accepted at the invitation of Archbishop Thomas Cranmer in 1547. In order to convince his former religious associates of his new faith, Tremellius, whom the *Realencyclopaedie für protestantische Theologie und Kirche* calls "a renowned theologian and an outstanding scholar of the Hebrew language,"[45] composed in 1551 a Hebrew catechism (considered by Hugh J. Schonfield to be a translation of John Calvin's *Catechism*[46]) which included the Pater Noster, the Apostles' Creed, and many New Testament passages, and some prayers. Under the pompous Hebrew title *Sepher Ḥaynuk Beḥirey-YH* [*The Book for the Instruction of God's Elect*][47] and the more sober English title *Catechism for Enquiring Jews,* the work went through several editions[48] and was "still in use as a missionary weapon" at the beginning of the twentieth century.[49] As he states in the preface to his *Catechism,* just as many missionaries after him Tremellius was inspired by the appeal of Roger Bacon, who had challenged Christians in the thirteenth century to learn Hebrew (and Arabic) rather than engage in crusades. For while it was doubtful whether shedding blood in the Holy Land was pleasing to God, "countless Jews are perishing in our midst because no one can preach to them in their own language. . . . Oh the unspeakable loss of souls, where it would be so simple to convert innumerable Jews."[50]

Another convert from Spain was Mataeus Adrianus (1460?–

1524?), also called Hadrianus, who was appointed professor of Hebrew language at Wittenberg in 1520 at the recommendation of Luther. He translated the Ave Maria, the Pater Noster, and several Christian prayers into Hebrew. Desiderius Erasmus and Johann Reuchlin also praised him for his knowledge of the Bible, but later he fell out with Luther, who then wrote of him: "I have done nothing to him, and yet he persecutes me, and tries to instruct me in the Gospel when he does not understand his own Moses." Melanchthon suspected him of being a mere pseudo-Christian, like so many other converts.[51]

A third convert, Johann Pfefferkorn, the notorious "Dunkelmann" of the controversy over suppression of Jewish books and the author of *Juden Spiegel* (published at Nuremberg in 1507), also translated the Ave Maria, the Pater Noster, and other Christian prayers into Hebrew "in order to convert the Jews," but as Reuchlin wrote on June 19, 1514, his translation "was justly criticized by Adrianus Hispanus," the above mentioned Mataeus Adrianus.[52]

Elias Schadäus (1540–1626), a pastor and professor at Strasbourg, established the first Hebrew press in Germany. He published the books of Luke, John, Acts, and the letters to the Romans and the Hebrews. These were in Middle Yiddish, or as he describes it in his preface, "he published them at his own expense in the German idiom but in Jewish clothing, namely in Hebrew letters owed to the Jews."[53] His plan to translate the entire New Testament into Hebrew was frustrated by his death.[54]

Fredericus Petri translated the Gospel of Luke at Wittenberg in 1574. Four years later in Leipzig, Johannes Clajus published the *Evangelia Anniversaria* [*The Sunday Gospels*] in Hebrew. Conrad Neander brought out the Letter to the Hebrews in Hebrew in 1586. Phillip Gallus, who translated the Augsburg Confession ("Confessio Augustana") and a selection of passages from the New Testament in 1588, was followed by Theodosius Fabricius, who published in Hebrew not only the Passion and Resurrection narratives together with the *Compendium Theologicum* of Matthaeus Judex, but also (in 1582) Luther's *Shorter Catechism,* which had appeared in Yiddish in 1572.[55]

Even evangelical hymns and religious songs were translated into the language of the Old Testament by some hebraeophiles at Leipzig as early as 1662 "so that they could be sung with the traditional melodies (i.e., of the synagogal tradition)."[56]

Although nearly all these works were written in passable Hebrew, usually with rabbinic assistance, they are all characterized more by missionary zeal than by verbal fidelity. In passages which either patently or even possibly could permit christological interpretation, the translator rarely hesitated to exploit the opportunity of demonstrating an agreement between the two Testaments.

Equal to Sebastian Münster in both enterprise and linguistic ability was Elias Hutter (1553–1605?), whose *Polyglot New Testament* included among its twelve languages a Hebrew New Testament. The editio princeps, printed by himself at Nuremberg in 1599, was followed by a selection of pericopes in four languages (1602), and a smaller manual edition (1602–1603), as well as further reprints, all containing this first translation of all four Gospels into Hebrew.[57] On the quality of this work Delitzsch says: "His Hebrew translation reveals a grasp of the language rare among Christians and it is still worth consulting, for in instance after instance he has been most fortunate in striking on precisely the right expression."[58]

In his edition of the Hebrew New Testament published in London in 1661, the Rev. William G. Robertson corrected some of these "fortunate" passages which offended not only Jewish sensibilities but also the biblical principle of pure monotheism (e.g., attributing divinity to Jesus explicitly), although some of his other corrections were not improvements. A further revision of the first two Gospels in this version appeared at London in 1798 under the aegis of Richard Caddick.[59] Also deserving mention is the Letter to the Hebrews in Hebrew by Rabbi Alfonso de Zamora (Alphonsus Zamorensis, 1526), a Christian convert who participated in the preparation of the Complutensian Bible and held a professorship in Hebrew at the University of Alcalá until 1519;[60] the Rev. Thomas Ingmethorpe, who translated the Anglican catechism and a small selection of the New Testament passages at Durham in 1633; *Ha-eduth ha-Ḥadhashah* [*The New Witness*] of Dominicus Hierosolymitanus, alias Yomtob Jerushalmi (1550–1621?), who was born in Safed and whose translation of the four Gospels is preserved only in two (pointed but almost illegible) manuscripts in the Vatican Library, dated 1615 and 1616;[61] and also the translation of the Letter to the Hebrews at Leipzig in 1676 by the Protestant convert Friedrich Albrecht Christiani (Baruch ben Moshe), a translation which was based on the Greek text and was both tendentious and defective.

In the spirit of the age, nearly all the Hebrew grammars and primers of the sixteenth century contained at least the Pater Noster and usually also the Creed, the Ave Maria, and some other New Testament passages, ostensibly as examples of usage as well as devotional incentives for the study of the biblical language. A roster of only the most significant editors of such textbooks would include:

Conrad Pellicanus (1504)
Johann Reuchlin (1506)
François Tissard (1508)
Agathias Guidacerius (1513)
Wolfgang Fabricius Capito (or Köpfel; 1516, 1518)
Johannes Böschenstein (1518)
Matthew Aurigallus (1525)
Alfonso de Zamora (1526)
Johannes Campensis (Jean de Campen; 1528)
Theodosius Fabricius (1528)

Sébastien Gryphius (1528)
Augustus Sebastianus (1530)
Theodor Buchmann (or Bibliander; 1535)
Emmanuel Tremellius (1541)
Henricus Uranius (1541)
Petrus Artopoeus (1543)
Johannes Vallensis (1545)
Johannes Quinquarboreus (1547)
Francesco Stancari (1547)
Martinus Martinez (1548)
David Kyber (1552)
Andreas Placus (1552)
Abdias Praetorius (1558)
Antonius Cavallerius (1560)
Wigand Happel (1561)
Petrus Martinius (1568)
Robert F. R. Bellarmine (1578)
Marco Marini (1580)
Conrad Neander (1589)
Elias Schadaeus (1591)

Many other hebraists of the Reformation and of the Catholic church could also be cited.

Quotations from the New Testament and paraphrases are often found also in Jewish polemics of the Reformation period. One example is the book *Shebeṭ Yehudah* [*Tribe of Judah*] of Salomon ibn Verga (1460–1554), who had fled to Turkey after his forced baptism in Spain; returning then to Judaism he argued against Christianity from both Testaments.

David Nasi from Candia (1516–1580?) reversed the polemical tables, and in his work *Hoda'at beʿal ha-Din* [*The Witness of the Prosecution*] cited the New Testament verbatim to prove the truth and permanence of Judaism. The *Kabhod 'Eloqim* [*Glory of God*] by Abraham ibn Megas (1521?–1589), physician to the Turkish sultan, is as much an apologia for Judaism as an attack on Christianity, demonstrating the "inner contradictions" of the latter from the New Testament.

Finally, one should not overlook the *Ḥizzuq ha-'Emunah* [*Faith Strengthened*] by the Karaite Isaac ben Abraham de Troki (1533–1594), which Voltaire praised as "a masterpiece." In its 150 chapters this magnum opus not only discusses nondogmatically and rationally all the controversial passages of the Old Testament, but also cites some two hundred New Testament passages from Matthew to Revelation to dispute the divinity and messiahship of Jesus as well as his intention to found a new religion.

One more sixteenth-century work should be noticed because it probably represents the only translation of the four Gospels into Hebrew made by a rabbi in the land of Israel. Of Sephardic origins, Jehuda Jona was born in Safed in 1588, where at the age of eighteen he received the title of rabbi.[62] In 1617 he emigrated to Amsterdam, where he taught for seven years in the Jewish community until he was called to the rabbinate at Hamburg. A year later King Sigismund III of Poland sponsored him in baptism and bestowed upon him the name Giovanni

Battista together with expensive gifts. The newly baptized kept his family name, but latinized it to Jonas. In 1638 he moved to Rome where he served first as lector in Hebrew at the Archigymnasium Romanum, next as Hebrew scriptor in the Vatican, then as instructor in the House of Catechumens founded in 1543 by Pope Paul III (the support and missionary program of which was the financial burden of the Jews in the pontifical state from 1554), and finally in 1650 as master in rabbinics in the Vatican Library. In this position Jona had many students, among whom was Bartolocci, who refers to him as "praeceptor meus" ("my teacher"), often quoting him and his works.

Although he protested that like Moses he was "slow of speech and of tongue,"[64] Jona left five polemic manuscripts, including "Dialogus in quo contra Hebraeos disputatus" ("Dialogue in which is an argument against the Hebrews"), under the eponym "Alae Columbae" (Heb. *knpy ywnh,* apparently after the silvered "wings of a dove" in Ps. 68:14 [Eng. v. 13], Tremellius and Franciscus Junius version), as well as a *Refutatio* of the *'Eben Boḥan,* for whose author he shows deep enmity. But his principal work is a Hebrew rendering of the Gospels called *Quatuor Evangelia Novi Testamenti ex Latino in Hebraicum sermonem versa* [*Four Gospels of the New Testament Translated from Latin into the Hebrew Language*]; it was published at Rome in 1668 in a Latin-Hebrew edition, fully pointed and at the expense of the Congregation for the Propaganda of the Faith. The volume was dedicated to Pope Clement IX, who is called *qdwš hkhn hgdwl* ("holy high priest") on the title page. In his prefatory statement Jona justifies the translation by the necessity that the Gospels—which already "are available in Arabic, Syriac, Greek, and Latin"—should also "be translated into the language in which almost all the books of the Old Testament were written." Besides, a faithful Hebrew translation would be of the greatest importance, because the "iniqua et impia Hebraeorum mens" ("the Hebrews' biased and wicked mind") had misinterpreted practically all the evidence pointing to the Christ. Jona translates "Evangelia" on the title page and in the preface as *'bny hglywnym* ("Stones of the Revelations"; sing. *'bn glywn*), rendering it in Latin as "petra manifestata." He explains this in his introduction by the fact that "the New Law was concealed in the Old . . . this was implicit on Mt. Sinai in the two stone tablets of the Ten Commandments, which represented (symbolically) the Old and the New." He concludes that Matthew, "who wrote his Gospel in Hebrew," called it *'bn glywn* ("The Stone of Revelation"). In this the Evangelist was attacking "the rabbis" who had distorted the true meaning of the term by changing the *beth* (ב) to *waw* (ו) [and the *aleph* (א) to *ayin* (ע)], thus making the "stone" (*'bn*) into "sin" (*ʿwn*).[65]

Simon acknowledges that Jona's translation "is pure Hebrew," but he calls this argument "a completely Jewish form of reasoning, more worthy of a cabalist than of a Christian."[66] In view of the origins of "Rabbi Jonas" (as many Christian historians call him despite his baptism) in what was then the stronghold of cabalism, this should not be taken simply as an expression of disparagement. It cannot be denied that many passages in Jona's writings reveal a mystical penchant. Delitzsch is less enthusiastic over the Galilean's skill as a translator, contending that Jona "achieves less than one should expect from a Jewish scholar of no little significance born in Safed of Upper Galilee."[67]

Generally it can be asserted that Jona's *Revealed Stones* represents the best and most fluent of all Hebrew translations of the New Testament up to his time. His work combined for the first time a profound knowledge of the biblical language with a positive intention to present a devotional as well as an accurate version of the Vulgate text without a carping undertone as in Ibn Shaprut. His success may be seen in the following verses, which are characteristic of the quality of most of his Hebrew text.

(a) Matt. 26:26 *wb'klm lqḥ yšwʿ hlḥm wybrk wybṣʿ wytn ltlmydyw wy'mr qḥw w'klw zh hw' gwpy* "Now as they were eating, Jesus took the bread, and blessed, and broke (it), and gave (it) to his disciples and said, 'Take, eat it; this is my body.' "

(b) Mark 14:2 *wy'mrw l' bywm hḥg pn yʿśh š'wn bʿm* For they said, 'Not on the day of the feast, lest it cause a tumult among the people.' "

(c) Mark 14:28 *w'ḥry qwmy mhmtym 'qdym 'tkm glylh* "But after I am raised up from the dead, I will go before you to Galilee."

(d) Luke 22:20 *hkws hzh hw' bryt ḥdšh bdmy 'šr yšpk bʿdkm* "This cup is the new covenant in my blood which is poured out for you."

(e) John 1:11 *wyb' bšlw wmywdʿyw l' qblwhw* "He came to his own, and those who knew him did not receive him."

(f) John 8:7 *my mkm bl' ḥṭ' yhyh r'šwn lydwt lh 'bn* "Whoever among you is without sin shall be the first to throw a stone at her."

Although about 5 percent of his vocabulary is derived from the Talmud, Jona attempts to give his text an Old Testament character. For example, he uses both the construct state and the waw-consecutive consistently and correctly (e.g., in Luke 22:61 *wypn h'dwn wybṭ lkyp' wyzkwr* "and the Lord turned and looked at Peter, and he remembered") and renders the ablative absolute correctly by the Hebrew infinitive (e.g., Mark 14:22 "et manducantibus illis" *wb'klm* "and as they were eating"). Further, he observes the distinction between the christological "filius hominis" (*bn h'dm* "son of man") and the generic "man" or "men" (*'nšym* and *'nwš; 'dm*). "Magister" ("teacher") as a title is always translated appropriately as *hrb* "the master, rabbi"; the Temple is *hykl,* even when only the courtyard is indicated (and not *mqdš* or *byt hmqdš* "house of the sanctuary," as in Ibn Shaprut); all Old

Testament quotations are taken verbatim from their sources; "principes sacerdotum" are *śry hkhnym* "chiefs of the priests"; "summi sacerdotes" ("highest priests") become *r'šy hkhnym* "heads of the priests," and while Caiaphas is called *śr hkhnym* "chief of the priests," it is Pope Clement IX who is called *hkhn hgdwl* "the great priest" in the dedication! Similarly John 11:24 "in resurrectione in novissima die" ("in the resurrection on the last day") becomes the Jewish *btḥyt hmtym* "in the resurrection of the dead"; Mark 14:12 "quando pascha immolabant" ("when they sacrificed the Passover lamb") is corrected to *bzbḥm 't hpsḥ:* the apostles are *šlwḥym* "those sent"; Peter is always *kyp'*; Luke 22:14 "et cum facta esset hora" (lit. "and when the hour had been accomplished") becomes *wbšʿt hkwšr* "and when the hour was suitable"; Mark 15:14 (etc.) "crucifige eum!" ("crucify him!") becomes *tlh 'wtw!* "hang him!" following the Old Testament (Esth. 7:9 [Eng. v. 10]); Luke 22:15 "desiderio desideravi" ("I have earnestly desired") becomes good Hebrew *'bh 'byty;* and "a stone's throw" in v. 41 becomes *kmṭḥwy 'bn* on the analogy of Gen. 21:16 *kmṭḥwy qšt* "a bowshot." John 8:32 "and the truth will make you free" *wh'mt tḥpš 'tkm* sounds no less biblical, although the hapax legomenon *ḥpš* from Lev. 19:20 had to be adapted for the purpose. The woes pronounced on the Pharisees (Matt. 23) and the numerous passages against "the Jews" in John (e.g., 8:44) which Jona renders with literal fidelity sound almost too harsh in Hebrew.

Apart from numerous errors in pointing, which may have been due to the typesetter, and some inconsistencies in translating parallel themes and passages, the following mistranslations deserve attention:

(a) Judas Iscariot is translated variously as *'śqrywṭh, 'śkrywṭh,* and *'śq'rywṭ'*. Latin names also, such as Caiaphas, Pilatus, and Lazarus, are hebraized inconsistently.

(b) Matt. 26:7 "Alabastrum unguenti" *m'bn lbn . . . mrwqḥ . . .* "from a whitestone . . . an ointment." The Italian "alabastro" was understood here as a color, and "unguens" in its usual medical sense. Since many Jews were physicians and skilled in medicine, Jona may well have studied pharmacology.

(c) Matt. 26:13 "What she has done will be told in memory of her" *wy'mr šʿśth z't lzkrwnh.* Here the woman with the ointment becomes a publicity seeker, who anoints Jesus for the fame it will bring her.

(d) Matt. 26:16 "Oportunitatem" *hzmn mwkn* "the established time." This is somewhat awkward.

(e) Mark 14:3 "Unguenti nardi" *šmn ndrym* "oil of vows (pl.)," instead of *nrdymwn* or *nrdy*. Did Jonas have the Nazirite vow in mind? Or is this merely a misprint?

(f) Mark 15:3 "Et accusabant eum" *wylšynwhw* "and they slandered him.'' Since ''accusare (Jesum)'' is always translated elsewhere by ''to denounce,'' perhaps Jona was reminded of the phrase in the ʿAmidah prayer *wlmlšynym 'l thy tqwh* ''and to those who malign (us) do not be a hope.'' Or possibly the long and bitter experience of late medieval Jewry had led to a fusion of the terms ''accuse'' and ''denounce''?

(g) Luke 22:63 ''They mocked and struck him'' *lʿgw bw wbhktw* ''they mocked him and when he struck . . .'' This makes Jesus the one who strikes, rather than the one who is struck.

(h) John 1:1 ''In principio'' *br'šwn* ''in the beginning.'' It is not clear why the more biblical *br'šyt* (cf. Gen. 1:1) was not used.

(i) John 8:28 ''Cum exaltaveritis Filium hominis'' *bhrymkm bn h'dm* ''when you lift up the Son of man.'' Since the hiphil form of *rwm* almost invariably refers to elevating physically, and the spiritual alternatives are *lhdr* or *lrwmm* (which Jona must have known from the daily prayers of his youth), there seems to be a clear allusion here to the crucifixion of Jesus. The context of an angry dialogue with the ''unbelieving Jews'' strengthens this suspicion, as does also an often-cited polemic in one of the objections in *'Eben Boḥan*. The latter compares ''the lifting up of the Son of man'' (John 3:14) with the earlier serpent of Moses (Num. 21:9) in a clear allusion to the cross. Jona was quite familiar with this text, as his aspersions on Ibn Shaprut demonstrate.

(j) John 8:42 ''Ego enim ex Deo processi'' *ky 'ny h'ṣlty mh'l* ''for I have taken away from God.'' It appears that although the right verb has been chosen here, the form is inappropriate. In the Old Testament only God can be the subject of the verb *'ṣl* (''lay aside'') in the causative form. But since there is actually no Old Testament parallel for ''procedure'' in this sense, Jonas was forced *faute de mieux* to employ a Hebrew term with a Neoplatonic cabalistic meaning corresponding to ''emanate.'' His use of the hiphil form rather than the qal appears to be merely a grammatical slip.

(k) John 11:12 ''Si dormit salvus erit'' *'m hw' yšn bwšʿ* ''if he sleeps he will be saved.'' Although the disciples were thinking here only of the therapeutic value of sleep, Jesus soteriologized the passage to connote the redemption of the soul of Lazarus.

(l) John 11:27 ''Tu es Christus Filius Dei vivi'' *'th mšyḥ bn 'lqym ḥy* ''you are (the) Messiah, son of the living God.'' Either Jona hesitated to pluralize the Latin ''Deus'' to match the Hebrew grammatical form, or he intended specifically to construe the adjective ''living'' with ''Christ.''

(m) John 11:30 ''In castellum'' *btyrh* ''in the enclosed-village.'' This sounds like a feudal medievalism.

Excessive literalism is represented in the following, which are typical of about one hundred other examples:

(a) Matt. 26:17 "Prima die azymorum" *bywm r'šwn mhmṣwt* "on the first day of the Unleavened Bread."

(b) Mark 14:1 "Erat pascha et azyma" *wyhy psḥ wmṣwt* "it was Passover and Unleavened Bread."

(c) Mark 14:5 "Et fremebant in eam" *wygʿrw ngdh* "and they rebuked her."

(d) Mark 14:14 "domino domus" *l'dwn hbyt* (instead of *bʿl hbyt*)

(e) Luke 23:4 "Nihil invenio causae in hoc homine" *'yny mwṣ' b'yš hzh šwm sbh* "I do not find any case against this man." Although the Latin word "causa" clearly implies juridical guilt, the Hebrew word does not.

(f) John 11:13 "De dormitione somni" *'l tnwmt šynh* "by the slumber of sleep." The context here demands "the repose of sleep," but both Jerome and Jona have simple tautologies.

Despite all of its undeniable excellences, Jona's work remains the last of the great prescholarly translations. Its unevenness and inconsistencies witness to its spontaneous nature, prepared without the aid of dictionaries, lexica, and concordances. It is also the last to be based solely on the Latin Vulgate text, without reference to Greek sources. And yet it seems to have enjoyed extensive popularity, at least among missionaries. New editions continued to appear well into the eighteenth century, including a large tetraglot edition in 1746 which was published in German and Yiddish "so that even uneducated Jews will be able to understand it and profit from it."[68]

4. *From Baroque Philosemitism to the London Society for Promoting Christianity amongst the Jews*

Of the five types of relationship classified by Hans-Joachim Schoeps under the term "philosemitism,"[69] only three have had any effect upon Hebrew worth mentioning: (1) the Christian missionary type, which continues today to produce a Hebrew literature aiming at "the conversion of the Jews"; (2) the biblical-chiliastic type, whose fanatical "Jewish" interest so often leads to an interest in hebraisms; and (3) the religious type, the rarest of the five, whose representatives may master Hebrew the best, but who are irrelevant to our purpose because they nearly always end in being themselves converted to Judaism. The first two are scarcely to be identified as "philosemitism" in the strict sense, because the missionaries traditionally associate with Jews only to dejudaize them, while the Jewish fascination of chiliasts, pietists, quintomonarchists, and other such religious utopians comes down in the final analysis—to an extent even today—to advising the Jews in all friendliness to renounce Judaism.

A fusion of these two types is found in the British form of "hebraism" and doctrine of special election, which has produced such remarkable efforts to learn the Hebrew language. In conformity with the Missions Bull of Pope Clement V in 1312, there had long been a nominal lectureship in Hebrew at Oxford (as well as at Paris, Bologna, Salamanca, and Avignon) dedicated "to leading the erring (i.e., Jews) into the way of truth,"[70] but it was not until the sixteenth century that such a program was actually developed.[71] From 1524 Hebrew was printed in England; in 1549 the use of Hebrew was permitted in private worship—although the laws that banned Jews from the British Isles since 1290 were not repealed. Hebrew medals were struck as early as 1545 under Henry VIII, and in 1549 the German hebraist Paul Fagius was called to Oxford. He was followed in his chair at Oxford, and later at Cambridge, by a succession of converts, outstanding among whom was Emmanuel Tremellius of Ferrara (1510–1580), mentioned above.[72]

Not until the seventeenth century were Jews permitted to teach Hebrew in a university. The first to do so was "Rabbi Jacob" at Cambridge, whose students included some of the "forty-seven learned men" who undertook work on the new King James Version of the Bible in 1607.[73] These scholars were responsible for the fact that in England most of the Old Testament proper names were dehellenized (e.g., Elijah instead of Elias), that dozens of Hebrew expressions became an integral part of the English language, and that the names and sermons of the later Puritans—and even the muster rolls of Oliver Cromwell's army—were so influenced by the Old Testament.[74] Cromwell thought that the British were descendants of the "ten lost tribes" of Israel; he further held that because they had been lost since the destruction of the Northern Kingdom in 722 B.C.E. they had taken no part in the crucifixion of Christ, and consequently their British descendants could claim all the promises of the Old Testament as their proper inheritance. From this idea there was developed in the nineteenth century the British-Israel World Federation, which did not hesitate to support the claim of genealogical identity with Israel by etymological arguments: their leaders, including members of the nobility, the clergy, and the scholarly community, asserted that the very word "British" itself was simply the Hebrew expression *bryt-'yš* "Covenant-Man"![75]

The Dane Holger Paulli (1644–1714) argued along similar lines in claiming that his great-grandfather Simon Paulli was a Jew, a descendant of the royal line of David, whose name "Paulleli" was a combination of the Greek "Paulus" and the Hebrew *Eli,* meaning "God supplies the inadequacy." Further, he claimed that at the age of thirteen he had made a blood covenant with God, who exchanged a *yodh* (י) for the *he* (ה) in his baptismal name, thereby altering Holger to Oliger as a sign that "through him Jesus would be brought to the Jews." And further, the name Oliger also held an allusion to the olive leaf of Noah's dove.[76] To eliminate the scandal of the Christian Messiah who did not triumph, Paulli "proved" in several hundred pages sparking a brisk theological controversy that Jesus did not cry out "My God, my God, why hast thou forsaken me?" (Matt. 27:46; Mark 15:34) but "Why hast thou glorified me!" This, he contended, was because the Aramaic *šbqtny* in the "original Gospel" should be derived not from the Hebrew verb *šbq* "leave" but from *šbḥ* "to glorify."[77] Although Paulli's desire to help the Jews is certainly above suspicion ("No true Christian is an enemy to the Jews" was one of his favorite sayings), few were attracted to the enthusiasms of this "Apostle to the Jews from the North."

Among the fathers of the Jewish mission was also Johann Christoph Wagenseil (1633–1705), the jurist and orientalist of Altdorf, who envisioned a "great conversion of Jews" and sought to promote it by studying the language of the Bible: "In order to draw them (the Jews) out of the depths of unbelief in which they are mired, it is necessary to win them by becoming like them, and writing in their own dialect. . . ."[78] Among the first pietists to accept this challenge were the Herrnhut Brethren, whose hymnal included since 1731 the following hymn[79]:

I. "Der Tolah[80] ist mein Herr und Gott,
mein Goel[81] und mein Heil,
und werd' ich aller Welt zum Spott,
der Tolah bleibt mein Theil."

II. "Baruch Haschem[82] in Ewigkeit,
dass ich kann Maimin[83] sein,
ich bin Bewaddai[84] nun befreit
von Schire Lev[85] und Pein."

III. "Das ist Ikker,[86] wer es glaubt
und sich darauf verlässt,
wer's Modeh[87] ist und frey behaupt,
hat Olam Habbo[88] vest."

1. The *Crucified One* is my Lord and God
My *Redeemer* and my Savior,
Though ridiculed by all the world,
My lot is the *Crucified One*.

2. *Thanks be to God* eternally
That I can faithful be,
For now I am free *indeed*
From *suffering* and pain.

3. This is *the truth:* whoever believes
and trusts completely,

who *knows* and freely perseveres
is assured of the *Age to Come*.

As noted by Siegfried Riemer, who has done yeoman service in research on these Jewish-German hymns, it is quite understandable "that the frequency of Hebrew expressions in the songs struck contemporary critics as pompous and inappropriate."[89] Further it seems that this pious language mix contributed neither toward "Jewish participation in the Christian worship services"[90] nor to "making Jews feel at home in the Church,"[91] as Count Nicolaus Ludwig von Zinzendorf (1700–1760) undoubtedly hoped it would. Since Jesus is called "Tolah" here and "Ose Ish"[92] in another hymn, both of which are medieval Jewish paraphrases for the Nazarene familiar from the notorious *Toledot Yeshu,*[93] it would appear that the count was the victim of a subtle mockery. It may be, of course, that he proudly wished to accept this ridicule as a kind of crown of thorns, which may be suggested by the third line of the first verse cited above.

The following hymn approaches the grotesque with its mixture of German, Yiddish, and Hebrew:

"Am Schabbas[94] sind wir stille
und ruhn in der K'hille,[95]
wir tun uns was zu gut,
wir acheln[96] von dem Tolah,
der für uns ward ein Olah,[97]
und trinken auch von seinem Blut."[98]

On the *Sabbath* we are quiet
and find rest in the *church,*
we do it for our good.
We *eat* of the *Crucified One*
who became a *sacrifice* for us,
and we also drink of his blood.

The blunt "acheln von dem Tolah" here stands in contrast to the sensitive use of the Old Testament expression *'Olâ* to bring Jesus' self-sacrifice into association with Abraham's near-sacrifice of his only son Isaac (Gen. 22:6ff.). No less biblical despite its Yiddish pronunciation is the following verse from another hymn of the Herrnhut community.

"Welch ein gute B'sore[99]
sein Blut ist die Cappore,[100]
wir sind dadurch erlöst.
Es schreit für uns Mechile,[101]
Gott hört's, schenkt die Meile,[102]
das Herz fühlt's und wird getröst't."[103]

What *good news!*
His blood *atones,*

And by it we are saved.
It cries for our *forgiveness,*
God hears, bestows *pardon,*
the heart feels it, and is comforted.

The hymnal concludes with Hebrew translations of two hymns, the first of which ("Christi Blut and Gerechtigkeit") is still found in the German Evangelical hymnal.[104]

The only translation of Matthew based on the Syriac Peshitta of the fifth-sixth century is from the hand of a distinguished Sabbatarian, Moses ben Aharon "Kohen min Cracow," who accepted Christian baptism after the gematrically determined "messianic year" 1695 had passed, and who took the new name Johan Christian Jakob Kemper.[105] About 1699 he left Niederwerrn-bei-Schweinfurt for Sweden, where he served from 1700 until his death in 1714 as "Sprakmästar i Hebreiskan" at the University of Uppsala, training a whole generation of Swedish scholars in oriental and rabbinic studies. Since "Rabbi" Johan Kemper, as he was known after his conversion, knew no Greek and as a convinced Lutheran (or because of the strong rabbinic criticism of Jerome?) was distrustful of the Vulgate, his choice of source texts was no less original than some of his translations. For example, in his preface he calls Christians *mšwḥym* "anointed ones"; Peter in Matt. 4:18 is theologized as *piṭûr* (instead of *pāṭûr*) "freed" (i.e., by his faith he had been freed from his sins); the treatment of the woman with an issue of blood in 9:20 reminds him of the prophet Elisha (who did similar things in Elijah's day), yet he analyzes his name as *ʾl-yšʿ* to explain him as a "type" of Jesus. Finally, in commenting on 24:5 Kemper states that Jesus foresaw both Simon Bar Kokhba and Sabbatai Zvi "who falsely claimed to be the Messiah," and he cites Ezek. 13:10 ("they have misled my people, saying, 'Peace,' when there is no peace").[106] Of the ninety pages of this translation, only the title page was printed, but in 1714 a Latin translation of Kemper's commentary on Matthew was published under the title *Meʾirat ʿEnaim* (*Illuminatio Oculorum,* from Ps. 19:9), in which the number of rabbinic parallels and examples anticipates the work of Paul Billerbeck.[107] The manuscript of Matthew is still in the library of the University of Uppsala.

One of the most interesting translations of the eighteenth century is *Ha-sepher shel we-ʾangilu shel ha-Noṣarim shel Yesh"u* [*The book of the Gospel belonging to the followers of Jesus*]. It contains all the books of the New Testament and was translated about 1750 by a certain Ezekiel Raḥabi (not Rakibi, *pace* Franz Delitzsch[108]) in an uneven and faulty Hebrew with a strong anti-Christian bias. From the style of the handwriting, the first part[109] is the work of a half-educated rabbinic Jew of Sephardic background; the second part,[110] consisting of Acts through Ephesians and Revelation, was penned by his assistant, who came from Germany (as even Gustaf Dalman agrees[111]). The polemic tendency, which is well attested in the text itself, is confirmed explicitly by the final words on page 70b of Ms. no. Oo 1:32, which reads: "Heaven is my witness that I have not translated this, God forfend, to believe it, but to understand it and know how to answer the heretics . . . that our true Messiah will come. Amen."[112]

In comparison with the translation of Matthew in Ibn Shaprut's *'Eben Boḥan,* the clumsy vigor of this attempt at a Hebrew translation is reminiscent of the first Latin translations of the Talmud by the Church's hebraists in the late medieval period. But that is another story.

The most important translations of the New Testament from the German late Baroque and Enlightenment periods are the following:

The Letter to the Hebrews published at Leipzig in 1676 by the convert Friedrich Albrecht Christiani (alias Baruch ben Moshe) was rightly praised by his publisher as written in a "pura, tersa et nitida (pure, concise and neat)" style.

Under the aegis of the Institutum Judaicum which was founded in Leipzig in 1728, the Gospel of Luke (through 22:14) appeared in Hebrew in 1735 in a translation by the proselyte Dr. Heinrich Christian Immanuel Frommann. Franz Delitzsch extolled it as "the best ever written by a Jewish Christian in the Hebrew language."[113] Over a century later (1855) Frommann's rabbinic commentary on Luke appeared in a revised form, edited by Dr. Joachim Heinrich Raphael Biesenthal.[114] Frommann also translated a second book into Hebrew, the Acts of the Apostles, which he completed in 1736 but never published; also as early as 1729 he had translated and published a Yiddish edition of Acts and 1 John.

The well-intentioned but deplorable attempt of Johann Heinrich Callenberg (1694–1760), the founder of the first Institutum Judaicum at Halle, and of his students to trick faithful Jews into proselyting conversations is described in his *Bericht von einem Versuch das arme jüdische Volck zur Erkänntnis und Annehmung der christlichen Wahrheit anzuleiten* [*Account of an Attempt to Lead the Poor Jewish People to a Recognition and Acceptance of Christian Truth*].[115] They greeted Jews with "Shalom Immanu!" ("Peace be with us!") instead of the usual "Shalom aleḥem!" ("Peace be with you!"). On Friday evenings they appeared in the synagogues and opened up their Hebrew Old Testaments to passages not appointed for that Sabbath, and handed out missionary tracts written in Hebrew by "Joḥanan Kimḥi"—as the Pastor Johannes Müller translated his name—to suggest a false association with the renowned medieval rabbinic family of Provence (Joseph, Moses, and David Kimḥi).

Missionary writings of the nineteenth century such as the *'Edut le-Israel* [*Witness to Israel*] of Theophil Lucky; the *Ḥizzuk 'Emunah 'Emet*

[*Strengthening True Faith*], a Jewish-Christian answer to the *Ḥizzuq 'Emunah* of the Karaite Isaac ben Abraham de Troki; and the *Shirey Shaḥar* [*Songs of Dawn*] of Constantin Schlottmann[116] contained long quotations and paraphrases from the New Testament whose literary quality seldom matched the missionary zeal of their authors.

All of this was far surpassed in England at the beginning of the last century, where in 1809 the London Society for Promoting Christianity amongst the Jews was founded, essentially as the result of efforts by a German Jewish Christian, Joseph Samuel Christian Friedrick Frey (1771–1850). In the words of Pastor J. F. A. De Le Roi, the cool and objective historian of Jewish missions, writing about this son of a rabbinical assessor who began his career as a shoemaker[117]: "The heart of it all was Frey. It was he who brought the Society into being and gave the Jewish mission the evangelical cast it retains in our own day."[118] Delitzsch reported later: "It was not very long before the London Society came to appreciate the task of (Hebrew) translating as of inestimable importance but still inadequately achieved, and was excited by a noble enthusiasm for the work."[119] The impetus for this work came from the Rev. Claudius Buchanan, who after many years of pastoral work in India returned in 1810 with a considerable collection of Hebrew manuscripts he had discovered on the Malabar coast in 1806 "in one of the synagogues of the Black Jews of Cochin."[120] The collection, which he later gave to the Cambridge University Library, included among other items a homiletical commentary on the Pentateuch, a fragment of the Talmudic tractate *Ḥullin,* a commentary on the first part (*'Oraḥ Ḥayyim*) of the *Shulḥan 'Aruḥ* [*Table Prepared*] of Joseph ben Ephraim Qaro, a Sephardic *Maḥzor,* a chronicle of the Jews of Malabar and Cochin,[121] and the Hebrew New Testament (noted above) whose translator (or transcriber?) appears as *kbwd m'lt hrb rby rḥby yḥzq'l nwḥw 'dn* "Honored to the degree of the great Rabbi Raḥabi Ezekiel, may he rest in peace." Even Buchanan, whose knowledge of Hebrew was evidently excellent, speaks of him as "a learned rabbi"[122] who disputed with the Syrian Mar Thoma Christians of his area. Nevertheless, the remark in the eighteenth chapter of the Malabar chronicle seems reliable: *'bl zh yḥzq'l 'ynw rby wmšpḥtw rḥby* "But this Ezekiel is not a rabbi nor his family Raḥabi."[123]

Buchanan proposed to the Society that a new translation of the New Testament be undertaken on the basis of the Travancore text. Since a cursory review of the Indian manuscript showed it to be "too full of rabbinisms," and the work of Elias Hutter was "not in pure Hebrew," and neither William G. Robertson's nor Richard Caddick's edition had received approval, it was decided that a new translation should be undertaken. The project was launched in 1813 by Thomas Frey and William Bengo Collyer, with the assistance of "a learned

Jew, Mr. Judah d'Allemand, from Germany.''[124] Matthew was published the same year, followed in 1815 by Mark, and in 1816 by Luke, John, and Acts. A year later the epistles and the Apocalypse were published, and then the entire New Testament in a new octavo edition.[125] Since the sole purpose of this fully pointed (although occasionally faultily vocalized) translation was ''the conversion of the Jews''—in the preface the editors echo medieval tradition in speaking of ''the Jews laboring in constant blindness''[126]—great emphasis was placed on simplicity and clarity of expression, often at the expense of grammatical accuracy and stylistic elegance.

The fact that this was the first Hebrew translation to be made from the Greek Textus Receptus is reflected in the great number of hellenisms which replaces the earlier high incidence of latinisms. For example:

—Matt. 17:15 ''selēniázetai'' *mkh-yrḥ* ''be moonstruck''

—Matt. 26:27; Luke 22:17, 19 ''eucharistḗsas'' *wywdh* ''he gave thanks''

—Mark 15:1 ''euthỳs prōì'' *pt'wm bbqr* ''suddenly in the morning''

—Luke 21:7 ''didáskale'' *mlmd* ''instructor''

—Luke 21:32 ''héōs àn pánta génētai'' *ʿd ky yhyw kwlm* ''until all of them come to pass''

—John 1:13 ''haimátōn'' *mdmym* ''of blood''

—John 4:25 ''ho legómenos Christós'' *hnqrʾ qrysṭ* ''the one called Christ''

Most grating is the use of the verb *bpṭs* (and *bpṭz*) for ''baptize,'' so that Matt. 20:22 reads *wlhbpṭyz bbpṭysmʾ ʾšr ʾbpṭyz* ''or to be baptized with the baptism (with) which I am baptized,'' which is not only absolutely un-Hebrew but is also unnecessary because the verb *ṭbl* ''dip'' is completely satisfactory. No less un-Hebrew are the Old Testament quotations, which are almost without exception back-translations from the Septuagint, as are also such neologisms as *mhgym* for ''mágoi'' (Matt. 2:1), *ywḥnn bpṭysṭys* for John the Baptist, and *šmʿwn pṭr* for Peter.

In response to criticisms of language and style which only increased following the appearance of the second edition of 1819 and the third edition of 1821,[127] the Society decided on a basic revision of the text. This was accomplished in 1837–1838 by Alexander McCaul and the proselytes Johann Christian Reichardt, Stanislaus Hoga, and the Rev. (later Bishop) Michael Solomon Alexander. The finished revision, partly dehellenized and with correct Old Testament quotations, appeared in 1840 in a new edition, followed in rapid succession by further editions in 1844, 1846, 1852, and 1853. Another duodecimo edition with accents added (*ṭʿmy hmqrʾ* ''accents of the reading'') followed in 1863–1866. "We will not discuss here whether this accenting of the New Testament text is an innovation serving any useful purpose at all," said Franz Delitzsch, and in his further comments he left the reader in no doubt of his absolute opposition to it.[128]

In 1831 a further revision of the original Hebrew edition of 1813–1817 appeared, prepared by William Greenfield, editorial superintendent of the British and Foreign Bible Society, and taking into account criticisms of its language made by competent German as well as English hebraists. It was published by Samuel Bagster in London in a Hebrew-English edition and also in the same year in a miniature edition, apparently as a curiosity, almost illegible to the unaided eye.[129] Between 1857 and 1863 the revised text of 1840 was again thoroughly revised by a committee of nine members, eight of whom were either Jews or of Jewish background.[130] The resulting text which appeared in London in 1866 was characterized by Delitzsch the following year as "no improvement" over the earlier editions.[131] "Even the title of the latest edition is incorrect (*ktby hbryt hḥdšh nʿtq mlšwn ywnyt ʾl lšwn ʿbryt* [*Writings of the New Testament translated from the language of the Greeks to the language of the Hebrews*])," wrote the great Leipzig hebraist, who had also objected to the title of the first edition (*bryt ḥdšh ʿl py mšyḥ nʿtq mlšwn ywn llšwn ʿbry* [*New Testament according to the Messiah translated from the Greek language to the Hebrew language*]).[132]

The Hebrew version of the *Book of Common Prayer,* the liturgy of the Anglican church, was the magnum opus of the Anglican Mission to the Jews, based on the work of three generations of converts. The first Hebrew translation, made in 1717 by the proselyte Abraham Bar Jacob, was never printed. About 1815 another convert, Christian Czerskier, translated it into the language of the Bible in Warsaw. Both versions were reviewed by Reichardt and Alexander, who collated and coordinated them in a single text which they published with great confidence in London in December 1836. All the archbishops, bishops, dignitaries, and theologians of the Anglican church received copies of this magnificently designed edition. Services following this liturgy were observed in London (Palestine Place Church) from 1837, and in Jerusalem (Mount Zion) from 1838. Alexander used it for his consecration to the episcopacy in 1841, and a few months later for the blessing of the cornerstone of Christ Church on Mount Zion.[133] The hope which his church placed in this work was expressed at the time by Bishop Edward Henry Bickersteth of Exeter: "It is no small thing that the Liturgy of our Church has been translated into Hebrew . . . and has proved to so many Israelites that we hate idolatry even as they and worship Him Who is a Spirit in spirit and truth."[134] Despite the high cost of production and a relatively restricted circulation, a second fully-pointed edition of three thousand copies appeared in 1841. Three characteristics strike the reader of this text.

(a) The many anglicisms, such as:

—"He took again his body, with flesh . . ." (Article IV) *wlqḥ 't gwytw 't hbšr*.

—"The realm of England" *mmlkt 'ngl'nd*.

—"Parliament" *prl'mnṭ*.

(b) The technical terms of the Church which are left untranslated:

—"The homilies" *h'wmylywt*.

—"The litany" *lyṭ'ny'*.

—"Phronema sarkos" *prwnmh srqws*.

(c) The artificial hebraizing of many theological terms:

—"Confirmation" *htqymwt* (lit. "self-establishment").

—"Consecration" *htqdšwt* (lit. "the setting apart of oneself").

—"Holy Communion" *hthḥbrwt hqdš* (lit. "the making of a holy alliance").

—"Justification of Man" (Article XI of the Thirty-nine Articles). This is mistranslated by the use of the reflexive hithpael form (*hṣṭdqwt bny-'dm*, lit. "mankind's making itself justified"), resulting in a distortion of the Pauline doctrine of justification.

With regard to one part of the book (*šḥryt* "Morning Prayer," *m'ryb* "Evening Prayer," *t'nyt* "fasting"), the Israeli who thinks in Hebrew can agree with the London Society's *Report* 31 (1839): "The ministrations and liturgy of our Church are peculiarly suited to the mind and habits of the Jews."[135] Actually, there are whole pages which sound like excerpts from the Psalms or the synagogue *Siddur*. But Delitzsch is largely right in saying of the rest of the liturgy that "these works are anything but Hebrew, what with Old Testament phrases pieced together with no sense of correct usage, to say nothing of gracefulness. The translators' good intentions far exceed their stylistic abilities; they are altogether lacking in the basic principles and the sensitivity to rhythm so necessary for expressing the message of the New Testament in Hebrew forms."[136]

A sober review of this Hebrew version of the liturgy naturally raises the question: for whom was this text actually produced at such great expense? By far the majority of the Jews in England at the time did not understand enough Hebrew to read the book, much less use it devotionally; their rabbis and those familiar with the Torah would have had difficulty suppressing amusement at the awkward attempts to Judaize Christian terminology; and those Jews along the fringe who were most susceptible to the Jewish mission would undoubtedly have preferred to use the texts in their original English form. To judge from the Society's distribution lists, the work may have found its greatest use among the clergy of the Anglican church, in stimulating their interest in the study of Hebrew.

5. The *Ha-berit ha-Hadashah* of Franz Delitzsch

Franz Delitzsch (1813–1890), the theologian, exegete, and one of the best informed Christians on Hebrew literature, wrote in 1870: "We would not ourselves have attempted a new translation (of the New Testament) if we thought that the London Society had succeeded in the three stages of their approach to this goal. But we are not so persuaded."[137]

Even as a young instructor he had been concerned with the task to which he devoted fifty-two years of his life and the greater part of his scholarly efforts. Echoing Johann Wolfgang von Goethe he wrote in 1884: "I have long been divided between a purely scholarly interest in the literature of the Jewish people, and a spiritual concern for their conversion."[138] It often seemed that his two great passions for Judaism and the Jewish mission, which were so often in mutual conflict, could find their final solution only in a Hebrew translation of the New Testament. His philological confession in the year 1838 is most revealing:

> The New Testament . . . was written in the Greek language. The Holy Spirit made use of the language of the gentiles, not the language of Abraham and his people, for the literary transmission of the New Testament revelation in order to show that the Church should comprise not only the old Israel, but the new as well. . . . The Jewish people rejected . . . the revelation of the New Testament. . . . If the Jewish people had not rejected their Messiah and the Hebrew language had developed within the Church, it would certainly have taken a different direction, developing through quite different cycles of growth, with a completely different range of vocabulary. . . .[139]

Delitzsch criticized all the Hebrew versions of the New Testament, from the *Evangelium iuxta Hebraeos* [Gospel According to the Hebrews] once copied by Jerome to the versions made by proselytes in the nineteenth century.

> Jewish-Christian literature in Hebrew offers only rare examples of writers adequately prepared either by nature or by training to mold a new Hebrew idiom for the formal expression of newly recognized truths when faced with a lack of any precedent. It is most interesting to observe how the Jewish convert struggles with Chris-

tian ideas when writing in Hebrew, and how difficult it is for him to express his Christian faith in Hebrew forms.[140]

He himself admitted that the new translation which he felt was so necessary "could not be the work of a single individual," and yet as someone had to make a beginning of it the young instructor decided to undertake it: "I am appending to this essay a sample of a new translation which is faithful to the spirit of the Hebrew language and not merely to its vocabulary. May the friends of Israel support this effort to its completion!"[141] Then follows a Hebrew version of the apostolic Hymn to Love (1 Cor. 13) in a pure Biblical Hebrew, fully and correctly pointed, and in a poetic diction of a sublimity that borders on the rapturous. It should also be noted that these thirteen verses pose no great theological or semantic difficulties, that their vocabulary and train of thought are essentially related to the Old Testament, and that Delitzsch's Jewish Hebrew teacher, Dr. Julius Fürst, reviewed and corrected it. From 1883 to 1890 the responsibility for revising, correcting, and vocalizing the Leipzig hebraist's version of the New Testament in Hebrew was entrusted to the Jewish scholar J. J. Kohan.

Since the "friends of Israel" who were addressed in this preliminary effort practically ignored it, Delitzsch turned in 1864 to his missionary periodical *Saat auf Hoffnung* with a call for assistance in "reorienting first the four strictly Jewish Christian books of the New Testament to their origins, i.e., the Gospel of Matthew, the Letter of James, the Letter to the Hebrews, and the Apocalypse . . . (and to) permit the people of Israel to read them in the holy language of their fathers." To make the proposal more attractive, Delitzsch emphasized that the new version would differ from the London edition based on the text of Desiderius Erasmus by being based on "the earliest witnesses, now including the recently discovered codex from Mount Sinai." Although he himself claimed no remuneration "as the director of the project and as one of the translators," this appeal also fell on deaf ears.

Undeterred, Delitzsch continued his work, and in 1870 published his translation of the Letter to the Romans.[142] As Delitzsch indicates in his preface, the methodology for this and his later translations was set by both of the purposes governing this long-range project.

> We made no attempt to hide the fact that the major practical purpose of this undertaking is primarily . . . to give to Israelites in a more attractive, easier, and direct form a knowledge and experience of the New Testament writings. . . . We hope that the noble souls who read the Gospels in the Hebrew language will find it convincing, but this we leave to God, and we forswear all unworthy tricks to force the issue. . . . Together with this practical goal there is combined a scholarly purpose. . . . A translation of the

> New Testament into Hebrew involves far more (than translations into other languages), because it requires not only a basic understanding of the New Testament text, but also an understanding of the language which conditioned the thought and expressions of the sacred writers even though they were writing in Greek. The role of scholarship consists primarily in distinguishing the various Old Testament, rabbinic, and hellenistic components in the early Christian ways of thinking and speaking.[143]

The great number of hebraisms which prompt Delitzsch to speak repeatedly of ''thinking back'' provide fully adequate evidence for his hypothesis. Over several decades and through successive revisions Delitzsch developed the early outlines and ideas of his own methodology which found its justification in the joint promotion of his overall purposes of scholarship and mission. As the following statement shows, throughout his life the theologian in Delitzsch recognized his need of the philologist for his scholarly well-being. In 1864 he wrote: ''The task facing the translator of the New Testament is to combine faithfulness with proper usage and taste, so that the New Testament will not only be intelligible to Israelites, but will also engage and hold their interest.''[144] Several years later he discussed how this could be done.

> It has been my endeavor to present the text as the writers of the New Testament conceived it in Hebrew and would have written it in Hebrew, taking all due consideration of the transition from Biblical to Mishnaic Hebrew.[145] The translator should not avoid rabbinic usage when it provides words or expressions reflected in the Greek text, but medieval and philosophical expressions are certainly to be avoided, even when translated into biblical words.[146]

Delitzsch continued to define his basic principles.

> The orthography of the text, including scriptio plena and defectiva, should resemble that of the Old Testament as much as possible. . . . We should attempt to translate sentences as complete units, rendering them idiomatically. Even if they do not correspond to the Greek in every detail, they should convey the whole idea the writer wished to express. . . . When the choice is between a classical but free translation and a less classical but more faithful translation, the latter is to be preferred because it is far more important to be faithful to the original text of the Word of God than to weaken it for the sake of a proper Hebrew style. . . . The spirit of the New Testament has its own special forms of thought and expression, and the New Testament writers, St. Paul and St. John in particular, have their own styles. It was my endeavor not to hide

> it from the Jewish readers when the form of the original is stiff, monotonous, or unpleasant. . . . We should not try to improve on the human form of the New Testament. . . . I admit quite frankly that I have sacrificed consistency and eloquence to faithfulness in passages where both cannot be achieved together.[147]

As a result of these principles Delitzsch did not attempt to be consistent in the translation of certain words—such as ''kósmos'' (''world''), ''kairós'' (''time''), ''cháris'' (''grace''), and ''parousía'' (''presence'')—whose meaning in Hebrew differs by context. He frequently translated several Greek words by a single Hebrew word, or vice versa, occasionally ignoring a ''kai,'' ''gè,'' or ''dé'' where it does not alter the meaning. True to his principle of maximal similarity to Old Testament usage, he employs Mishnaic Hebrew (with which he assumed at least Paul and Matthew were familiar) only where the Old Testament offers no genuine equivalent. Thus in Romans he used only 109 postbiblical words—less than 2 percent of the text, and about 5 percent of the total vocabulary. For example:

—*'brym* ''members'' (Rom. 6:13, 19; 7:5, 23; 12:4–5)
—*'pšr* ''possible'' (5:7; 12:18)
—*blbd* ''only'' (Gk. ''mónon''; 5:3, 11; 9:10)
—*nlwy* ''revelation'' (16:25)
—*ṭbylh* ''baptism'' (6:4)
—*sbh* ''opportunity'' (7:8, 11)
—*ʿtyd* ''future'' (8:38)
—*ṣlb* ''crucify'' (6:6)
—*tḥyh* ''resurrection'' (1:4; 6:5)

Despite all his efforts, the Hebrew version of Romans received only a small favorable response and little sales. Since no publisher could be found in Germany to finance a complete edition of the New Testament in Hebrew, Delitzsch turned to the British and Foreign Bible Society, which agreed after some hesitation to sponsor it. The first edition, which appeared in London in 1877, was based largely on Codex Sinaiticus. The second edition followed in 1878, and at the request of the conservative Society it was corrected to the Greek Textus Receptus. Suggestions for improvements contributed by numerous Christian and Jewish scholars were incorporated (when approved by Delitzsch) in the third edition in 1880 and the fourth edition (of fifty thousand copies) in 1882.

Encouraged by his long awaited success, Delitzsch concentrated on an intensive program of careful revision, examining afresh every sentence and every word. After his fifth edition appeared in 1883, representing a thorough revision of the text, he was appointed an honorary member of the Society. An improved sixth edition appeared in

1885, a seventh in 1886, an eighth in 1888, an improved ninth edition in 1889, and at the beginning of 1890 the tenth and last edition to be overseen by this tireless perfectionist himself.

Delitzsch's words on January 29, 1890, a few weeks before his death, recall something of his conscientiousness as a scholar.

> The typographical composition of a book of about thirty quires such as the New Testament is not something to be tossed off lightly in passing, but demands at least six months' attention. And this demand becomes the more urgent when the text is the New Testament Word of God, and the variety of questions involved, both small and large, constantly suggest the possibility of further improvements.[148]

During his final illness in February 1890, he decided to entrust the editing of a new edition of his New Testament to his disciple and friend, Gustaf Dalman, and until the day of his death he continued to review with him with keen interest the principles, corrections, and footnotes of the new edition. This eleventh edition, which represents the definitive form of the final revision achieved by Delitzsch and (after his death) Dalman, appeared in 1892 and served as the base for the three further editions that have since been published.

Theological Terms and Idioms Lack of space precludes discussion here of any more than half a dozen theological terms from Romans. The longest of St. Paul's letters and a basic expression of the apostle's theology, the translation of this book was revised most frequently by the Leipzig hebraist.

(a) Rom. 1:1 "Euangelion" ("gospel"). Delitzsch translates the term consistently as *bśwrh* "good news," although literally it should be *bśwrh ṭwbh* (with the attributive adjective). Two cogent reasons, one linguistic and one theological, led him to this decision. The Old Testament term *b^{e}śôrâ* is always translated in the Septuagint as "euangélion" (or "euangelía"). Further, Delitzsch wished to establish an explicit association with Isa. 61:1–2, both on the verbal level and on the deeper level of content, for all the "Gospel" passages of the New Testament—in the tradition of Luke 4:17–21, where Jesus appears as the proclaimer of the Good News foretold by Isaiah. Therefore the verb "euangelízesthai" ("to proclaim") is also regularly translated by *bśr*.

(b) 1:4 "Pneûma hagiōsýnēs" ("Spirit of holiness"). Not only the words, but also the genitive of description points to the term *rwḥ hqdš* "holy Spirit," which is found twice in the Old Testament: (1) Ps. 51:13 (Eng. v. 11), where the context demands the meaning of an inner moral power which inspires mankind to uprightness of life[149]; and (2)

Isa. 63:10, where the reference is to the guiding presence of God in the life of Israel. In both instances the Septuagint translation is "pneûma hagiōsýnēs." So although *rwḥ hqdš* means literally "the spirit of holiness" and Delitzsch generally avoids Mishnaic Hebrew in favor of Old Testament terminology, here he translates *rwḥ hqdšh*. The reason seems to be that he recognized in Rom. 1:3–4 an early Christian formula ("katà sárka" ["according to flesh"] and "katà pneûma" ["according to spirit"]!) in which the concept of the "Holy Spirit" already shows a tendency toward a degree of personification or hypostasis that is sufficiently alien to the Old Testament to make the term *rwḥ hqdš* no longer appropriate. The option of the postbiblical *rwḥ hqdšh*, which is distinctly a stage removed from the original Old Testament expression, is consequently more suited to represent the (later) Christian implication of personification.[150]

(c) 1:4 "Anastáseōs nekrō̃n" ("resurrection of the dead"). Here the words and their grammatical construction clearly imply *tḥyt hmtym*, which occurs four times in the Mishnah (e.g., *Sanh.* x.1, 3).[151] But Delitzsch intentionally avoids this and translates instead *t*ᵉ*ḥiyâ mēʿim hamēṯîm* (lit. "resurrection from [being] with the dead"). The reasoning seems to be that Jesus arose from the dead, while the dead remained dead.

(d) 2:4 "Metánoia" ("repentance"). The Greek term corresponds naturally to *tšwbh*, as Delitzsch correctly translates. But there is a clear philological distinction between these two concepts, as Franz Rosenzweig describes it.

> Our obduracy is a fact, and our "alienation from God" (if indeed it is alienation and not original distance from God) can be healed only by returning, and not by conversion. The concept of repentance is represented in Hebrew by "returning," and the fact that this Hebrew word *tešubah* is "metánoia" and therefore "repentance" in the New Testament represents one of the points where world history is recorded in the dictionary.[152]

(e) 5:1 "Dikaiōthéntes ek písteōs" ("justified by faith"). It is Pauline theology that mankind is affected from birth by original sin and cannot become righteous by his own efforts (in contrast to *j. Mak.* i.6 *yʿśh tšwbh wytkpr lw* "he will repent [lit. "make a return"] and be covered for it") but only through the atoning death of Jesus and by faith in this divinely given atonement. This doctrine is expressed grammatically by the passive form of the verb *ṣdq* "be righteous," which does not occur in the Old Testament with this meaning. (It should be remarked parenthetically that the Qumran texts reveal conceptions of justification more closely related to Paul's.) That this distinction is more than a mere grammatical quibble is demonstrated by the London version (by a predominantly Jewish Christian committee), where Paul's "justification" is consistently rendered as *hṣṭdqwt* "self-justification"[153] and this passage (Rom. 5:1) is *hṣṭdqnw* "we justify ourselves" on the analogy of Gen. 44:16.

The transition from the Old Testament to the New Testament concept is found in the Letter to the Galatians. Delitzsch translated the key passage Gal. 2:16ff. "ou dikaioûtai ánthrōpos" ("man is not justified") with the biblical phrase *l' yṣdq 'dm,* and "hína dikaiōthṓmen" ("in order to be justified") in the next line with the Old Testament phrase *lmʿn nṣdq*. But then he follows Paul in altering the citation from Ps. 143:2 antinomistically to *ky l' yṣdq kl bśr mmʿśy htwrh* ("for no flesh is righteous before the law"), thus preparing the theological basis for the semantic change in the next verse (2:17). It is interesting to note here that the Septuagint renders the *qal* form of the Psalm's *yiṣdaq* with the passive form "dikaiōthḗsetai" (as it does similarly in Isa. 43:9, 26; 45:25). Paul adopts this, but in a quasijuristic sense of "made right in the divine court" rather than in the moral context of the Old Testament. Delitzsch rightly rejects the Septuagint passive for the Old Testament qal here, but not in the next verse (Gal. 2:17), where he follows Paul's lead by rendering "zētoûntes dikaiōthḗnai" ("endeavoring to be justified") with the novel niphal *bbqšnw lhṣdq*. This niphal occurs also in Rom. 4:2 as *ky 'm nṣdq 'brhm* "for if Abraham was justified"; in 5:9 as *nṣdqnw* "we are justified"; and in 5:1 as hophal *'ḥry hṣdqnw* "since we were made just," to the surprise of the Hebrew reader. Delitzsch also seems to have sensed this, for from the fifth edition of the New Testament he contented himself here also with the more easily acceptable niphal *'ḥry nṣdqnw b'mwnh* "since we were justified by faith." He relies here on an obscure passage in Dan. 8:14 (*wᵉniṣdaq qōḏeš* "sacredness shall be restored"), which is understood by most Jewish exegetes as concerned with the purification or restoration of the sanctuary—completely unrelated to Paul's doctrine of justification.

(f) 8:2 "Nómos toû pneúmatos tês zōḗs" ("the law of the Spirit of life"). The expression certainly does not have for Paul the meaning of its literal translation *twrt rwḥ hḥyym.* While *rwḥ hḥyym* means "the breath of life," referring at Gen. 6:17; 7:15 to the biological fact, in this context it is theologized as the antithesis of the Torah.

Similar difficulties surround such terms as "grace," "justification," "sin," "spirit," "atonement," "to be saved," and "sons of God," all of which have clear, unequivocal meanings in the Old Testament differing radically from their use in the letters of Paul. The unbiased reader of Hebrew can only regard them as confusing homonyms.

6. The Posthumous Delitzsch Edition by Gustaf Dalman

When Franz Delitzsch, shortly before his death in February 1890, entrusted to Gustaf Dalman the manuscript and press sheets for the eleventh edition of his Hebrew New Testament, they were both correct in speaking of a "new edition," because it was to be distinguished from its predecessors by more than one thousand alterations and corrections. A number of these improvements admittedly consisted of returning to the readings of earlier editions; but these instances did not mark the interruption of a trend so much as simply Delitzsch's capacity for recognizing to the very last when he had made a poor judgment and his ability to learn from it. The indefatigable hebraist took most seriously the saying of Jesus that "not a dot will pass from the law" (Matt. 5:18), as is shown among other things by the fact that secondary translation problems such as the dubious *yodh* (י) in Isa. 29:13 (*wthw yr'tm 'ty* or *wthy yr'tm 'ty?*), which he needed for Matt. 15:9, became for Delitzsch the occasion for an extended and profound correspondence.

In spite of all his love and respect for his mentor, Dalman did not regard it as his duty to carry out obediently the principles and decisions of Delitzsch. He had two scholarly reservations that stood in the way.

> First, I could not agree completely with Delitzsch's principle of "translating the text as the New Testament writer would himself have conceived it in Hebrew and written it in Hebrew," because I could not convince myself that the New Testament writings had generally been conceived in Hebrew, and I suspected that Jesus and his disciples in the Palestinian environment spoke not Hebrew but Aramaic.[154]

This last fact, as well as the hypothesis that some presynoptic collections of logia or similar "primitive Gospel" must have been compiled in Aramaic, the "mother tongue" of Jesus, became the theme of Dalman's later work *Jesus-Jeshua.*[155] This work represents a kind of "anti-Delitzsch" statement in New Testament scholarship because it offers reconstructions of the principal pericopes, logia, and key passages of the New Testament in Aramaic. Delitzsch was naturally well aware of the popular use of Aramaic in Jesus' day, yet he asserted that "the Hebrew language always remained the language of worship, of law, of scholarship, and of literature."[156] In his view, Aramaic was "the popular everyday language, used by the common people as well as by scholars for conversation . . . but Hebrew continued to be the holy language of the temple, of prayer, of blessings, and of the Law."[157]

Therefore Delitzsch concluded that "it was most unlikely that Matthew would have written in Aramaic."[158]

No less important than Dalman's "Aramaic protest" is his reservation about Hebrew: "A major difficulty with the type of language chosen by Delitzsch is that it represents a mixture of Old Testament and talmudic Hebrew which is his own creation, and not paralleled in any Jewish document."[159]

Fifty-seven years after the death of Delitzsch a bedouin goatherd found a collection of scrolls in a cave not far from the Dead Sea which offered at least partial support for the Leipzig hebraist. Jean Carmignac writes:

> Since the discoveries at Qumran we are now aware of a third kind of Hebrew (besides Biblical Hebrew and Mishnaic Hebrew) which must be acknowledged. Qumran Hebrew is certainly much closer to Biblical than to Mishnaic Hebrew . . . but it cannot be dismissed as simply a subvariety of the former. And since it was used for religious purposes in the time of Jesus, it ranks as a prime candidate among the varieties of Hebrew idiom in our search for the Semitic backgrounds of the Synoptic Gospels.[160]

Since Dalman was not in full agreement with Delitzsch's "scholarly purpose" for his version of the New Testament,[161] he concentrated his efforts on the goal of Jewish mission or, as Delitzsch referred to it, the "practical purpose." This inevitably led to a rethinking of the underlying linguistic principles, which Dalman described with something of condescension on the eve of the renaissance of the Hebrew language.

> Special considerations are required by the practical nature of the work. Expressions which might well be precise translations of the original text have to be avoided if their connotations for the contemporary reader are alien to the meaning of the original. And yet no real concession should be made to the poor taste of the contemporary reader. The kind of Hebrew in common use among Jews today is an arbitrary mixture of elements from all periods of the Hebrew language, frequently with a considerable number of German elements thrown in. Further, what is sometimes called "Classical Hebrew" may not be classical at all. . . . Expressions should be avoided which may themselves be quite accurate historically, but which are no longer a part of the common Jewish vocabulary. Thus the historical terms for civil and military dignitaries are often replaced by more common terms. The cohort ("speîra") becomes simply *gdwd* "ranks," "bouleutḗs" ("member of a council") fades into *ywʿṣ* "an adviser," and in

Acts 14:12 Zeus, who is evidently not mentioned in any of the early rabbinic literature, becomes *Bel* (from Isa. 46:1).[162]

With a touch of inconsistency Dalman departs from the Aramaic thesis he has just been discussing to conclude his introduction in a pietistic vein: "It remains a symbol of the judgment incurred by Israel for rejecting salvation that the Gospel which was originally revealed in their midst and in their own language was given to the world in a Greek form and not in Hebrew, and is now coming in full circle back to its origins as a translation."[163] In the four editions from the eleventh to the fourteenth (which finally appeared as a reprint in Tel Aviv in 1962), Dalman introduced a great number of changes, most of which were quite trivial and did not alter appreciably the basic structure of the work. It is quite appropriate that all the British and Foreign Bible Society editions of this Hebrew New Testament are still identified by the name "Professor Franz Delitzsch."

Delitzsch bequeathed three monuments to posterity. The Institutum Judaicum which he founded in Leipzig (and is now in Münster) is called by his Christian colleagues and students the Delitzschianum. Significantly, Delitzsch was probably the first missionary to the Jews to elicit so many deeply appreciative obituary memorials from rabbis and Jewish scholars in the Jewish press and literary world. David Kaufmann of the Rabbinic Seminary in Budapest wrote:

> It was the major concern of his life to make the New Testament available and translate it into Hebrew. No man was better qualified to recognize these writings as a product of Jewish literature. . . . His reading of the New Testament into the Old may be accounted a defect of his biblical exegesis, but in this perspective it becomes conversely a most valuable asset. He can discern its development within its own setting, appreciating it in its proper context as an expression of the Jewish life of the time. . . . Delitzsch's New Testament is a priceless enrichment of Jewish literature. . . .[164]

Even more valuable than these two epitaphs is the continuing influence of Delitzsch's work in Israel today. His Hebrew New Testament is found on the reading desks of the Hebrew University in Jerusalem where early Christianity, religious studies, and church history are taught in his "beloved Hebrew." The first Hebrew-Greek concordance of the New Testament, published in Tiberias in the autumn of 1974 under the auspices of the United Christian Council in Israel, was based on his translation. And finally, all new translations of the New Testament into Modern Hebrew undertaken in recent years depend upon his magnum opus as their base and point of departure. He could hardly have imagined a better memorial.

7. The Salkinson-Ginsburg Version of the New Testament

The last Hebrew version of the New Testament produced in the nineteenth century was the work of Isaac Edward Salkinson (1822–1883), son of the well-known Hebrew author Salomo Salkind, who was converted to Christianity in 1848, and later worked as a Jewish missionary in England and in Austria-Hungary. He gave proof of his knowledge of Hebrew in his early youth by a poetical translation of John Milton's *Paradise Lost* and of William Shakespeare's *Othello* and *Romeo and Juliet* in the language of the Bible. Before his death he achieved the translation of all the New Testament books except the Acts of the Apostles, which was completed and revised after his death by Christian David Ginsburg. The first edition appeared in London in 1885 under the auspices of the Trinitarian Bible Society, and between 1886 and 1961 it was reprinted fifteen times at London, Vienna, Warsaw, and Philadelphia; only the second edition of 1886 presented any significant textual changes.

As early as 1855, in the preface to his Hebrew translation of the Letter to the Romans, Salkinson criticized the earlier version of the New Testament which had been published by the London Bible Society: "It abounds unduly with Aramean forms, vulgar expressions, and rabbinical idioms, all of which appear to the lover of genuine Hebrew incompatible with the character of inspired Scripture."[165] In order to avoid such errors Salkinson later succumbed to a kind of exaggerated biblicity which often tends toward artificiality and more frequently misrepresents the meaning of the New Testament. For example, at Rom. 1:5 he translates "apostolē̄n" ("apostleship") as *ml'kwt* "deputation," and later even as *ml'kwt-YH* "labor of God" in allusion to Cant. 8:6 *šalhebet-YH* "flame of God" (Franz Delitzsch *šlyḥwt* "mission"). Salkinson calls the first apostle *mttyhw* after Ezra 10:43 or after the father of the Hasmoneans (Delitzsch *mty*). Rom. 1:8 is translated *'mwntkm 'śth śm* "your faith is made thither," to avoid the rabbinic *mpwrsmt* "proclaimed." Rom. 14:10 has *ks hmšyḥ* "throne of the Messiah" (where Delitzsch has *ks' dyn h"* "judgment seat of God"). Salkinson is inconsistent in avoiding *bśr* "flesh" in "katà sárka" at 1:3, replacing it with the medieval philosophical expression *lpy hḥmr* "according to (the mouth of) clay," but then mistranslating the key passage Matt. 26:26 as *zh hw' bśry* "this is my flesh" (Delitzsch correctly *zh hw' gwpy* "this is my body") despite his awareness of the pejorative Pauline use of the word "flesh." The same *ḥmr* appears again at Rom. 2:29, where "grámmati" ("book") is rendered *ḥmr hktwb* ("inscribed clay"), an expression Paul would scarcely have recognized (in the second edition Ginsburg improved this to *lpy 'wt hktb* "according to the written letter"). Equally inappropriate is *'wtywt h'ty-qym* "copied letters" at 7:6, which Delitzsch renders better and literally as *lpy yšn hktb* "according to the old writing." Salkinson's *hwn b'rṣ* "wealth in the earth" for "tòn bíon toû kósmou" ("worldly goods") at 1 John 3:17 approaches the ridiculous; Delitzsch renders it far better as *nksy h'wlm* "riches of the world."

On the other hand Salkinson has also made some improvements, such as at Matt. 27:1 *nwsdw yḥd 'l yšw'* "sat together (in conclave) against Jesus" from Ps. 2:2 (Delitzsch *hty'ṣw 'l yšw'* "conspired against Jesus"); at Matt. 27:1 *hbqr 'wr* "the morning dawned" (Delitzsch *wyhy lpnwt hbqr* "it came to pass before morning"); 1:19 *ldbt 'm* "to whisper with," thus "defame" (Delitzsch *lḥrph* "to reproach her"); 4:10 *gš hl'h* "move away!" as at Gen. 19:9 (Delitzsch *swr mmny* "turn aside from me!"). At Matt. 27:2 Pilate is rendered *hpḥh* "the governor," following Neh. 12:26; Ezek. 23:6 (Delitzsch *hhgmwn* "the official"). The mocking cry at Matt. 27:29 is *yḥy mlk hyhwdym* "Long live the king of the Jews!" (which is more literal and rings truer than Delitzsch's *šlwm lk mlk hyhwdym* "Peace to you, king of the Jews!"); and at Phil. 2:4 *lṭwbt r'hw* "to his friend's welfare" is simpler and more biblical than Delitzsch's *l'šr lḥbrw* "to what is his fellow's."

The remarkable combination of hyperbiblicism and poetical license characteristic of Salkinson's version is due to the linguistic principles which he formulated in a letter to Delitzsch on June 11, 1877, and which the latter published twelve years later.

> My plan is to take a good share of liberty in regard to words and phrases, and to be faithful only to the sense and spirit of the text, which must neither be added to nor taken from in anything. . . . But we must remember that our New Testament is intended chiefly for our unconverted brethren. Therefore it may be of some service to have it in a style which the Jews have not yet forgotten to appreciate, that is, the biblical Hebrew. . . .[166]

Rabbi David Kaufmann describes how effective Salkinson's version was for many Jewish readers.

> Salkinson's version was more popular among many people (than that of Delitzsch) because it was more "Hebrew," i.e., actually un-Hebrew but truer to the kind of poor taste which delights in the mischievous and finds crudeness and confusion the hallmark of true literary genius.[167]

Eighty years later an American biblical scholar, who recently published a new version of the Gospel of Mark in Hebrew, summarized the verdict of a later generation. Robert L. Lindsey writes: "Although there are those who prefer the Salkinson translation until today it is undeniable that most Hebrew-speaking students and scholars have continued to approve the Delitzsch translation."[168]

As for the character of the New Testament translation itself, it should be noted that Salkinson and Delitzsch frankly borrowed from each other—Delitzsch openly admitted as much.

> It cannot have escaped anyone who has compared both versions that Salkinson's is based on mine, and that its differences are largely in his embellishments and improvements on it. It was only to be expected that in many instances his version would surpass mine, and so it has. In effect, it provides a most welcome contribution to a further revision of my own.[169]

Delitzsch had begun translating the New Testament long before Salkinson, and after Salkinson's death he produced five further editions in which he incorporated a great number of Salkinson's improvements. As he was also the more penetrating and pedantic scholar, he and his work may justly be said to have had the last word.

V

Christian Neo-Hebraica in the State of Israel

"Translating the New Testament into Hebrew involves more than an exercise in style or rhetoric," wrote Franz Delitzsch in 1870 in defense of his life's work.[1] Yet there are hints in several of his writings that doubts about the practical value of his work continued to worry him to the very end. And rightly so! However one may admire his linguistic virtuosity, his theological sensitivity, and his ardent missionary zeal, in retrospect it is difficult to escape the impression that this achievement of a century ago was a philosophical tour de force, reminiscent in a way of the medieval windows in the cathedral at Cologne—undoubtedly a masterwork, imposing, but unfortunately much too lofty to be appreciated by more than a handful of experts. Even the number of potential readers of Delitzsch's version has been steadily decreasing. About 1870, when Delitzsch published his *Letter to the Romans* in Hebrew, the Haskalah movement, a Jewish Enlightenment whose members advocated a return from the ungrammatical Hebrew of the medieval period to the biblical style preferred by Delitzsch, was already in cultural decline.[2] About 1875, when Delitzsch completed his translation of the whole New Testament, the Hebrew poet J. L. Gordon gave expression to the disillusionment of all who believed in the continuing vitality of Hebrew literature.

> Who can know the future? Who can say
> Whether I am not the last poet of Zion,
> Or you the last to read in Hebrew?[3]

What remained were the rabbinic exegetes, whose books were principally dedicated now as before to hebraic problems; several still unknown enthusiasts of the *Ḥibbat-Zion* ("Lovers of Zion"), a precursor of Zionism, who dreamed of Israel in Hebrew; and a half-dozen Hebrew journals, the first of which, *Ha-maggid* [*The Messenger*] (founded in 1856), ranked very low in Delitzsch's esteem. In denouncing Isaac Edward Salkinson's version of the New Testament Delitzsch wrote: "The difference between Salkinson's version and mine has always been that I have never gilded the New Testament text in imitation of the Jewish mosaic style, or what is called the maggid style, after the title of one of the most popular of the Hebrew journals, which floods the Jewish reader with all kinds of poetic elegance and flowery expressions."[4]

And yet in 1880, when Delitzsch's third edition of the New Testament appeared, it was in *Ha-maggid* that another Don Quixote of the Hebrew language issued a glowing appeal which historians today identify as the beginning of the renaissance of the Hebrew language[5]: "Hebrew is our national language. For each of its words, its letters, even its vowel points, the blood of our forefathers was shed like water. . . . But can it survive if we do not put it in the mouths of our children, if we do not revive it, if we do not bring it once more into daily use?"[6] The young Eliezer Ben-Yehuda (1858–1922) who wrote these words was later to complete the epoch-making sixteen-volume opus *Millon ha-Lashon ha-ʿIbrit* [*A Complete Dictionary of Ancient and Modern Hebrew*], or *Thesaurus Totius Hebraitatis,* in the purest of Biblical Hebrew, which even Delitzsch would certainly have lauded.

From this time forward the inherent conflict of Delitzsch's magnum opus only grew more acute. As the renaissance of Hebrew language and literature developed, the number of people who wrote and read the Hebrew from Jewish-religious or nationalist-Zionist motives also increased, and for them there could have been no thought of reading the New Testament at all, especially not in the "holy language," which represented the true antithesis of the Diaspora for these survivors of Christian persecution. To put it bluntly, practically none of the Jews who would be likely candidates for conversion (and who were ultimately the concern of Delitzsch) was sufficiently familiar with Hebrew to understand his classical version, while the rabbis, Zionists, and authors (such as Mendele Mokher Sefarim ["Mendele the Itinerant Bookseller"; Shalom Jakob Abramowitz, 1835–1917], Ḥayyim Naḥman Bialik [1873–1934], and David Frischmann [1865–1922]), who could have been impressed by his style and his skill in translating, were in no frame of mind to approach the book seriously.

This situation was changed only by the renaissance of the language of the Bible and its metamorphosis into the national language of Israel. The milestones of this unique development are too well known to require more than the briefest review here.

1882–Ittamar Ben-Avi, son of Ben-Yehuda, was born in Jerusalem and, thanks to his father's hebraeomania, became the first child of the modern era to learn Hebrew as his native tongue.

1892–Teachers proposed the establishment of Hebrew as the exclusive national language of education throughout Palestine.

1906–The Hebrew Gymnasium of Haifa adopted this principle for higher education.

1921–The British Mandate for Palestine recognized Hebrew as one of the three official national languages, along with English and Arabic.

1925–The Hebrew University in Jerusalem established Hebrew as the sole language of instruction in all academic disciplines.

1948–With the founding of the State of Israel Hebrew regained the significance lost to it 1985 years earlier by the fall of the Hasmonean monarchy. It became the national language of its old homeland, not only officially but in actuality as well.

A survey undertaken in 1918 showed that among the entire Jewish population apart from Jerusalem, the number of Hebrew speakers totalled about 40 percent.[7] In 1954 it was estimated that some 60 percent of the population used Hebrew as either their principal or only language.[8] The census of 1961 reported that 75 percent of all adult Israeli Jews spoke only Hebrew, while for children of two to fourteen years the number rose to 93 percent.[9] Today Hebrew publications include thirteen daily papers, hundreds of periodicals, and more than 1,500 books a year. Five universities and colleges use Hebrew to provide instruction in practically all academic disciplines.

1. *Which Hebrew?*

Despite stylistic differences and the thousands of new words required for expressing modern ideas and concepts, the Modern Hebrew of Israel today stands closer to its biblical ancestor in many ways than does the Mishnaic Hebrew of 1700 years ago. Anyone who doubts this should observe the school children who visit the Dead Sea Scrolls in the Shrine of the Book every day, and see how they are able to read even the oldest manuscripts of the Old Testament as fluently and understand them as well as they do the latest newspapers from Tel Aviv.

And yet Modern Hebrew is by far richer than any of its predecessors, from Mishnaic Hebrew to the language of the Haskalah, because Eliezer Ben-Yehuda, and after him the Waʿad ha-Lashon ("The Language Commission") which he founded, and since 1954 the Academy of the Hebrew Language with its twenty-nine technical committees, have almost daily incorporated new words into the old language, most of which are not really neologisms but good Hebrew words or roots which are modified or modernized. Thus Ben-Yehuda honored the motto that "the greatest virtue a new word can possess is that it is not really new."[10] Similarly Prof. Zeev Ben-Chaim of the Academy of the Hebrew Language explained in 1965: "We are generally not interested in making new words. Our main efforts are rather toward the restoration of words which have long been a part of the vocabulary."[11] What Gustaf Dalman once disdainfully called "a random mixture of elements from all periods of the Hebrew language"[12] is actually typical of the whole development of the Hebrew language, and is even characteristic of the daily prayers, some of which are two thousand years old.

Strictly speaking, a "pure Hebrew" has never existed, for even the language of the Bible contains loan words and foreign words taken from Egyptian, Assyrian, Sanskrit, Sumerian, and Aramaic. To cite only one example, Naphtali Hertz Tur-Sinai has demonstrated that the word *sēp̱er* "book," which is regarded as an original Hebrew term, actually represents a loan from Babylonia derived from *šipru* "message" and related to the verb *šaparu* "send."[13] One well-known theory even defines Early Hebrew as a "hybrid language."[14] However this may be, the form of the talmudic and mishnaic language would be inconceivable apart from the addition of infusions from Aramaic, Persian, Greek, and Latin, which contributed hundreds of words and concepts to postbiblical Hebrew, nor can the philosophy and mysticism of the medieval period be imagined apart from the innumerable arabisms from Spain.

On the other hand, never has the process of mixing been so intensive and systematic as since the beginning of the twentieth century. Chaim Rabin describes the effect in these words: "With oversimplification it could be said that the word forms of today's Hebrew are generally taken from the Bible, the syntax borrowed from the Mishnah, and the words themselves from all periods and styles."[15] To illustrate quantitatively how the language has grown from the desks of creative writers to popular usage in the course of a few decades, we will note only that while the biblical vocabulary comprises 7,704 different words, the standard dictionary, *Ha-millon ha-Ḥadash* [*The New Dictionary*] by Abraham Eben-Shoshan (1958–1962; revised ed., 1966–1970), contains 28,185 words. The most recent (1970), *Millon ʿIbri Shalem* [*The Complete Hebrew Dictionary*], by Reuben Alcalay, brings this number to well over 45,000 words and forms.

Qualitatively this broadening and deepening of the language has not only increased considerably the number of expressions available to authors and translators, but has also enabled them to distinguish between finer nuances where previously there were no alternatives. Modern Hebrew has, for example, the biblical word *tʿh* with the meaning "be confused, lose one's way," and assigns the corresponding talmudic word written with a *ṭeth* (ט) *ṯʿh* the abstract meaning "err, mistake for true." Similarly Old Hebrew *kṭn* is "small," the postbiblical diminutive, *qṭnṭn* "tiny"; the biblical *zʿyr* today means "little," and the corresponding Aram. *qṭyn* has the legal meaning "juvenile." Finally, Aram. *zwṭ'* means today "mini" or "miniature." In the same way earlier synonyms have gained specialized meanings; for example, Hebr. *ḥd* is (physically) "pointed," and Aram. *ḥryp* is (spiritually or gastronomically) "sharp." No less important is the distinction today of multiple levels, which makes it possible to distinguish near-synonyms sociologically. Thus *mtnh* is "gift" in normal usage; *tšwrh* is "present" in more formal circumstances, as with public ceremonies; the postbiblical *šy* is a "present" on a special occasion (such as on Hanukkah or Purim); Gk. *dwrwn* is a "gift" in lofty language, and the biblical *mnḥh* is a "gift" (an offering) in poetry.

Especially significant for such matters as New Testament translation and Christian Hebrew usage are the following three characteristics of Modern Hebrew today.

(a) *Its Dynamic Growth.* Modern Hebrew is dynamic, a constantly growing language whose terminology, structure, and idiom today, two generations after its rebirth, are still riding the crest of further development—development which as Tur-Sinai has observed often breaks all the rules of semantics.

> So many ancient Hebrew words and phrases are now used in ways that must be considered definitely wrong from the viewpoint of a biblical or talmudic scholar. Still, he is unable to change what has become part of actual, living speech.[16]

Beyond this are also, as Rabin states, "the daily neologisms coming from the journalists and from authors,"[17] as well as the germanisms, slavisms, yiddisms, arabisms, and all the other linguistic imports brought to Israel by a million immigrants from the five corners of the world—only the most striking and apt of which will be able to sink their roots into the national language. The admitted openness of the language to growth is attested by the fact that many of the entries in Ben-Yehuda's *Complete Dictionary of Ancient and Modern Hebrew,* which was completed in 1958 by Tur-Sinai, already sound archaic, and that its successor planned by the Academy of the Hebrew Language, *The Historical Dictionary of the Hebrew Language* [*Sepher ha-Mekorot: Ha-millon ha-Hisṭori la-Lashon ha-ʿIbrit*], is already long overdue and is still in the first stages of its compilation.[18]

(b) *Its Scholarly Openness.* In contrast to the purism which inspired Ben-Yehuda, the Academy of the Hebrew Language today is characterized by an open-mindedness in its basic approach, and in the spirit of the times in Israel today it is cosmopolitan in outlook. Its president wrote:

> While E. Ben-Yehuda believed in the necessity of finding a Hebrew expression for every foreign term, we now realize that this

is often impossible and not even desirable. While reviving our national language, we do not want to sever our links with the great cultural heritage of the world.[19]

This more liberal policy may well have resulted partly from the recognition that new technical terms in Hebrew (e.g., "university," "telephone," "microscope") could not simply be naturalized by decree from above. Rather, the overwhelming majority of all Israelis not only transcribes international terms like these into Hebrew, but also hebraizes them if it is at all possible by creating grammatically correct (verbal, nominal, etc.) derivative forms. In the development of the language, as in so many other areas of official life, it is not always the authorities but rather the people who constitute the decisive factor.

(c) *Secularization.* When a language which has served for centuries as a "sacred language" primarily for prayer, biblical exegesis, and religious writings must adapt itself in a relatively short period of time to the demands of modern technology, scholarship, and everyday usage, its partial secularization is an inevitable accompaniment. Thus in Israel today *twrh* does not refer solely to the books of Moses but to doctrines or teachings of any kind, from Charles Darwin to Mao Tse-tung. Similarly, *ʿbwdh* for "temple service" has come to mean simply "work"; the verb *lhqdyš* loses the implication of sanctification and usually means "dedicate"; *lkhn* is derived from *khn* "priest," but it now means merely "to officiate"; the biblical sentence of condemnation *ḥrm* now usually means "boycott"; *trwmh* once referred to the priestly heave offering (and was the title of a talmudic tractate), but now means a "contribution"; the pious *ḥsyd* now means the secular supporter of any party, theory, or cause. The most frequent talmudic circumlocution for God, *rbwn,* is the political term for a "chief executive"; *ḥnwkh* is not only the Hasmonean celebration of consecrating the altar but any formal "opening" (e.g., of a kindergarten or a new library); *ywbl,* which is translated as the year of Jubilee (so RSV; TEV "year of restoration") has been secularized to mean an anniversary; and *qn'y* "zealot" (usually for the Torah or the glory of God) is now pejorized to mean "fanatic." The list of these and similar secularizations in current usage could easily be extended, but these examples are sufficient to show the implications of this phenomenon for Christian translations.

Now let us observe the actual use of Hebrew in Christian communities in the State of Israel.

2. *The Pioneer: Fr. Jean-Marie Paulus Bauchet, S.S.S.*

The first hebraizer of Christian texts in the State of Israel was a French Eucharistine, Fr. Jean-Marie Paulus Bauchet (b. 1900), who began his study of Hebrew in 1929 in Orleans "from love of the holy language," and has since continued to teach and study "in hebraicis," working on a Hebrew glossary of Christian terminology. In the years 1939–1941, while serving as secretary to the Roman Catholic archbishop in Baghdad, he developed a novel method of transcription to simplify learning Hebrew, based on the capitalization of radicals (e.g., *be-Re'Shit BaRa 'Elokim et hash-ShaMayim we-et ha'aRets*). By 1941 he had transcribed the entire Hebrew Bible in this way, together with phonetic notes and grammatical comments, and introduced it in several seminaries as a teaching aid. In 1940 he published in Baghdad a Hebrew language text, *L'Hebreu pour tous,* with the Imprimatur of the "Archiepiscopus Babyl. Latinorum," printed at the Maronite press in Aleppo. In seventy pages this work takes its readers through an appreciation of an Old Testament chapter in the original, even to the details of pronunciation, yet without introducing a single Hebrew letter. Bauchet sent a copy of this book to Archbishop Giovanni Battista Montini (later Pope Paul VI), who responded with an expression of "sincere gratitude."

While he was studying and teaching in Baghdad, Bauchet also found time to compose poetry in Hebrew, one example of which earned him the praise of Eugène Cardinal Tisserant. The Cardinal also advised him to follow his own example and gain a command of Modern Hebrew in Jerusalem. Tisserant's reasoning, according to Bauchet, was that "the Church needs specialists who are capable of following rabbinical exegesis and research as it is pursued by modern Jewish scholars."[20] Accordingly Fr. Bauchet went to Jerusalem late in 1941, where he studied for five years (1945–1949) at the Hebrew University, with Joseph Klausner and Harry Torczyner (now Naphtali Hertz Tur-Sinai) among others, to receive his doctorate in 1951 for a five hundred-page dissertation on "Onomatopoeia in Northern Semitic." His qualification as a hebraist is attested by Meir Medan, the scholarly secretary of the Academy of the Hebrew Language, who writes: "He has a good command of the Hebrew language and is quite familiar with Hebrew literature."[21] The well-known lexicographer Abraham Eben-Shoshan calls Bauchet's Hebrew style "clear, natural, and fluent." Before he left Israel for reasons of health in 1952, Bauchet had composed in Hebrew or translated into Hebrew about one dozen books and essays, a few of which should be reviewed briefly here.

(a) *'Or we-'Osher* [*Light and Salvation*]. This Hebrew catechism of 357 pages, written at the request of Msgr. Luigi Barlassina, patriarch of Jerusalem, and largely based on the German catechism of the Diocese of Trier, bears the imprimatur of the Franciscan Custodia di Terra Santa at whose press it was printed in 1945. The spirit of Jewish mission is apparent on nearly every page, but for clarity it is further confirmed specifically in the dedication: "This work is offered to the 204,504

Jews who were converted to Christianity in the nineteenth century." Apart from the Christian prayers, Bible quotations, and church hymns, which appear in the Old Testament Hebrew, the language of the book is completely Modern Hebrew, the text is unpointed, and despite numerous typographical errors and some few violations of Hebrew grammar and syntax, its style is generally quite easily understood.

In rendering Christian terminology into Hebrew (on the advice of his friends, including Eben-Shoshan and Reuben Alcalay) Bauchet avoided neologisms as much as possible, deriving Christian expressions which are foreign to Hebrew from familiar Hebrew roots, and resorting to Hebrew transcriptions instead of translations only when the alternatives were obscure, ambiguous, or disqualified by pejorative associations. "Only two neologisms," he writes, "could not be avoided."

(1) *Qnwm* "(divine) person" (pl. *qnwmym*), borrowed from Syriac *qnwm*' and corresponding to Arabic '*wqnwm*, was first used with this meaning in 1658 by Rabbi Giovanni Battista Jona in his Hebrew catechism *Limud Mešiḥim* (*Instruction for Christians*).[22] Cardinal Tisserant, with whom Bauchet conferred on this neologism, gave his written approval.[23] Since this concept is lacking not only in Hebrew but in many European languages as well, it was unnecessary and rather confusing theologically to seek etymological parallels such as '*yš* ("man") and '*yšywt* ("personality") as Bauchet suggested several years later. He was quite wise in rejecting a priori the medieval *prṣwp*, which Mishnaic Hebrew adopted from Gk. "prósōpon"[24] and which meanwhile in Modern Hebrew had added to its literal meaning of "physiognomy" the associations of "parvenu" and "rascal." It would have been interesting to recall the Lurian-cabalistic use of "parzuf" with the meaning of a divine manifestation, but Bauchet ignored this.

(2) *Mwrwn* for "chrism," cognate with the biblical *mwr* "myrrh" from Exod. 30:23 and also derived from Syriac, was a second neologism Bauchet felt necessary because *šmn* as "cooking oil" and *mšḥh* as "(tooth) paste" or "(cosmetic) cream" were too secular to use for consecrated ointment.

In examining the following Hebrew renderings of church terms one should remember that these are the achievements of a talented pioneer working entirely without precedent, whose only models came from the medieval and early modern periods. The only fresh coinage in the Christian area by Eliezer Ben-Yehuda was the word *mnzr* "monastery" from *nzyr* "Nazirite" (later "monk"), and none of the "fathers of the Hebrew language" who came after him had the slightest interest in developing a Christian vocabulary in the newly revived language.

(1) "*Original sin.*" *Hḥṭ' htwrsty* (lit. "hereditary sin") has a

Germanic ring, sounding too much like a technical biological term to the Israeli ear (cf. *twrt htwršh* "laws of heredity" or "genetics") for any association with theology. Jakob ben Reuben's translation *ḥṭ' qdmwn* "ancient sin" from the twelfth century,[25] or Profiat Duran's *ḥṭ' h'dm hr'šwn* "sin of the first man" from about 1400,[26] would have been more apposite and closer to the Latin concept of "peccatum originale."

(2) "*Incarnation*" (*swd hhtgšmwt*). The medieval terms for this concept were either too long, such as Ben Reuben's *hnbr' btbnym bśr* "created in the image of flesh," or tinged with a suggestion of docetism, such as Profiat Duran's coinage *hlbšt yšw bbśr* "the clothing of Jesus in flesh." Thus Bauchet opted for the philosophical term *htgšmw'* "embodiment" used also by Rabbi Jonas. But since this word had meanwhile acquired in Modern Hebrew the primary meaning of "realization" (of dreams, hopes, plans),[27] and its root *gšmy* (which originally meant "material, bodily, physical") had gained the connotation "coarse" (e.g., *pnym gšmyym* "rough features"),[28] and the recently derived *gšmn* means "materialistic," Bauchet evidently attempted to reconsecrate the secularized *htgšmwt* by the addition of the word *swd* "mysterious."

(3) "*Obscurantism*" (*mrydt-'wr*). Since the verb *mrd* "rebel" requires either the preposition *b* or *ʿl*,[29] the term would have to be rendered *myrdh b'wr* "rebellion against light." In current usage it should be *śn't dʿt* "hatred of understanding."

(4) "*Christian*" (*mšyḥyym;* cf. Arabic *mšyḥy* "Christian"). Since the word *nwṣry* still means "Nazarene" (i.e., a native of Nazareth, a place called home today not only by Jews and Christians but also by Moslems) and since eighteen centuries of Christian diaspora have further given it a negative connotation, Bauchet returned to the original meaning of Gk. *christós* and *christianoí.* Yet he had to retain such common abbreviations as *Lsh"n* (*lpy spyrt hnwṣrym* "according to the counting of the Christians") whenever he wanted to add "A.D." after a date. By analogy "Christianity" became *mšyḥywt,* but to be converted to Christianity was expressed by *lhtnṣr.* In three instances the typographical error of an omitted *yodh* (י) changed "Christians" into "Messiahs" (*mšyḥym* for *mšyḥyym*).

(5) "*Religious truths*" (*'mtwt h'mwnh*). Although nothing is grammatically wrong with the plural of *'mt* "truth," the form never occurs in Jewish literature despite the dozens of idioms and proverbs about *'mt.*[30] Bauchet may have had in mind the rare medieval usage *'mth* (meaning "axiom, premise," as in Moses Maimonides' *Guide for the Perplexed* [*Moreh Nebuḥim*] ii.36), which may occur in the plural but is rather affected.

(6) "*The Pope.*" Here Bauchet experimented with *hkhn hgdwl* "the High Priest," perhaps in terms of the theology of Hebrews (Heb.

7:24–28; 10:21),[31] then with *hkhn hgdwl hmšyḥy* "the Christian High Priest," and later with the apostolically modest *r'š h'dh* "head of the congregation." The term *'ppywr* which had been in use for centuries would have been simpler and more intelligible; it is not encumbered with any negative associations and probably represents a Hebrew corruption of the Greek title *páppas hierós* "Holy Father."[32]

(7) "*The Church.*" In the sense of a religious community Bauchet uses *'dh* "congregation," which is associated with communities of faith in the Old Testament (e.g., Num. 20:27), midrashic literature (e.g., *Mekilta* on Exod. 14:15 [35a], where Israel is called *'dh qdwšym* "congregation of the holy"), and also at Qumran (cf. *'dh qdš* "holy congregation" in CD ix). In the sense of the (invisible) ecclesia Bauchet uses the term *knsyh* "church," and for the church building *byt tpylh* "house of prayer." Modern Hebrew is still content with *knsyh* for all three meanings.

(8) "*Mass.*" The service was at first called *hzbḥ hqdwš* "the holy sacrifice," but later followed a synonymous arabism, *hqrbn hmqwdš* (*'lqrbn 'lmwqdš*). Since following the abolition of the biblical sacrificial system *qrbn* became spiritualized to refer to an offering of the mind or heart, and in Modern Hebrew it still suggests the context of the temple service, it is a perfect term for this central element of the Christian liturgy—especially as it represents for Christians the fulfilment of the covenant sacrifice (Exod. 24:5–8) and the later temple offerings (Heb. 9:9–14).

(9) "*Transubstantiation.*" *Hštnwt h'ṣm* "change of the substance" is taken from the medieval philosophical vocabulary,[33] although the reflexive hithpael distorts the theological significance.

(10) "*Transfiguration*" (*htglwt hkbwd*). This is hardly a translation so much as an apposite theological explanation which should be clear to any Israeli reader at all familiar with tradition. "Revelation of the (divine) glory" suggests more than the Latin original and corresponds more closely to the New Testament term "metamorphoûsthai." *Hštnwt hṣwrh* "change of the form" would be more faithful to the Latin term but also less intelligible. The reflexive hithpael is more appropriate to the spirit of the synoptic account (Matt. 17:1–2 par.), although the Greek has the passive form.

(11) "*Host*" (*hmṣh hmqdšt* "sanctified matzo"). The bread is translated here appropriately as "unleavened bread," as it is also at Jesus' last Passover supper, although the bread offered in the Western churches is not always *maṣṣâ* bread. The Hebrew translation here goes back logically to the origins of Christianity.

(12) "*Christmas*" (*ḥg hwldt yšw'* "festival of the birth of Jesus"; cf. Arab. *'d 'l-myld*). Here Bauchet protests[34] against the long popular *ḥg hmwld* "festival of the birth" because among other things *mwld* is

also a postbiblical synonym for *ksh* (Ps. 81:4 [Eng. v. 3]) in the meaning of "new moon." That this has never disturbed anyone is attested by the fact that all standard dictionaries, such as those by Eben-Shoshan, Kena'ani, Alcalay,[35] and others, as well as Christian institutions continue to use the customary term *ḥg hmwld* for Christmas. The same word in its Aramaic cognate form *maulodo* serves for Christmas in the Syrian Catholic church.

Bauchet quite prudently leaves a whole series of Christian terms untranslated in his catechism, such as Protestant, Catholic, sacrament, theology, and communion, but in many instances he supplies Hebrew footnotes or explanations.

(b) *Gephen Poriyah* [*A Fruitful Vine*]. Bauchet wrote this brief (seventy-five pages) biography of St. Francis of Assisi at the request of the Franciscans in Jerusalem. The title page bears the date 5706 as well as the address *mnzr hgw'l, yrwšlym, 'rṣ hqdš* "Convent of the Redeemer, Jerusalem, the Holy Land." The title of the book is evidently drawn from Ps. 128:3; Isa. 32:12. The text is written in unpointed Modern Hebrew, and with few exceptions in a fluent and easily understood style. The following renderings in Hebrew should be noted.

(1) "*Immaculate Conception*" (*hhrywn hblty nktm*). This is too literal in its translation of "undefiled," because neither in Biblical nor in Modern Hebrew does it express "innocence" in the sense of freedom from original sin, which is the essential element here.

(2) "*Stigmata*" (*mḥṣy-rz* "secret wounds"). This fresh coinage does have the virtue of suggesting Isa. 30:26 (*mḥṣ mktw yrp'* "wounds inflicted by his blow"), and the originally Aramaic (or Persian?) *rz* as "mystery" (Dan. 4:6 [Eng. v. 9]) lends an aura of the mysterious to the expression—but no uninitiated Israeli would ever guess its meaning.

(3) "*Laity*" (*ḥylwnyym*). This would make sense to any Israeli because the Hebrew word has been familiar for centuries, first as the antithesis of the holy and later of the religious. Originally it meant "nonpriestly" in the sense of Num. 18:4; today it has the additional meaning of "secular" and "nonreligious," but the difference here is slight. The Hebrew language has no precise equivalent for this antithesis to the priest, because there is a genealogically established division of the whole people into three groups of Priests-Levites-Israelites. The use of the word *hdywṭ* "common person" (from Gk. "idiṓtēs") is inappropriate, for Hebrew also has the term *khn-hdywṭ* to refer to the average priest (*Yebam.* ii.4).

(4) "*The place of Paul's conversion*" (*mqwm tšwbt p'wl hqdwš*). However the experience of Saul of Tarsus on the Damascus road may be understood, it is certainly not to be translated as *tšwbh* "return" or "repentance." Today his conversion to Christianity is usually referred

to more practically if not precisely as *htnṣrwt p'wlws* ''Paul's conversion.''

(5) ''*Christian priests.*'' Bauchet is quite justified in resenting the commonly accepted expression *kōmer,* which is used in the Old Testament to refer to priests of false gods (2 Kgs. 23:5; Zeph. 1:4). It was also used in the medieval period to describe all who professed the Christian faith in any religious order,[36] as a practical synonym for *glḥym* ''clergy'' (from *glḥt* ''tonsure''). The controversial writings of Joseph the Zealous, Ben Reuben, Rabbi Yomtob Lipmann, and others employ *lšwn glḥw'* ''Catholic language'' for ''Latin,'' and *glḥwt* for the clergy. In view of the pejorative implications today of the terms *glḥ* and also *kmr* (or *kwmr*), Bauchet insists on the introduction of *khn qtwly* ''Catholic priest,'' and adds the following warning:[37] ''If some Jews are unwilling to understand this, they inevitably invite a degree of Christian distaste for the Modern Hebrew language.'' Although official publications of the Ministry of Religion in Jerusalem have avoided these medievalisms for years and refer to both Christian priests and Moslem dignitaries as *khny dt* ''priests of religion,'' most dictionaries have remained true to popular usage.

(c) *Toledot Nephesh* [*The History of a Soul*]. A better title for this work would be *Toledotiyah shel nephesh.* This Hebrew translation of a devotional life of St. Teresa of Lisieux (St. Teresa of the Child Jesus and the Holy Face; 1873–1897) contains 271 pages and bears the imprimatur of the vicar of the Franciscans in Jerusalem, whose press published it early in 1948. The title page shows the Hebrew date 5708, identifies the place (shortly before the founding of the State of Israel) as *yrwślym, 'rṣ-yśr'l* ''Jerusalem, Israel,'' and the work is dedicated to ''Professor E. Zolli, earlier chief rabbi in Rome, now returned to his homeland.''[38] Here again Bauchet experimented with Hebrew Christian terminology, only two examples of which are still relevant today.

(1) ''*Martyr*'' (*'d-yšw'* ''witness of Jesus''). Historically speaking, the act of religious ''witness,'' in which is ultimately implicit the sacrificial offering of life itself, can be traced back to Jewish sources, although in contrast to Greek the Hebrew expression for martyrdom has nothing to do etymologically with ''witness.'' According to Second Isaiah (Isa. 43:9–11), before the tribunal of ''the peoples and the nations'' which is to decide who is the One God, Israel will appear as witness for the true God: '' 'You are my witnesses,' says God, 'whom I have chosen, so that people will recognize me and believe me, and understand that it is I . . . I, and I alone who am God.' '' Twice in this context this fateful declaration is repeated: '' 'You yourselves are my witness,' says God'' (v. 12); ''You are my witnesses. Is there any God beside me?'' (44:8).

It is in this quasijudicial sense that the devout priest Eliezer and Hannah with her seven sons became witnesses (''mártyres'' in the Septuagint) when Antiochus IV Epiphanes forced the Jews to ''live no longer by the laws of God'' (2 Macc. 6:1). The last words of the seventh son indicate that these protomartyrs must have thought of the words of Second Isaiah when they died: ''Therefore I will face death unflinchingly, he said. Never will I betray the cause for which my brothers gave their witness (''martyría'' in Codex Alexandrinus)'' (4 Macc. 12:16). Christian respect for these Jewish martyrs is echoed in the Letter to the Hebrews (Heb. 11:35). Later in the Church's typological hermeneutic Augustine interpreted them as Old Testament models of the crucified Christ himself, while other Church Fathers such as Ambrose, Gregory of Nazianzus, and Cyprian asserted only that they died ''in the name of Christ.''[39]

These statements in conjunction with the cult of the Maccabees, which began as early as the fourth century in Antioch and for which there is also medieval evidence, especially at Cologne (the Church of the Maccabees at Greesberg was consecrated to the martyrs in 1134), must certainly have contributed to making the Jewish ''witness to God'' in its Greek translation an embodiment of the highest form of religious heroism. But Judaism had rejected the essentially juridical and colorless term *ʿd* ''witness'' (cf. Num. 5:13; 35:30; Deut. 17:6–7; 19:15) as a synonym for ''martyr.'' *Qdwš h''* ''sanctifying the Name of God'' is the Hebrew term (cf. Lev. 22:32) for Jewish religious martyrdom, especially since the mass murders by the Crusaders. Here the focus is clearly and pointedly upon the credal form of the Shema with its final antitrinitarian word, as it is told in the talmudic account of Rabbi Akiba's martyrdom and elsewhere: ''. . . He drew out the word *'ḥd* [''one''] slowly, and with it his soul passed from him. Then a voice from heaven said, 'Blessed are you, Rabbi Akiba, that your soul passed with the word ''One'' ' '' (*Ber.* 61b).

The literal back-translation *ʿd-yšwʿ* which Franz Delitzsch used at Rev. 17:6 is not only essentially obscure, but it could be relevant only in a special sense to Stephen, who according to Acts 7:55–60 suffered death because of his faith in Jesus. It is not appropriate for the later Christian martyrs, who died almost without exception for their rejection of the cult of Caesar or of polytheism.

It is interesting that in Islam the term *śhyd,* which originally had the juridical meaning of ''witness,'' came to mean ''martyr'' under Christian influence through the Syriac *shd'*, which corresponds to ''mártys.''[40]

(2) ''*Antichrist*'' (*hmtngd lmšyḥ,* lit. ''the adversary to Christ''). This Greek expression which Bauchet uses with the meaning of 1 John 2:22 as ''one who does not believe in the Christ,'' and which is also

found in the plural as at v. 18, is a loaded term for religious Jews, because none of them could be considered antimessianic, and yet all of them would deny the title to Jesus. A more precise form would be *hmtngd lyšwʿ kmšyḥ* "the adversary to Jesus as Messiah," but even this is not a happy solution. The strongly satanic component in the antichrist concept gives the application of the term to those who do not believe in Jesus an acutely polemic tone.

(d) *The Gospels of Matthew and Mark.* These slightly revised versions of Delitzsch's New Testament are based on the Greek text edited by Marie-Joseph Lagrange, O.P., of the Dominican École Biblique in Jerusalem. The commentaries on Matthew and Mark were prepared at the request of Cardinal Tisserant, and published in Jerusalem in 1948 and 1950, respectively. In the interim the city of Jerusalem was divided, and because the Franciscans with their library and press remained in the Jordanian part of the city, the address on the title page no longer read *ʾrṣ yśrʾl* "Land of Israel," but more ecumenically *ʾdmt hqdš* "The Holy Land." Both are pocket editions, fully pointed[41] and quite legible, bearing the name of Delitzsch, and with brief Latin prefaces and extensive exegetical notes which attempt to deal with such theological and philological problems as "alma-parthénos" (Isa. 7:14), the "brothers and sisters of Jesus" (Matt. 13:55–56), and the date of the Passover Supper (Mark 14:12). Bauchet did not have time to revise the rest of Delitzsch's version for, as noted, he was forced to leave Jerusalem for reasons of health in 1952.[42]

The following passages in Matthew offer interesting expressions.

(1) 1:18 *Wbṭrm yšbw yḥd* ("before they lived together") certainly does not mean "*prìn ḗ syneltheîn autoús*" ("before they came together"). It was probably a monastic prudery that displaced textual fidelity here. I see no reason to criticize Delitzsch's biblical *wbṭrm bʾ ʾlyh.*

(2) 16:18 *ʾTh kypʾ wʿl hkp hzh ʾbnh ʾt ʿdty* ("you are Peter and on this rock I will build my church") is an ingenious translation of the Petrine succession, since the word *kp* corresponds in Hebrew to Aram. *kpʾ* and has the same meaning "rock" (Jer. 4:29). Both the alliteration and the rhythm of the sentence here are faithful to the original, although *knsyty* (for *ʿdty* "my congregation") would have been closer to modern usage, and the verb for "build" usually takes a definite (even if spiritualized) object in Hebrew.

(3) 26:27 *Wyqḥ kws wywdh* "and he took a cup and gave thanks" is translated literally but erroneously, because Gk. "eucharistēsas" represents Heb. *brk* "bless, praise" here, just as does "eulogēsas" ("blessed") in the preceding verse.[43]

(4) 26:49 *Wbrgʿ ngš* "and he came up at once." Bauchet prefers the somewhat more colloquial *brgʿ (bw brgʿ* "in a moment" would have been more correct) to Delitzsch's *wmyd* "immediately" for translating the frequent "kaì euthéōs" ("at once") in Matthew and Mark. Gustaf Dalman thought that this reflected an original Aram. *myd,*[44] while Marie-Joseph Lagrange believed it corresponded to Aram. *ʾdyn* or *bʾdyn* meaning "then."[45] Yet Jean Carmignac is persuaded that it represents the plain and simple Heb. *ʾz,*[46] which can mean "then, thereupon, therefore" as well as "immediately." But again, Henry Barclay Swete believed he could distinguish in it the biblical *whnh* "behold,"[47] because the Septuagint translates this idiom as "kaì euthýs" at Gen. 15:4; 24:45; 38:29 (although it translates it more correctly elsewhere as "kaì idoú" ["behold!"]. Since the expression occurs no less than seven times in Matthew for forty times in Mark, it is necessary to distinguish between the meaning "immediately" (e.g., here in Matt. 26:49 and in Mark 1:42), which is best translated today as *wmyd,* and the more numerous instances where the context requires either "then" or "thereupon" (e.g., Matt. 24:29; Mark 1:12, 21, 23), and where *ʾz* or *wʾz* would seem most appropriate today.

(5) 27:25 At the "Jewish self-incrimination" Bauchet adds the following note which strikes Israelis as frankly amazing: "This is where the responsibility of the people of Israel for the death of God's Messiah becomes clear."

(6) 28:19 *ʾt kl hʿmym* "all nations" is probably the only way missionaries in Israel today can translate "pánta tà éthnē," although Delitzsch's *ʾt kl hgwyym* is probably more correct in relating it to the gentile mission. And yet no Israeli would be aware of any relevance to himself in this latter rendering, because for centuries *gwyym* has referred only to "gentiles."

In Bauchet's slightly modernized form of Delitzsch's version of Mark the following passages should be noted.

(1) 1:9 *Wyṭbl ʿl ydy ywḥnn* "and was baptized by (lit., "by the hands of" or "at the side of") John" is an exact translation of the Greek, reproducing Delitzsch's version unchanged. Yet it is interesting to recall Leo Baeck's comment with regard to the (Essene?) *ṭwbly šḥryn* "morning immersion" (*Ber.* 22a), also called *ṭwbly-šḥryt* (*j. Ber.* 6c) and known as hemerobaptism:

> The Hebrew and the Aramaic words for baptising, *tabhol, tebhal,* are used, in relation to human agents, exclusively as intransitive verbs. The people who came to John the Baptist were not baptized by him; they baptized themselves, they became, so to speak, baptists like him. . . . It was the man himself who . . . cleansed

himself through this baptism. It was not administered to him by someone else.[48]

The reading of **D** (Codex Bezae Cantabrigiensis) at Luke 3:7 "baptisthēnai enṓpion autoû" "to be baptized in his presence" or "in his sight" (not "hyp' autoû" ["by him"]) seems to suggest this self-baptism, which is the only form observed in Judaism even to the present. And yet the Christian idiom has meanwhile also been accepted in Modern Hebrew, so that today the distinction is made between Christian baptism (*ṭbylh nwṣryt*) which takes the passive verb (*lhṭbl; nṭbl; hṭbl*), and Jewish proselyte baptism (*ṭbylt zrym* "baptism of strangers") which takes only the active verbal forms (e.g., *Yebam.* 46b; *Gerim* i).

(2) 1:22 *Kbʿl šlṭwn* "as one who possesses authority" is too close to secular "power" to express the meaning in this context of "exousía," which Delitzsch translated with the biblical *kbʿl gbwrh*—where *gbwrh* "strength" (e.g., *Meg.* 31b) means the divine power, and *bʿl gbwrh* is used as in the liturgy for "God." This gives it christological force and makes the Hebrew reader feel the close identification of Jesus with God. The New Testament passage, however, is describing the difference between the way Jesus taught and the methods of the Pharisees, who based their statements on the principle of tradition with certain hermeneutical rules. The readiest translation would be *kbʿl ršwt* "as one who has control," one with plenary power and independent authority. And yet *ršwt* is also used with the special halakhic meaning of rabbinic jurisdictional competence. Hans Kosmala properly objects to this halakhic *ršwt* as a translation[49] because a supernatural power is intended here rather than academic teaching credentials. What has been said about *bʿl šlṭwn* is true also for Matt. 7:29, where Bauchet translates *k'yš šlṭwn* "as a man of authority," an expression which suggests to Israelis a member of a South American military junta rather than a man of God.

(3) 6:3 *Hl' zh hw' hngr* "Is this the carpenter?" is undoubtedly better and more faithful to tradition than Delitzsch's *hl' zh hw' hḥrš*, because *ḥrš* means either a "manual laborer" or merely a "smith" (Exod. 35:35; Deut. 27:15), while *ngr* "craftsman," as David Flusser says, can also mean someone "particularly knowledgeable."[50] In talmudic times when a particularly difficult (halakhic) problem was under discussion, the question would often be asked: "Is there a craftsman or the son of a craftsman present?"[51]

(e) *A Hebrew Church Glossary.* Since there has never been a standard for church terminology in the national language of Israel,

Bauchet attempted for several years to supply this lacuna by an English-Hebrew glossary, but without general success. In 1966 this glossary comprised 520 terms in a nine-page list, and it has since been expanded into a bilingual dictionary with more than 2,500 lexemes supplied with translations, exegesis, commentary, and some rather penetrating excursuses. As it is impossible to discuss analytically all of his suggested translations here, only a few of his key concepts will be mentioned.

(1) *"The Eight Beatitudes" (of the Sermon on the Mount).* Bauchet proposes *šmwnh-ʾšry* "Eight 'Blesseds,'" patterned after the *šmwnh-ʿśrh* "Eighteen Benedictions" of the ʿAmidah prayer. Although each of the Beatitudes begins with *ʾšry* "Blessed is . . ." and in Hebrew the sections of the Torah as well as prayers are often identified by their first words, it is doubtful that the analogy will find popular acceptance.

(2) *"Bishop."* Bauchet proposes *hgmwn* "official" for Catholic bishops, a usage which dates from the medieval period, and *mbqr* (lit. "one who seeks") for Protestant bishops. Although the latter word is found in the Qumran Scrolls (CD xiii.5, etc.) representing almost the precise equivalent of the "epískopos" in the early Church (cf. Acts 20:28: RSV "custodians"), in Modern Hebrew it has the meaning of "supervisor, inspector." This is not exactly an appropriate description of the episcopal office, although it might be apt for the district superintendent of an evangelical church.

(3) *"Charisma."* Bauchet's proposal *mgdyh* is evidently an arabism, since Arab. *madšid* corresponds to Heb. *pʾr* "beauty," *kbwd* "glory." The biblical term *mgd* means "choicest, best (gifts)" in the Pentateuch (Deut. 33:13–16), "the choicest fruits" in the Song of Solomon (Cant. 4:13; 7:14 [Eng. v. 13]), and "delicacies" in Modern Hebrew.[52] It is in this sense that *mgd* is used today for the most popular salad oil in Israel. In Greek "chárisma" refers rather to an imparted quality in the sense of a particular gift of grace (cf. "gratia infusa"), while *ḥsd,* which corresponds most closely to it, describes a close personal relationship of loyalty. For special acts or gifts of God's grace Hebrew also uses the plural form *ḥsdym.*

(4) *"Congregation, community"* (*yḥd*). This usage corresponds to the terminology of the Qumran community. In this form the term could easily be widely accepted in the sense of a community led by a priestly caste, thanks to the extensive popularity enjoyed by the Qumran scrolls in Israel.

(5) *"Worship, veneration"* (*sgydwt*), *"worshipper"* (*swgd*). Both terms must be rejected because both in the Old Testament (e.g., Isa. 44:15, 17, 19) and partly in Modern Hebrew usage as well *sgd* "prostrate oneself" clearly refers to the veneration of idols. Because of

these associations the words are never used with reference to Jewish worship. Yet *msgd,* from the closely related Arab. *sadšada* "prostrate oneself," has become naturalized for "mosque" without any implication of idolatry.

(f) *The Battle over "Trinity" in Hebrew.* Bauchet's battle waged for a quarter century against the use of the Hebrew word *šlwš* "three" in the meaning of "trinitas" is an example of the stubborn longevity of old words, even in a newly revived language, as well as of the difficulty facing any attempt to modify controversial theological terms. As early as 1945 he wrote in his Hebrew catechism: "We reject the expression *šlwš* for 'Trinity' because Jews have used the term to express the plurality of the (Christian) Godhead. Therefore *šlwš* is completely unsatisfactory to describe the true nature of the Christian belief."[53] A philosophical excursus followed defending this position and concluding with the proposal "to translate henceforward the unity of the three Persons as *hšlšh hqdwšh* ["the holy three"]" analogously with *nkdh* "granddaughter" and *ʿglh* "calf," as he explains later in his glossary.[54]

From the historical viewpoint Bauchet is partly right. Ever since the *Milḥamot ha-Shem* [*Wars of the Lord*] of Jakob ben Reuben in the twelfth century[55] *šlwš* has been used in innumerable Jewish manuscripts, and almost invariably in the derogatory sense of tritheism or a quasitritheism. Thus Joseph the Zealous[56] (and many others after him) wrote polemic works partly in the form of a dialogue between *hmšḥd* "the monotheist" or "Jew" and *hmšlš* "the tritheist" or "Christian." In contrast to Jewish religious polemics another perspective is offered by Jewish religious philosophers. According to the Halakhah, Christianity and its doctrine of the Trinity differed from paganism and idolatry (*ʿbwdh zrh,* lit. "foreign worship") on account of *štwp* "syncretism" (i.e., including the veneration of many divine powers along with the worship of the One God). The Christian, like the Moslem or a half-proselyte (*gr twšb;* cf. *Tosafot b. Sanh.* 63b), was regarded as one who "accepted the Seven Commandments (the first of which is the rejection of idolatry) which the sons of Noah acknowledged" (*b. ʿAbod. Zar.* 64b). The Talmud (*b. Sanh.* 63a) indicates that while this "conjunction" detracts from the purity of monotheism, it does not constitute a mortal sin (as does idolatry), so that the offense of Israel in worshipping the Golden Calf may be viewed more leniently, because they said: " 'These are your gods, O Israel, who have brought you out of the land of Egypt' " (Exod. 32:4). Since they used the plural it shows that they did not worship the calf itself, but "the Name of the Holy One, praised be He, in conjunction with the alien rites" (therefore *štwp*). Consequently they were spared complete destruction. This *štwp* as a form of theological syncretism, to be regarded as inferior to Jewish monotheism, corresponds to the Islamic *Širk* which is essentially quite close to polytheism as it is expressed in the Koran (6:94; 10:18).

Saadia (882–942), the head (Gaon) of the School at Sura, was the first Jew to discuss the Trinity philosophically. Despite many objections (*ʾEmunot we-Deʿot* ii.5), he saw no essential offense against monotheism in the "subtle perception" of the doctrine of the Trinity, although he considered it an error "to conceive such divine attributes as being, life, and wisdom as independent." But this can be attributed to the inadequacy of human language, as he explains it.

> We have already established that our three characteristics constitute but a single attribute, only they cannot be combined verbally in a single word as they can be combined in a single cognition. For it is just as one might say that he does not worship fire, but something burning, giving light, and ascending upward, and yet in reality it is the same as fire.

Yet he devotes a careful discussion to the refutation of the Christian doctrine of the Trinity, prefacing it with the following remarks:

> In presenting this refutation I do not have in mind the common crowds who have only a crude conception of the Trinity (*šlwš*)—such a refutation would not be worth the space, because it would be too obvious and simple. I intend rather to refute the more thoughtful among those who imagine they believe in a deeply speculative and subtly apprehended Trinity (*šlwš*).[57]

Judah Halevy (1075–1141) goes still further in his religious dialogue on the conversion of the "King of the Kusars." In all fairness he has the Christians in the book *Kuzari* describe the doctrine of the Trinity as follows: "There is the Messiah, called the Son of God, and there is the Father, the Son, and the Holy Spirit. We maintain that these three are in reality a single being, for although our words imply a threefold nature (*šlwš*), yet nonetheless we believe in the unity of God."[58]

Without digressing into any further details of the exhaustive medieval debates on the nature of the Trinity, it may be stated in summary that all Jewish thinkers rejected practically all forms of the Christian Trinitarianism, and that they expressed this doctrine in Hebrew by the term *šlwš*.[59]

Yet Bauchet supports his proposal with further arguments, e.g., grammatically *šlwš* is a *nomen actionis* from the piel of the verb *šlš* "to treble," meaning "triplication, trebling." This is not quite accurate, because three different meanings may be distinguished for *šlš* in current usage: (1) "to divide into three parts"; (2) "tripartite," as in *bryt mšlšt* "Triple Entente"; (3) "to do a third time."[60] As a Frenchman,

Bauchet adds that in his own language the word *šlwš* suggests a near-homophone with obscene associations (''chie-louche,'' ''a dirty leer''). Then proceeding to positive counterproposals, Bauchet offers these five suggestions:

(1) *htšlyš,* an arabism patterned on the common Arabic expression *sir et-tathlith*

(2) *šilšâ,* from 1 Chr. 7:37, where Shilshah is the name of one of the sons of Zophah

(3) *šlšwt,* which has the phonetic virtue of resembling *'ḥdwt* ''unity''

(4) *mišlôš,* from Gen. 38:24, where a three-month period is described as a single unit of time, comparable to English ''fortnight,'' whereby a plural content is expressed by a singular form

(5) *hṭrynyṭh hqdwšh,* an untranslated transliteration with the advantage of freedom from any historical or linguistic associations, as well as of clarity for multilingual Israelis—but at the expense of remaining an alien expression

Faced with resistance to change on the part of Christians in Israel, whose prayer books and church texts (to the extent that they were hebraized) had for years accepted the term *šlwš,* Bauchet turned to the church authorities in Rome, Jerusalem, and North America. One of the first to lend him support was Cardinal Tisserant, who wrote to him on April 7, 1965: ''For 'Trinity' I prefer *šelšâ.*''[61] Less impressed were Msgr. Hanna Kaldany, the Catholic bishop of Nazareth, and Msgr. Beltritti, then the adjutor to the patriarch of Jerusalem, who merely promised to consider his proposal. Thereupon the undaunted hebraist attempted to gain support for his position from Jewish lexicographers in Israel. As he wrote to the author on June 29, 1970, the three leading scholars—Eben-Shoshan, Kana'ani, and Alcalay—indicated their willingness to include in the next edition of their dictionary the lexeme *šelšâ* as a dogma of Catholic theology, with an appropriate explanation. Indeed, Bauchet did score his first victory in the last volume of Eben-Shosan's authoritative lexicon, revised late in 1970; here the term *šelšâ* appears with the meaning ''trinitas,'' but with a note: ''a variant of *šlwš* in Catholic theology.''[62] Yet as of Spring 1971 most authoritative Hebrew dictionaries continue to offer the word *šlwš* as the only translation for the Christian ''trinitas,'' even though some go into great detail (e.g., *Millon Megiddo he-Ḥadish* [*The Megiddo Modern Dictionary*]:[63] ''trinity—*hšlwš hqdwš.* Christian religion: The unity of the Father, Son, and Holy Spirit in a single Godhead'').

The chief reason for the persistence of this usage in all Christian Hebrew texts appearing in Israel to date is summarized by Yoḥanan Eliḥai, a French member of the order of the Little Brothers of Jesus.

> The word *šlwš* is derived from the radical *šlš* ''three.'' Its general meaning of ''treble, threefold plurality'' contains nothing in and

of itself that would make it inappropriate as a translation of "trinitas." It is no more inappropriate than the German "Dreifaltigkeit" ("a threefold reality," or literally almost "a triplicity"). There are Christians who oppose the use of this word because of its association with false interpretations of the Trinity in medieval rabbinic polemical writings. But the word itself is intrinsically no more involved in these errors than any other word derived from the root for "three." It says just what one wishes it to say, just as the French word "trinité" can also be misinterpreted by unbelievers.[64]

For these reasons, and probably other reasons as well, all five drafts of the then unpublished "Glossary of Christian Terms in Modern Hebrew" compiled by the United Christian Council in Israel have *hšlwš* as the only translation given for the term "trinitas."

To all these arguments pro and con is also a "Jewish" one that should be added, but which has been overlooked in the heat of the fray. In one of the Piyyuṭim in Morning Prayer for the Day of Atonement, the introduction of an early Kedushah[65] reads *bšlwš hqdwšwt mšlšym,* which may be translated "We repeat the threefold Sanctus thrice." Similarly in another Piyyuṭ, "All respond together with the threefold Sanctus (*šlwš gdwš*)," whereupon follows the Trisagion ("Holy, holy, holy is the Lord of hosts," proclaimed by the angelic hosts). And although the Trisagion (Isa. 6:3) has served since the High Middle Ages as the locus classicus for Christian theologians demonstrating the origins of the Trinity in the Old Testament,[66] no Jew has yet taken offense at this liturgical *šlwš* passage in the synagogue service—despite the fact that in several instances the text of prayers and also of talmudic passages has been altered on the grounds of Christian influence or as a defense against the Church.[67] Only the future can tell whether Bauchet or the traditionalists will prevail in this controversy.

These few examples are typical of the problems, dilemmas, and ambivalences which no translator can avoid in attempting to render Christian concepts faithfully and accurately into Modern Hebrew. As for Bauchet's *Glossarium,* it may be said that some of his coinages may yet find their way into Hebrew textbooks, lexicons, and dictionaries.

3. *The Beginnings of the Roman Catholic Mass in Hebrew*

Br. Jean Leroy, a young French member of the Little Brothers of Jesus, first visited the State of Israel in 1949.[68] He came from southern Lebanon where he was active as a teacher in a Syrian Catholic village. He stayed only three days in Haifa and Jerusalem, and soon afterward decided to return again. In 1953 he visited Nazareth where the founder of his order, Charles Eugène de Foucauld, had spent several years of his life, and later in Jerusalem Leroy assisted in establishing a group of Little Sisters of Jesus, the women's branch of the order, in the Jewish part of the capital of Israel.

On closer contact with Israeli Jews he was impressed by three things: the necessity for "unqualified reparations on the part of Christianity"; the need to help in creating a real "Christian presence" in the Jewish state in the sense and spirit of "ora et labora"; and the possibility of worship again in the Holy Land in the language of Jesus and the apostles. So in 1955 Leroy left his position in Lebanon and sought his fortunes first in a Jewish religious kibbutz. Although he enjoyed it there and even laid aside the cross pendant which he had always worn, he felt that his deeper purpose could best be achieved by other means. Apparently the European association of the cross with the swastika was still too fresh for many kibbutz members, and several of the *ḥaberim* suspected him of being a missionary despite all their friendship, as he later recounted it.

Leroy left the kibbutz after three weeks, and together with an associate opened a ceramics workshop in Jaffa where they eked out their living, studied Hebrew, and worked at night on a Hebrew translation of the Mass. For a basis Leroy chose the Missal of the Syrian Catholic church, whose liturgy he was familiar with from Lebanon. Their Missal, like that of the Maronites and of the Chaldean Catholic (also called Assyrian) churches, was written in the Aramaic language, the so-called Palestinian Christian Aramaic of the Galilean Jewish farmers who were forcibly baptized during the Justinian persecution of the sixth century.[69] Since the nineteenth century, however, the Arab clergy had translated the people's responses, the Creed, the Canon, and a part of the priest's oral prayers into Arabic. Leroy translated these Arabic parts of the text into a mixture of Modern Hebrew and synagogal Siddur Hebrew, which was easily understood without sounding secular. In the winter of 1955 he returned to France for ordination to the priesthood, and while there he received permission from the superior of the order to mimeograph the text he had prepared and to celebrate the Mass in Hebrew and Aramaic (corresponding to the mixture of Arabic and Aramaic in the Syrian Catholic church). This license was possible due to Rule No. 3 of his order, which had permitted since 1933 the use of local national languages for the observance of worship, and also to the fact that the Uniate churches, among whom a great many of his fellow religious were working in Lebanon, Syria, and North Africa, had received the recognition of Rome since the last half of the eighteenth century with permission to continue the celebration of the liturgy in their traditional languages. Since this was most likely the first Modern Hebrew church text to be accorded official sanction for use in celebrating Mass, it should be noticed briefly.

As is usual in the Syrian Catholic church, the translator divided the Mass into two books. The first was an altar book (*spr lmzbḥ*) containing in thirty-one pages a Hebrew transliteration of the prayers of the priest (*hkhn*) and of his deacon in the Palestinian Christian Syriac original (which the Syrian Catholics called Aramaic), with only a few key passages such as the Anaphora of the priest and the following Epiphora of the people translated into Hebrew. This was obviously an incomplete work that would soon require revision. More important is the second book, intended for the members of the congregation and bearing the subtitle *tšwbwt hqhl* [*Responses of the People*]. Common to both books is the general title *Hqrbn hqdwš lpy hmnhg h'rmy* [*The Holy Sacrifice according to the Aramaic rite*]. In fourteen pages it contained in a slightly abbreviated form a Hebrew translation of what was basically the Syrian Catholic Mass, also known as the Anaphora of the Twelve Apostles,[70] with the words of the celebrant of this antiphonal liturgy given both in the Aramaic original (transliterated into Hebrew) and in Hebrew translation. The words of the deacon and the responses of the people, however, are given in only partly pointed Hebrew. The name of God, which appears in the original Aramaic as *Mor*, is written (inaccurately) with the double *yodh* (״י) of the Jewish prayer books.

As might be expected, the character of the original frequently tempted the translator to commit aramaisms, almost invariably with homonyms. There are also a few conspicuous judaisms, e.g., the lessons for the Mass are called *pršwt mspry htn"k* "chapters from the books of the Bible"; the apostle Paul is called *š'wl hšlyḥ* "Saul the messenger," and the deacon is called *ḥzn* (the present term for the precentor or cantor in the synagogue).

One easily understood translation error is *'lrwḥw ḥy' wqdyš'* "unto his living and holy spirit," which Leroy renders as *lrwt hqdš hmḥyh*, although "living" is *ḥy'* and *mḥyn'* would be "lifegiving" in Aramaic. And yet to avoid dividing the Hebrew phrase *rwḥ hqdš* "Holy Spirit" by the adjective "living," he placed it following; thus the Holy Spirit, perhaps for reasons of sentence cadence (or meter), is called "lifegiving."

It is interesting that neither the Aramaic nor the Hebrew requires the word "persona" in the definition of the Trinity. It says of Jesus *wythw ḥd mn tlytwytw qdyštw* "and he is one of the holy threesome," which Leroy translates literally and correctly *w^{e}hû' 'eḥāḏ min hašelšâ haqdôšâ*, adopting Bauchet's translation of "Trinity."

In 1956 Leroy combined both Missals in a single diglot text of forty-seven pages including a French as well as a Hebrew translation of this (abbreviated) Aramaic Mass, with the Hebrew text now fully pointed and considerably improved. Leroy celebrated the Mass according to this text regularly until March 1957, when other events led to a new Missal.

In 1953 Fr. Bruno Hussar, a young Dominican of Jewish background who had been baptized several years earlier, approached Eugène Cardinal Tisserant with the request that he be permitted to work for his order in Israel. Hussar envisioned the establishment of a small monastic brotherhood in Jerusalem which would stand as an anti-Torquemada witness, for it would be at least a symbolic disavowal of the Jewish persecutions which were once instigated and prosecuted by the Spanish inquisitor who like Bruno was both of Jewish origin and a Dominican: "Only in Israel can Jewish-Christian dialogue achieve full credibility. To prepare the way for this we must first accept the Jewish State, become fully integrated into Israeli society, and come to know the Jews as they actually are today." In Rome Hussar followed these arguments to a conclusion which he considered unavoidable: "To accomplish these purposes we must learn Hebrew in Israel, and not only to speak, but to worship in Hebrew. Our Breviary consists largely of Hebrew Psalms; why should we recite them in Jerusalem in Latin?!"

Cardinal Tisserant, who had studied Modern Hebrew with Eliezer Ben-Yehuda and Joseph Klausner during his student days in Jerusalem, was essentially in agreement with Hussar's plan, but suggested that the Mass be read for a while in the Aramaic text of one of the Uniate churches, while the Antiphons, which are read or sung in Arabic by the Maronites, Syrian Catholics, and Assyrians, should in Israel be translated into Modern Hebrew. But this translation would need approval in Rome before final permission for its use in celebration could be granted.

When Leroy took his Hebrew-Aramaic text of the Mass to France in the winter of 1955, it was approved by his order, as noted above, after due consultation with the Vatican. At Hussar's request he was invited to prepare a memorandum discussing the linguistic and theological aspects of rendering the Roman Catholic Mass completely into Hebrew. Meanwhile as a first step Hussar received permission to read the New Testament lessons from the Delitzsch version, and the Trisagion and other Old Testament portions of the Mass in Hebrew. Hussar and his brothers read the rest in Latin. Before returning to Israel in late February 1956, Leroy and Hussar met in Rome where they celebrated together their first Hebrew Mass in the catacombs. At the beginning of 1957 Leroy submitted his memorandum on a completely Hebrew text of the Mass to Cardinal Tisserant, who discussed it with Pope Pius XII. The cardinal's support of a Hebrew rendering of the Mass, which Leroy's evidence and sample texts proved both possible and desirable, was based chiefly on the following arguments, as he explained it later to

Hussar: when Cyril and Methodius, the apostles to the Slavs, approached Pope John VIII for permission to translate the Bible into Slavic, the pope approved because the proposal seemed to be justified by Ps. 150:6 ("Let everything that breathes praise the Lord!").[71] This decision must a fortiori apply to Hebrew, which was counted by early Church tradition to be one of the three holy languages.[72] Nor did Tisserant forget to remind Pius XII of his own encyclical of 1943, "Divino afflante spiritu," in which it is indicated that "the Holy Scriptures are a source of comfort," and wherein the pope had given the exhortation to study the Scriptures, especially in their original texts. Late in February 1957 Leroy received permission by telegram from Rome to nominate a Catholic priest to whom the Holy See could grant a faculty for Hebrew. Leroy proposed Hussar, who within days received the written faculty.

March 18, 1957, was for both an historic day. On that day five priests gathered to celebrate the first (mainly) Hebrew Mass on Israeli soil in Haifa at the residence of Msgr. Vergani, vicar general of the patriarch of Jerusalem, Alberto Gori, and since 1951 representative of the patriarch in Israel. Besides Leroy and Hussar the following persons participated in the simple ceremony.

(a) Fr. Joseph Stiassny, superior of the Ratisbon Institute in Jerusalem, for almost a century a property of the Order of the Notre Dame de Sion. As a specialist in the field of Jewish Hellenism, Stiassny was also a recognized hebraist and had given substantial assistance to Leroy in the preparation of the new text of the Mass.

(b) Father Jean-Roger, an Assumptionist father of Jewish origins, known in Israel as "king of pilgrim guides" and generally popular because of his remarkable fluency in Modern Hebrew which he speaks and writes like a "Sabra" (born Israeli). In his own words, "I cannot imagine myself apart from Hebrew—I mean that it is simply impossible to have a real understanding of Christianity apart from the language of the Bible."

(c) Msgr. Vergani, the host himself, who remarked to several journalists shortly after assuming his office that he saw "no reason why the Vatican and Israel should not enjoy the best of mutual relationships—and that officially. There is nothing in Catholic doctrine requiring the Church either to reject or to support a Jewish state."[73] Since he made these remarks in fluent Hebrew, and repeated them on later occasions as well, he was soon accounted one of the most popular ecclesiastical dignitaries in Israel.

The nine-page text which was printed especially for this inaugural Mass bears the title *Hqrbn hqdwš lpy hmnhg hlṭyny bśph hʿbryt* ["The Holy Sacrifice According to the Latin Rite in the Hebrew Language"]. On the last page the date of March 18, 1957, appears also in Hebrew:

the fifteenth day of the month 'Adar in the year of Creation 5717. This day was most probably chosen for the saint it commemorates: Bishop Cyril of Jerusalem, a "Confessor and Teacher of the Church," renowned for his catechetical instruction, and whose Proper was read at the High Mass. Quite appropriately the following note is added immediately below the date: "In memorial of the Holy Sacrifice offered for the first time in Hebrew, in the holy language"—for the text was a translation into Old Testament Hebrew (Gradual, Sentences from the Psalms, Introit, etc.), Piyyuṭ Hebrew (Confiteor, Gloria, etc.), and a mixture of both styles (Credo, Collect, and Communion).

Linguistically and theologically the following passages are of particular interest.

(a) In the first trinitarian formula at the beginning of the Introit the translator considered it necessary to add after "of the Father, the Son, and the Holy Spirit" the words "One God," apparently to give special emphasis to the Triunity of God for the Hebrew reader. The same motive seems to appear also at the end of the Gloria with the insertion of the emphatic connective *yḥd* between "Jesus Christ" and "with the Holy Spirit," which is lacking in the original. But this concern is thwarted by the presence of a *yodh* (י) (typographical error?) in the Munda Cor prayer, where the words "per Dominum nostrum" ("by our Lord") are translated with an ambiguous plural *ʿl ydy ʾdwnynw,* which is found in this form in the Bible only with the Tetragram (e.g., Ps. 8:2, 10 [Eng. vv. 1, 9]; Neh. 10:30 [Eng. v. 29]), which is not used here, and only in the sense of the Lord God ("Kýrios"). The plural of *ʾdwn* "lords" can mean both "the Lord" (1 Kgs. 22:17; 2 Chr. 18:16) and "lords" (Deut. 10:17) in the Bible. The liturgy of the synagogue does not have the plural form *ʾdwnynw* for "God" at all, but frequently uses the simple form without the suffix *ʾdwn* "dominus" as a periphrasis for the name of God, e.g., *ʾdwn ʿwlm* "Lord of the universe" in the daily Seliḥah ("penitential") prayer, and in the *ʾdwn bpqdk* ("Lord when you visit") on the eve of the Day of Atonement.

(b) It seems inconsistent when the reference to "Peter and Paul" in the Confiteor reverts to the Aramaic form *Kephaʾ* for the first when the Latin form "Paulus" appears for the latter, especially as he was called *šʾwl* in the Syrian Catholic Mass a year earlier.

(c) The translation of "beatus" and "sanctus" also appears inconsistent. Mary, Michael, and John the Baptist, who are all called "beati" in the Confiteor, become *qdwšym* together with all the saints ("omnes sanctos") in Hebrew; but "sanctis apostolis" is *ṣdyqym* "righteous." Admittedly, according to Rabbi Yoḥanan (*Sanh.* 92b–93a), "the righteous are greater than the angels who serve," and according to 4 Ezra 7:97, "their countenance will yet shine like the sun and be made like the light of stars." But this superhuman glorification and transfiguration of the *ṣdyqym* does not correspond to the doctrinal assumptions of the Catholic veneration of the saints, which is expressed in formal canonization, in the index of those sanctified in the Canon, and in their "elevation to the honor of the altar." Since the ecclesiastical status of sainthood depends upon a papal act, perhaps the best translation of "sanctus" would be the pual participle (mepual) of the verb *qdš*, i.e., *mqdš* "consecrated."

(d) The vocative "Domine Deus" is quite appropriately rendered in Hebrew as "Lord, our God," because an impersonal God who is not related to "us" is alien to the language of the Bible.

(e) "Sub Pontio Pilato" is neutralized by the translation "*bymy* Pontius Pilatus" ("in the days of Pontius Pilate")—which restricts the relationship between the death of Jesus and the Roman procurator to their simple contemporaneity. In the historical and New Testament sense, "under Pontius Pilate" would better be translated as *bšlṭ* Pontius Pilatus" ("in the reign of Pontius Pilate") or, on the analogy of Ruth 1:1, "*bymy šlṭ* Pontius Pilatus" ("in the days when Pontius Pilate ruled").

(f) Since "passus" in the Creed does not mean merely "suffered" but "suffered death," as the following "et sepultus" makes quite evident, *sbl* "suffer" may be true to the text, but it is not true to its meaning. To solve this dilemma the translators inserted the word *mt* "he died" between the two verbs. In the place of the two words *sbl . . . mt,* a terse, unequivocal "humat" ("he was killed") might have been preferable.

The translators were soon no less aware of these and similar secondary impressions than of the fact that in this unprecedented work philology often edged over into theology, and that with all its variety of styles Hebrew still frequently lacked a precise equivalent for technical church terms. So the circle of assistants and consultants grew as they attempted to deal with the problem they had set themselves. Their first choice was an Israeli who had lived in the country since early childhood and spoke Hebrew fluently as his native tongue as well as school language. Baptized in his fifteenth year, Joshua Blum was not only a major in the Israeli Army Reserves, but also convinced that his nationality and his newly found faith were not in the least contradictory. He was only trading his uniform for the black cowl of the Benedictines, and by his own wish he stayed in their Abbey of the Dormition on Mount Zion for the extent of his novitiate (which he did not complete). During this period he assisted his abbot, Leo von Rudloff, in his Hebrew studies, and was quite willing to review the text of the Mass, eliminating obvious unevennesses in word order, dissonances of rhythm and word usage, as well as typographical errors. Further, Blum also thought the text should come at least somewhat closer to Modern

Hebrew, because of his interest in its value for a religious approach to his fellow Jewish citizens. He proposed, e.g., in the Creed *kl hsmwy* (instead of *hblty nr'h*) for "all things unseen"; *bhdr* (instead of *kbwd*) for "in glory" ("cum gloria") despite its biblical-liturgical associations, because the former is more familiar to the average Israeli than is *kbwd* and the latter usually means "honor, esteem" in Modern Hebrew. Blum rejects *šwh l'b bʿṣm* "being like the Father in substance" for "consubstantialem patri," but without finding a more satisfactory alternative. For "catholicam" he proposed *mqyph,* which means "comprehensive" but lacks the universality implied by the Greek word. On the title page Blum altered *lpy hmnhg hlṭyny* ("according to the Latin rite"), which corresponds to ecclesiastical usage in Jerusalem, to *lpy mnhg rwm'* ("according to the Roman rite"), which is Modern Hebrew and idiomatic, but which also recalls the distinction between regional synagogue rites found at the beginning of Jewish prayer books (e.g., *kmnhg pwlyn* "as the Polish rite" or *kmnhg Frankfurt* "like the Frankfurt rite").

In the Munda Cor prayer he made the improvement of "evangelium tuum . . . nuntiare" ("to announce your good news") from *lhkryz . . . 't bśwrtk* ("to proclaim . . .") to the simpler and more biblical form *lbśr 't . . . bśwrtk* ("to bring tidings . . .").

Meanwhile the number of hebraists contributing to the improvement of the Hebrew Missal was increasing. To mention only the most important among them:

(a) Fr. Alfred Delmée, a Belgian diocesan priest who from 1958 lived in Jaffa with responsibility for a Catholic parish and began in 1959 to observe an increasing number of his services in Hebrew

(b) Hans Kosmala, the director of the Swedish Theological Institute in Jerusalem, and earlier the director of the Delitzschianum (the Institutum Judaicum), first in Leipzig, then in Vienna

(c) Fr. J. Marcel Dubois, the colleague of Bruno Hussar and coinitiator of the Dominican Institute of St. Isaiah, and from 1968 the first monastic instructor (in medieval philosophy) at the Hebrew University

(d) Fr. Shmuel Stehman (until his death), a Belgian Benedictine of Jewish origin, who suggested the famous solution to the question "who is a Jew?" when it was under debate in the Knesset: "A Jew is a person who weeps when the shofar sounds at the Wailing Wall"

(e) Fr. Ludwik Semkowski S.J., for many years director of the Pontifical Biblical Institute in Jerusalem, who collaborated with Augustin Bea (later Cardinal) and four other hebraists in 1944–1945 on the preparation of a new Roman translation of the Psalter from Hebrew into Latin

(f) Fr. Joseph Samuelov, a native of Jerusalem and son of a Jewish

Orthodox family, who was baptized in 1945 while an English soldier, later fought as a member of the Zionist underground organization Eṣel, and in 1948 entered the Trappist monastery in Latrun shortly before the founding of the State of Israel

All of these, together with a few other hebraists, assisted in the preparation of an improved text of the Mass which received the imprimatur of Patriarch Gori shortly before Easter 1958, due to the fact that in the meanwhile five priests had been granted the "Hebrew license." Since Gori was reluctant to grant his imprimatur (as he also later opposed the proposal of several priests to transfer the Sunday Mass in Hebrew to the Sabbath), the new text of the Mass was printed by an understanding with Cardinal Tisserant and the superior of the Dominican order in Rome with the note on the title page: *hqrbn hqdwš lpy mnhg rwm' wmnhg hdwmynyqnym* ("The Holy Sacrifice according to the Roman Rite and the Use of the Dominicans"). This text represents substantive progress over its predecessors, which Leroy now refers to as "prehistoric." Significant changes may be recognized in the following passages.

(a) "Crucifixus pro nobis" ("crucified for us") has been improved by replacing the colloquial *bʿdnw* "on our behalf" with the liturgical *lmʿnnw* "for us," which recalls for Jews the phrase *ʿśh lmʿnk 'm l' lmʿnnw* "do for yourself if not for us" from the "Our Father, Our King" prayer.

(b) "The world to come" is now clearly *ʿwlm hb'*, and Joseph, the "castissimus sponsa" (therefore the "fiancé" of Matt. 1:18), appears in the Benedictus Deus prayer as *bʿl,* which juridically means clearly "husband" (cf. Exod. 21:3, 22), and assumes the consummation of marriage.

(c) "Immaculata conceptio" ("immaculate conception") is translated here with the pual participle (mepual) of the verb *hrh,* which can mean "conceive" (Num. 11:12) and "be pregnant" (Gen. 16:4): *mrym hmhwryt ll' ḥṭ'* "Mary who has been made pregnant without sin." This unique verbal form is apparently inflected to avoid the suggestion that the birth of Jesus (instead of Mary) is intended. The form was coined on the analogy of the hapax legomenon (in this biological sense) *hwrh gbr* "a child is conceived" in Job 3:3, although biblical scholars are still not certain whether the form in Job is pual, hiphil, or qal. The literal translation *hrywn ll' ḥṭ'* "conception without sin" would be understood by most Hebrew readers as a reference to the virgin birth, which is not intended here. In any event this is a real improvement over Jean-Marie Paulus Bauchet's literal *hrywn blty nktm* "conception not stained."

Two events in rapid succession soon after the revision of this text seem to have given fresh impetus to the Roman Catholic trend toward Hebrew translations. The "Constitutio de sacra liturgia," the first Constitution passed by the Vatican Council II at the end of its second session and promulgated on December 4, 1963, by Pope Paul VI, states clearly in Article 36: ". . . since the use of the mother tongue, whether in the Mass, the administration of the sacraments, or other parts of the liturgy, may frequently be of great advantage to the people, the limits of its employment may be extended." It seemed to be confirmed personally by the pope only a month later that this reference to "mother tongues" applied also to Hebrew, when on January 5, 1964, he was greeted on Israeli soil by President Schneur Zalman Shazar with a state reception, and responded with a speech of gratitude which concluded with the biblical words "shalom, shalom!" A few hours later the pope heard a thirty-six member mixed choir of the Basilica of the Dormition on Mount Zion sing the Magnificat and the Tu Es Gloria from the fifteenth chapter of Judith. Not only the Hebrew translation but the musical setting and the printing of the texts were the work of Catholics of Israeli nationality.

In dozens of instances adaptation to Hebrew had led to Israeli naturalization. For example, Brother Leroy became an Israeli citizen in 1960, hebraizing his name, as did so many thousands of other immigrants, to the biblical Yoḥanan Eliḥai; and thenceforward he celebrated the Sunday Mass on the Sabbath. His example was followed by a number of Assumptionists, Carmelites, and Dominicans, whose predecessors would doubtless have accused them of "judaizing" for such deviations and had them burnt at the stake.

Until the papal visitation the "prehistoric" Hebrew Missal texts were still incomplete and published only in simple tentative pamphlet formats, but on March 3, 1964, the first professionally printed and attractively bound edition of the Ordinarium Missae [Order of the Mass] appeared, illustrated in color and with the nihil obstat of the Jesuit Superior Semkowski and the imprimatur of Msgr. Hanna Kaldany, the first Israeli Arab to be consecrated to the episcopacy (by Pope Paul VI himself on his visit to Nazareth). Lest it appear absurd that a Polish Jesuit and an Arab bishop should pronounce on the quality of the Hebrew of the Catholic Mass, it should be noted that like many other Christians in Israel, both had a thorough command of the biblical language. In addition to the Mass, this sixty-page book also included the Confession (*hdwy*) and other prayers such as the Magnificat (*Zmr mrym* "Song of Mary"), Regina Coeli (*Mlkt hšmym* "The Queen of Heaven"), Te Deum (*'wtk 'nw mhllym* "Thee We Praise"), Benedictus (*Zmr zkryh* "Song of Zechariah"), and the stations of the cross (*ntyb hṣlb* "path of the cross").

Many of the philologically interesting passages in the Missal show that despite eighty years of labor by translators there were still a great many theological terms that remained elusive, and that the language must still be recognized as *in statu nascendi*. The mixture of Biblical and Mishnaic Hebrew, of Piyyuṭ idiom and an increasing number of words from Modern Hebrew in the usage of this Missal also raises questions. The following review considers the more important among the new coinages in the language.

(a) "Ordo missae" is *sdr hqrbn hqdwš* "Order of the Holy Sacrifice," which recalls the *sdr psḥ* "Passover seder" that is theologically akin to the Mass.

(b) "Deacon" is *sʿd* in Modern Hebrew in the sense of "aid and support," but it is also used on occasion for subdeacon, lector, and acolyte. Hebrew terminology for distinguishing the various orders is still vague.

(c) *Twdyh* is a new coinage intended to avoid both the word *twdh*, which means "thank offering" (Lev. 7:13) but is now the colloquial word for "thanks," and also the word *hwdʾh (hwdyh)*, which means a religious thanksgiving (*b. Ber.* 29a: *j. Ber.* 3d) but in current usage can mean "confession, agreement"—although both correspond etymologically to "Eucharist." The neologism not only has the advantage of sounding liturgical, but is legitimately derived from the verb *ydh* "give thanks" on the analogy of such words as *twdʿh* "consciousness" from *ydʿ* "know."

(d) "Canon missae" is *hsrk*, which corresponds to the "discipline" of the religious community of the Qumran scrolls. This is a well-chosen word because it comes from the period of the early Christian Church and is close to the concept of the Canon of the Mass.

(e) "Lesson," which was earlier judaized to *pršh mhtn"k* "section of the Bible," is now quite ecumenically *mqrʾ* "reading" and can refer to lessons from either Testament.

(f) "Secreta" ("silent prayers") is rendered as *mʿtr hyḥwd* "private prayer," an expression unrelated in either form or content. The Latin derivation is from "secernere" ("to set apart"), while the piel of *yḥd* as a religious term means "to confess the unity of God, to pray the Shema" (which is certainly also a quiet prayer but has nothing in common either formally or liturgically with the secreta and their assumptions with regard to the offering). On the other hand, in the cabalistic-ḥasidic view *yḥwdym* means contemplative prayer which leads beyond the world of the *spyrwt* "emanations" to the knowledge of the Oneness of God. This meaning corresponds more closely to monastic prayer or the practice of the solitary. But then, since the verb *yḥd* is also used colloquially with the sexual meaning "coire" ("to copulate") this translation is not recommended.

(g) "Host" (the triple "hostiam" of the Unde et Memores prayer) and "oblatio" ("offering") (in the Hanc Igitur prayer) are translated *ʿwlh*, the Old Testament burnt offering (e.g., Exod. 18:12; 29:18; Lev.

1:9), which consisted of a whole sacrificial animal which is burned completely on the altar. A more appropriate term would probably have been *šlm* "peace offering" (also a meat offering), which could be associated verbally both with the Eucharistic "prayer for peace" and concluding "kiss of peace" immediately preceding the Communion, and also with *šlm* as a "communion sacrifice"[74] which is essentially a description of the Mass.[75] An essential parallel with the Mass is also found in the fact that when the *ʿwlh* was burned nothing remained, while in the *šlm* the meat was enjoyed by the one making the offering together with his family and his friends. The principal reason why the Host, or the Bread that is transformed into the Body of Christ, was translated by *ʿwlh* seems to have been Christian typology. In the Genesis account of Abraham's sacrifice the "lamb for the burnt offering" is mentioned twice in rapid succession (Gen. 22:7–8), and since the third century the lamb (*hśh*) has been understood to prefigure the "Agnus Dei," although it was a ram (*'yl*) that was actually sacrificed (v. 13). The editors of the Jerusalem Bible note, ad loc., "In the sacrifice of Isaac the Fathers saw a prefiguring of the Passion of Jesus, the only-begotten Son."

The use of the neologism *tqrwbt* is both inconsistent and incorrect for "oblatio" (in the prayer of self-offering Suscipe Sancta Trinitas) and "munera" ("gifts," in the prayer Te Igitur), for although it is etymologically derived from *qrbn,* it has the secular meaning today of "attendance, entertainment." Finding this rare word used in the liturgy is reminiscent of Martin Buber's rendering of *qrbn* in his 1925 German translation of the Bible as "Darnahung" ("approach"), which is undoubtedly close to the original meaning of the biblical sacrifice but has as little chance of being understood in Germany as the word *tqrwbt* for "sacrifice of the Mass" does in Israel. For "offering" in general the oldest Old Testament term *minḥâ* might be recommended, a term used in Gen. 4:3 simply for the presentation of an offering.

(h) The translations of "Pentecost" as *ḥg hšbwʿwt* "Feast of Weeks" and of "Easter" as *psḥ'* are purely Jewish, although the latter is an Aramaic form, possibly to suggest a distinction between the related *psḥ* "Passover" and the Feast of Easter.

(i) "Communion" is called *hwḥdh* from the newly formed hiphil of the Qumran community's *yḥd* ("community") which many theologians trace to sources close to the early Church. Since the piel of the verb *yḥd* can also mean "unite," it need not be associated exclusively with the Qumran community, as in the case of "canon" (*srk* "order"), which is known only from Qumran. But since the words *srk hyḥd* occur in the Qumran scrolls as a fixed formula, the translators may have been reminded of the Dead Sea documents at this point. True to the causative sense of the hiphil, it is used only of the priest who administers the Host (*hkhn mwḥyd 't ʿṣmw*), while the action of the lay communicants is translated with the passive niphal (*hnwḥdym*).

The colloquial word *htyḥd,* which is quite close to "communicare" ("to share, commune") in the spiritual sense, is avoided because the reflexive form conflicts with the Catholic sacramental position which requires for its validity the (causative) ministration by a fully authorized minister to a faithful and willing recipient. The relationship between the celebrant and the communicant in communion can be expressed properly only by the hiphil (for the priest) and niphal (for the laity).

"Let us partake of the divinity of him who" is rendered *tn lnw štwp b'lqwtw* in the prayer Deus qui Humanae Substantiae. Not only is the style of the Hebrew here somewhat complicated (*štwpnw b . . .* would be briefer and more graceful) but also somewhat offensive, because the word *štwp* has historical connotations similar to those of the word *šlwš*.[76] It was used, as has been mentioned, in the medieval period with the theological meaning of "association" for all who were monotheists but who placed other beings in association with God as did the Christians (from the rabbinic viewpoint) in the doctrine of the Trinity.[77] Here, then, the shorter *štpnw* or the synagogal *śym ḥlqnw ʿm* "set our share with" should be recommended.

Among the numerous improvements characterizing this text, the following should receive special notice.

(a) The frequent "Deo gratias" which was earlier translated with the colloquial expression *twdh l'l* "thanks to God" is now more liturgically *šbḥ l'l* "praise to God." The banality of "thank God" is similarly avoided in English by the fuller expression "thanks be to God."

(b) The equally frequent "per Dominum nostrum," which was earlier translated with the simple instrumental *drk* "through" and *ʿl ydy* "by," is now rendered by *bʿd ḥmšyḥ,* which can mean "pro" ("for") as well as "per" ("through") in Hebrew. "Dominus noster" ("our Lord") is now changed to the singular form *'dwnnw* following the usage of the synagogue liturgy.

(c) "Hoc est corpus meum" ("this is my body") is no longer rendered *zh hw' gwpy* but rather *zh hw' bśry* "this is my flesh," which approaches more nearly the doctrine of the Incarnation. Since *bśr* in the Old Testament means "body" as well as "flesh," and *gwp* is postbiblical, this improvement also has these further advantages:

(1) "Flesh and blood," into which the offerings of the Mass are changed, is a Hebrew idiom indicating the whole person (e.g., *ʿErub.* 19a; *Ber.* 28b; Matt. 16:17), corresponding to the doctrine of transubstantiation, according to which the Bread and the Wine are changed into the "Living Christ."

(2) Since *bśr qdš* "holy flesh" is an Old Testament synonym

for flesh that is offered (Jer. 11:15; Hag. 2:12), this again emphasizes a verbal affinity to the offering of the Mass.

(3) "My blood of the covenant" in Matt. 26:28 (from Exod. 24:8) is now harmonized with Matt. 26:26 "this is my body (*bśry*)," which recalls Gen. 17:13 "my covenant in your flesh." This harmonization brings together in relation to the Old Testament both these central logia of the Lord's Supper.

(d) "Eternal life" ("vita aeterna") as a reward of the righteous has been a religious theme in Hebrew as *ḥyy ʿwlm* since Dan. 12:2, and became an accepted part of the liturgy.[78] This text of the Mass, however, speaks of *ḥyy nṣḥ* "everlasting life," apparently following the Qumran scrolls where the term occurs twice (CD iii.20; 1QS iv.7) in clearly eschatological contexts which come close to the future hope of Luke 20:35ff.[79] Since *ḥyy ʿwlm* does not necessarily have a transcendental reference, but can also be used of remarkable longevity,[80] this is a model example of the subtle interplay between theology and philology.

By the end of 1968 twenty-two of the Propers had been translated into Hebrew and made available for experimental use. They were later revised and expanded along the lines of the new liturgical calendar and adapted to the Motu Proprio "Paschalis Mysterii" of February 14, 1969, and the Apostolic Constitution "Missale Romanum" of April 3, 1969.

A significant contribution to the Mass was made by the Carmelite Father Daniel (Oswald Rufeisen), who became famous in 1962 when he appealed to the Supreme Court for Israeli citizenship under the Law of Repatriation, on the grounds that both his parents were Jews and that his own subjective loyalties were Jewish. "My religion is Catholic," he insisted, and added in the spirit of St. Paul, "I became a Christian not to desert my people, but in order to increase my Jewishness. I think of myself as completely Jewish." And yet the court decided after extensive debate and with a close majority that the son of a Jewish mother who has converted to another religion cannot be regarded as a Jew in terms of the Law of Repatriation, and that this accords with the widespread feeling today that although a Jew need not have an active religious affiliation, and may well be an atheist, yet he cannot be a member of another religion. Nevertheless, although the genuineness of his convictions and the number of times he had rescued other Jews from Poland were unquestioned, Father Daniel soon afterwards became an Israeli citizen as an immigrant, a basis available to all non-Jews. As a Zionist and son of a traditional Jewish family, who called himself Daniel because he was saved from the lion's den of Adolf Hitler's regime, his knowledge of Hebrew was sufficient for him to observe a part of his prayers in Hebrew soon after his arrival at Stella Maris, the

Carmelite house on Mount Carmel in Haifa. Although one of his brothers, Father Elias (alias Friedmann, a baptized Jew from South Africa) had already received a "communicatio in privilegio" in 1958 to say the hours of the Breviary in Hebrew, "in 1960 it was still illegal for me," Father Daniel still recalls.

As for the Mass, although on the basis of Article 36 of "Constitutio de Sacra Liturgia" Patriarch Gori had possessed since 1963 ecclesiastical competence with regard to its observance in the vernacular for Israel, Jordan, and Cyprus, he refused to authorize its official celebration in Hebrew before at least ten Catholic priests were duly qualified for it. Since the persons involved were almost without exception Jewish Christians, it is interesting to note that Gori set the synagogal quorum of ten (minyan, the number required for a valid community service) as the minimum number of celebrants for a Hebrew mass. In February 1965 the number was completed. Gori granted authorization at a single time for the celebration of the Mass in Arabic, Greek (for Cyprus), and Hebrew, once the translations in these respective languages received the approval of the appropriate diocesan bishops. Since the hebraizers had received permission from Bishop Kaldany to print the (tentative) text of the Mass on March 3, 1964, they were the first of the three language groups to take advantage of this authorization. On March 7, 1965, this first Hebrew Mass was celebrated by eleven priests in the Roman Catholic diocesan church in Haifa. Only the Canon was said in Latin and not in Hebrew at the express wish of several of the priests because they were not yet sufficiently familiar with the Hebrew form of this central part of the Liturgy.

On August 11, 1968, Father Daniel celebrated the whole of the Mass in Hebrew for the first time, from the preparation at the steps to the dismissal. Since then he has read the Hebrew Mass every Sunday afternoon in the diocesan church at Haifa for a congregation averaging 150 Catholics, about one-third of whom are Arabs, as well as several Jewish Christians, with some dozen monks and nuns of various orders, and the remainder comprising a number of Catholic partners of mixed marriages who had come to Israel from Europe in the last twenty-five years. Before the mass attended by the author in May 1969, several young Arabs vied (in Hebrew) for the privilege of serving "Abuna Daniel" as acolyte.

Since the majority of Catholics coming from Europe had difficulty reading the Hebrew text, Father Daniel published a Latin transcription of the text of the Mass. This transliteration represents a phonetic and graphic compromise between the rules of the Academy of the Hebrew Language and the Polish, Hungarian, and Czech orthographies—the three major language groups represented among the ex-Europeans in his parish.

As in many other lands, the Catholics in Israel have begun since 1970 to reform their Hebrew text of the Mass in the spirit of the "editio typica" of the new Roman "Ordo Missae," and it is quite clear that they are making full use of the permission "to prepare editions in the vernacular . . . that are not merely literal translations."

To date only the Ordinarium (*hqbwʿ*, lit. "the fixed") has been printed as a provisional trial text—without imprimatur—with the intent that after a trial period and subsequent revisions it may become duly authorized. Because of the tentative nature of this trial version only the most fundamental change will be noted here, that which appears on its title page. The Mass is no longer called "The Holy Sacrifice" (*hqrbn hqdwš*), but "The Lord's Supper" (*sʿwdt hʾdwn*). One reason for this change of names is that Israeli Christians who would tell their friends that they had to leave home at six o'clock, for example, "to offer the Sacrifice" (*lhqryb ʾt hqrbn*) found their friends visibly shocked. Indeed, such a rite in modern Israel almost inevitably involves a particular association: the bloody sacrifice of the Passover lamb as performed annually by the Samaritans according to the prescriptions in Exod. 12:1–11 and in the presence of hundreds of visitors and tourists on Mount Gerizim. When the Jewish friends explain this association and the Christian with all good intentions points to the inner connection between the Passover and the Mass, it becomes very difficult to avoid the impression that the Mass is a retrospective anachronism. Yet since for Christianity this kind of cultic offering (described in 2 Chr. 30; Ezra 6:19–22; Ezek. 45:18–24) is declared in Hebrews as accomplished once and for all time (Heb. 9:14; 10:10–13; 13:20), and because as Paul says, "Christ, our Passover lamb, has been sacrificed" (1 Cor. 5:7), it was considered both theologically and literally desirable to transfer the emphasis to the second basic element of the celebration, namely the Supper. For the "Last Supper," which Paul later called the "Lord's Supper" (11:20) and Franz Delitzsch translated literally as *sʿwdt hʾdwn*, had become a Jewish family meal even before the time of Jesus. Thus it was six days before Pesach that Jesus came to Jerusalem (John 12:1), sending his disciples ahead to prepare for it carefully (Mark 14:12–16), and saying, "I have greatly desired to eat this *psḥ* with you" (Luke 22:15). It is also with this in mind that Anselm Schott says, "The celebration of the Holy Mass is essentially a communal celebration . . . (and) it finds its natural climax in the shared offering of a communal meal."[81] Similarly the Jerusalem Bible notes at Exod. 12: "The Jewish Passover hence becomes a rehearsal for the Christian Passover: the lamb of God, Christ, is sacrificed (the cross) and eaten (the Last Supper) within the framework of the Jewish Passover (the first Holy Week)."

But the parallel is also of an eschatological nature. Just as the Mass is replete with anticipations of the Parousia (e.g., in the Credo, Sanctus, and Pater Noster), the Jewish Passover Haggadah also contains numerous messianic references and allusions. For example:

(a) The cup on the seder table for Elijah the prophet, who will proclaim the salvation of Israel (Mal. 3:23 [Eng. 4:5]).

(b) The Piyyuṭ of Eliezer ha-Kalir: "At midnight (pray to God) 'Hasten the day that is neither day nor night . . . . Then, O Lord, thy hand will be victorious . . . as in that night in which the first Passover was established.' "

(c) Rabbi Joshua ben Ḥananiah (*ca.* 90 B.C.E.) explained the meaning of Passover night in simple words: "In this night we were rescued; in this night we shall be saved."

(d) In the final Piyyuṭ those assembled at the table join in prayer for the long desired salvation: "Bless, O Lord, the faithful stock of Jacob."

(e) Finally, as the last course of the meal the mystical piece of matzo, which is veiled at the beginning of the seder liturgy, is broken with a special blessing (". . . in praise of the Holy One, blessed be he and his presence, through whom he is both concealed and revealed, in the name of all Israel"); this is called *Afikoman,* from Gk. "Ephikómenos" ("the coming one"), in Hebrew *hb*ʾ, and in Aramaic ʾ*th*—all words having soteriological implications.

Besides the solemn Sabbath meal (*sʿwdt-šbt*) with its *zemirot* ("hymns") so full of eschatological hope, the word *sʿwdh* itself has at least four clearly messianic associations.

(a) *sʿwdh šl ṣdyqym* "the feast of the righteous" (1 En. 62:14; *Midr. Esth.* 1:4)

(b) *sʿwdt gʾwlh* "the feast of salvation" (*Pesiq. R.* 41; *Midr. Ps.* 14:7)

(c) *sʿwdt lwytn* "the feast of the (sea monster) Leviathan" (1 En. 60:7ff; *B. Bat.* 75a)

(d) *sʿwdt šl gn-ʿdn* "the feast of Paradise" (*Exod. Rab.* 45; *Num. Rab.* 13)

All of these are rabbinic synonyms for the future feast of the Day of Salvation, for which the Apocalypse uses a no less esoteric and poetical expression, the "marriage feast of the Lamb" (Rev. 19:9).

To the best of the author's knowledge as of August 1974, 286 Israeli Catholics were participating in the Hebrew Mass at least once a week, mostly on the Sabbath. This number comprises three different groups in eight parishes in Jerusalem, Jaffa, Haifa, and ʿAfula: Jewish Christians (laypersons as well as priests), some of whom were born Israelis and considered Hebrew their native tongue, although all were at least bilingual; Arabs who preferred the Hebrew-language churches either for the prestige attached to the "first language of the country" or for the convenience of their being nearby; and Catholics of European origin who were either partners in mixed marriages and as parents of Hebrew-speaking children wished to worship in the language of their children but in their own church, or priests and members of religious orders (from seven different countries) who for religious reasons wished to worship in "the language of Jesus." In this last group were also seven Arab monks and nuns from Lebanon, Syria, and Egypt.

Apart from these were also about eighty priests, monks, and nuns (from nine countries, including Lebanon, Syria, and Egypt) who celebrated the Hebrew Mass at irregular intervals, but at least three times a year. Since 1968 the number of celebrants and participants in the Hebrew Mass has grown slowly but steadily.

In June 1970 Father Dubois, the director of the Institute of St. Isaiah, the Dominican center for Jewish Studies in Jerusalem, wrote of the Hebrew Mass:

> The first significant event . . . was the celebration of Easter Mass in the Church of the Holy Sepulchre. It is important to mention this. Actually it is not nearly so surprising that Israeli Christians worship in their own language on Easter at the site of the Easter event, as it is that so many are unaware that Israeli Christians worship in Hebrew, celebrating the liturgy in their own national language, which is also the language of the Bible.[82]

4. *The Greek Catholic Liturgy of the Mass*

Fr. Jacob Barclay, born of Canadian Jewish parents, was baptized a Catholic in 1956, came to Israel in 1957, and entered the Greek Catholic church in 1958.[83] At Nazareth in 1961 Archbishop George Hakim of Galilee ordained him to the priesthood in this Uniate church of about 22,000 souls, which was until 1967 the largest Christian minority in Israel.[84] During his theological studies in Jerusalem he came to realize that until the end of the eighteenth century the language of worship used by the Melchites, as his church was called in the east, was Syro-Melchitish, a dialect of Palestinian Aramaic[85] which was gradually displaced by Arabic in the course of the nineteenth century. Barclay formed a resolve to revive the original form of his church liturgy which evidently may be traced in part to Jewish-Christian worship in Galilee.

In his language studies Barclay also became convinced that the majority of the Arabic-speaking Melchites in his archdiocese (which included Akko, Haifa, Nazareth, and several villages in Galilee) were descendants of Jewish Christians whose worship seemed to derive partly from the circles of the early Church. The report by Saadia Gaon, which has been further confirmed by Eduard Y. Kutscher, that about

930 he had met Jewish peasants in Galilee who still spoke Aramaic[86] further encouraged Barclay in his endeavor "to prove to the Arabophone Israelis in Galilee that they were not as Arab as they imagined themselves to be, and to demonstrate to my Jewish brothers that they were neither linguistically nor ethnically distant from their Arab fellow-citizens, but actually came from the same cradle."

But when the project to restore the Aramaic form of the liturgy was frustrated by linguistic and other difficulties—in particular by the lack of original texts, the lack of interest within the church, and the lack of apparent relevance for contemporary church life—Barclay decided to render it in Hebrew. In this scheme he received unexpected assistance from two Trappist monks who had come to Israel in 1960–1961, and being converted to the Melchite church, were now contemplating the founding of a lavra in Galilee, the first Greek-Catholic monastic community. Br. Ja'aqov (Jaap) Willebrands, a Dutchman and a distant relative of Cardinal Willebrands, and Br. Thoma (formerly Thomas) Farelly of St. Louis, Mo., were certainly no hebraists, but after six months in Israel they resolved to translate their worship services gradually into Hebrew.

With the assistance of Fr. Joseph Samuelov from Latrun, Br. Yoḥanan Eliḥai (Jean Leroy), Joshua Blum, and several Jewish friends, Barclay was able by the beginning of 1962 to prepare a translation of the Greek Catholic Sunday liturgy of St. Chrysostom into Hebrew. After Eliḥai had examined the text, Archbishop Hakim gave his sanction for its publication, and on March 25, 1962, the first two hundred copies of this fifty-one-page liturgy were printed with the title: *hqrbn hqdwš kmnhg qwsṭ'* "The Holy Sacrifice according to the rite of Constantinople [the Byzantine rite]." The fact that this text was largely based on translations of the original in English, French, Spanish, and Arabic in its respective parts (apparently due to the lack of any knowledge of Greek!) is obvious in the Hebrew version. Nor is it any less apparent that the most important theological terms, the creeds, and other essential elements were copied directly from the Roman Catholic Mass—including mistranslations and two typographical errors! And yet it should also be duly noted that specifically Greek prayers, such as the "Cheroubikon" (or "Cherubic Hymn"; *hmnwn hkrwbym*) and the "Kathagiasmos" (translated as the synagogal *qdwš* "sanctifcation," and corresponding to the prayer of consecration in the Roman Catholic Mass) are translated in the best Piyyuṭ tradition of the synagogue, even though the quality is achieved sometimes at the expense of textual fidelity.

It is too early yet to discuss further the linguistic details of the text in its present experimental form, which is regarded by its editors as a tentative model. To the best of the author's knowledge the liturgy is presently serving only four persons for their regular devotions: Father Barclay, a Belgian postulant, and the two ex-Trappists who have lived since 1966 in their Lavra Netofa on a hillock in Galilee between the Arab village of Deir Hanna and the Jewish settlement of Jodfat.

Brother Willebrands believes that "the Melchites are direct successors of the primitive Jewish-Christian community," that "a majority of the so-called Arabs of Israel are of Jewish origin," and that "there is a wealth of Jewish tradition in the liturgy, exegesis, and theology of the native church awaiting investigation by a religious historian."

At present the Greek Catholic breviary and the liturgies of St. Basil and St. James are in advanced stages of translation into Hebrew, thanks to the initiative of these leaders. It was reported in October 1971 that Archbishop Joseph Raya, then the ecclesiastical superior of the Greek Catholic church in Israel, promised his support to these hebraizers, furthermore indicating his interest in considering whether some prayers from the Liturgy of St. Chrysostom in its Hebrew version could in the future be introduced into his church.

5. *Hebrew in Christian Worship and Hymns*

A. Worship in Hebrew. The first Protestants in Israel to observe a part of their worship service in Hebrew were the Norwegian Lutherans, who have administered since 1951 the two churches built in Haifa and Jaffa by the German Lutherans and Templars in 1893–1896. In 1959 on the initiative of the Rev. Magne Solheim, who represented both the Lutheran World Federation and the British and Foreign Bible Society in Israel, two Jewish Christians in his congregation of some sixty members prepared a new Hebrew liturgy which has been celebrated every fortnight since March 1960 in Haifa and since September 1969 in Jaffa. It also provided a part of the consecration service for the new Church of Elias which was celebrated in Haifa on May 23, 1960, with Bishop Fridtjov Birkeli, primate of the Norwegian national church, the Greek Catholic Archbishop Joseph Raya, and representatives of the Israeli government in attendance.

The "judaizing" influence exercised by this liturgy on worship services written originally in other languages, especially in German, English, and Norwegian, is to be found in the fact that some of them are held on the Sabbath, that the Lord's Prayer is almost always said in Hebrew, and that a Menorah (the seven-branched candlestick of the temple, or of the vision of Zech. 4:2ff., which was adopted in 1948 as the state symbol of Israel) stands on the altar of the Church of Elias, which also has Isa. 56:7 inscribed in large Hebrew letters across its front.

The name of the three-page liturgy is *Sdr-ʿbwdh* "Order of Worship." In Rabbinic Hebrew this indicates the Jerusalem temple worship service on the Day of Atonement (and later, the oral tradition of this service in the synagogue) as it is referred to in *Yoma* iii.8 and in the *Shebeṭ Yehudah* [*Tribe of Judah*] (lxiv.10) of Salomon ibn Verga, who cites the description of a Roman eyewitness.[87] The only verbal difference in the titles is the definite article, which is lacking in the Lutheran liturgy, presumably because it did not wish to suggest that it was *the* worship service (in an exclusive sense) as the temple service once claimed to be. Since the transition from the cultic temple service to its corresponding synagogue worship after 70 C.E. is confirmed specifically in the rabbinic *Sipre* on Deut. 11:13 ("as the Altar Service is called service *ʿbwdh,* so also prayer is called God's service"), this term can be used liturgically for an "order of worship"—especially as *Siddur* is the name for the common Jewish prayer book containing the order of worship for the synagogue. The only difficulty is the fact that in Modern Hebrew this expression is used for a "work schedule" as posted on notice boards in factories and kibbutzim.

The following terms and expressions found in this liturgy are of special interest.

(a) For the evangelical, whose concept of the "universal priesthood" of all baptized believers does not recognize a basic distinction between priests and laity, the pastor is not *kohen* as in the Catholic Mass, but *khn-dt* (lit. "priest of religion"), the Modern Hebrew expression for (non-Jewish) clergy.

(b) Similarly the community of worshippers is not the sacral *ʿdh* of the Catholic Mass but *qhl,* corresponding to Martin Luther's translation of the New Testament "ekklēsía" by "Gemeinde." It seems inconsistent that the word "church" is then translated *qhlh* in the Creed, although this agrees with Franz Delitzsch's Protestant translation of Matt. 16:18. The latter term refers in postbiblical Hebrew rather to the local parish. Since *qhl* refers to the whole body of God's people in Num. 16:3; 20:4; 1 Chr. 28:8, etc., the opposite should be expected, with *qhlh* as the individual church, following the common Jewish usage today, and *qhl* as the whole church, as in the Old Testament. But in Modern Hebrew *qhl* has the secular meaning of "a public lecture." In effect, since the concern here is with a text in Modern Hebrew, it would be better to use *knsyh* for the "whole" church on the analogy of the Knesset of Israel, and *zbwr* for the worshipping group; this would meet the requirements of the Hebrew liturgy and also sound appropriate to Israelis.

(c) "He suffered death" is translated *nʿnh,* which is Modern Hebrew for "he was heard" or "he was answered." This is apparently a christological use of Isa. 53:7, where it is said of the Servant of God that "he was abused." But since the whole Creed is translated here into Modern Hebrew, consistency demands *ʿnh* "he was tormented" or *hwmt* "he was killed."

(d) "Hosanna in the highest" from Mark 11:10 is at least obscure in Hebrew, if not meaningless, especially when the same petition is directed in the previous sentence to one "who comes (on earth)." No less obscure is the Greek dative in Matt. 21:9 "Hosanna to the Son of David!" which seems to agree with Mark 11:10 in suggesting that in the Koine Greek of the New Testament "Hosanna" has been misunderstood as a kind of greeting or acclamation. In order to correct this without altering the New Testament text, the editor resorted to the expedient of placing an exclamation point after both "Hosanna" and "in the highest." But this only leaves the cry "in the highest" without a context, and it is still meaningless.

Since there is no authorized common form of evangelical worship service, and most Protestant churches do not wish to place restraints on the spontaneous freedom of the individual worshipper, only a few churches of the Augsburg Confession in Israel have formulated written orders of worship for their services. Šalhebet-YH ("Flame of the Lord"), the Finnish mission school in Jerusalem,[88] has only a one-page mimeographed order of worship for the Sabbath celebration and a few pietistic hymns translated from Finnish or German and distributed on a separate sheet. But when singing such Christmas hymns as "Ich steh an deiner Krippen hier" ("A Babe Lies in the Manger"),[89] or Advent hymns and Easter cantatas with their European melodies, the Hebrew translations quite frequently differ from the originals in rhythm and meter. Miss Havas, the founder of the school and its director until 1969, reports that Jewish Christians who lead in the weekly worship service are quite eclectic; Ps. 51, a variation of Ps. 118, and the Kyrie Eleison sung to a melody by Jean Sibelius rank as favorites.

Of interest for their vocabulary are two small booklets translated into Hebrew in 1960 by Prof. Aimo Murtonen from Helsinki for use in the Finnish mission: Martin Luther's *Shorter Catechism* (*Shoʾel u-Meshib Qaṭon*), and *On the Liberty of a Christian Man* (*Ḥeruto shel ʾAdam Meshiḥi*).[90] Since the texts are for the elementary grades, their Modern Hebrew style is clear and easy to understand, with no difficult passages needing any simplification. The following points should be noted.

(a) "Bishop" is mistranslated as *mšqyp,* which means "observer" instead of "overseer," as this office was originally called at Phil. 1:1; Acts 20:28ff. The word *pqyd* which Delitzsch used here sounds no less inappropriate today because, although it was used to indicate the presiding member of the *yḥd* ("community") at Qumran, in Modern Hebrew it means "employer." The proper expression derived from Qumran is *mebaqqer,* which is the accepted Protestant term in Israel today.

(b) "Sacraments" is translated as *qdšy hqdšym,* which not only sounds sanctimonious but is also unidiomatic; in Hebrew as well as in Latin this expression is used exclusively in the singular.

(c) "Passus est" ("he suffered death") is translated as *ntʿnh,* which places greater emphasis on pain than the shorter pual *ʿnh* "he was afflicted" (but none on death, which is not even mentioned here).

(d) "Was crucified" is translated as *hwqʿ ʿl hṣlb* "hanged on the cross," apparently to portray the form of execution more vividly. The niphal of *ṣlb* "crucify" would have been adequate.

(e) The somewhat inaccurate translation *kōp̱er* "ransom" is given for the "Indulgences" against which Luther inveighed. In the sense of a fine this does have the connotation of ransom (e.g., Exod. 21:30), but it also implies an element of indemnification to the one suffering loss[91] which is not present in the ecclesiastical absolution of sins (according to the Church's doctrine of Thesaurus). From the Lutheran viewpoint an expression such as *dmy kprh* "expiation fee" would have damned this practice more effectively.

Among the other Mission publications, most of which are translated from Finnish, only one more need be mentioned: a translation into simple Hebrew (*trgwm ʿibry pšwṭ*) of the Aramaic chapters of the book of Daniel, explicitly relating to Jesus the passages which can be interpreted christologically.

Until 1967 the school enrollment averaged about fifty children, but by the summer of 1969 the last of its Jewish pupils was withdrawn due to the efforts of a Jewish religious group. In their place twenty-eight Arab children from Ramleh were admitted (twenty-four Greek Orthodox and four Roman Catholics), whose parents agreed to a "generally Christian" education and the condition that the language of instruction, of the Scripture readings, and of worship continue to be Hebrew.

Another Lutheran institution is the Ecumenical Sisterhood of Mary from Darmstadt, which was founded in 1947 by Mother Basilea Schlink and has been active in Israel as a nursing order since 1957. In 1961 they bought a house in Jerusalem where they undertook the care of older victims of the Nazi Reich. Their motivation: "We are here because we Germans have sinned most grievously against the Jewish people. We cannot bring the dead back to life, but we want to express our remorse and our love for Israel by our service."[92] Their solidarity with Israel, "the Covenant People of God," finds expression in fasts on the Jewish Day of Atonement, in the Ner Tamid (Eternal Light) which burns in their chapel in memory of the six million Jewish martyrs, in a religious festival which they celebrate annually on the State of Israel's Independence Day, in the kosher food they serve in their house which is called Bet-Abraham and where each of the halls and walls is decorated with scenes such as Hebron, Beersheba, Ain-Mamre, and Moriah. Every Friday evening the four to six Sisters of Mary, who are assigned annually to service in Israel from Canaan, the mother house in Darmstadt, celebrate for their guests a Hebrew Sabbath ceremony consisting of passages from the Bible and Psalms together with brief poems and antiphonal choruses, designed by Mother Basilea and translated by her hebraist assistants. In consideration for Jewish sensibilities the Divine Name is represented in these texts consistently by the letter *he* (ה). Since some of the older guests (almost all Central European Jews) understand less Hebrew than their hosts, every setting at the Sabbath table is provided with a German translation of this composite liturgy, which is recited and sung by the sisters in Hebrew. Some of the books by Mother Basilea, such as *Israel, mein Volk* [*Israel, My People*], *Um Jerusalems Willen* [*For the Sake of Jerusalem*], *Die Stunde des Messias* [*The Hour of the Messiah*], and *Juden und Christen* [*Jews and Christians*], have been published in Hebrew by the sisters, sold in the bookstores, and exhibited in the Jerusalem book fairs. On Jewish feasts the sisters send postcards to their Israeli friends with sayings of their founder in Hebrew or appropriate words from the Old Testament in Hebrew.

A small Protestant group from the Federal Republic of Germany maintains a similar rest home for Nazi victims called Bet-El with a similar worship service arranged in Hebrew. Bet-El is also the name of a Jewish-Christian mission school in Haifa with about forty children ranging from kindergarten to the fourth grade. Since the founders of this institution were mainly baptized Jews of a chiliastic tendency with their base in the United States, most of their worship service is translated from English. The New Testament texts are all taken from Delitzsch's version.

The most active American missionaries are from the Southern Baptist Convention, with a congregation today of about 350 members, mostly Arab. Under the direction of Robert L. Lindsey, who has lived in Israel since 1945, eight Baptist and two Mennonite missionaries are at work in Nazareth, Kana, Rama, Touran, and Akko. In the Jewish sector new centers have been active for several years in Ramat-Gan, Haifa, and Tel-Aviv, with services observed regularly in Hebrew. The main office of the mission is the Baptist House in the center of Jerusalem, which has been active since 1925. In Baptist Village (*kpr hbpṭsṭym*), a vocational school not far from Petaḥ-Tiqwah, about fifty children (except for three Jews, all Arabs and Moslems) receive elementary education and agricultural instruction leading to matriculation.

The majority of the staff are Jews and Jewish Christians who teach in Hebrew.

Since Baptists believe in unrestricted spontaneity in worship, their only Hebrew prayer book is an 85-page manual for children entitled *Nitpallel* [*Let Us Pray!*] which has been recognized as the best child evangelism text in Israel today for its form, typography, illustrations, and content. The list of special days for which page-long prayers are provided reflects an ecumenical spirit: Christmas, Hanukkah, "the Day of Jesus' death," Passover, "the Resurrection of Jesus," Purim, the Feast of Weeks, "the Day of Inspiration by the Holy Spirit," the Day of Atonement. The only Jewish day that is not christianized in simple language easily understood by ten year olds is the Israeli Independence Day, when God is thanked for "our state," and the conclusion echoes the Jewish petition: "prepare our hearts for the coming of the messianic king. Amen." Thus the prayer on Purim thanks God for "rescuing me through Jesus my savior (*yšwʿ mwšyʿy*)" from a foe worse than Haman, "from the hand of Satan. Amen." On the day of Atonement the Creator is thanked "for granting us atonement through the blood of the Messiah, who offered himself for us." On Hanukkah it is recalled at the lighting of the candles that "Jesus is the light of the world, who came to us in the darkness of sin to bring us light."

The transition from Jewish to Christian motifs is so seamless and smooth that the blend is not often detected at first reading. All ideas that could sound at all "un-Hebrew" have been adapted to the natural idiom of the age group intended by the writer. For example, Sunday is simply *ywm rʾšwn* "first day," although in the middle of the Sunday prayer *ywm hʾdwn* "the Lord's Day" appears in quotation marks. Christmas is easily adapted from the usual Heb. *ḥg hmwld* "Festival of the Birth" to the more explicit *ywm hwldtw šl yšwʿ* "Birthday of Jesus," and on Passover the Passover Lamb (*śh hpsḥ*) becomes the Lamb of God (*śh lh"*)—just as the Ascension of Jesus (*ywm ʿlyt hmšyḥ hšmymh* "day of the ascension of the Messiah to heaven") suggests the hope of the parousia (*ʾnw mṣpym lšwbk* "we await your return . . .").

The Baptist publishing house and translations of the New Testament will be discussed later.

The Church of Scotland maintains churches and chapels in Jaffa, Tiberias, Nazareth, and Jerusalem, holding regular Hebrew services in the first two cities. Especially active is the young Rev. Hugh Kerr in Tiberias, the successor of John M. Snoek, a clergyman of the Dutch Reformed church, who served as secretary of the Committee on the Church and the Jewish People for the World Council of Churches in Geneva since mid-1970. Together with Samuel Paul Re'emi, a Jewish-Christian presbyter of the Scottish church, the young Scotsman is responsible for daily morning prayers, weekly Sabbath evening services, and a monthly sermon, all in Modern Hebrew. These services, which were designed partly by Snoek and partly by Re'emi and Kerr, are based on the Jewish *Siddur*, Delitzsch's New Testament, translations from the Scottish Prayer Book, and their own intuition.

The Messianic Assembly of Israel (*qhlh mšyḥyt yśr'lyt*) is located in Jerusalem, belongs to the international Pentecostal Movement, and has about forty members, only three of whom are "gentile Christians" from Europe or America. The others are all Israeli citizens who serve in the army, emphasize their Jewishness, call their place of worship *byt hqhlh* ("parish house"), their worship hours *'spwt* ("meetings"), and their three clergymen "Rab" ("rabbi"). Only the director of the group, the Rev. Ze'ev Kofsman, signs his name as *rwʿh hʿdh* "shepherd of the congregation," which corresponds approximately to the title "Pastor." Their quasi-Ebionitic creed, which ignores Jesus' divine sonship and apotheosis, the Trinity, and the virgin birth, and exhibits distinctly Jewish and Zionist traits, is printed regularly in boldface on the first page of their periodical *Ha-lappid* [*The Torch*], which is defined as "an organ of the Israeli church, a revival (*hḥy'h*) of the original Messianic Church." Their five-part creed (after the Mosaic Pentateuch?) reads in translation:

> We believe:
> in the unity of God (the Divine Name is *h*″, as in proper Jewish usage).
> in the messiahship of Jesus, the son of David, who was born according to the Holy Scripture in the time of the Second Temple in Bethlehem, suffered death (*hwmt*!) for our sins, arose from the dead on the third day, ascended into heaven, and sits on the right hand of the Power (*gbwrh*) in the highest, and will certainly come again (*šwb yšwb*) to establish the kingdom of heaven on earth.
> in the Holy Spirit.
> in the *tnk* (sic!) as the Word of God.
> in the political (*mdynyt*) and spiritual return to Zion, in accordance with the promises of God.

The weekly Hebrew worship services, held on the morning of the Sabbath as well as on Sunday and Wednesday evenings, include three lessons—the weekly pericope from the Old Testament, the haftarah from the Prophets, and a pericope from the New Testament; the Lord's Prayer; a sermon; and some songs from their own hymnal. The latter is a collection of fifty-four excerpts from the Old Testament which are quite rightly described in the introduction as largely "a part of Israel's traditional folk songs" (e.g., Exod. 3:8; Num. 24:5; Ps. 68:1; 133:1; 137:5–6; 150:6; Isa. 2:3; 35:1; 55:12; Amos 9:13). The only reference to Christianity appears in hymn no. 33, which has the title "The Lord's

Supper'' (*sʿdt hʾdwn*) and is composed from Lev. 17:11 and Isa. 53:5, 3, 6; by some slight rephrasing and transposition of verses the purpose of the (Servant's) self-sacrifice is ''made clear'' in the light of the priestly altar prescriptions in Leviticus, but without mentioning either Jesus or Christ by name. The title of the hymnal, ''For the Choirmaster: a Song, a Psalm'' (Ps. 66:1), is interpreted by the church in a military sense as ''To the Conqueror, a Song, a Psalm''; this is possible because in Modern Hebrew the word *mnṣḥ* can have both meanings, and the second verse following (66:3) speaks of God's victory—as the prayer leader frequently explains with reference to the Six Day War. A new edition of the hymnal features a programmatic element in its bibliographical notice: United Jerusalem, the capital of Israel, Pessach Eve 5729.

The Jewish Pentecostals circumcise their sons, abstain from pork, celebrate all the Jewish feasts with particular emphasis on salvation at Passover and religious-national independence at Hanukkah, while their house of worship is without any Christian symbolism or inscriptions. The common expression for Christians, *nwṣry*, is also taboo because of its historical associations for Jews. The name they have adopted, *mšyḥyym,* represents a construction literally parallel to ''christiani,'' and is preferred today by most Protestants in Israel. In 1962 the small community, which also has several members in Haifa and Tel-Aviv, was successful in organizing a World Conference of Pentecostals in Jerusalem, with more than three thousand fellow believers from nineteen countries participating.

The Anglican church today no longer has the significance it possessed during the period of the British Mandate when it was the unofficial ''state church'' of the establishment, but it is still the largest of the Protestant communities in Israel with a membership numbering approximately 1,200. Under the English regime the two branches of this church were almost completely independent: the Arab Evangelical Episcopal church with about one thousand members in Haifa, Nazareth, Jaffa, Akko, Jerusalem, and three Arab villages, was separated from its mother church, the Anglican Church in Jerusalem, by an inability to come to a common agreement on mutual recognition, despite the efforts of Canterbury to achieve a reconciliation. It was not until 1968, after the reunification of Jerusalem, that an understanding between the Arab and English churches was achieved, resulting on April 12, 1970, in the official recognition by the State of Israel of the United Evangelical Episcopal Church in Israel. This made it the first Christian church to be recognized by Israel as an autonomous religious community, a tenth addition to the list of churches enjoying self-government since Ottoman times, and the first Protestant church to be awarded this status in the land of the Bible.

In connection with this legal "emancipation," which also increased Anglican prestige in the eyes of other denominations, negotiations were initiated between the Rt. Rev. George Appleton, erstwhile "Archbishop in Jerusalem" (interchurch negotiations in 1841 had led to this compromise title which was regarded as less presumptuous by the leaders of the older churches than "of Jerusalem"), and a group of about forty Israeli Jewish Christians of evangelical convictions who had hitherto deliberately avoided any formal church relationships. "Entering any establishment church could quite easily bring us into contact with anti-Semitism, from which none of the older hierarchies is free," the spokesman of the group said frankly to the archbishop.[93] In the course of their conversation which was intended to consider an eventual affiliation on the part of the Jewish-Christian group, this group defined its theology in the following way (while emphasizing that "it has not yet been thoroughly formulated"): Jesus came as Messiah to the Jews, and it is to them that he will come yet again; the Pauline letters, such as Galatians, were intended for gentile Christians and are therefore irrelevant for Jewish Christians; the "resurrection" of Israel as an independent nation is an omen of the last days; gentile Christians will be saved only after the Jewish Christians (but according to some, only through the Jewish Christians).

Their worship, which is still in the experimental stage, is held in Hebrew on the Sabbath, but it has not yet been formulated definitively, nor has it been written down. The members of the group call each other *'ḥym* "brothers" or *m'mynym* "believers," but wish to avoid sectarianism both in appearance and in fact. They join from time to time in common worship and Bible study with pentecostals and other Jewish Christians. They all share in an effort to return in spirit and in faith to the "original church of Israel." How this can be accomplished today authentically and practically is not quite clear to anyone, and is the subject of frequent discussion. Appleton's question about the relation of the Jews of Israel to baptismal candidates received the unanimous answer that there is noticeable a growing tolerance, especially on the part of the young native generation, which regards religion as a private and individual matter. When the spokesman for the evangelical group came to the matter of the eschatological significance of the State of Israel and the religious basis for the Jewish return (to Palestine), the Anglican representing a church of 80 percent Arab membership could not refrain from remarking: "I do not believe in any New Testament Zionism," and later: "You are just as chauvinistic as my Arabs!" Although no effective affiliation was achieved, the door was left open for further conversation—and for common worship. Meanwhile the Anglican Immanuel Church in Jaffa and the Anglican Christ Church in Jerusalem (the latter only after the reunification of Jerusalem in 1967) held worship services in Hebrew regularly, using a twenty-five-page booklet entitled *Tephillot le-Yaminu 'Anu* [*Prayers For Our Days*], printed in Tel-Aviv in 1957. The first words in its preface are unfortunately not quite accurate in claiming that "these prayers were written for Jewish as well as for Christian use." Although the book contains special prayers adapted for Israeli use, such as "for officers and soldiers in active service," "for border settlements," and "for families of soldiers," yet six of the twenty prayers refer to "Jesus the Messiah" in such a way that no Jew could possibly use them devotionally.

In February 1975, following the pattern of several churches in Israel today which are rendering their liturgies into Modern Hebrew, the Anglican evening prayer service at Christ Church was revised and simplified from the form in which it had first been introduced in 1838 and revised in 1842 by several rabbis and Michael Solomon Alexander, the first Anglican bishop in Jerusalem.[94]

A number of evangelical sects and missionary societies such as the Adventists, the Church of Christ, the Church of the Nazarenes, the Brethren, the Christian and Missionary Alliance, and others hold regular services in Hebrew in fourteen other worship centers in Jerusalem, Tel-Aviv, Haifa, Beersheba, and Ashkelon. From conversations with the leaders in these centers it appears that the total number of worshippers of Israeli citizenship in these houses varies from sixty to eighty. No data could be obtained on "conversions" during the last ten years.

The Protestant village of Nes Ammim ("A Light to the Gentiles," after Isa. 11:1–5, 10, 12ff.), which has cultivated a piece of land between Akko and Nahariyyah since 1964, today comprises ten families of young settlers from the Netherlands, Switzerland, Germany, and America, whose goal is "to help our Jewish brothers build their state in the land which God promised them and to which He has returned them."[95] While they resolutely dissociate themselves from Jewish mission, the group affirms that "through an experience of solidarity we wish to make possible a new conversation between brothers, in which each is true to his own faith and each respects the faith of the other."[96] This solidarity is expressed not only in the choice of a Biblical Hebrew name for their village and its overtones, but also in the partial hebraizing of its worship. This trend is promoted by the polyglot composition of the group which makes Hebrew the lingua franca of all the settlers today. So the people of Nes Ammim on Friday evening take their Sabbath meal together after Dr. Pilon, the director, the Rev. W. H. Zuidema, a Dutch clergyman, or the Rev. J. Schoneveld, a theologian who studied in Jerusalem, has pronounced the blessing over the bread and wine, and the table fellowship has sung a Sabbath hymn such as "Lekah Dodi" ["Come, My Friend"] or "Shabbat-shalom" ["Sabbath Greeting"]. After the meal verses from the Psalms usually follow in the Ḥasidic tradition as it is observed in many of the neighboring kibbutzim. Ingrid Hindenberg, a German teacher from Essen, has written about this weekly celebration which has now become a custom in the village.

> A visitor could well consider it all very peculiar. Here are young Christians from Europe observing a Jewish tradition, on the Sabbath eve! Isn't it all artificial, an empty gesture? But the question should not be dismissed too quickly. I have myself experienced the Sabbath celebration in Nes Ammim as an attempt to come closer to the goal of the settlement, of being "a sign for the peoples" and achieving a communion with those we have unfortunately known in the past only as aliens.[97]

The Christmas celebration arranged in 1969 by the Rev. Schoneveld was interesting. Strictly speaking it was a post-Christmas celebration (*nʿylt ḥg hmwld*), held on December 26, with more than one hundred Jewish and Arab friends attending from neighboring settlements. A seasonal homily in Hebrew was followed by Christmas carols in all the languages of the settlers with the following lessons interposed: Gen. 1:26–2:3 in Hebrew, Mic. 4:1–5 in German, Eph. 2:11–22 in Arabic, and Luke 2:22–38 in Dutch. Schoneveld then gave an ecumenical sermon, and in response to the Israeli Supreme Rabbinate's call for all Jews throughout the world to offer prayers for the Jews in the Soviet Union, all joined in reading Ps. 20 in unison. The service concluded with the Lord's Prayer in Hebrew, sung by all in an arrangement by the Sisters of Zion in Jerusalem. Similar ecumenical experiments were also planned for 1976.

B. *Hebrew Church Songs.* The first church hymnal to appear in Israel was the evangelical anthology *Shir Ḥadash* [*A New Song*], which was published in Tel-Aviv in 1957 under the aegis of the so-called International Church of Jerusalem (*knsyh bynlʾwmyt šl yrwšlym*). The title (after Isa. 42:10, "Sing to God a new song!") was considered appropriate for members of the "New Covenant" (Jer. 31:31). Yet little is to be found in the 385-page, attractively bound volume that can be called new, since practically all the 211 hymns, cantatas, and psalms are translations from the familiar church music of the seventeen Protestant churches representing nine different national traditions. The printing of the vocalized Hebrew texts and of the musical notes is correct and clear, but the quality of the Hebrew—the work of a dozen different hebraists—is not only uneven but often quite strained. This is, however, not so much the fault of the translators, who were almost without exception as competent linguistically as they were biblically knowledgeable, as it is due to the procrustean demands made by the German,

English, and Scandinavian melodies on the language of the Bible. To make the texts singable, all the resources of Biblical Hebrew, the Piyyuṭ style, and Modern Hebrew were exploited, resorting sometimes even to Sabra slang in an effort to satisfy the musicologists' demands, but in the process producing a rare linguistic mixture at the expense of the philologists. Although the syntax, grammar, and sentence rhythm are usually acceptable, there is still an awkward element in the Hebrew form of such hymns as the Lutheran "Ein feste Burg ist unser Gott" ["A Mighty Fortress Is Our God"], the pietist "Herr Jesu Christ, dich zu uns wend," "O Heil'ger Geist, kehr bei uns ein," and the militant march "Onward Christian Soldiers."

Some neologisms are rather noticeable, such as *kbsny mkl ʿwny* ("wash me from all sins") which sounds like a laundry advertisement in contrast to the biblical *rḥṣny* for "washing clean." "Arch-enemy," meaning Satan, cannot be expressed as *'wyb zqn* by any poetic license; nor can *hmṣy'* be used to translate "Jesus brought atonement," because in today's usage it would mean that Jesus "invented" atonement. "No, not one" repeated in the chorus of a hymn with the meaning "there is no one like Jesus" cannot be translated as *'yn 'ḥd;* it should be either *'yn kmwhw* or *'yn zwltw*. But these errors are merely exceptions which do not detract seriously from the profoundly religious spirit clearly expressed in nearly all the hymns. The hymnal is used by all the Protestant Hebrew congregations in Israel today, as well as in several Bible colleges in America where it is used as supplementary material for the study of Hebrew. A new and improved edition, with the errors, dissonances, and vulgarisms removed, was planned for 1976.

The hymnal *Shiratnu* [*Our Song*] published in 1968 by Samuel Paul Re'emi, the presbyter of the Scottish church in Tiberias, is more modest and smaller. Following an old Jewish usage, Re'emi is signed in his Hebrew works as *špr,* "grace" or "loveliness," which actually represents the acronym for his name: S(amuel) P(aul) R(e'emi). The book contains nineteen hymns, including eleven from the Scottish church hymnal, one from Billy Graham, and the rest from various English hymn collections. It is interesting that "the Lord" (as "kýrios") is always rendered as *yšwʿ* (as is also "Jesus"), and "God" is always rendered by Jewish paraphrases. The translation departs from the original whenever literalism would produce an unhebraic construction or an expression or image that would be un-Jewish. The translator also avoids conscientiously any lyrical enthusiasm (found occasionally in English) which could appear to compromise the monotheism of the texts.

The most recent Christian hymnal is called *'Ashirah le-YH* [*I Will Sing to the Lord*], taken from the beginning of the Song of Moses in Exod. 15:1). It is the work of Sr. Maroussia Legrain of the Order of

Zion, begun in 1966 and completed in the winter of 1969. The editor, who is also a music teacher and serves as the superior of the Sisters of Zion in the Ratisbon Convent in Jerusalem, began to study musicology and Jewish liturgics shortly after her arrival in Jerusalem in 1963. After four months her mentor, Mrs. Gerson-Kiwi, dismissed her with the words: "Your musical sensitivity is purely Jewish." Sister Maroussia spent the next seven months in an Ulpan (an intensive Hebrew language course), which gave her a good if not perfect familiarity with the language. Among her first compositions were the Magnificat (*zmr mrym* "Song of Mary") and the Thanksgiving to Judith "O thou pride of Jerusalem" (*'t kbwd yrwšlym*) from Jdt. 15:9–10, which are in the tradition of Gregorian chant, but with a free rhythm that is reminiscent of the synagogue style. When Pope Paul VI visited the Basilica of the Dormition on Mount Zion on January 5, 1964, Sister Maroussia directed a mixed choir of religious that performed these compositions in Hebrew to their credit. Encouraged by the pope's words of gratitude which were communicated to her later by Abbot Leo von Rudloff, Sister Maroussia proceeded to devote all of her free time to church music, and by the end of 1966 she completed a setting for the entire Kyriale in the Hebrew translation of Yoḥanan Eliḥai. At the beginning of 1967 the deputy mayor of Jerusalem, Prof. André Chouraqui, commissioned her to write an ecumenical setting for the Jewish table blessing (*brkt hmzwn* "blessing of the food") that had been adopted by several circles in the capital. When the apostolic delegate, Msgr. Sepinski, heard Sister Maroussia sing the Ave Maria (*šlwm lk mrym* "Peace to You, Mary") in the spring of 1967 and learned something more of her work, he asked for a copy of the Kyriale and sent it to the pope in Rome. On February 12, 1969, when the superior of the Sisters of Zion in Spain, Mother Esperanza de Sion, spoke on Radio Vatican describing the first consecration of a synagogue in Madrid since 1492, Sister Maroussia accompanied her on the broadcast with the Jewish Shema and with Kiddush prayers which she recited to her own settings. By mid-1972 music for the whole of the Missal (in the Catholic edition by Eliḥai) was complete: the Kyrie (*h" rḥm* "Lord have mercy") as a choral cry for mercy, the Gloria (*kbwd l'l* "Glory to God") as a joyful song of praise, on the pattern of similar settings from Simḥat Torah ("Feast of the Law"), two different settings for the Credo (*'ny m'myn* "I Believe"), three variations for the Sanctus (*qdwš*), one fervent but discreet Pater Noster (*'bynw šbšmym* "Our Father Who Art in Heaven"), and a solemn dismissal (*nʿylh* "Concluding") which reminded many Jews of the ʿAlenu prayer settings.

By the end of 1972 settings for all the prayers of the feasts for the church year (*hqbwʿ šl ʿwnwt hšnh*) and of the saints' days (*qdwšym*) to the month of August were completed and printed, as well as settings for twenty-seven Psalms, five Christmas carols, eight Easter songs, several Scripture lessons and pericopes—some arranged for solo voice, some for choir, and some for antiphonal choirs. The first edition of this 154-page collection, which is constantly being expanded by new additions, is mostly written in roman transliteration. The reason for this is given in a Hebrew footnote: "After an attempt to point the text in Hebrew, we returned to transliteration because experience taught us that most of us who knew Hebrew could not read notes, while the majority of us who could read the music had difficulty with Hebrew. We hope to publish this collection of songs in Hebrew in the future." The latest compositions to appear in a sheet-music edition by November 1972 fulfilled this promise halfway: the titles at the head and the full text at the foot of each page are printed in unpointed Hebrew, while the syllabically divided text of the lyrics is given in roman letters in the score. The hymnal is in use today not only in all the Catholic parishes where services are observed in Hebrew, but it has also been received in several convents, churches, and groups which worship in different languages. The number of requests Sister Maroussia has received from different groups for instruction in her radical settings of the worship service would suggest that an increasing number of Catholics of European and Arab origin are interested in singing at least a part of their liturgies in Hebrew. To date the musicologist has not yet written any of her own texts in Hebrew, but only provided musical settings for excerpts from the Old Testament or Christian translations by other hebraists. In the future, however, she hopes to write hymns herself.

C. *The Marriage Service.* To the best of the author's knowledge, by the end of 1974 there were only two written texts that could be called Jewish-Christian marriage services, the first because of the persons participating, and the second because of its content.

The first ceremony of this kind took place in Haifa in January 1969, designed by a Jewish-Christian pastor (*rwʿh-ʿdh* "shepherd of the congregation") who performed the service for two Israeli Jewish Christians of a Protestant group. The two-page text bearing the proper Jewish title *sdr qdwšym* "Order of Betrothal" is an abbreviated and slightly adapted version of the Anglican marriage rite, with the surprising omission of the most Jewish part of the Christian ceremony, where the minister blesses the two with the words: "O God of Abraham, God of Isaac, God of Jacob, bless these Thy servants . . . as Thou didst send Thy blessings upon Abraham and Sarah. . . ." Apart from the New Testament passages which are taken from Delitzsch and the Old Testament quotations which appear in their original form, the text is written in Modern Hebrew with an occasional hint of an overly literal dependence on the text of its English original.

The second ceremony was held on October 1, 1969, in the Baptist House in Jerusalem, and offered a more original synthesis. Pastor Robert L. Lindsey and Prof. David G. Flusser concelebrated in Hebrew the marriage of a young gentile Christian couple—two American students who met in Jerusalem, studied Hebrew, and sought to find the roots of their Christian faith in Judaism. On their Hebrew-English invitation the date was given in Hebrew (nineteenth day of the month Tishri 5730) as well as in Christian usage (October 1, 1969), and the place of the ceremony (Jerusalem) was identified as "the city of the great king" (*ʿyr mlk rb*), as the Jewish capital was also referred to by Jesus in Matt. 5:35 (echoing Ps. 48:3 [Eng. v. 2]).

After a few introductory comments in Hebrew by Lindsey, Flusser pronounced five of the traditional seven blessings which form an essential part of the Jewish wedding. The omitted elements were the blessing of the wine chalice and the purely Jewish *berakah* ("benediction") which concludes with the words "who blesses his people Israel with Ḥuppah [lit. "a canopy," thus "protection"] and holy marriage." Lindsey then said a few transitional words leading to the reading of Gen. 2:23–24 and Eph. 5:21–32. The final verse (v. 32) provided him the occasion to speak on the mystical love of Jesus for his church (as a Baptist he phrased it *ʾhbt hmšyḥ lʿdt mʾmynym* "love of Christ for the community of believers") "as it is also expressed in the drinking of wine and the breaking of bread, as a sign of the love of our Lord, of the mutual love of the two present, and of their love for their Lord."

The bridegroom then put on his Kippah (skullcap), pronounced the Jewish blessing of the wine, drank from the cup, and gave it to his bride to drink. Then he broke a piece of bread, sprinkled it with salt, pronounced the Jewish blessing of the bread, and shared the bread with his bride. Next he consecrated his bride with the wedding ring, altering the traditional Jewish formula but without christianizing it; instead of the last five words of the sentence "by this you are consecrated to me, with this ring, by the faith of Moses and Israel," the bridegroom said "*kʾmwntny, ktqwtnw, kʾhbtnw*" ("by our faith, by our hope, by our love"). After a brief silent prayer by all present (about 150 Christian, Jewish, and Moslem guests), Lindsey pronounced "this man and this woman now joined in marriage," and concluded the service with Matt. 19:6, changing only one word of Delitzsch. Instead of *ḥbr* "united," he said *zwg* "joined," which in Hebrew has primarily a sexual connotation. Whether as a hebraist and student of Jewish literature he was relating the *unio mystica* in Eph. 5:31–32 to the *zwwgʾ qdyšʾ* "holy union" of the cabalists (both of which have sexual reference) is an open question.

D. *Ecumenical Worship.* Although this is an area related only indirectly to the concerns of this study, the most important milestones should be noted.

The first ecumenical service in Israel was held on February 26, 1967, on Mount Zion. Participating in this "Prayer foı World Peace" were the Rt. Rev. Charles P. Greco, Roman Catholic bishop of Alexandria, Louisiana (with a group of American Catholics), Rabbi Samuel G. Natan of the Jeshurun Synagogue in Jerusalem, and Sheik Taufiq Asaliya, the qadi of Jaffa. Since all three monotheistic religions have sacred sites and places of worship quite close together on Mount Zion, the location in the court between the Coenaculum, where there is a mosque, and the tomb of David seems almost predestined to be ecumenical. After each of the clergy prayed in his own language, Abbot von Rudloff concluded the brief service with the Lord's Prayer in Hebrew.

The ecumenical service held on February 12, 1969, in the Dominican chapel of the Institute of St. Isaiah in Jerusalem commemorating the nine Jews and two Christians who were executed as Zionist spies in the marketplace of Baghdad on January 27, 1969, was a religious experience. Fr. J. Marcel Dubois opened the devotions with a sermon in English and French. The Rev. Gardiner Scott of the Scottish church read Ps. 103 in English. The Assumptionist Father Jean-Roger said a Yizkor ("may [God] remember") prayer of his own composition in Hebrew. The Rev. Peter Schneider of the Anglican church said a prayer of supplication for all who are persecuted, and Canon Allison of Christ Church read the promises of peace from Isaiah and the Sermon on the Mount. He was followed by the Melchite priest Elias Chacour, who prayed in Arabic for "peace on earth" and the mercy of God. The service closed with the Aaronic blessing ("The Lord bless you and keep you . . .") in Hebrew, Arabic, English, and French, followed by the Lord's Prayer in Hebrew. Participating in the service were the deputy mayor of Jerusalem, the director of the Israel Inter-Faith Committee, and a number of Jews as well as clergy and religious from seven churches.

Ecumenical prayers frequently conclude the weekly meetings of the *Ḥwg byndty* (Inter-Faith Circle) in Tel-Aviv, which comprises some thirty Jewish members of two Reformed synagogues together with about ten Christians and Jewish Christians. In the articles of the Circle, which was founded in 1964, it is stated: "The intention is not for any member to convert another member, but for all to be mutually supportive in the worship life of each in his own tradition."[98]

Neweh-shalom ("Oasis of Peace," from Isa. 32:18) is the name of a collective village inspired by the Dominican Fr. Bruno Hussar and soon to be constructed in the neighborhood of the Trappist monastery at Latrun. The purpose of this village, whose name was suggested by a sentence from Pope Paul VI's farewell address to President Shazar of Israel on January 5, 1964 ("May this holy land be an oasis of peace!"), is formulated in its constitution in the following words: "It will be a meeting place for Jews, Christians, and Moslems . . . , inspired by an honest desire to promote mutual understanding in dialogue, and to achieve a genuine peace with justice between men, nations, and peoples."[99] When the first group of volunteer helpers returned to France in October 1970, a farewell service was held in Crusader Hall, now standing among the first wooden houses in the new village, with prayers offered for the success of the Jarring mission.[100] First to lead in prayer was the imam of Abu Ghosh, an Arab village near Jerusalem, with two muktare (mayors) from neighboring villages who read excerpts from the Koran (5:20–21, 70; 2:40, 47, 49ff., 62) in which the Children of Israel are extolled. They were followed by a young Orthodox Jewish student who said the Maʿarib (Evening Prayer), and Father Hussar, who read from the encyclical "Pacem in Terris" (*šlwm ʿly ʾdmwt*) of Pope John XXIII in Hebrew and concluded with the Hebrew Peace from the Mass. Thanks to the initiative of the Israel Inter-Faith Committee, a group of Jewish and Christian hebraists translated this encyclical into Hebrew and published it in a sixty-six-page deluxe edition in 1963—the only papal encyclical so to appear. It contains also a preface by Professor Flusser and as an epilogue an account of the ecumenical memorial service held in Jerusalem on June 20, 1963, in honor of the late Pope John XXIII.

A brief ecumenical prayer is used to open the sessions of the Regenbogen group, a gathering of nine Jewish and nine Christian biblical scholars who meet monthly to discuss such themes as "The Image of the Jew in Karl Barth's Theology" and "The Influence of Bar Kokhba's Revolt on Jewish Self-understanding." The Ecumenical Discussion Group of students in Jerusalem, founded in 1965 by visiting students from Europe, meets twice a month for a program of lectures and panel presentations on current religious questions such as "Atheism and Theocracy in Israel," "Who is a Jew?" and "Synagogue Liturgical Reform." These evening programs are also begun with Jewish and Christian prayers, the latter frequently read partly in Hebrew. Since early 1970 this group, which now includes about one dozen Arab members, has met under the new name Student Christian Forum, expanding its activities to include excursions for the study of Jewish-Christian relations *in situ,* especially on the Arab-Jewish level.

Among the various groups and institutions which on occasion observe ecumenical worship services (partly in Hebrew) may be counted the Ecumenical Theological Research Fraternity in Israel, an interchurch group founded in Jerusalem on February 28, 1966, which stated among its purposes "the fostering of Christian relationships with Jews, with Judaism, and with Israel."[101] There is also the United Christian Council in Israel, an umbrella organization for nearly all the non-Catholic churches (which will be discussed later); the Israel Inter-Faith Committee founded in 1959 by a group of professors, rabbis, qadis, and

Christian dignitaries under the patronage of Martin Buber to promote understanding among all the religions in Israel; and a Dutch-speaking group of about eighty Jews, Catholics, and Protestants from different cities and settlements in Israel who assemble annually to discuss religious questions.

In mid-January 1970 Msgr. John M. Oesterreicher, director of the Institute of Judaeo-Christian Studies at Seton Hall University, New Jersey, said a public penitential prayer in the 'Ohel Yizkor (Tent of Memorial) of Yad Vashem, the Jerusalem memorial to martyrs and heroes, in the presence of Christian pilgrims and Jewish guests. In this prayer he included the following words from the Hebrew table blessing: "Have mercy, O Eternal One, our God, on Israel your people, and on Jerusalem your city, and on Zion the place of your glory." And he ended his prayer with the words: "*ʿm yśrʾl ḥy!* ("the People of Israel lives!"). Amen."

Three Hebrew inscriptions in churches and Christian buildings should also be mentioned here.

(a) The Ten Commandments, the Lord's Prayer, and the Apostles' Creed inscribed in gold letters on four tablets decorate the wall behind the altar in the Anglican Christ Church in Jerusalem. They result from the initiative of Michael Solomon Alexander, the first Anglican bishop in Jerusalem, whose successor, Bishop Samuel Gobat, consecrated the church in 1849.

(b) The building of the YMCA (Young Men's Christian Association) in Jerusalem (New City), whose membership belong to all three monotheistic religions, symbolizes this ecumenicity by three stone inscriptions. On the north side in large letters is the central sentence of the Jewish Shema in Hebrew: "The Lord our God, the Lord is One." The south side has the Islamic creed in Arabic: "There is no God but God." On both sides of the forty-six-meter Tower of Jesus, which commands a view of all Jerusalem, are the words of Jesus in Aramaic: "I am the Way."

(c) In the Chapel of Elijah on the summit of Mount Carmel a series of black marble tablets adorn the wall, covered with the biblical verses of 1 Kgs. 18:27–31 in Hebrew.

E. *Christian Publishing Houses.* Only the most important of the publishing houses that issue Christian literature in Hebrew can be mentioned here.

The Franciscan Press in Jerusalem, which has published the writings and Hebrew translations of Fr. Jean-Marie Paulus Bauchet since 1945,[102] also published in May 1969 a fifty-four-page illustrated booklet entitled *Kenesiyat ha-Beśorah* [*Church of the Good News*] dedicated to the newly-built Basilica of the Annunciation in Nazareth. Despite a few printing errors, its typography and its Modern Hebrew style deserve high commendation, as does the fact that the Jewish builders, artists, and architects who assisted in the construction of this monumental Near Eastern church are given public recognition.

Dugith (cf. the fishing boat from which Jesus preached on the Sea of Gennesaret) is the name of a Christian art gallery in Tel-Aviv, and also from 1956 of a publishing house as well, specializing in Christian historical and theological writings. Among its publications are Roland H. Bainton's monumental *History of Christianity* (*Twldwt hnṣrwt*) and *The Reformation of the Sixteenth Century* (*Hrpwrmṣyh šl hm'h hšš'śrh*), as well as a new translation of the Gospel of Mark (which will be noted in the next section).

Hwʿd hm'wḥd lmšyḥyym byśr'l (United Christian Council in Israel, or UCCI) is identified by its emblem of two fish and an anchor, and has published three small service books; a convenient directory of all the churches, chapels, and pilgrimage sites, with their telephone numbers, addresses, and service hours; and also a half-dozen "devotional" missionary books, such as *Why I am a Christian, Our Faith,* and *Mau-Mau Youth* (the story of a conversion).

Dolphin, with insignia featuring the Christian fish symbol, provides the market with books by Billy Graham (*Peace with God*), Paul P. Levertoff (*The Son of Man*), and C. S. Lewis (*Mere Christianity*), as well as similar works of an inspiring and challenging character written in a simple Modern Hebrew style.

Yonah ("The Dove")—apparently taken from the symbol of the Holy Spirit in Matt. 3:16—specializes in missionary tracts, Christian hymnals, and anthologies of New Testament passages proving the messiahship of Jesus "according to the Torah," under the sign of the Dove of Peace.

Ha-lappid ("The Torch") is the Jewish Pentecostal press, publishing its own periodical as well as occasional challenges, manifestoes, and appeals, such as *Shemaʿ Yiśra'el!* and *Can a Jew Be a Christian?*

There is also a veritable flood of missionary literature in Hebrew of all denominations, sizes, and levels, which is distributed to Jews from Nahariyyah to Eilat by mail, by person, or through some dozen "Bible shops." According to unofficial estimates, there are from 400 to 600 Christian missionaries active, frequently masked as pilgrims, teachers, seminarians, and the like, whose main interest is "the conversion of the Jews." Their effect will be discussed in the concluding section (cf. pp. 180–81).

6. *Modern Hebrew Versions of the New Testament*

In the last five years three Gospels have been translated by different Christian translators, and a completely new translation of all the New

Testament books and letters into Modern Hebrew has been undertaken. All four works share the basic recognition that although Franz Delitzsch produced a masterpiece—albeit artificial, his Hebrew is almost faultless—his idiom no longer represents the living national language of Israel. Indeed, the Hebrew language has proceeded to develop with its own dynamic and logic and is today no longer identical with the language of the Bible.

These translations also share the tacit hope of the "passive mission" which inspired Delitzsch earlier: "That to someone (Israeli) at some time the Gospel read in the Hebrew language will yet speak with its power of conviction."[103] Although this strategy of evangelism should emphasize clarity and intelligibility as the first commandment for translators, yet as the following analysis of their texts will show, each one differs considerably from the others in linguistic method and approach.

A. *The Gospel of John by a Catholic.* In 1966 the newly baptized Joshua Blum decided to translate the Gospel of John into Modern Hebrew. He gave his friends two reasons for his selection of the Fourth Gospel for his first attempt at translating. Despite its being the most "un-Jewish" of the Gospels in its theology, the most difficult in its language, and undoubtedly the most anti-Jewish in attitude, as literature it is the most attractive, and christologically the most eloquent. Since Blum knew no Greek and little Latin, he relied primarily on the Delitzsch edition aided by German and French versions. The text he produced was then reviewed (evidently in haste) by Fr. Joseph Stiassny, Br. Yoḥanan Eliḥai, and Fr. Ludwik Semkowski, and published in the spring of 1967 as a fifty-eight-page booklet under the title *Ha-beśorah lepi Yoḥanan* [*The Gospel According to John*]. The text was unpointed except for Old Testament quotations, hellenisms, and aramaisms. It was divided into paragraphs, and printed in an easily read typeface. Further, the prologue (John 1:1–18), which must be particularly difficult for any Hebrew reader, is divided into short sense lines to suggest its poetical nature formally as well as stylistically—a goal well achieved but for a few slips. The quality of the translation, its experimental character as well as its missionary intention, made it appear more prudent to forego the otherwise (even then) usual nihil obstat and imprimatur.

With regard to particular words and phrases, the following analyses are of interest.

(1) Blum found an original solution for the basic problem of reference to "the Jews," which is also one of the main problems of Jewish-Christian relations in the New Testament field. "The Jews" occurs seventy-one times in John (as opposed to five times each in Matthew and Luke, and six times in Mark), many times indicating an inhabitant

of Judea, more often for the Jewish people as a whole, but most often as simply a synonym for the enemies of Jesus who usually appear in the Synoptic Gospels as "high priests," "scribes," and "Pharisees," or as specifically named persons. By carrying over the Johannine dualism (light-darkness, truth-lie, God-Devil) into semantics, Blum divides "hoi ioudaîoi" into two groups: the enemies of Jesus (as in John 1:19; 2:18, 20; 5:10, 15–16; 6:41; 7:1) are renamed *hyhwd'ym,* while the "good Jews" (as in 8:31; 11:31) appear with their legitimate name as *yhwdym.*

The word *yhwd'yn* occurs in the Bible only in Dan. 3:12, a hapax legomenon in Aramaic meaning simply "Jews." From this passage is derived the phrase still in use today, "*khlkt gwbryn 'hwd'yn*" meaning "in the Jewish manner."[104] Blum sometimes identified Jesus' opponents with the "Judaeans," since it is from this area that most if not all of his opponents came, but it must be objected that in the Bible the "Judaeans" are called either *'îš yᵉhûḏâ* "men of Judah" (Isa. 5:3; Jer. 4:4; 17:25) or *bᵉnê yᵉhûḏâ* "people of Judah" (Jer. 50:4; Hos. 2:2 [Eng. 1:11]; Joel 4:6 [Eng. 3:6]). It is only in the Aramaic documents of the Jewish colony in Upper Egyptian Elephantine (Yeb) of the time of Nehemiah that the term *yhwd'y* is found as a Jewish self-designation, and there it is used as synonymous with *'rm'y* "Aramaean."[105] The only Israeli citizens today who still speak of "Judaeans" (apart from scholars and biblical students) are the Samaritans, who still condemn them for making Jerusalem the center of Jewish worship in the reign of King Solomon.

As an old neologism *yhwd'y* as "Judaean" is conceivable on the analogy of *ḥ'p'y* "a Haifaite," but this would be a purely geographical term completely unrelated to the Johannine personification of disbelief and opposition to Jesus. The dichotomy is artificial and even borders on absurdity, especially in such passages as John 7:11–12, where the distinction is drawn so closely that "the Jews who were looking for him at the feast" are called *yhwdym,* yet in the immediate sequel (v. 13) "for fear of the Jews" speaks of *yhwd'ym.*

(2) To make the text sound contemporary for Israeli readers, Blum avoided the waw-consecutive, the casus pendens, and all such archaic biblicisms (which Delitzsch so favored), and adapted numerous passages to modern Israeli idioms. For example, Simon Peter (John 1:40 passim) is called *šmʿwn ṣwr,* a common Israeli name that no one would think of associating with the Gospel, or even with Christianity. Nathanael, "an Israelite indeed" (v. 47), becomes "a genuine Israeli" (*yśr'ly 'mty*), and "little children" (13:33) is reduced to the "dear children" (*yldym ḥbybym*) of the common Israeli elementary school phrase. The cohort (18:12) which took Jesus captive is for Delitzsch (a century before the Israeli army) still a *gdwd* as in 1 Kgs. 11:24, where

the Revised Standard Version and the Jerusalem Bible translate it as "a (marauding) band." But since this word has gained the specific meaning of "a battalion," Blum (an ex-major) properly corrects it to *plwgh* "company," which represents approximately the strength of a Roman cohort and gives the scene in Gethsemane a contemporary military flavor. However, it is inconsistent that the "captain" of this cohort should be called *śr h'lp* "commander of a thousand," as he is by Delitzsch following the Greek text (*chilíarchos*) and the Bible (1 Sam. 18:13), whereas Blum should know that the Israeli term for "captain" today is *srn,* following the biblical example (Judg. 16:30; 1 Sam. 29:6).

The translation of sandal-thong in John 1:27 by *rṣwʿt hsndl* "sandal strap" is more correct and better Israeli usage than Delitzsch's *śrwn-hnʿl* (following Gen. 14:23), for it corresponds not only to the original Greek text and to the footwear of Jesus and the apostles (cf. Mark 6:9), but also to that of Israeli youth today.

It seems rather crude, however, to attempt to conciliate the Israeli reader by omitting the words (ostensibly) of Jesus "in their law" at John 15:25, although it naturally borders on the incredible that a pious Galilean should refer to the Torah as "their law" when speaking to fellow believers—especially in Hebrew!

Even more embarrassing are frequent colloquialisms, bordering on Modern Hebrew slang, such as the following examples.

(a) 1:21 "What then?" becomes *'z mh?,* which is close to the familiar "So what?"

(b) 1:42 "He brought him (to Jesus)." Blum translates *hwbyl 'wtw,* using a verb associated today primarily with transporting freight, cattle, or cars. Delitzsch's *hby' 'wtw* could be taken in the same sense, but it is more tasteful.

(c) 1:46 "Anything good" is unnecessarily crass as *mšhw ṭwb,* which is used only for material produce or culinary delicacies in today's slang. Here as so often elsewhere Delitzsch's translation is both modern and superior: *hmnṣrt yṣ' ṭwb?* ("Can good come forth from Nazareth?").

(d) 8:45 "Because I . . ." is translated here and frequently elsewhere by Blum as *mpny š . . . ,* which every Israeli middle-school teacher decries as a vulgarism. In proper Modern Hebrew "because" is either *mšwm š* or *hywt w* or *ky.*

(e) 11:43 "Come out!" is translated *ṣ' hḥwṣh,* which is both street slang and tautological, because the verb *yṣ'* means "to come out" and does not require the supplemental "outside."

(f) 14:8 "We shall be satisfied" should be not *zh mspyq lnw,* because this expression belongs to a lower level of colloquial usage than Philip's statement suggests. A precise equivalent of both its meaning and its form is to be found in the well-known Passover Piyyuṭ called

Dayyenu from its refrain. Since any half-educated Israeli would associate this expression (which means precisely "it satisfies us") with the great events of the Exodus from Egypt, this would be the simplest and best translation.

It is linguistically interesting to observe how the semantic development of particular Hebrew words has forced the translator to introduce changes into the text in order to avoid expressions that would appear trivial or even comic. The following examples illustrate this point.

(a) 8:23 "You are from below, I am from above" was translated by Delitzsch using the rabbinical terms *tḥtwnym* and *ʿlywnym* which contrast the "mortal" and the "divine."[106] But since today *tḥtwnym* has the meaning "underpants," Blum had to rephrase the passage: *mwṣ'km mmṭh; mwṣ'y mmʿlh* "Your origin is from below, my origin is from above."

(b) 8:23 "Of this world" can only be *mn hʿwlm hzh,* as both Delitzsch and Isaac Edward Salkinson attest. By the irony of circumstances, however, *hʿwlm hzh* is the name of one of Israel's most popular weekly magazines (in which pornography is not unknown), so that Blum felt compelled to insert the preposition *mšl* "of" at the least, in order to avoid the appearance of an allusion to the magazine.

(c) 14:16 "Another Counselor" is translated by both Delitzsch and Blum as *prqlyṭ 'ḥr* in literal fidelity to the Greek, but erroneously. This rabbinic hellenism (derived from "paráklētos," lit. "one who appears in another's behalf") not only has the purely juridical meaning of "lawyer (solicitor)," but in the phrase *prqlyṭ hmdynh* "district attorney" it also has the meaning "prosecutor," which is the precise opposite of the original meaning as "defender."[107] A better solution would be *mlyṣ* (from Job 33:23) "mediator," or perhaps *mlyṣ-ysr,* the "advocate" of the Additional Prayer (Musaph) for the Day of Atonement.[108]

(3) Blum's treatment of bilingual passages in the Gospel is inconsistent.

(a) 1:38 "Rabbi (which means Teacher)" he translates simply with the word "Rabbi"—although Delitzsch found it necessary to add here *prwsw mlmdy* "its explanation is 'Teacher.' "

(b) 1:41 "Messiah (which in translation means Christ)," however, Blum translates literally: *hmšyḥ z't 'wmrt krsṭws*. Here the "translation" of the word which is itself originally Hebrew seems ridiculous, unless Blum intends to point out to Israelis the affinity of the words Messiah and Christ.

(c) 1:42 "Cephas (which in translation means Peter)." Blum overtranslates here: *kyp', mšmʿ ṣwr* "Cephas, to be understood as 'rock.' "

(d) 19:13 "The Pavement, in Hebrew Gabbatha." By translating literally (*rṣpt 'bnym—blšwn hʿbrym gbt'* "the pavement of stones—in the language of the Hebrews, Gabbatha") Blum surprises most Israelis, who know that *gbt'* is Aramaic and not Hebrew. The translator of the New Testament should recognize that John called the Palestinian Aramaic of Jesus and his disciples "Hebrew," as Eusebius reports Papias did also.[109] But even apart from this it would be more logical and linguistically accurate to say *b'rmt . . . gbt'* "in Aramaic, Gabbatha."

(e) 20:16 "In Hebrew, Rabboni (which means Teacher)." John errs here both in his identification of the language and in his translation of the Aramaic title (as Gustaf Dalman has shown[110]), which is an intensified form of the usual "Rabbi" and should properly be rendered as "my lord and master." Therefore Blum's *blšwn hʿbrym rbwny kl-wmr: rby* "in the language of the Hebrews, Rabboni (this means Rabbi)" is doubly erroneous, and should be corrected to *b'rmyt mwry wrby* "in Aramaic, Teacher and Rabbi."

(4) Matters of theological significance are of concern in the following peculiarities of Blum's version.

(a) 1:34 "That this is the Son of God." While Delitzsch is content with *zh hw' bn h"*, Blum makes the more precise statement *zh hw' hbn lh"*; the former associates the uniqueness with God, while the latter [by adding the definite article to *bn* "son"] emphasizes rather the uniqueness of the Son.

(b) 8:24; 13:19 "I am he." In both passages Blum translates "*egṓ eimi* as *'ny 'šr 'ny* "I am I," which is most probably intended to remind his readers of the divine self-revelation in Exod. 3:14 (*'ehyeh 'ašer 'ehyeh*). This does not quite correspond to Johannine christology, where Jesus can say "I and the Father are one" (John 10:30), implying the unique relationship of the Father and Son (1:14, 18) while still clearly distinguishing both persons. On the one hand he speaks of "believing in the name of Jesus" (1:12; 2:23; 3:18), and "asking in the name of Jesus" (14:13–14; 16:23ff.). Yet again, Jesus reveals the name of God (17:6, 26), and prays that the name of God be glorified (12:28), and says that he has come "in my Father's name" (5:43). He even goes so far as to insist that his appeal to God is not a way of seeking "his own glory" (7:18; 8:50; cf. 5:44). This does not imply as complete an identification of Jesus and God as is found almost consistently in this Hebrew version. A modest *'ny hw'* would be more acceptable for Israeli readers and idiomatically unexceptionable—without "judaizing" the Johannine theology.[111]

(c) 13:2 "To betray him" (lit., "to hand him over"). Delitzsch translates this literally *lmsrw* "to hand him over," but Blum makes it an overt act of betrayal *lbgd bw* "to betray him." This corresponds to Christian tradition, but not to the Greek text, nor to various theories since Johann Wolfgang von Goethe which have interpreted Judas' handing over of his master as an act of faith with the intention of inducing the crisis which would force Jesus to act in deliverance.[112]

In summary it must be stated that this version is a roughhewn work, linguistically uneven, and that it represents an unintegrated mixture of all possible styles ranging from Old Testament usage to modern slang. It offers nothing new toward the solving of vexed problems in the field of theological terminology, but adopts practically all the expressions of Delitzsch-Dalman.

B. *The Gospel of Mark According to Robert L. Lindsey.* In October 1966 Robert L. Lindsey, the leader of the Baptist Convention in Israel, published a new, fully-pointed Hebrew version of the Gospel of Mark[113]—the result of six years' work. This thirty-nine-page booklet marked a distinct advance linguistically over the works of Franz Delitzsch and Jean-Marie Paulus Bauchet, yet the translator was not satisfied. After three more years of language studies and textual analysis he presented a second and considerably improved version of Mark at a press conference in Jerusalem on October 19, 1969. The new 159-page *Sepher ha-Beśorah ʿal pi Marqus* [*The Book of the Gospel According to Mark*] is the first Greek-Hebrew diglot edition of the Gospel. This scholarly version was produced with the cooperation of a group of Christian hebraists and Jewish biblical scholars, especially David Flusser, although Lindsey bears the final responsibility, as he emphasizes, for the text which appears under his name.

An interesting by-product of this work is a new solution of the Synoptic problem suggested to the translator by the philological difficulties encountered while translating it into Hebrew. This is essentially a variant of the two-source theory, based on the application of literary criticism to the similarities, differences, and peculiarities of the three Synoptic Gospels (in Hebrew translation) and issuing in the following conclusions.[114]

(1) A Proto-Luke is the first of the three synoptic writers, whose Gospel was written about 65 C.E. and derived from one or more Hebrew sources ("or at least from some Semitic document or documents so much like Hebrew that in retranslation it was impossible to tell the difference," p. 13). His work contains no traces of literary influence derived from Mark or Matthew. Its content, syntax, and grammar make it the easiest to translate "back" into Hebrew, and it contains the least number of Greek "non-hebraisms."

(2) Mark, "a skilled midrashist and preacher" who is identical with Paul's companion John Mark (e.g., Acts 12:12, 25; 15:37), wrote the second Gospel on the basis of Luke, the "Source" (Q), and a protonarrative, as well as borrowing on occasion from the first five

Pauline letters and the Acts of the Apostles. This Jewish-Christian "student of the Torah from Cyprus" was "really a kind of word-magician" (p. 64) who did not simply depend on the oral teaching of Peter as he cited Jesus from memory, transcribing as he listened (as Papias suggested so misleadingly about 135 C.E.); on the contrary, he "was determined to seek some written authority not only for his basic text but also for the materials he uses for replacement into this text" (p. 65). Mark had a genius for dramatic presentation, and he made use of Aramaic, Hebrew, and Greek sources to which he applied his redactional skill masterfully in the rabbinic tradition of *darešehu we-sarsehu* ("homilize it [i.e., a scriptural text], and twist it around"; cf. *B. Bat.* 119b) shortly before the destruction of the Second Temple.

(3) Matthew, the last of the three Synoptics, did not know Luke but based his Gospel on Mark, the "protonarrative," and "Q," using the latter two documents to correct his principal source Mark on occasion, because he was evidently aware that they represent the historical Jesus and his words more faithfully than Mark.

Lindsey published an essay in 1963 on his theory of the priority of Luke,[115] and he plans to edit a Hebrew "back-translation" of the Gospel of Luke which will provide more evidence for his claims together with further philological support. Professor Flusser, who greeted Lindsey's research as "a revolutionary advance in the understanding of the New Testament," reminds us that his own book *Jesus*[116] is also based on Lindsey's solution of the Synoptic problem; in his foreword to Lindsey's translation of Mark he recommends that New Testament scholars take seriously the concluding challenge of Lindsey's introduction: to refute or defend this theory with due recognition given to Judaistics, which together with the Greek texts form the basic tools for this kind of inquiry.

Although the Hebrew text represents a completely new translation of the Greek (Nestle[117]) text, Lindsey also made use of earlier works as well as the last edition of Delitzsch-Dalman. Remembering the dozens of English New Testament versions, each of which makes its own claim to textual fidelity, Lindsey decided to prepare a very literal preliminary translation in simple Modern Hebrew, and circulate it among biblical scholars, students, and teachers for their criticisms. Some of the responses indicated a preference for Biblical Hebrew and others for Mishnaic Hebrew, while the majority recommended the Modern Hebrew of the contemporary Israel generation. Therefore, the final draft was based on the following compromise of maximum fidelity to the original text (where it could be reconstructed) with ease of comprehension, which was ultimately Lindsey's principal goal.

(1) The logia and preaching of Jesus were translated into Old

Testament Hebrew, which Lindsey took to be the original medium of these primary units from their intentionally hellenized archaisms and syntactic peculiarities (the frequent "kaí," "de," and "kaì idou").

(2) Controversies, dialogues, and conversations of Jesus with individuals were translated into Mishnaic Hebrew, occasionally enriched with Qumran expressions, for this was probably the idiom of the scholarly preachers and rabbis of the Second Temple.

(3) The parts of the text which are Mark's own narration are rendered in standard Modern Hebrew, avoiding as much as possible both extremes of pomposity and slang, as well as semantic anachronisms. Only where the Greek text suggests a Hebrew base is the translation literal. Where a Hebrew base has obviously been adapted for a Greek audience, as in the hellenization of "kingdom of heaven" to "kingdom of God," the original Hebrew idiom has been restored.

Finally, three matters of typography and format contribute to the usefulness of this translation for scholars: (1) the Greek and Hebrew texts are arranged in a parallel format on facing pages, (2) the Hebrew is printed in large clear letters and fully pointed, and (3) the Old Testament quotations and references are identified in footnotes on each page.

Special problems and aspects of New Testament terminology in Hebrew include the following.

(1) "*The Son of Man.*" In his first edition of 1966 Lindsey translated this multifaceted title with the Aramaic term *br-'nš* after the "one of human appearance" who is coming on the clouds in the last days to judge, and who is described distinctly in Dan. 10:16, 18 as one "who looked *like* a man." This expression occurs also in the Talmud[118] with the simple meaning of "an ordinary man," and in Modern Hebrew in the apocopated form *brnš* it is further reduced to the meaning of "fellow" or "chap."[119] Therefore, Lindsey changed it in his second edition to *bn-h'dm,* which may remind the biblicist of the way the prophet Ezekiel was so frequently addressed by God (cf. Luke 13:33). Nevertheless, it differs from the modern term *bn-'dm* "mortal man" by a single central letter, the article *h,* which was an unpronounced guttural[120] in the time of Jesus. This only increases the triteness of this obscure but key term, especially as one of the three groups of "Son of Man" sayings in the New Testament (e.g., Matt. 8:19–20; Mark 2:28) refers simply to "man." The humanizing of the title, which still retains an aura of the mysterious in Greek, is especially critical in Hebrew in such passages as Mark 9:31 ("the Son of man will be delivered into the hands of men") and 14:21 ("the man by whom the Son of man is betrayed"), in which Jesus and his opponents are placed practically on the same level. In order to create a difference between the two in these instances, Lindsey uses *'nšym* for the former (Delitzsch has *bny-'dm*), and for the latter, where Judas is intended, *'dm* (Delitzsch is better with

'yš, which plays on *'yš-qrywt* "Iscariot"). This verbal levelling corresponds to the Jewish construction of the historical Jesus as well as to the rabbinic understanding of the Messiah.

(2) "*Amen.*" Mark uses this Hebrew emphasis marker thirteen times at the beginning of statements, in contrast to the usage of the Old Testament, the New Testament letters (e.g., Rom. 1:25; 11:36; 15:33; Gal. 1:5; 6:18), and contemporary usage. Lindsey is convinced that "there is no need to suppose that Jesus deliberately broke with normal Hebrew idiom," and that "it remains improbable that Jesus used the word as an adverb beginning a sentence."[121] He offers four different solutions to the problem.

(1) In six instances, such as in Mark 9:1 where the "Amen" can be construed as emphasizing an immediately prior statement in an unpunctuated Greek text, Lindsey translates *'mn. 'ny 'wmr lkm* "Amen! I tell you . . ." (cf. Nestor Hakkomer, above, p. 25; and Delitzsch).

(b) In 3:28 he biblicizes it with a *waw* (ו): *w'ny 'wmr lkm.*

(c) In 8:12 he paraphrases it with "the truth": *h'mt 'ny 'wmr lkm* "the truth I say to you."

(d) In the five remaining passages Lindsey is somewhat inconsistent in letting the text stand unhebraically: *'mn 'ny 'wmr lkm.*

It would have been better to paraphrase in these passages also, either as in (b) or (c), or to follow Joshua Blum's example of *hn* "behold" and *'kn* "truly."

Among the many modernizations and improvements of Delitzsch's text owed to Lindsey, the following words and passages are particularly noteworthy.

(1) 1:5, 8, etc. References to baptizing are changed from the qal, which is used today for Jewish proselyte baptism of "dipping" (14:20), to the "Christian" hiphil as required by a sensitivity to Israeli usage.[122]

(2) 1:10 "He saw the heavens torn asunder" becomes literally *nqr'ym hšmym* (instead of Delitzsch: *npthw hšmym* "the heavens were opened"), an improvement that now suggests a response to the petition in Isa. 63:19 (Eng. 64:1).

(3) 1:15 "The time is fulfilled" is no longer translated literally (in a way that violates both biblical and hebraic usage), but as *hnh ml'w ymym* "behold, the days are full (or "accomplished")," recalling Gen. 29:21; 1 Sam. 18:26.

(4) 1:39, etc. "Synagogue" is translated by Delitzsch as *knsywt* (which still referred to synagogues in *Exod. Rab.* 21), but today this appears rather a jarring christianization because the word is now used exclusively for "church." Lindsey wisely replaces it with *byt hknst* (lit. "house of the congregation"). This is a little awkward in 5:35 ("from the house of the ruler of the synagogue"), where Lindsey follows

Delitzsch verbatim: *mbyt r'š hknst* "from the house of the head of the synagogue." This certainly corresponds to "archisynágōgos" in Rabbinic Hebrew,[123] but in today's usage, when *knst* means the Israeli parliament (after the "Great Synagogue" of *Pirqe 'Abot* i.1), the meaning of this phrase becomes in effect "from the house of the chairman of the Federal Parliament."[124] In the Mishnah *knst* may mean "synagogue"[125] or "(parish) community," but not in Israel, where the term *byt hknst* has long since become well established. In order to avoid repeating the word *byt* (*mbyt r'š byt hknst*), Lindsey has omitted the second *byt* at the expense of clarity. It would have been better and more faithful to the Greek text (which lacks the word "house") to have omitted the first *byt*.

(5) 2:24 "That which is not lawful" becomes *'šr l' yʿśh* "what (one) does not do" for Delitzsch, with a suggestion of categorical imperative. Lindsey improves this by translating *'šr 'swr lʿśwt* "what is forbidden to do," which is truer to the rabbinic disciplinary authority of the time,[126] as well as to the Modern Hebrew idiom.

(6) 6:1 "To his native town" surely does not mean *'l 'rṣw* "To his country," as Delitzsch puts it, but by saying *'l mqwm mwldtw* "to his birthplace," Lindsey contradicts the whole Matthaean birth story (Matt. 2:1–12), as well as the slaughter of the infants at Bethlehem (vv. 13–18), which is closely related to it.

(7) 6:3 "The carpenter," which became *ḥrš* for Delitzsch (i.e., a cabinet maker[127] or craftsman [Jer. 10:3]), now returns to his proper trade as *ngr* (cf. Bauchet on Mark 6:3, above, p. 110).

(8) 7:34 "Ephphatha, that is, 'Be opened.'" Delitzsch translated the Aramaic imperative here with the Hebrew hithpael *htpth!*, corresponding to the Aramaic *'tpth* "open yourself"—the word underlying the Greek misconstruction, according to Gustaf Dalman's conjecture.[128] It is peculiar that *ntpqḥ*[129] should be said to a deaf man (and here Jesus is addressing a deaf-mute) who is healed, just as in the Talmud *ntptḥ*[130] is said to a blind man who receives his sight. But since the meaning of *htptḥ!* has become in Modern Hebrew "Work it out!", it was necessary for Lindsey to change the word to the niphal *hptḥ* for it to mean "open up."

The situation is different for the two following aramaisms.

(a) 3:16, etc. "Peter." The problem of translation here can be dealt with in four different ways.

(i) Reproduce the Greek text faithfully, transliterating "Peter" in Hebrew letters, as Delitzsch did.

(ii) In the spirit of the Old Testament, change the Aramaic original back into the Hebrew *kp* (Job 30:6), as Bauchet did.

(iii) Translate the term into Modern Hebrew to make it intelligible to the modern reader (with biblical overtones), as Blum did with *ṣwr*.

(iv) With faithfulness to the authentic logion, reproduce its original Aramaic form *kyp'* as Lindsey did (following John 1:42; 1 Cor. 15:5).

Against options (i) and (iv) is the fact that both words are unintelligible to the Israeli reader. Against (iii) is the inaccuracy of the translation: "petros" means "stone" (*'bn*), as some modern translations of the New Testament also phrase it in John 1:42, while "petra" corresponds to the Hebrew *ṣwr* or *slʿ*. The best solution is (ii), with a footnote to explain Simon's name in both Greek and Aramaic.

(b) 5:41 "Talitha cum, which means, 'Little girl, I say to you, arise.'" It may have been possible in the past to explain to Greek readers (and later to European readers) how the two words in Aramaic are equivalent in meaning to five words in Greek (or to seven in English), but in Hebrew this is simply impossible. To force the issue as Delitzsch and Lindsey do is to forfeit credibility, because any Israeli knows that *ṭlyt' qwm* (and some manuscripts have *qwmy*) can mean nothing but *yldh, qwmy*. Therefore it would be better to render the two Aramaic words with their similar Hebrew equivalents and discuss the matter in a footnote.

(9) 8:37 "In return for his life" is deepened by Delitzsch to *kpdywn npšwn*, "ransom for his life," which has soteriological overtones, and is translated as *lýtron* in the Septuagint seven times.[131] Lindsey de-theologizes the mainly commercial "antállagma" ("medium of exchange") to *tmwrh*, which can mean not only "ransom" (Ruth 4:7) and "price," but "substitute on the personal level" as well.[132] Although the Septuagint translates *kōp̱er* "ransom" in Isa. 43:3 with "(ant)állagma," this may be one of its many mistranslations comparable to its rendering of the substitutional *taḥaṯ* "instead of" in the next verse (v. 3) with "hypér" ["for the sake of"] instead of "antí").

(10) 10:30 "A hundredfold" is a rare example of Delitzsch being more modern than Lindsey. While the former translates this with the common everyday expression *m'h pʿmym* "a hundred times," the more contemporary Lindsey goes back to the biblical blessing of Isaac (with which Jesus' answer to the question about wages has a certain affinity) for the expression *m'h šʿrym* "a hundredfold." But this does not sound at all archaic in Israel, because everyone knows the Orthodox Quarter of Jerusalem which is called by the same name, and also the reason for its name (Gen. 26:12).

(11) 14:41 "It is enough." Since it is impossible to make this statement in Hebrew without indicating who it is enough for (cf. Deut. 3:26), the decision is left to the translator. Delitzsch has Jesus say *rb ly* "it is enough for me," and construes the phrase with the next sentence: "the hour has come." This heightens the theological implications of these two small words. But Lindsey construes them with the preceding

sentence: "Sleep on and rest." Jesus adds the words *rb lkm* "it is enough for you" (meaning perhaps, "you have done enough"), which simplifies the meaning but seems to contradict the command in the next verse (v. 42): "rise, let us be going." And yet, in view of the rather childish picture the evangelist sketches of the fainthearted apostles (e.g., 4:13, 41; 6:51–52; 7:18), there is the possibility that Jesus is speaking here to the Twelve with the same sarcasm as in 8:17–21. Of course, if a long pause is to be understood as following "sleep on and rest," then Jesus can say afterwards *rb lkm* "it is enough for you," meaning "you have had enough (sleep)."

Words and passages which need improvement are primarily the following.

(1) 1:11; 9:7 "My beloved Son." Here Delitzsch translated literally with *bny ydydy* (following Deut. 33:12; Ps. 2:7). Lindsey christologizes the voice from heaven to *bny yḥydy,* reminding Jews of Isaac, and consequently also of Abraham's readiness to sacrifice his "only son" (Gen. 22:2, 16). The Jerusalem Bible comments on the sacrifice of Abraham: "In the sacrifice of Isaac the Fathers saw a prefiguring of the Passion of Jesus, the only-begotten Son," and yet it translates both verses in Mark literally like Delitzsch with "my Son, the Beloved."

In view of the text and the christology of the Fourth Gospel, Blum probably had no alternative in John 1:18 than to translate as Lindsey did. But in Mark there is no necessity to flout Jewish readers with an expression that misrepresents the text and appears to contradict explicitly the word of God in Exod. 4:22 ("Israel is my first-born son"). Flusser accepts Lindsey's position,[133] and appeals to an interpretation by C. H. Turner[134] which understands "agapētós" as meaning "only beloved," only to continue translating the Greek verbal adjective in the sequel as "loved, beloved, dear, precious." Shlomo Pines found evidence for the literal translation "loved" in an Arabic manuscript from the tenth century containing anti-Christian polemic and evidently derived in part from a Jewish-Christian source. This manuscript cites Mark 1:11 almost verbatim, with "agapētós" appearing as *ḥbyby* "my loved one."[135] Pines has discussed in a monograph[136] the use of the Exodus passage in tenth-century Islamic polemics to refute (on the basis of Jewish-Christian sources?) the apotheosis of Jesus.

(2) 2:23 "To pluck ears of grain." Delitzsch translates this with *mlylwt,* which means "ripe ears"—as the lexicographer A. Eben-Shoshan defines it, "ears that are fully ripe, so that their kernels can be freed by a slight friction."[137] Lindsey translates with *šblym* "ears" (Ruth 2:2). The translation by Delitzsch supports Flusser's view: "The general opinion was that on the Sabbath it was permissible to pick up fallen ears of grain, and rub them between the fingers; but according to R. Jehuda, also a Galilean, it was also permissible to rub them in one's

hand."[138] Flusser comments further, "The Greek translator of the original was unacquainted with the customs of the people, and to make the scene more vivid, added the statement about plucking the ears of corn as well, thus introducing the one and only act of transgression of the law recorded in the synoptic tradition."[139]

If Delitzsch has divined the text of the original account correctly, it must be assumed that together with his derived verbal form must also have appeared the cognate *mll* meaning "to rub" or "to shake." Such an etymological parallelism of verb/nomen actionis is characteristic of biblical style (e.g., Lev. 26:35; Josh. 9:20; 1 Sam. 18:17; Isa. 30:14; Jer. 30:3). These particular words (*hmwll mlylwt šl ḥṭyn* "Whoever rubs a head of wheat") occur also in the Mishnah,[140] where the practice is described as a legitimate one: "Whoever grinds a head of wheat need not pay a tithe of it." This hypothesis finds support in the tenth-century Arabic anti-Christian manuscript mentioned above, in which a Jewish-Christian text (according to Pines) is cited as saying of the disciples merely that "they rubbed (*yprwqwn*) and ate the ears."[141] This version also agrees with the Arabic *Diatessaron.*[142] From the author's own farming experience it should be added that in Israel it is absolutely unnecessary to pluck ripe heads of wheat (in the sense of expending any significant effort) in order to enjoy their fruit, because the kernels of the standing wheat fall into one's hands at the slightest rubbing. If this hypothesis is correct, it invalidates one of the main arguments of such theologians as Ethelbert Stauffer[143] and Herbert Braun,[144] who attempt to brand Jesus as a lawbreaker or apostate. In the author's mind it would be best to recommend a return to Delitzsch's translation: *mlylwt.*

(3) 10:23 "Those who have riches." Lindsey's attempt to modernize this concept leads to *bʿly hwn,* which means "capitalist" in Hebrew, thus branding Jesus as the socialist revolutionary which many youth of the radical left today would like to make him. Delitzsch's translation *bʿly nksym* "owner of riches" corresponds precisely to the idea of "ho tà chrēmata échontes" because *nksym* like "chrēmata" is closer to "goods" (including houses and lands as well as money), while *hwn* is limited to financial capital.

(4) 14:22 "This is my body." Delitzsch stresses the bodily presence of Jesus in the bread by the emphatic *zh hwʾ gwpy,* which corresponds to the "estin" in the original and in 1 Sam. 16:12. Lindsey, however, weakens this to *zh gwpy,* which comes nearer to Ulrich Zwingli's understanding of the Last Supper (which interprets "is" as "represents"). Fidelity to the text in any sense requires Delitzsch's translation.

(5) 15:27 "Two robbers." Both Delitzsch's translation *šny pryṣym* (cf. Jer. 7:11) and Lindsey's *šny pwšʿym* (cf. Isa. 53:12, "transgressors") are theologically based, the former appealing to the logion

of Mark 11:17, while the latter reflects the description of the death of the "servant of God" in Second Isaiah. The former (*pryṣ*) has the disadvantage of being identified in the classical literature of Modern Hebrew (e.g., Ḥayyim Naḥman Bialik, JaLaG [or YaLaG; Judah Loeb Gordon], Mendele Mokher Sefarim), with the Polish landlord, the central figure in the Jewish ghettos to whom a tax was paid for protection.[145] The latter word (*pwšʿ*) means simply "criminal, malefactor" without specifying the nature of the crime as does "lēstḗs" ("robber"). The corresponding word in Rabbinic Hebrew is the Greek loanword *lysṭyn* (or *lysṭys*), and in Modern Hebrew it is *šwdd*. But it would hardly be fair to use *pwšʿ* without adding a footnote to explain that the same Greek term of abuse was used by Strabo and the Seleucids for the Hasmonean freedom fighters, and by Josephus and the Romans to condemn the Zealots, a usage reflected also in 14:48.[146]

In summary, it should be remarked that Lindsey's version is by far the best and most modern in Modern Hebrew today, and that his intentional mixture of styles only rarely disturbs the harmony between the content and its expression. Vocabulary, syntax, and simplicity almost consistently produce the combination of easy comprehension and dignity which he defined as his goal. Biblical students and New Testament scholars in Israel are eagerly looking forward to the Gospel of Luke he has promised, which will not only profit from his experience in translating Mark, but also presumably provide in greater detail the defense for his theory of the priority of Luke.

C. *The Gospel of Matthew According to Blum-Eliḥai*. The basic text of this version was prepared by Joshua Blum, then revised by Yoḥanan Eliḥai in some four hundred passages, and further reviewed by two other Catholic hebraists in Jerusalem. It was printed in June 1970, and published as a ninety-three-page booklet by the end of September 1970. *Beśorat Yeshuʿa ha-Mashiaḥ lepi Matityahu* [*The Gospel of Jesus the Messiah According to Matthew*] is written in a Modern Hebrew style with primary emphasis on ease of reading. For this reason long sentences are frequently divided into their simpler components. Word order is often altered for the sake of clarity. Biblicisms and classicisms are avoided even when required by the context, and modernizations are numerous. Although the basic text is presented without pointing, not only Old Testament quotations and foreign words but also words that might be ambiguous or beyond the range of daily usage are pointed in full, as is usual in Israel in texts designed for primary school children and new immigrants. As Eliḥai emphasizes, this text is experimental in nature and still far from satisfactory. The translators hope that it can be thoroughly revised in the light of further experience and criticisms after a few years, when a more or less final Roman Catholic version of Matthew in Hebrew can be published.

Of first interest are some of its more striking modernizations and improvements in comparison with the Delitzsch edition, which has enjoyed the widest distribution in Israel to the present.

(1) 1:16 "Mary, of whom Jesus was born." The Greco-Latin *'šr mmnh* "who was from her" has finally been simplified to the Hebrew *šlh nwld* "to whom was born."

(2) 1:18 "She was found to be with child of the Holy Spirit." The literal *mrwḥ hqdš* "from the Holy Spirit" has been biblicized to the ethical dative *lrwḥ hqdš* "of the Holy Spirit." While this is not exactly the modern idiom, it does indicate the relationship of the biological father of the (yet unborn) child.

(3) 1:23 "Emmanuel (which means, God with us)." Modern translators correctly suppress the explanation of the name, which they have duly pointed for clarity.

(4) 2:17, etc. "Then was fulfilled what was spoken." Here and in all the prophetic fulfillment passages the new text correctly avoids not only the literal *ml'* "be filled" but also such formulae as *'z hwqm dbr* "then the word was upheld," and substitutes the talmudic and modern idiom *'z ntqym* "then it may be fulfilled.[147]

(5) 3:9 "From these stones to raise up children to Abraham." By a simple transposition of words the original play on words is now made both audible and visible: *lhqym bnym l'brhm mh'bnym hllw.*

(6) 3:17 "This is my beloved Son." This has been changed to the more literal *bny h'hwb* "my son, the beloved," because Delitzsch's biblical *bny ydydy*[148] can also be understood today to mean "my Son, my friend."

(7) 4:6 "Throw yourself down." This is rendered by Delitzsch with a germanism *npl lmṭh* "falle hinab!" ("fall down!"), while *hpl ʿṣmk!* "throw down your body!" sounds more natural.

(8) 5:33 "You . . . shall perform to the Lord what you have sworn." Delitzsch followed the Mishnah in translating *šbwʿwtyk* "your swearing."[149] Here it should be related to Ps. 50:14 and translated *wšlm lh" ndryk* "and complete for the Lord your promises," which would be more generally understood today.

(9) 5:46, etc. "The tax collectors." Delitzsch translates literally with *hmwksym,* which has quite different associations today although it refers to the same profession. Since tax collectors in today's Israel, as in every other country, simply exercise their function in the service of the state and within its own borders, the New Testament collocation of "tax collectors and sinners" as practically synonymous becomes unintelligible. They represent, in fact, the antithesis of the tax farmers of Jesus' day, who collected bridge tolls, city taxes, shipping tariffs, etc., at a high personal profit for the despised Romans and Herodians, so that arbitrariness, avarice, and "collaboration with the enemy" were among the associations of their function.[150] To come closer to the

meaning rather than to the literal wording of the text, the new version has *gwby hmsym* "customs collector," which is inaccurate from a purely historical perspective because the imperial head taxes and land taxes (mentioned in Matt. 22:17–21; Luke 2:1–3; Acts 5:37) were generally collected by Romans under the authority of the governor. And yet an historically inaccurate translation comes closer to the meaning of the original here than would a literal translation.

(10) 5:48 "You, therefore, must be perfect, as your heavenly Father is perfect"; 19:21 "If you would be perfect." Delitzsch translates all three instances of the Greek word "téleios" with *šlm,* following the Mishnah which says of Abraham that by circumcision he was made "perfect" like his Creator.[151] The second biblical possibility would be *tmym,* as in Gen. 17:1. But since today the former word means simply "complete," and the latter means generally "innocent" or "naive," the new text correctly translates Matt. 19:21 with *mwšlm,* although 5:48 remains (through oversight?) the archaic *šlm.* For consistency all three instances should be translated by *mwšlm*, which today has the meaning of "perfected" or "perfect."

(11) 7:12 "For this is the Law and the Prophets." While Delitzsch translates this apodictic conclusion to the Golden Rule quite literally, the new version inserts the word *kwwnt* "the intention" to make it read now: "this is the intention of the Law and the Prophets." This comes closer to the related saying of Hillel without involving the Hebrew Scriptures in a reductio ad absurdum.[152]

(12) 16:18 "You are Peter, and on this rock." The name of the apostle is best given in Hebrew here, for the original play on words which depends on the Greek text ("Pétros . . . pétra") and is lost in a translation would then become obvious: *'th ṣwr wʿd hṣwr hzh . . .* "You are *Ṣwr* and on this *ṣwr* . . ." The association of the word *ṣwr* with God, however, as in so many prayers as well as in the Israeli Declaration of Independence,[153] suggests the advisability of an alternate word such as *slʿ* which also means "rock."

(13) 16:26 "Give in return for his life." Delitzsch has theologized the word "antállagma" ("something given in exchange"), which is primarily commercial, by translating it as *pdywn* "ransom." The new version replaces this with *tmwrh,*[154] which can also mean "a substitute" on the level of human affairs.[155]

(14) 18:19 "If two of you agree." Delitzsch perpetrates a germanism here with *yhyw lb 'ḥd* "be of one heart, of one mind," which the new version improves to *hgyʿw lydy hskm* "come to an agreement." But since this expression has juridical overtones, *tmymy dʿym* "unanimous" would be ever better.

(15) 19:12 "He who is able to receive this, let him receive it." Delitzsch translates this erroneously as *my šywkl lqbl yqbl,* which repre-

sents the physical sense of "chōreín" ("to contain") but not its spiritual sense of "understand, comprehend." The new version improves this by means of a hebraism *hmbyn ybyn* "he who understands, let him understand," which may also have stood behind the Greek text.

(16) 21:7 "The ass and the colt . . . and he sat thereon." Since Matthew (or one of his copyists) unfortunately took the biblical parallelism of Zech. 9:9 too literally, Jesus was made to enter Jerusalem astride two animals. The English eliminates the difficulty (by "thereon") as does the German (by "darauf"), but the Hebrew translation *ʿlyhm* "on them" does nothing to alleviate the embarrassing literalism.

(17) 22:20 "The image and the inscription." This pair of words can serve as a classic example of the semantic change that has occurred in many Hebrew words during the past century. In 1870 when Franz Delitzsch completed his first Hebrew version of the New Testament, hebraists could still express this meaning by *hṣwrh whmktb,* but a century later these words can only mean for Israelis "the form and the letter." Today the equivalent of the Greek text is *hdywqn whktwbt,* as the new version has given it.

(18) 22:37 "And with all your mind." Delitzsch attempts to suppress this arbitrary alteration of the Jewish Shema (Deut. 6:5) as best he can by translating the Greek "diánoia" ("mind") with *mdʿyk,* which sounds almost like the original biblical *mᵉʾōḏeḵā* "your might." The new version returns completely to the Old Testament original to avoid a discordant effect for the Israeli reader.

(19) 27:2 "Pilate the governor." Following rabbinic usage[156] Delitzsch still hellenizes the title as *hgmwn,* but in today's usage this would make Pilate a Christian "bishop." The new text is quite right in calling him *mwšl,* which means a "ruler" or "commander."

No less interesting linguistically are certain paraphrases which cannot be called errors but which are most probably tendentious. In some instances the tendency may have been the by-product of "back-translating" into Hebrew (or rejudaizing?), but whatever the cause, these deviations from the Greek text produce significant changes which go beyond the limits of simply translating.

(1) 4:18 "Simon who is called Peter"; 27:17, 22 "Jesus who is called Christ." In all three instances Delitzsch translates the Greek "ho legómenos" ("who is called") literally as *hnqrʾ*. But the new version has *hmknh,* which is closer to the Greek "epikaloúmenos" as used, e.g., by Josephus for "John, who is also known as the Baptist."[157] As Paul Winter says, "The expression ʿho legómenos Christós (which is intensified by *hmknh*) indicates that 'Messiah' is not regarded as his true name, and suggests Jewish rather than Christian usage."[158] *Hnqrʾ* would have been better.

(2) 1:16 "Joseph the husband of Mary" is *bʿlh* in Delitzsch, clear-

ly indicating the consummation of their marriage, because the root *bʿl* today as in biblical times refers to marriage in terms of consummating conjugal relations.[159] But since this contradicts the Roman Catholic dogma of the perpetual virginity of Mary, in the new version Joseph becomes *'yšh šl mrym,* which is also a biblical expression,[160] but is seldom used today.

(3) 1:18 "Before they came together." In Delitzsch the simpler biblical *ybw' 'lyh* "he went in to her" has a straightforward sexual meaning (as in Gen. 16:2, 4). To transform this cohabitation into a platonic "living together" the new text reads *bṭrm ybw'w zh'l zh,* which can also mean "before they met each other." This prudery is reminiscent of Jean-Marie Paulus Bauchet's paraphrase which pays similar lip service to the Greek text, but distorts its meaning nonetheless.[161]

(4) 2:4 "Where the Christ was to be born." Delitzsch translated this almost literally with *ywld,* which can be taken grammatically as a conjunctive meaning "where the Messiah (whom Herod fears and whose birth he refuses to believe) might have been born." The new version changes this possibility into a (theological) necessity with *ṣryk lhwld,* meaning "he must or should be born," which is alien to the Greek text.

(5) 3:11 "I baptize you with water . . . but he who is coming after me . . ." The contrast between the two baptisms which the Greek text expresses simply with "mèn . . . dé" is translated in a similar vein by Delitzsch as *hn . . . w.* The Catholic version sharpens this contrast which is so theologically important to it with *'mnm . . . 'bl* "truly . . . but," to glorify Jesus explicitly despite the text.

(6) 9:3; 26:65 "He blasphemes." In both instances Delitzsch translates with the piel of *gdp,* which means blasphemy in the broad sense of speaking arrogantly against the Torah, as Jesus does (according to the view of many rabbis) in both these pericopes of the healing of the lame man and the trial before the Sanhedrin. But since this and other kinds of blasphemy (which today can also mean "railing, swearing") are punishable according to rabbinic law by scourging (*Sipra* Lev. 24:11ff.) instead of by death,[162] the Roman Catholic version adds to the verb in both passages the words *šm šmym* "the name of names"; this makes Jesus a "blasphemer against God" in the sense of Num. 15:30, i.e., one who curses the Tetragrammaton in the presence of witnesses—an act which is never reported of Jesus in any of the four Gospels. And since only such a flagrant blasphemer against the holy Name of God could be condemned to hanging[163] or render plausible a unanimous death sentence by the Sanhedrin (Matt. 26:66),[164] Jesus is twice described here—and that by rabbinic authorities—as *mgdp šm šmym* "reviling the name of names," in direct contradiction not only to the general usage of the Greek term "blasphēmeín," but to the events of the Gospels themselves.

(7) 24:15 "When you see the desolating sacrilege spoken of by the prophet Daniel, standing in the holy place (let the reader understand)." As the parenthetical signal to the reader suggests, this conflation of two quotations from Daniel (Dan. 9:27; 11:31) was intended as an allusion to the coming destruction of Jerusalem. But in contrast to Delitzsch, the Catholic version does not wish to leave anything to the reader's imagination, and departing from the text it identifies "the holy place" more explicitly as "the temple" (*mqdš*) and then proceeds to transpose it for fuller emphasis to the beginning of the sentence: "When you see in the temple the desecrating sacrilege . . ."

(8) 26:17–19 "The passover." Gustaf Dalman commented on 26:17:

> No instructed Jew could have called the eve of the Feast "the first day of the Feast" . . . . When I was editing Franz Delitzsch's Hebrew New Testament, I felt strongly what a difficult task was that of a translator of a biblical text which he is not allowed to alter, however awkward it may sound in the language into which it is being transferred, in this case Hebrew.[165]

Delitzsch, then, and Dalman as well, preserves the literal translation of "tò páscha" (*pasḥa'*) as *hap-pesaḥ*. But the Catholic version does not, attempting instead to cover the embarrassment by coining a new word *sʿwdt hpsḥ* "Passover meal," which has never existed in Hebrew! This word does not refer to the traditional Passover supper which follows the slaughter of the Passover lamb on the day of preparation for the Feast, the fourteenth of Nisan, and which has been called *Seder Pesaḥ* since the time of Rashi.[166] Rather, it indicates an ordinary meal on any of the eight days of the Feast, and therefore one that could also occur "on the first day of Unleavened Bread." This verbal pseudosolution of the famous question of the date of the Last Supper implicitly deprives it of practically any Passover symbolism, and for the Jewish reader this is the significant aspect.

(9) 27:20 "Now the chief priests . . . persuaded the people." While Delitzsch translated with the verb *hsytw* "they incited," the Catholic version has *sknʿw,* which means "they convinced." This places both the chief priests and the people in a far better light: neither demagoguery nor stratagem is involved for persuasion, but rather it is a logical argument that convinces the crowd.

(10) 27:24–25 "He . . . washed his hands before the crowd . . . and all the people answered, 'His blood be on us.' " Unfortunately the Jerusalem Bible still translates both words as did Delitzsch with "people" (*ʿm*), which is both erroneous and anti-Jewish. This fateful passage has been cited for more than fifteen hundred years as evidence of Jewish self-condemnation, because despite all logic and in a single stroke of theological eisegesis the "óchlos" ("crowd") of v. 24 has been equat-

ed with the "pás ho laós" ("all the people") of the following sentence (v. 25).

The fact that the inner court of the Fortress Antonia, where Pilate pronounced his judgment, could accommodate no more than four thousand people at most, which would be about 2 percent of the population of Jerusalem at that time (particularly when crowded with Passover pilgrims),[167] is as irrelevant for popular theology as the words from the Cross, "Father, forgive them; for they know not what they do" (Luke 23:34). Clemens Thoma has summarized incisively the bias which is read into these sentences: "It is here that the Jewish people cursed themselves and sealed their rejection. Here they became the quintessential example of fratricidal Cain, inheriting also his divine condemnation to live on earth with neither destiny nor homeland."[168] The continuing vigor of this kind of vindictive pseudotheology in the 1970s is sadly but amply attested by the textual analyses, interviews, press reports, and individual reactions to the Oberammergau Passion Play.[169]

Even if the average Israeli is not familiar with all the eisegesis involved here, any citizen of Israel who has wandered through the Old City of Jerusalem in the last eight years is well aware that only a small fragment of "the people" could possibly have agitated for the crucifixion of Jesus. To accommodate this fact and to detheologize this passage (at least in Hebrew), the Roman Catholic translators found an ingenious solution: (a) "the crowd" before which Pilate washed his hands (v. 24) is translated as *qbl-ʿm,* which incorporates the word *ʿm* "people," but means idiomatically "coram publico" ("in public, overtly");[170] (b) "all the people" in v. 25 becomes consistently *hhmwn* "the crowd," so that unlike the underlying Greek text, there is no quantitative difference implied in the two group references.

The following examples of translation errors are limited to awkward modernizations of Old Testament expressions and idioms which render the Hebrew in some way alien to the biblical idiom, whether intentionally or not. The translator of the New Testament should not forget that practically every school child in Israel encounters the Bible two or three times as often in his or her curriculum as does the average contemporary student in Europe. The Bible is central for the Israeli's instruction in history and forms the foundation of his literary education; it is a source of topographical information, and in religious schools it is studied again as Holy Scripture. It is no surprise, then, when the street urchins in the Bible insult each other with curses from the Prophets, and schoolchildren draw on the Song of Solomon for their first love letters. Consequently it sounds condescending to translate "Fear not!" (1:20) as *ʾl tḥšwš,* when every middle-school child is familiar with the biblical *ʾal-tîrāʾ* (e.g., Gen. 15:1; 26:24; 46:3). Other unnecessary modernizations are:

(1) 5:3, etc. "The kingdom of heaven." *Mmlkt hšmym* is altogether too this-worldly, because the word is used today solely in political contexts, as in "The United Kingdom (*hmmlkt hm'wḥdt*) of Great Britain."

(2) 5:3 "The poor in spirit." This cannot be rendered as *hʿnyym brwḥm* without risking the implication of "stupidity"—just as *ʿny bdʿh*[171] means "ignorant." Alternatives include *nkh-rwḥ* "contrite in spirit" from Isa. 66:2, *dk'y-rwḥ* "the crushed in spirit" from Ps. 34:19 (Eng. v. 18), and *špl-rwḥ* "a humble spirit" from Isa. 57:15; these are sufficiently well known apart from the related expression *ʿnwym* from the Qumran Thanksgiving Scroll (1QH xviii.14) and Delitzsch's *ʿnyy hrwḥ* in the sense of "humble."

(3) 5:43 "Love your neighbor." This quotation from Lev. 19:18 is too well known in its original form for it to be reduced now to *'hb 't rʿk.*

(4) 9:13 "Go and learn" is the standard expression *ṣ' wlmd* familiar to every student at least from the Passover Haggadah[172] if not from the Midrash.[173] It is odd rather than contemporary to rephrase this as *lkw, lmdw* "go, learn."

(5) 10:6 "The lost sheep of the House of Israel" is probably derived from Jer. 50:6 and should therefore be cited in its original form as *ṣ'n 'wbdwt,* not corrupted to *hkbśym h'bwdym.*

An example of the many modernizations which are susceptible of being easily misunderstood, with considerable distortion of meaning, is found at 10:39: "he who loses his life." This should not be translated as *hm'bd 't ʿṣmw* (lit. "he who loses [or "destroys"] his body"), because it could be taken in the sense of "suicide." Delitzsch is much nearer to both the text and its meaning with *hm'bd 't npšw* "he who loses his soul."

Finally, one should be alert to the use of common daily expressions bordering on slang. These may well lend a contemporary flavor to passages on occasion, but almost always with a compromise of stylistic standards.

D. *The New Translation Project of the United Bible Societies.* On February 13, 1969, seventeen representatives of various non–Roman Catholic Christian religious communities met at the Lutheran Center in Jaffa together with Dr. R. C. Stevenson of the British and Foreign Bible Society from London to discuss a new version of the New Testament in Modern Hebrew. The meeting itself could be viewed as a kind of de facto recognition of the Modern Hebrew language on the part of the Society, which almost a century earlier had underwritten and published the translation of the New Testament by Franz Delitzsch. As a result of this interchurch discussion, Joseph Aṣmon, an Israeli Jewish Christian, was commissioned to prepare a draft of Romans, which was given a preliminary review and then duplicated to serve as the basis for further discussion in May 1970—precisely a century after Delitzsch's *'Iggeret Paulus ha-Shaliyaḥ 'el ha-Romayim* [*Letter of Paul the Apostle to the Romans*] had appeared in Leipzig as the first of his New Testament translations. A committee was appointed to review the text, drawn from hebraists of all Christian confessions, and a translators' seminar was held in Jerusalem from October 19–30, 1970; here the Rev. H. K. Moulton and Dr. Stevenson from the Society lectured on the problems of theory and praxis in New Testament translation, using the Aṣmon text as a sample for thorough examination. On November 19, 1970, the revision was completed, and a third stage of the Letter to the Romans was sent to the members of the text revision committee. This keystone of Pauline theology was published early in 1972. The closely related Letter to the Galatians followed in 1973, and three further Pauline letters in 1974, with the remainder of the New Testament in Modern Hebrew scheduled to appear in a few years. In any event, the exhaustive nature of the preparations, and the large number of some fifteen qualified scholars—hebraists from all traditions—engaged in revising and correcting the text, lead one to expect this Hebrew version of the New Testament to be of the highest scholarly order.[174]

A few concluding remarks on the problem of hebraizing the New Testament in Israel are now in order. When Martin Buber invited Franz Rosenzweig to join him in undertaking a new translation of the Bible into German, Rosenzweig wrote in response: "Translating is serving two masters. No one can do it." But the very fact that he finally accepted the invitation demonstrates that ultimately (in his own words) Rosenzweig achieved "the courage of discrimination, which does not demand of itself the impossible, but only the recognition of immediate necessities."[175] Most translators of the biblical text and of the liturgy in Israel seem to have followed the same line of reasoning, although nearly all have been guilty on occasion of such tendencies as:

(1) Attempting to reconstruct the "original Hebrew text" underlying the Greek New Testament

(2) Adapting the text to the modern colloquial usage of the readers, for better or for worse

(3) Theologizing or detheologizing passages that are either ambiguous or capable of interpretation on different levels, depending on the context and the present meaning of certain words

(4) Increasing the harmony within a Gospel, a letter, or a worship service by translating certain key terms uniformly where there is diversity in the Greek text

(5) Overfidelity to the literal text

(6) Changing the sense of the text by an inept paraphrase

(7) Promoting the "rejudaizing" of Jesus and/or of his environment by vocabulary choices, at the expense of textual fidelity

All of these deviations, which have been somewhat facilitated by the present transitional state of the Modern Hebrew language, can be brought together into a single catalogue under these heads:

(1) Mission. Whether intentionally or subconsciously, practically all translators of the New Testament engage in a passive Jewish mission. Even Rosenzweig, when he decided to translate the Hebrew Bible into German, wrote to Buber: "And thus we will be missionaries."[176]

(2) Commission. None of the versions completed to date is free of the "seven sins" listed above.

(3) Omission. Words in the text which are awkward or "un-Hebraic" are often simply omitted.

In Israel today three schools of New Testament translators can be distinguished. J. Marcel Dubois, O.P., has written about the first two, leaving no doubt as to where his own sympathies lie.

> Opinions are divided between the two extremes. For some the traditional Hebrew language, that of the Bible and of the Siddur, provides extremely rich expressions of religious experience and prayer. It therefore seems ideal to adopt these formulas and inscribe in them the sentiments of the Christian liturgy, to rediscover the Hebraic expressions, with their full meaning, in the formulas of the New Testament. For others it is, above all, important to understand and be understood and, consequently, the ideal would be to translate the prayers and the readings as nearly as possible into everyday language. To pray in church in the language of Dizengoff Street![177] The debate between these two tendencies will last until the end of time. . . . On one side stand the proponents of a more eternal, mysterious and sacerdotal style, a language which, so to speak, has created, through sacred usage, its own religious framework. On the other hand there are those who prefer a more realistic and committed style which risks being more common and more subject to change.[178]

In defense of his conviction that Christian texts in Modern Hebrew should retain a characteristically lofty biblical style, the Dominican father points out that Israel is probably the only country on earth where the Bible (*Tana"k*) has not been translated into the current vernacular despite the growing distance between the language of the Torah and the idiom of the young native generation. What he looks for in a good Hebrew version of the Mass, the New Testament, and in Christian worship, is an expression of Jewish-Christian continuity clothed in a diction which any educated Israeli, whether Jew or Christian, would associate with the Holy Scripture. Such a style should be "hieratically" (sic!) inspiring, as clear as the *Siddur,* and natural. Still, it should be as lofty as the prophets, without relying on the daily vernacular usage—which will have changed in twenty to thirty years and meanwhile risks "banalizing the mysterium of the faith."

Br. Yoḥanan Eliḥai is of the opposing view, which prefers the "Dizengoff style." He would like to make "the truth of the faith" intelligible "to the laborers" as well, but without engaging in any kind of missionary activity. He argues that the Aramaic which Jesus most probably used in his preaching was no less a "vernacular language" than the Koine Greek of the Synoptic Gospels. To use a more refined style would not only build a barrier around the kerygma, but change its nature as well. In Blaise Pascal's words, the Creator is "not the God of the philosophers,"[179] nor is Jesus "the savior of the theologians," but of ordinary people, and it is in their language that the Gospel should be translated.

Hans Kosmala, the director of the Swedish Theological Institute in Jerusalem, who is generally consulted as an expert in matters of Christian translations into Hebrew, is well aware of this dilemma. He suggests half-seriously that two versions of the New Testament should be made: one in the Hebrew that Jesus might have used, and another in the Hebrew of today's Israeli youth. The first would be for scholars, theologians, and students, and the second for the use of Jewish missions.

Robert L. Lindsey believes in the possibility of a compromise, demonstrating in his translation of Mark a subtle graduation of styles according to the content and tone of the sentences that has won the approval of most critics. A similar stylistic versatility is characteristic of modern masterpieces by young Israeli authors, e.g., Moshe Shamir's *A King of Flesh and Blood,* Shmuel Yosef Agnon's *A Guest for the Night,* and Aharon Megged's *The Living on the Dead,* to mention only three examples.

The problems of translating have naturally not all been solved, but the tension between the rival schools seems to have stimulated the creative efforts of many hebraists. Three new translations are now in progress, and all the versions already published are in process of revision. Bible translating is in any event a painstaking form of service, but translating Christian texts into the language of the *hebraica veritas* seems to have attracted some of the best hebraists.

7. *The Church Glossary of the United Christian Council in Israel*

Greek, Latin, and other languages were used to describe the incar-

> nation, the resurrection, the totally human and totally divine natures of Jesus Christ, the trinity of God: . . . the mysteries of atonement and enthronement, of the sacraments. . . . All the respective dogmas could not possibly have been phrased in the language of the Torah, the Prophets, the Psalms, or of the Mishnah and Talmud. Hebrew and Aramaic did not become the Christians' primary tool of expression.[180]

In these words Markus Barth stated a semantic truism that has intrigued and frustrated all the Hebrew translators of the New Testament since Franz Delitzsch.

Despite the pervasive presence of the Old Testament in the Synoptic Gospels, the numerous Old Testament quotations in the Christian liturgies, and the many hebraisms in the New Testament (e.g., "hallelujah," "amen," "hosanna," "Satan," "Messiah," "Sabbath," "rabbi," "Passover"), and despite the ubiquity of biblical idioms (e.g., "in the name of the Lord," "in all eternity," "the Holy Spirit," "our Father in heaven," "the blood of the covenant," and so many others) apart from which a Christian vocabulary is inconceivable, the new christology and soteriology introduced by Paul made it necessary to forge new expressions and definitions which could in no way derive, either verbally or conceptually, from the Hebrew Bible. Translating these theological terms into Modern Hebrew—taking advantage of all its many levels of expression which provide the translator today with a much larger vocabulary than was available to Delitzsch—is the concern of the United Christian Council in Israel. This umbrella organization comprising eighteen evangelical churches of exclusively European and American backgrounds was formed in 1956 as a kind of microecumene "to work for a deeper Christian community in cooperation with all Christian churches and institutions . . . and to promote the strength and unity of the native church."[181]

The final section of the UCCI constitution explains one of the chief motives for the work on Hebrew translations which has engaged the efforts of the best hebraists in Israel (Protestant, Catholic, and Jewish consultants as well) since 1961. For more than a decade the problem of a "Jewish church" within the religious community of Israel has been a matter of lively discussion in all the sessions of the UCCI. Although the Jewish Christians constitute one of the smallest minorities in the Jewish nation (numbering no more than six to eight hundred altogether) and are further subdivided into a half-dozen confessions and churches, they are characterized by a growing emphasis on solidarity with their Jewish compatriots, an increasing independence of their overseas patron-churches, and for the past several years a trend toward the development of a native Hebrew liturgical tradition.

Some theologians cannot help associating this development with the first schism in the first-century Church between the original community and the followers of Paul (Acts 15)—especially since a considerable element among the Israeli Jewish Christians tends toward the position of Peter rather than of Paul in the controversy over judaizing (Gal. 2:11–14), observing not only circumcision but also the food laws and the feasts of the Jewish calendar. It is hardly surprising that many clergy speak openly about the danger—or the prospects—of a new "Jewish church," a development which Martin Buber commented on in Jerusalem when discussing Adolf von Harnack's theology: "Life in Israel prejudices one for agreement with Jesus and against Paul."[182] One among many evidences of this is a Catholic group of Jewish Christians in Jerusalem who call themselves the Community of James, worship regularly in Hebrew, and hebraize many Christian terms in the New Testament (e.g., rejudaizing the name Paul to Saul [*š'wl*]).

Although Roy Kreider, a Mennonite from the United States and President of the UCCI, pleaded recently for a "new relationship, a *hyhd* ("koinōnía") of the spirit, that would include our native brothers and their leaders,"[183] there has been an increase of local complaints from both the Arab-Christian and the Jewish-Christian sides against a kind of ecclesiastical colonialism. Emil Nusair, the Arab leader of the Baptist school in Nazareth, counselled the Fourteenth Annual Conference of the UCCI, meeting in Tiberias in November 1970: "Do not tell us 'This is the way we do it in Texas.' We are in Israel, and we must do things here in an Israeli way!"[184] In the same session the Jewish-Christian Dominican Fr. Bruno Hussar explained: "In the future we must make our own liturgy—a liturgy which is inspired by the synagogue and takes us back to the roots of the olive tree, which is the Jewish people. We are seeking for the basis of a dialogue of faith, for the mystery of unity which can be found only among the Jews."[185]

Ricky Maoz, a Protestant Jewish Christian, expressed the same aspiration in an open letter.

> They (the foreign Christians) do not follow Israeli customs . . . , they enjoy pork in public, they serve milk and meat together. . . . I should say that a fundamental and thorough rethinking of things is necessary, Brothers in Christ from abroad, if you wish to achieve the contribution you should be making in Israel. Until you are prepared to stand aside and make it possible for the faithful in Israel to forge their own forms of devotion, of witness, and of doctrine, so that the Israeli churches (Arab as well as Jewish) may be born of God, I do not believe we will be able to cooperate in a spirit of love.[186]

Support for this trend toward indigenization (not just for Jewish

Christians) came from Archbishop George Appleton, who asked the UCCI assembly: "Should we not be Jews? Should we not say the Kiddush on the eve of the Shabbat and celebrate Pesach? Should we not recite Kaddish when someone dies? Should Jews who come to Christ break with the synagogue if they wish to keep their Jewish identity?"[187]

It appears that five other motivations also favor the hebraizing of church terminology.

(a) A new kind of hebraiophilia exists, harking back to the "hebraica veritas" of Jerome, which he promoted through his own study of Biblical Hebrew. The same attitude was expressed more than a thousand years later by the Reformer Andreas Osiander of Nuremberg: "God did not desire that Jewish books should be burnt for the sake of Christianity. Rather that by means of the Hebrew language Christians might come to a proper understanding of their own faith."[188]

The discovery of the Qumran scrolls and other Hebrew manuscripts from the period of Simon Bar Kokhba, the growing shift of emphasis in biblical scholarship toward philology and Hebrew studies together with the new trend in biblical scholarship to dehellenize the early traditions about Jesus and to give greater consideration to his Jewish backgrounds, and finally the revival of the Hebrew language—all these factors have increased the number of Jerome's emulators in our own times, many of whom have followed his footsteps to the land of the biblical language.

More naive but also more vigorous than Dante Alighieri, who considered Hebrew "the first language of man,"[189] is the assertion of Br. J. Maigret, O.M.I., the French initiator of the Friends of Hebrew Language Study, which has many supporters among the Roman Catholics in Israel: "Everyone knows that God spoke Hebrew. And now, my students, you have also experienced the fact (that) Hebrew is the best medium for fruitful biblical studies."[190]

This insight, expressed in many ways, has led during the past decade to a steady growth in the number of Christian students (mostly clergy or members of religious orders) enrolled in Israeli ulpanim,[191] as well as the establishment of their own Hebrew courses in three theological seminaries in Jerusalem. The number of hebraisms used by "gentile Christians" in Israel in their daily conversation has also increased. Thus the English periodical of the Baptists is called *Ha-yaḥad* (*The Community*), church tradition is often called Halakhah by theologians, a French Catholic quarterly is called *Shoresh* (*Root*) in allusion to Rom. 11:18, completion of a New Testament translation is celebrated as a *sywm* "graduation," and reformers in the ecumenical area are lauded as *ḥlwṣym* "pioneers." Furthermore, the evangelical settlement in Galilee founded in 1962 by Christians from the Netherlands, Germany, the United States, and Switzerland is called Nes Ammim ("A Light to the Gentiles," from Isa. 11:10), and the new

Catholic retreat center built in 1970 not far from Latrun is called Neweh-shalom ("Oasis of Peace"), from Isa. 32:18.

(b) "Ecumania" is the label given facetiously in Jerusalem to the recent ecclesiastical trend which has prompted an increasing number of Christian institutions in Israel and from abroad to sponsor interfaith discussions, Israeli seminars, and Bible conferences in Jerusalem. Participation in genuine dialogue here requires a knowledge of Hebrew, as attested by the three colleagues from the Institutum Judaicum at Tübingen[192] who attended the Fifth World Congress of Jewish Studies in Jerusalem: "The fact will have to be accepted that Hebrew can no longer be restricted to the familiar role of a *lingua sacra;* it is also the lingua franca of the World Congress of Jewish Studies. . . . In such a forum the knowledge of Hebrew is a prerequisite."[193] The appeal of this "ecumania," which has contributed to the growing number of Christian scholars and Bible students visiting Israel, may be related to the insight of Joseph Ernest Renan (1823–1892), who called the land of Israel "the fifth Gospel,"[194] without a knowledge of which neither Jesus nor his message can be rightly understood. Today it is no longer unusual for ecumenical worship, international symposia, and interconfessional study conferences to be held in Hebrew.

(c) Hebrew has become the lingua franca not merely of many conferences on the Bible and on Judaism, but in many instances it is the only common language shared by Christians from throughout the world when they meet in Israel.

(d) The proclamation of the gospel will naturally always be integral to the life of the Church. The biblical basis for this vocation is traditionally identified primarily with the final verses of Matthew, which call for "making disciples of all nations ("tà éthnē") and baptizing" (Matt. 28:19)—which literally and specifically commissions a gentile mission and makes no mention of a Jewish mission.

In 1920 Wilhelm Dantine wrote an acute theological criticism of both overt and covert Jewish missions.

> If we consider the Jewish mission basically from a theological perspective, we cannot avoid recognizing that to the extent the whole enterprise is understood to be a special case or aspect of the gentile mission it represents a fundamental misunderstanding. In terms of theological responsibility, the Jewish mission as a deliberate program of the Church . . . is an absurdity. . . . We should not be blind to the fact that by characterizing this whole activity as a "mission" to the Jews their claim to their very existence as Israel is challenged. In all honest Christian conviction one cannot blame Jews for holding the suspicion that the Jewish mission is basically nothing but a pious, Christian-humane way of achieving a final

> solution: destroying the essence of post-Christian Judaism by christianizing it.[195]

Although almost all the Jews in Israel are of this view, there are also Jewish views that draw an opposite conclusion.

> We should have confidence in our own ability to convert the missionaries—not to Judaism, but to friendship with Israel. . . . With the benefit of age and experience it now appears to me that our fear of the missionaries is exaggerated and unwarranted. What can possibly happen to us? Throughout the relatively long history of Christian missions in Israel the number of Jewish baptisms has always been remarkably small.

These were Schalom Ben-Chorin's[196] words at a time when debate had flared up again over whether Israel should enact antimissionary laws such as most Islamic countries have had for years.

Whatever the front Jewish missions may assume, their meager "success" despite their use of Modern Hebrew (among sixteen other languages) appears to confirm Ben-Chorin's position! Overall statistics on Jewish conversions to Christianity are not available, partly because mission reports to their mother churches are usually somewhat exaggerated, but also because some neophytes keep their baptism secret, and a small number of converts apparently emigrate shortly after baptism. Yet the following numbers presented to the Cabinet by the late President Levi Eshkol on March 1, 1964, may be reasonably considered as quantitatively representative.

> 900 Jewish children attend eleven Christian schools, three of which proselytize actively. This represents 0.17 percent of the Jewish school population in the country. Hebrew is the language of instruction in two of these three mission schools, where ninety-five pupils are in attendance. . . . Since 1950 a total of eleven children have been converted to Christianity. . . . The total number of Jews converted to Christianity and to Islam during the last fifteen years amounts to about 201 persons.[197]

But on the other hand, from the founding of the State of Israel to the end of 1968 4,010 people petitioned for acceptance into Judaism, 2,288 of whom were received after examination and probational period of one to four years; about 85 percent of these were Christians.[198]

For missionaries in Israel today it seems still to be much as it was for Paul, who "to the Jews became as a Jew in order to win Jews" (1 Cor. 9:20), and for this purpose preached "in Hebrew" (Acts 21:40); yet he was frustrated in his approach to the Jews (13:44–45; 18:5–6), so that he turned "to the gentiles" (13:46; 18:6). Some of

Paul's followers today have traced the same pattern, leaving Israel in disappointment for more fruitful endeavors in Africa and Latin America, while others have come to love Israel so much that they defend it morally and "theopolitically" no less passionately than the Apostle to the Gentiles did in his Letter to the Romans (Rom. 9–11).

(e) Finally, there are some Christian theologians—such as Maas Boertin, formerly secretary of the UCCI (until 1967), and Robert L. Lindsey, who served as chairman of this body to the end of 1969—who believe that the Hebrew language can be useful as a kind of catalyst for Christian unity in the land of the Bible. In this hope Lindsey is now working for an autonomous Israeli federation representing all the Protestant churches in the country which he hopes to call ecumenically "the Church of Israel,"[199] while Boertin has devoted most of his free time since 1961 to the compilation of a Hebrew-English church glossary. After nine Christian and six Jewish hebraists promised to assist him, the UCCI appointed a Glossary Committee of six members, and in 1963 their first draft of about three hundred terms was circulated to forty hebraists within Israel and abroad. Roman Catholics participated regularly in the monthly sessions of the committee, and the Metropolitan Isidoros Myrsiades, head of the Greek Orthodox church in Israel (until 1967), notified Boertin in 1962 that although "unfortunately he had no competent hebraists" in his communion, he would be glad to accept in the future the terminology compiled by the UCCI.

As a first step in the difficult process of coining new forms, the Glossary Committee began in 1964 by establishing an ecumenical text of the Lord's Prayer, which the various churches had until then prayed in a half-dozen different versions; since 1965 it has been uniform in all the churches in Israel observing Hebrew worship services. Since this prayer is not only purely Jewish in origin and diction, but also contains no fewer than eight phrases which appear to be derived from the morning worship of the synagogue, its translation into Hebrew actually posed no essential difficulties. The rendering of "tòn árton . . . tòn epioúsion" (Matt. 6:11) is of particular interest.[200] In translating this key phrase the UCCI vacillated between Exod. 16:4 (*lḥm ywm bywmw* "bread for the daily needs") and Prov. 30:8 (*lḥm ḥqnw* "our allotted bread"). The first form has the intrinsic strength of repeating the "today" of Matt. 6:11, as well as echoing Jesus' moral challenge to blind trust in God's providence (vv. 25–34); indeed, the Old Testament pericope of the manna also emphasizes that "the people shall gather *only* their daily need. . . . This is how I will test them" (Exod. 16:4). Still clearer and also closer to the theme of Matt. 6:32b, 34a is *Mek.* Exod. 16:4 (55b), where Rabbi Eliezer says: "Whoever has enough to eat and says, 'What shall I eat tomorrow'—he has little faith . . ." Jesus also calls those who worry about the morrow "you of little faith"

(Matt. 6:30). The disadvantage of this translation lies in its evident pleonasm, with the word *ywm* occurring three times in a single line. The second possibility, however, has the advantage of coming from a petition to God which is almost identical with Jesus' petition for bread: "Let me eat my allotted bread." Since this interpretation expresses the literal meaning of "epioúsion" as well as the humble trust in God characteristic both of the Lord's Prayer as a whole and of the pericopes which follow (which could be contrasted with "for the morrow" or "daily"), a Solomonic decision is indicated. And v. 29 ("even Solomon in all his glory . . .") seems to suggest that Jesus himself may have been thinking of the king and his proverbs.

After two more years of interfaith discussions, drawing on the efforts of a great number of hebraists, biblical scholars, and lexicographers of all the churches, an achievement was recorded. On July 30, 1966, the first sketch of a church glossary containing 557 terms with dozens of notes, alternative translations, and question marks was sent by Boertin to all the members of the UCCI and to participating consultants, with a request for their immediate comments, criticisms, and suggestions for improvement, and expressing the optimistic hope that the document could be edited in final form by the end of 1966. But problems began with the very title of the future glossary. Some wished to call it *Mwnḥym lknsyh byśr'l* ["Terms for the Church in Israel"] and others *Mwnḥym lṣrky hknsyh byśr'l* ["Terms for the Use of the Church in Israel"]. The tentative form of the glossary which was circulated in 1966 was arranged in English alphabetical order with the fully-pointed Hebrew equivalent printed opposite in a parallel column. At the request of several UCCI experts it was decided to expand the compilation to accommodate four languages (English, French, Hebrew, Arabic), with the Roman Catholic consultants undertaking the preparation of the French component. Despite intensive efforts, the change to a tetraglot form together with an increasing amount of critical commentary received by Boertin made it impossible for the Glossary Committee to agree on a convenient format for their work during the first half of 1967. In July 1967 Boertin left Israel to accept a position at the Univeristy of Amsterdam as professor of Semitic languages.

In January 1969 Boertin returned to Jerusalem for a brief visit and presented to the Glossary Committee, which was now chaired by Lindsey, a brief tetraglot list of 134 key terms which he had painstakingly classified under three major heads.

A. God and his works (*'lqym wm'śyw*)
  1. General (*klly*)
  2. The earthly life of the Christ (*ḥyy hmšyḥ*)
  3. The Holy Spirit (*rwḥ hqdš*)
  4. God's relationship to man (*'lqym byḥs l'dm*)

B. The Holy Scriptures (*ktby hqdš*)

C. The Church (*hʿdh hmšyḥyt,* or *hnwṣrwt*)

Although this rather modest draft had taken most criticisms into account, discussion soon arose over the term to be used for the common faith of all the members. Should Christian (and also Christianity, etc.) be rendered by *mšyḥy* or by *nwṣry*? Arguments in favor of the former include:

(a) The associations of *mšyḥy* for Hebrew-speaking Christians in general, and for Jewish Christians in particular.

(b) The literalness of its translation from Gk. "Christós" and all its derivatives.

(c) The associations of the word *nwṣry* even today in the popular Jewish Israeli mind.

(d) The fact that *nwṣry* can also mean "a Nazarene," a citizen of the city of Nazareth, which is populated today by Moslems, Christians, and Jews.

Arguments favoring the alternative include:

(a) Popular Hebrew usage in Israel.

(b) The fact that if *mšyḥy* is taken in the sense of "believing in the Messiah"—which is its literal meaning—then it must include all orthodox Jews, because belief in the coming of the Messiah is an essential element of their faith.

(c) The fact that the term *mšyḥy* is used by Israeli scholarship to denote all the (pseudo-)messianic movements that have attracted and misled the popular Jewish imagination from Theudas to Sabbatai Zvi.

(d) The suspicion commonly aroused in popular opinion that any substitution for the term *nwṣrym* is simply a new disguise for the old "Jewish mission."

The dilemma posed by this key term in the planned church glossary illustrates most clearly why, after so many further sessions and consultations, the work has not yet been printed.[201] Only a few of the fundamental terms can be reviewed here. Although they cannot yet claim ecumenical recognition, they are significant as enjoying a broad consensus or alternatively as reflecting the difficulties of expressing basic christological concepts in Hebrew.

(a) "Trinity." The term was translated as *šlwš* by Jakob ben Reuben in the twelfth century (cf. p. 26). In the glossary it has been translated by this customary usage on the basis of Yoḥanan Eliḥai's reasoning (cf. pp. 114–15), despite the numerous objections of Jean-Marie Paulus Bauchet (cf. pp. 112ff.). But in accordance with the rules of orthography, the middle consonant is given a dagesh forte.

(b) "Incarnation." Ben Reuben paraphrased the term formally

(cf. p. 26), and Nestor Hakkomer evidently translated it intentionally as *htlbš bśr* (cf. p. 24) with docetic overtones. Profiat Duran first rendered it in good medieval philosophical style as *htgšmwt* "embodiment" (cf. p. 39), only to correct it later from the Vulgate to *htbśrwt* (cf. p. 40). A half-millennium later Bauchet rendered it mystically as *swd hhtgšmwt* "mysterious embodiment" (cf. p. 103). Duran's later expression may have suggested to the translator of the Roman Catholic Mass the possibility of translating "this is my body" as *zh hw' bśry* "this is my flesh" (cf. p. 127) in the Canon. And yet, despite the three theological advantages of the Hebrew term for Incarnation (cf. pp 127–28), this literal translation had to be abandoned. The reason is that the homograph *htbśrwt* is not associated with *bśr* "flesh" nearly as readily as it is with the hithpael form of the verb *bśr* "report," as in 2 Sam. 18:31 ("May my king report good news!") and in several passages of the Talmud and Midrash.[202] Just recently when a Christian hebraist was lecturing to a group of Jewish students, they took the word *htbśrwt* in the sense of "message" until the lecturer explained his terminology more explicitly.

The best solution may be found by turning from the Latin Church Fathers back to the Greek tradition, which speaks not of "becoming flesh" ("incarnatio") but of "becoming man" ("enanthrōpēsis"),[203] a term which can be expressed happily in Hebrew as *ht'nšwt*. Although the word is not yet given in the hithpael form in any of the standard Hebrew dictionaries, the related piel and hiphil forms (*'nš, h'nyš*) are found in most lexica.[204] This term also has the Christian advantage of suggesting the Aramaic "Son of man" (*br-'nš*) of Dan. 7:13, which is cited in Matt. 24:30 and has messianic associations in Jewish as well as in Christian tradition.

(c) "Evangelium." Ben Reuben still translated the term as *'wnglyws* and referred to it polemically as *sprm* "their book" (cf. p. 26). This usage was displaced by Joseph the Zealous by its near homonym *'wwh glywn* "wicked scroll" (cf. p. 32), following Rabbi Yoḥanan in the Talmud.[205] It was transcribed by Joseph ben Isaac Kimḥi as a purely Greek term, *'wnglywn* (cf. pp. 51–52); "Rabbi" Giovanni Battista Jona rendered it mystically as *'bn glywn* "Stone of Revelation" (cf. p. 68). After Sebastian Münster (cf. p. 72) it has been translated almost exclusively as *bśwrh* "Message."

In 2 Sam. 18:25; 2 Kgs. 7:9 the word indicates "good news," as *Tg.* 2 Sam. 18:27 also makes clear (*bśwrh ṭwb*). But the Mishnah regards the word as ambivalent, and speaks of both *bśwrwt ṭwbwt* and *bśwrwt r'wt,*[206] as implicit in one of the messianic passages of the table grace: "May the Merciful One send us the prophet Elijah . . . to declare to us good news (*bśwrwt ṭwbwt*)."

But again it seems almost certain that *lbśr ʿnwym* "to bring good news to the poor" in Isa. 61:1—which is translated "euangelísasthai" in the Septuagint and which Jesus read in the synagogue at Nazareth to apply messianically to himself (Luke 4:16–21)—is the source of the Christian term "euangélion." Yet Robert L. Lindsey is correct in asserting that for the modern Hebrew reader *bśwrh* means merely "message" or "news." When one person tells another "I have a *bśwrh* for you," the immediate response is, "Is it good or bad?"[207] For this reason the UCCI hebraists vacillated between *hbśwrh* (the message "kat' exochēn," "par excellence"), *bśwrh ṭwbh* "good news," and the frankly interpretive *bśwrt hmšyḥ* "good news of the Christ."

To avoid the plural form "Gospels" as theologically awkward—inasmuch as Christianity recognizes only one Gospel of Jesus Christ—it was decided to translate the common word "Evangelium" more biblically as *spry hbśwrh* "Books of the Good News" on the analogy of the Torah, which itself comprises five books.

(d) "Sacrament." Since this term is found neither in Judaism nor in the New Testament, it has taxed the ingenuity of hebraists since the time of Joseph the Zealous (cf. p. 32). At first the term was simply transcribed, thus evading the problem; Efodi (Duran) then added a lengthy explanation and a list of the seven Roman Catholic sacraments (cf. p. 41). The synonym which he used for "sacrament" in some passages, *ʿqr* "principle" (cf. p. 41), is used today as the proper translation for "dogma."[208] The use of *qdwšwt* (lit., "consecrated things") in the Anglican *Book of Common Prayer* (cf. p. 81) carries little conviction, for the passive form of the word stands in contradiction to the dynamic role of the sacraments. To the best of the author's knowledge the word *qdwšh,* which is found for example in the Third Blessing of the daily ʿAmidah, does not have a plural. Since Judaism, as Leo Baeck reminds us, has "adopted so many commandments, and refused sacraments and mysteries,"[209] the Jewish Hebrew textbooks in Israel today still use untranslated the modified transcription *saqrament.*[210] In his book *Ha-naṣrut* [*Christianity*] Saul P. Colbi makes the attempt to translate literally, prudently following it with a transcription, when he refers to *hdbrym hmqdšym* "holy things."[211]

When the early Christian hebraists attempted to translate this key concept, theological differences frustrated any agreement on a common formula. Thus the Catholics even today adhere to the translation *maqdēš,* which stresses the instrumentality of the sacrament as an effective means of grace (*ex opere operato*). They regard *maqdēš* as designating the means of sanctification just as the analogously formed *mptḥ* (from *ptḥ*) indicates a means of opening, and *mrp*' (from *rp*') a means of healing.

But the Protestants for whom "the sacrament is never considered a means subject to man's disposal" because they share Martin Luther's fear of "man's arrogance"—which wishes "to control God and avoid the venture of faith"—emphasize that it is "an act of God—sola gratia," and that it "speaks only to those who accept it in faith."[212] Accordingly they translate the word as *taqdēš,* which not only has an instrumental meaning but emphasizes primarily the result of an act, such as *tqṣyr* (from *qṣr* "be short") means "resumé," *tqlyṭ* (from *qlṭ* "retain") "record" (on which something has been recorded, while *maqlēṭ* is the recording equipment!), and *tktyb* (from *ktb* "write") "dictation." The reason for avoiding the structurally closer form *tqdyš* is its use in the Words of Consecration (of the Bread and Wine) in the Mass.[213]

Semantically the choice of words is extremely limited because nearly all the other possibilities (e.g., *qdyš, qdwš, mqdš, hqdš,* and *hqdšh*) have already been requisitioned for Jewish liturgical use. Since some Protestant theologians also regard the sacrament as a "sign," both of God's grace and of the way it is communicated,[214] and Augustine saw the sacraments prefigured in the manna, the rite of circumcision, and the temple offerings of the Old Testament (as *signa foederis*), Calvinists and other evangelical-Reformed Christians would translate this New Testament concept with *'wt hbryt* "sign of the Covenant" (cf. Gen. 17:11). This also corresponds to the Protestants' understanding of themselves as the new "covenant people" (Jer. 31:31; Matt. 26:28 par. Luke 22:20), whose two "covenant signs" in the narrow sense of the word (i.e., Baptism and Eucharist) were instituted by Jesus himself.

The Greek Orthodox church, however, whose representatives were now and then consulted by the Glossary Committee, preserve the original meaning of "sacramentum" which was itself a rendering of "mystḗrion," and translate it correctly as *rz* "secret" (Dan. 4:6 [Eng. v. 9]). While this word is Aramaic (or Persian?) in origin, in Modern Hebrew it clearly means "mystery."[215]

(e) "Martyrs." This expression, which is rendered *ʿd yšwʿ* "witness of Jesus" by Bauchet (cf. p. 106) on the basis of Delitzsch's literal translation of "witnesses of Jesus" in Rev. 17:6, has been discussed and criticized elsewhere (pp. 106–7). In order to retain continuity with the basic idea of witness (by blood or death, "mártys") and avoid secularizing it with the juridical term *ʿd,* the Glossary Committee chose the (Aramaic) term *śhd* from Job 16:19, which means "witness" (and is related to the Arabic *śhyd* both in etymology and in meaning), hebraizing it to *śwhd.* This was also acceptable to Eliḥai, whose earlier translation (*hrwg mlkwt,* lit. "murdered for the kingdom'') had been criticized. But since *śwhd* was not approved by all the hebraists, it was decided to include the Jewish *mqdš h''* ''one who sanctifies the name of God'' (cf. p. 107) as an alternative.

(f) ''Eucharist.'' This central sacrament was rendered in three different ways by Efodi. In addition to simply transcribing the term, he translated it as *ḥn ṭwb* (lit. ''good grace''; cf. p. 41), which obviously indicates the effect of (the communication of) divine grace rather than the sacrament itself. The latter form echoes the regular Vulgate rendering of the Old Testament *ḥn* as ''gratia,'' i.e., the grace of God.[216] But then Efodi also described the outward form of this sacrament with a third rendering, *dbr hlḥm whyyn* ''the matter of the Bread and the Wine'' (cf. p. 41), where *dbr* can be taken to refer either to the Logos hypostatically, or to Augustine's definition of the sacrament as ''the visible Word of God.''[217] In either case, Efodi was apparently influenced by the usage of the Utraquists, who interpreted the dual form of the Bread and Wine as a single figure.

Closer to the Roman Catholic view of the Eucharist as a representation of the sacrifice of Jesus is the translation by Ḥasdai Crescas, who speaks of *qrbnwt lḥm wyyn* ''sacrifices of bread and wine'' (cf. p. 42), although the plural is better adapted to the Old Testament view with its many classes of sacrifices than to the ''once-for-all'' sacrifice of Jesus.

Bauchet returns to the original meaning in his (still unpublished) Hebrew church glossary where he proposes the postbiblical *hwdyh*, which suggests the ''thanksgiving'' expressed by Jesus in Matt. 11:25; John 11:41, and in the penultimate petition of the ʿAmidah which is called Hodah even in the Mishnah.[218] In the Talmud and in the synagogue liturgy this word is identical with *hwdyh* (cf. *j. Ber.* 3d) in the sense of religious thanksgiving. Similar thanksgivings are found in the Qumran Thanksgiving Scroll, which Yigael Yadin called the Hodayoth (1QH) for this reason. Since the word can also mean ''confession'' and ''sympathetic understanding'' in Modern Hebrew, the UCCI accepted the new coinage *twdyh* of the revised Roman Catholic Missal, whose virtues have been discussed above (cf. p. 125).

(g) ''Persona.'' This concept is very difficult for Jews to grasp. Ben Reuben transcribed it with the rabbinic hellenism *prṣwp* (cf. p. 26), which almost all later hebraists also used—some in the sense of the Lurian-cabalistic term *prṣwp* ''countenance'' with regard to manifestations of God. In spite of Eugène Cardinal Tisserant's approval, the Syriac term *qnwm* which was first used by Jona in his Hebrew Catechism (1658) and borrowed from him by Bauchet (cf. p. 102) is unsatisfactory. It does not help the Hebrew reader when a foreign concept is expressed by an equally foreign and unknown loanword. A fresh solution must be found, because in Modern Hebrew the word *prṣwp* has not only the primary meaning of "physiognomy," but also the secondary connotations of "parvenu" and "rogue" as well. Eliḥai proposed *h-'ny* "the 'I,' " and this was accepted by the Glossary Committee.[219]

Eliḥai's defense of his translation is interesting.

> If the blending of persons in the Trinity is a fusion of the respective individuals in an "I-Thou" relationship, as it may be found implied in such texts as "Thou art my son, this day have I begotten thee" (Ps. 2:7), and "as thou, Father, art in me and I in thee" (John 17:21), then it can be said that God exists as three I's.[220]

Yet most hebraists are convinced that this solution is at best only provisional, mainly because of two faults: (1) *h-'ny* has been the technical psychological term for the "ego" since the time of Freud; and (2) the usual plural form of the theological term "personae" as *'nym* (or *'nyw*', as Eliḥai proposes) sounds at least odd, if not unintelligible.

The following translations are also interesting, and like the UCCI terminology in general, they must still be regarded as experimental.

(a) "Sunday" (*ywm h'dwn* "the Lord's day"). The biblical order of days gives only the Sabbath a special name, distinguishing Sunday (like the other five workdays) only by its number in sequence (i.e., *ywm r'šwn* "the first day"). Because Christians observe the day of Jesus' resurrection as a weekly day of rest and prayer, the UCCI wished to name this special day "the Lord's day," following the tradition of the Latin and Romance languages (e.g., "dominica," "domenica," "domingo," "dimanche"). This disagrees partly with the Jewish Christians' understanding of the Sabbath, as well as the tendency of some Christian churches to observe their weekly celebration of the Mass and their day of rest on the Sabbath day following the general custom in Israel.

(b) "Gentiles." To escape the long traditional associations of the word *gwym,* which originally meant simply "peoples" and is used so frequently in the singular in the Bible to refer to Israel (e.g., Deut. 4:7; 32:28), the UCCI uses the Modern Hebrew word *l'-yhwdy* (lit. "not Jewish"), which is now quite customary.

(c) "The Holy Scripture." The inclusion of both the Old Testament and the New Testament in a single term was first attempted by lengthening the acronymic *tn''*k to *tᵉna''kba''ḥ,* an abbreviation of *twrh-nby'ym-ktwbym-bryt-ḥdšh* ("Law-Prophets-Writings-New Testament"). When Jewish hebraists suggested that such an abbreviation could hardly be considered seriously, the more general and comprehensive term *ktby hqdš* ''The Holy Scriptures'' was proposed, as Delitzsch has used it so appropriately at Rom. 1:2.

(d) ''The Bible.'' The term is translated as *spr hbrytwt* ''Book of the Testaments (or ''Covenants'')'' in the same sense, implying only the multiplicity of Old Testament covenants (with Noah, Gen. 9:8–17; Abraham, 15:7–18; Isaac, 26:4–5; Jacob, 28:13–15; Moses, Exod. 19:3–6; 24:4–8; etc.), and not necessarily the ''New Testament'' (Luke 22:20)—although at least verbally even this is derived from the Old Testament (Jer. 31:31).

(e) ''Biblical.'' This adjectival form has been translated as *mqr'y* without arousing any objections, and it is already being accepted ecumenically.

(f) ''Mass.'' This term, which was transliterated by Joseph the Zealous (cf. pp. 33ff.), was rendered by Bauchet first as *hzbḥ hqdwš* ''the holy sacrifice'' (cf. p. 104), and later arabized to *hqrbn hqdwš*. This was the form followed by Eliḥai in his first tentative Mass (cf. pp. 117, 119), but as an aramaism because his work was based primarily on the Syrian Catholic liturgy. During the current Roman Catholic liturgical reform Eliḥai and his colleagues altered this term in 1970 to *sʿwdt h'dwn* ''Lord's Supper'' (cf. pp. 130–31), which had meanwhile been accepted by the UCCI. All the Protestant members of the Glossary Committee were prepared to accept only *qrbn* as theologically correct for indicating the ''self-sacrifice of Jesus'' which was accomplished ''once for all'' (according to Rom. 6:10), while from all theological perspectives the ''Mass'' corresponds to the ''Lord's Supper.'' It is interesting to note that Jewish Hebrew texts still prefer to use the transliteration *msh,* following it with an explanation of its meaning.[221]

In connection with the still incomplete church glossary, reference should also be made to the Hebrew concordance of the New Testament which has been under way since 1965. Here again it was Professor Boertin, then secretary of the UCCI, who initiated the undertaking on the basis of the latest (1962) edition of the Delitzsch-Dalman New Testament, following the methodology of Edwin Hatch and Henry Adeney Redpath's Septuagint concordance.[222] Work was begun by J. Goldin in 1965, and after his death in 1967 it was continued under the direction of Samuel Paul Re'emi, the representative of the Scottish church in Tiberias. The first stage, comprising the preparation of a card file of about 100,000 units, was completed in February 1970. By transcribing these in alphabetical order it was discovered that a single Hebrew word may have as many as fifty different Greek equivalents or semiequivalents. As to the present state of this project, Re'emi reports that the letter *aleph* (א) takes 235 pages and *beth* (ב) 62 pages to account for all the different significant readings.[223] The work which

Re'emi was able to accomplish by the end of 1974 with the support of the UCCI and of several churches in the Netherlands comprises three volumes, two of which appeared in 1973.[224] It may be hoped that in the foreseeable future the United Christian Council in Israel will be able to present to international biblical scholarship two new *opera hebraica:* a church glossary and a Hebrew-Greek concordance to the New Testament.

VI

Supplement: Further Developments in Christian Neo-Hebraica

In the seven years since the original German edition of this book was published, several works in the area of Christian Neo-Hebraica have appeared which enrich this ancient and yet modern field of theolinguistics and extend its boundaries.

1. *The United Bible Societies' New Testament*

Outstanding among the new works is the new translation of the New Testament published in Jerusalem in 1976 after many years of preparation by the United Bible Societies' Israel Agency. The work was formally issued with a modest celebration on April 16, 1977, exactly a century after the appearance of Franz Delitzsch's version which had meanwhile become established as a classic. As the Norwegian Magne Solheim, then director of the Agency in Haifa, emphasized in his address, the new version represents partly a revival of the presynoptic Gospel and partly a fulfilment of the words of Leo Baeck, the last great light of the German rabbinate.

> In the old Gospel which is thus opened up before us, we encounter a man with noble features who lived in the land of the Jews in tense and excited times and helped and labored and suffered and died: a man out of the Jewish people who walked on Jewish paths with Jewish faith and hopes. His spirit was at home in the Holy Scriptures, and his imagination and thought were anchored there; and he proclaimed and taught the word of God because God had given it to him to hear and to preach . . . .
>
> When this old tradition confronts us in this manner, then the

> Gospel, which was originally something Jewish, becomes a book—and certainly not a minor work—within Jewish literature. . . . It is a Jewish book because—by all means and entirely because—the pure air of which it is full and which it breathes is that of the Holy Scriptures; because a Jewish spirit, and none other, lives in it; because Jewish faith and Jewish hope, Jewish suffering and Jewish distress, Jewish knowledge and Jewish expectations, and these alone, resound through it—a Jewish book in the midst of Jewish books. Judaism may not pass it by, nor mistake it, nor wish to give up all claims here. Here, too, Judaism should comprehend and take note of what is its own.[1]

In vocabulary, style, and diction this edition represents an uneasy compromise between the Qumran style of the Dead Sea Scrolls—an idiom contemporary with the early Church—and the colloquial usage of Israel today.

Awkward expressions are found in the following passages, among others, to take examples from only the Gospel of Matthew.

(1) 1:18 "Before they came together" *bṭrm ht'ḥdw*. This suggests a commercial merger rather than the consummation of a marriage.

(2) 1:23 "Emmanuel (which means, God with us)" *ʿmnw'l šprwšw 'lhym ʿmnw*. Translating a Hebrew expression into Hebrew is not only superfluous, but sounds overly pedantic.

(3) 2:4 "Scribes of the people" *swpry hʿm*. Since no such group ever existed in Judaism, this literal translation from the Greek sounds strange.

(4) 2:17, etc. "Then was fulfilled what was spoken." The expression is rendered here in the talmudic idiom *'z ntqym hn'mr bpy hnby'*. Unfortunately, mishnaic hebraisms which frequently lie behind the New Testament Koiné Greek expressions are usually translated elsewhere into Modern Hebrew.

(5) 3:2 "Repent . . ." *šwbw btšwbh*. This sounds pleonastic and is not justified by the Greek text.

(6) 5:3–11. In the Beatitudes the numerous allusions to the Psalms (Ps. 24:3–4; 34:16 [Eng. v. 15]; 37:9, 11; 126:5) seem to be ignored, as are also the overtones of the prophets (Isa. 51:1; 61:2–3; Amos 8:11; Zech. 8:16) which echo there so unmistakably for Jewish ears.

(7) 24:27, etc. "The Son of man" *bn-h'dm*. This attempt to take Jesus' most frequent self-designation and render it by a common idiom while making it distinctive is hardly successful. If an identification with Dan. 7:13 is intended, it should be *br-'nš*. The form *bn-'dm* would correspond not only to the prophetic idiom (e.g., Ezek. 4:1, etc.), but also to the Modern Hebrew for "everyman" or "anyone"—and sacrifice the distinctiveness of the title.

(8) 27:25 "His blood be on us and on our children!" The frequently gross expressions of anti-Judaism occurring in the Evangelists may arouse some embarrassment in Greek, German, English, and other languages, but in Hebrew they are extremely painful. Certainly there can be no question here of revision or cosmetic improvement of the wording: the Hebrew translation of the Gospels must let this characteristic trait stand out in all its clarity. Here is ultimately a literature in transition between a Jewish Jesus movement and a gentile church. The originally Jewish elements usually become distorted or ambiguous in Greek translation. Often one may recognize an expression that once was Hebrew or Aramaic and has not yet become good Greek. This inherently transitional character poses an insoluble dilemma for the Hebrew translator of the New Testament. No linguistic skills can conjure it away.

Another problem still awaiting a solution concerns the use of Old Testament quotations in the Christian canon. Although nearly all the authors adopt the Old Testament–prophecy/New Testament–fulfilment pattern, the "scriptural" character here is in many instances a matter of sheer assertion. Among the 450 or so Old Testament quotations and allusions found in the New Testament, some few are of very uncertain origin. Examples are the unknown Psalm quotation in Luke 13:27, the mysterious "word of the prophet" in Matt. 2:23, and a number of vague references as in Matt. 26:24; Mark 14:49; 1 Cor. 15:3.

None of these passages offers the translator any real difficulty. Although their source in the Old Testament cannot be identified, yet they are at home in the thought world of the Hebrew canon. But it is different with the Old Testament quotations that can be verified, which are almost invariably taken from the Septuagint and differ substantively from their source. A corrective back-translation to the Hebrew original is both linguistically and theologically advisable, as Delitzsch demonstrates in his editions of the New Testament.

The situation is again different for Paul. Of the eighty-two quotations from the Old Testament in Paul's letters, thirty-four agree with the text of the Septuagint and thirty-six differ from it in minor details. Of the remaining quotations, ten differ significantly from the Septuagint, and two taken from Job (41:3 [Eng. v. 11] in Rom. 11:35; 5:13 in 1 Cor. 3:19) are outright paraphrases, hardly paralleling the meaning of the Old Testament, much less its words.

It is understandable that Paul, who wrote and preached in Greek, should quote the Old Testament from the Septuagint. No Jew of his or any later period would take it amiss so long as the quotation remained generally faithful to the Septuagint text. This it does in about thirty such quotations in Romans and in a few further instances in Romans where deviations from the Septuagint still keep within the bounds of Old

Testament ideas, such as Rom. 4:3 (Gen. 15:6), 7–8 (Ps. 31:1–2 [Eng. 32:1–2]), 17 (Gen. 17:5). In 10:21 the addition of "kaì antilégonta" ("and contrary") may be due to a typical septuagintism which attempts to give the source passage in Isa. 65:2 a contemporary slant with a special emphasis.

Similar septuagintisms reflecting either a misunderstanding of the Hebrew text by the Septuagint translator or an intentional intensification of the original text may be found in Rom. 1:17 (Hab. 2:4); 3:4 (Ps. 50:6 [Eng. 51:4]); 9:17 (Exod. 9:16), 29 (Isa. 1:9); 11:9–10 (Ps. 68:23–24 [Eng. 69:22–23]), 34 (Isa. 40:13); 15:21 (Isa. 52:15).

On the assumption that if Paul had written in Hebrew (just as according to Acts 21:40 he preached in Hebrew) he would have followed the Hebrew text, Delitzsch restored the original form of the Hebrew text in many of the instances where differences occur. But Delitzsch did so only (as he stated) "where the words of the Hebrew text in the passage quoted were as well suited to the context as the more or less incongruent Greek translation."[2]

And yet when differences from the Old Testament text affect the sense of the Pauline passage, Delitzsch observed the principle that "where the apostle's memory or intention modifies the Old Testament text, the free spirit unrestricted by slavish literalism should be respected. The Hebrew text should unquestionably be adapted to the Greek modification wherever the apostle is not strictly quoting so much as incorporating a text into his own statement."[3]

Thus since Delitzsch Rom. 10:5 has been a free rendering of Lev. 18:5 (although Paul introduces his paraphrase with "Moses writes . . ."!). Rom. 10:6–8 is a free rendering of Deut. 30:12–14, but a precise translation of Paul. Rom. 2:24 is a blend of Isa. 52:5 and Ezek. 36:20–21, although Paul introduces this semi-quotation with the words "as it is written." Rom. 9:9 blends Gen. 18:10, 14, although the Pauline introductory phrase is "this is what the promise said." Rom. 9:25 is a combination of Hos. 2:1, 25 (Eng. 1:10; 2:23), and Rom. 9:27 combines Isa. 10:22–23 with Hos. 2:1 (Eng. 1:10), although the latter is prefaced with the words "Isaiah cries out concerning Israel." Rom. 9:33 is similarly a fusion of Isa. 28:16 and 8:14–15, just as Rom. 11:8 joins Isa. 29:10 with Deut. 29:3 (Eng. v. 4).

These "Old Testament quotations," as well as the florilegium-like sequence of passages in Rom. 3:10–18 which comprises six different and partly adapted Old Testament passages, may all be aptly described textually by Paul's own statement in this very context: "they have all turned aside" (v. 12).

Proof that this "rhetorical liberty" was already a matter of reproach against Paul in his own day is found in his emphasis on the superiority of the "Spirit" which inspires the "New Covenant" over the "Old Covenant" with its "written code (which) kills" (2 Cor. 3:6ff.).

According to the British and Foreign Bible Society, "this is an example of the creative adaptation of earlier material for a new conception."[4] This may well be the case in such examples of radical reinterpretations of familiar Old Testament passages together with significant textual changes as are found with Deut. 21:23 in Gal. 3:13, and with Ps. 143:2 in Rom. 3:10. But it is hardly true of the many nontheological changes in the Old Testament text, which are more probably due to Paul's speaking and writing extemporaneously, forced as he was to quote the Old Testament from memory because he could hardly carry his library with him on his long journeys. Since the majority of these "free Old Testament quotations" are from contexts which are part of a heritage familiar to everyone who reads Hebrew, their hellenization is surprising, and it undermines for Jews the credibility of the Pauline text, especially in Hebrew translation.

To the credit of Delitzsch it should be noted that even shortly before his death he was still attempting to solve the dilemma between fidelity to Paul and fidelity to the Old Testament by means of footnotes "which would anticipate the New Testament reader's embarrassment with such explanations as 'free, following the Septuagint,' or 'blending prophecy with fulfillment'. . . ."[5]

This and similar suggestions were frustrated by the British and Foreign Bible Society's decision that "all quotations from the Old Testament which differ from the text of our Old Testament must be translated literally from the Greek text, because the text of the New Testament is no less inspired than the text of the Old Testament."[6]

The paradoxical result of this guideline has been that all the editions, including the posthumous editions of Delitzsch and the new version of 1976, show a freedom to incorporate reminiscences of the Old Testament text—except in the Old Testament quotations where Paul's forgetfulness, the Septuagint's inaccuracy, and the superficial errors of later scribes and copyists have been officially canonized by the Bible Society. The question of the impression this makes on Jewish readers—who after all constitute the primary and ultimate target audience for the translation—has never been addressed.

To paraphrase Franz Rosenzweig, the Jewish scriptures cry out, "Eli! Eli! My God, my God"—and the Christian theologians shake their heads and translate, "He is calling for Elijah!"

2. *The Church Glossary*

In 1976, after fourteen years of preliminary studies, revisions, and corrections, the United Christian Council in Israel's Church Glossary finally appeared in an edition of one thousand copies for circulation among all the interested churches and communities in Israel, Europe, and America. It differed in numerous details from the earlier drafts which had occasioned such protracted ecumenical debates. The spirit of compromise within the interchurch Glossary Committee that produced this manual is apparent in its Hebrew title: *Munnaḥim Meshiḥim Noṣerim,* which is basically tautological, combining the self-designation of the Christians who worship in Hebrew (*mšyḥy*) with the common Israeli term for Christians (*nwṣry*).[7] The understated English subtitle, *Christian Terms in Hebrew,* is too modest, because the contents comprise the essential vocabulary of the church in four languages: English, French, Arabic, and Hebrew. The editor, the Rev. Robert L. Lindsey, who is also the publisher, writes in the preface:

> . . . The entire work was reviewed by a board of Protestant and Roman Catholic scholars, assisted by a representative of the Holy Orthodox Church. On a number of questions the advice of several Jewish scholars connected with the Hebrew University was also sought.
>
> It was of course not always easy to find the Hebrew equivalents which would please all. For theological and other reasons some equivalents had special appeal to this or that church or tradition. Usage of Hebrew terms in the liturgy or services of various groups had also to be considered. However, for the majority of words and expressions chosen, no difference of opinion or of usage was found. Where usage dictated differences, it has seemed wise to signify this: Roman Catholic usage is thus sometimes marked with an asterisk, while preferences of the Orthodox Church are occasionally marked with a small circle.

The 540 entries are not arranged as originally planned under three classifications, but in the following six major categories.

A. Theology
   1. General
   2. Life of Christ
   3. The Holy Spirit
   4. God and mankind
B. Scripture
C. Life of the Church
   1. Unity of believers
   2. Preaching and catechism
   3. Doctrinal
   4. Religious response
   5. Baptism, confirmation, and communion
   6. Liturgical
   7. Set times of prayer

D. Life of the believer
   1. Sin and spiritual struggle
   2. Repentance
   3. Dedication
   4. Prayer—general
E. Organization of the church
   1. Ministry
   2. Discipline
   3. Orders
   4. Feasts
F. Vessels, vestments, and buildings

The following are a few of the basic theologoumena which exemplify the essential character of the problems encountered here.

(1) "Trinity." The term was rendered both as *hšlwš* and *hšlšh,* but only after long argument.[8]

(2) "Incarnation." The new rendering *ht'nšwt* both parallels the Greek "enanthrṓpēsis" ("assuming manhood") and also suggests the Aramaic "Son of man" of Dan. 7:13.[9]

(3) "Gospel." This was translated in two different ways: *hbśwrh,* with the definite article emphasizing its uniqueness; and *bśwrt-hmšyḥ,* which over-translates in attempting to define the content of the Good News.[10]

(4) "Sacrament." No ecumenical consensus was possible here. While the Catholics preferred *tqdš* on theological grounds, the Protestants decided on *mqdš,* and the Greek Orthodox church translated this key term by *rz* as corresponding to the original meaning of "mystḗrion."[11]

(5) "Martyr." Here again two long debated terms remain as options: *śwhd* (from Job 16:19), and also *mqdš-hšm* with its Jewish connotations and later historical associations.[12]

(6) "Eucharist." Here the proposal of the new Roman Catholic Missal won unanimous acceptance, with *htwdyh* representing not only a neologism but also the literal sense of "thanksgiving."[13]

(7) "Persona." In the interests of precision this complex term is analyzed into three terms: (a) as a person of the Trinity it is rendered *h"ny"* (lit. "the 'I' "), a plural form *h'n'ym;* (b) as hypostasis it becomes *qnwm* following the Syriac usage, or alternatively *hwyh,* suggesting both "real presence" and the Tetragram; (c) and as "prósōpon" it is translated literally *pnym* "faces."[14]

(8) "Sunday." The Solomonic solution to this dilemma is two terms: (a) the purely Christian *ywm-h'dwn* "Lord's day" as in the Romance languages (e.g., "dimanche," "domingo," "domenica"), and the Old Testament *ywm r'šwn* "first day" from the book of Genesis, which is also the common Israeli term.[15]

(9) "The Bible." As a book of two Testaments, the term was translated after long discussion as *spr-hbrytwt* "Book of the Covenants," although it is still not clear that the "New Covenant" (Jer. 31:31) justifies a plural form for the word "Covenant."[16]

(10) "Mass." Both Catholics and Protestants translated the term as the Lord's Supper (*sʿdt-hʾdwn*), with the common transcription *msh* as a secondary option in parentheses. The Greek Orthodox church, however, insisted on *ʿbwdt-hqdš* "Holy Service," which has clear associations with the Jewish temple liturgy in Jerusalem.[17]

All in all, the ninety-four-page booklet may be described as a valiant attempt, although halting at times, to gain for the Church a foothold in its founder's homeland. Undoubtedly some of the terms will be further adapted in the course of actual usage; some concepts that are lacking today will surely be added in a second edition. But it remains an open question whether and to what extent these Christian expressions will take root in the churches in Israel and in the national Hebrew vocabulary.

3. *The Hebrew New Testament Concordance*

Last, but not least, all three volumes of the concordance to the Hebrew New Testament have now appeared,[18] and copies are found in all the major libraries in Israel.

The work is based, as has been noted, on the latest (i.e., the twelfth) edition of the Delitzsch-Dalman version of the New Testament, which most specialists prefer over the new United Bible Societies' translation of 1976. The reason for this is discussed by Prof. David Flusser in his foreword to the concordance.

> . . . I have not the least doubt that back of a great many of the texts of our Synoptic Gospels lie Hebrew documents, which can be understood fully, only when the interpreter is closely acquainted with both Greek and Hebrew. Moreover, there is no New Testament book which does not indicate the enormous influence of Jewish and Hebrew concepts, words and word formations, even when no actual Hebrew text stands directly behind it. Therefore, even the study of a Hebrew translation of the Greek Testament develops an understanding of the general message of the New Testament.
>
> Franz Delitzsch would have agreed with these words. . . . He was convinced that the first historical materials of Jesus' life appeared in Hebrew. In the process of translating the Greek text of the Synoptic Gospels he discovered that he was obliged to use both

> classical and Mishnaic Hebrew expressions; and this led him to the further discovery that many passages could only be understood adequately after they had been translated *back* into Hebrew. . . .
>
> The recovery of the Dead Sea Scrolls has proved that in the days of Jesus a whole community of Jews was indeed composing Hebrew literature in just this way. Like the rabbinical writings, the scriptures of Qumran show us a company of people who know the Hebrew Scriptures by heart and write interpretations of them in a Hebrew that is both classical and mishnaic in idiom. That Delitzsch came to his conclusions and was thus able in many instances to reconstruct the earlier Hebrew *Vorlage* long before the scrolls were discovered, underlines the high probability that his approach is correct. . . .
>
> I find myself constantly asking the simple question: "Now, how did Delitzsch translate this or that passage in the New Testament?" . . . I shall now, with the help of this new tool, start asking myself: "Did the great Delitzsch connect this and that passage through the use of a common Hebrew word?"

In his introduction to the volume, Dr. Samuel Paul Re'emi, the editor, comments on the uses of the work to which he devoted seven years of painstaking labor.

> The advantages of a concordance of this kind are several. . . . First, for those who remember a text, but not where it is found, they have to look in the concordance for the significant word of the remembered text in order to locate the passage. Secondly, the study of a series of uses of a given word, very often, sheds light on the meaning intended by the writer originally. Thirdly, a concordance, which correlates the Greek and Hebrew equivalents, enables the Hebrew reader to know how the Hebrew translator interpreted the Greek text. In this way the Hebrew version acts as a kind of a commentary.

Although the concordance shows no trace of the linguistic insights gained for New Testament research from studies of the Qumran scrolls, there are good prospects that this tool will also promote an appreciation of the Hebrew backgrounds of the Christian canon.

Another sign of the growing interest in Hebrew studies among Christian readers of the Bible is represented by *Yalquṭ ha-Beśorah ha-Qedoshah* [*Anthology of the Holy Gospels*], translated by Fr. Jean-Marie Paulus Bauchet, S.S.S., in England in 1975, printed in Belgium, and published in Rome. Since this pioneer of Christian hebraizers has already been discussed above (pp. 110–15), it is sufficient here to note that this anthology is limited to selections from the four Gospels, narrating in chronological order the life, death, resurrection, and post-Easter activities of Jesus of Nazareth in easily understood Hebrew.

The discovery of the Qumran scrolls, the shift in the biblical sciences toward Semitics, which goes hand in hand with an endeavor to dehellenize the Christian kerygma in order to break through to the historic Jesus—all these factors, combined with the revival of Hebrew in this century, have given impetus for a growing number of biblical scholars to go back to the sources of their faith and to learn the mother tongue of the scripture.

October, 1982

VII
Conclusion

In the course of one thousand years of history, the study of Hebrew by Christians was first colored by polemics, then by missionary motives, and not until the present day has it come to be predominantly a branch of theological and philological scholarship. In common with earlier historical revolutions the temper which moves in contemporary theology shares the trait of looking anew to the sources of its faith for fresh inspiration, sloughing off old patterns of thought, reinterpreting, and radically demythologizing.

> We stand today in a remarkable period of transition. On the one side the hellenistically structured form of the Christian faith is ebbing. . . . On the other side the Christian faith is experiencing what I would like to call a "hebraic wave." About thirty years ago the enduring and prophetic significance of the Old Testament for the Christian faith was discovered. It was realized that the New Testament cannot be read apart from the Old Testament, but that only when both are read together beside and with each other does the fullness of life in the faith unfold.[1]

The "hebraic wave," as Jürgen Moltmann calls it, was due in part at least to the coincidence of two events which came so closely together in both time and space that many Christians were led to suspect the operation of something more than coincidence: the discovery of the Qumran scrolls, which made international headlines, simultaneously with the founding of the Third Jewish State—a state which was to make the language of the Bible, so closely related to that of the Qumran scrolls, its official language, and whose name "Israel" represents a central concept in both religions.

As the example of hebraists like Jerome proves, Hebrew as the lingua sacra of the rabbis and theologians could never inspire such a "wave." Although Jerome learned the language of the Bible from scholars of the Torah, yet he could also speak of the "Judaic serpents . . . of whom Judas was the model,"[2] just as Johann Reuchlin, the precursor of all modern hebraists, felt obliged to apologize for his studies *in hebraicis* because "they were considered unworthy of a man of position."[3]

To give the ancient language prestige and contemporary relevance, a national renaissance was necessary—and this among the "people of the (ancient) covenant" who had survived and achieved their freedom in the land of the Bible.

> The revival of the Hebrew language in Israel is the almost miraculous fulfillment of a religious vision of scholars and priests. The Hebrew language has become fully alive again, just because of the fact that it started as an inspired vision, thus creating the will to make it a reality, as part of the vision of prophets and priests to return and to rebuild the Land of Israel's forefathers and of its glorious past.[4]

This view expressed by Naphtali Hertz Tur-Sinai, the president of the Academy of the Hebrew Language, is shared by many Christian theologians and biblical scholars who agree in the hope that a back-translation of the Gospels into Hebrew will shed new light on the religious life of Jesus. In the words of Jean Carmignac, a Roman Catholic scholar and editor of the journal *Revue de Qumran,* "Retranslating the Gospels into Hebrew, reconstructing the original texts, we find ourselves listening to the actual voices of the eyewitnesses of Christ's activity."[5] And Robert L. Lindsey, a Protestant hebraist who developed a new theory of the priority of Luke while preparing a new version of the Gospel of Mark,[6] confesses that his work "gave me the frightening feeling that I was as much in the process of 'restoring' an original Hebrew work as in that of creating a new one. . . . In this kind of translation, the tantalizing possibility is constantly held out that we may often discover the exact words of Jesus himself."[7]

This hebraic character of the Synoptic Gospels in back-translation is particularly striking in such a passage as Matt. 1:21 (which makes sense only in Hebrew) or in the "Zionism" of the disciples of Jesus which is so obvious in Acts 1:6. It further renders irrelevant one of the arguments in the sixteenth-century controversy over the Lord's Supper, for the critical verb in the key sentence "This is my body" (Matt. 26:26; Mark 14:22; Luke 22:19) is simply lacking in Hebrew.

No less instructive is the list of thirteen technical terms from Qumran which the Dead Sea sect shared with pre-Pauline Christianity. In discussing this David Flusser has concluded that these "terms . . . were evidently coined in the Hebrew language and passed in a Hebrew literary medium into Christianity."[8]

Insights such as these, and similar ones too numerous to discuss here, make the Hebrew language a spiritual bridge between a growing number of Christian and Jewish biblical scholars, leading them to a deeper understanding of their respective traditions. New Testament scholars today are insisting that "Jesus must be understood first as a Jew and as a child of his times,"[9] and that "the message of Jesus was addressed to Israel—indeed, only to Israel."[10] And today many Israelis read the Gospel (of the Synoptics) no longer as a "scroll of sin," or a "scroll of destruction,"[11] but rather to discover in its Hebrew version as did Leo Baeck "a document of Jewish faith (whose) religious language is peculiarly that of Judaism (and) whose message is addressed to the Jews."[12]

This new trend of the linguistic ecumene is still in its infancy. But the growing number of Christian students at the Hebrew University in Jerusalem engage in such fields as talmudic and midrashic studies, the cabala, and Jewish history. The growing number of doctoral works, monographs, and books on Christian and Jewish-Christian themes appearing in Israel, as well as the fact that specialists in biblical and Jewish studies from abroad are invited to Israeli universities for guest lectureships on Christian themes in Hebrew,[13] demonstrates that this tendency is becoming increasingly influential today.

Endnotes

I. *Hebrew: Lingua Sacra?*

1. United Bible Societies, *Scriptures of the World* (Stuttgart: 1982), p. 7.
2. E.g., Mark 2:27; 1:21; Luke 4:16.
3. John 11:55; Luke 22:7–13; cf. Matt. 27:15ff.; Acts 20:6; Mark 14:12–16.
4. Mark 1:11; Matt. 4:1–11; 16:15–17.
5. Matt. 23:8; John 1:38; 3:26.
6. E.g., Rom. 2:28ff.; 9:11.
7. E.g., Matt. 21:9; Mark 11:9; John 12:13.
8. Rev. 19:1–6.

9. "The fact that it sounded like calling for Elias makes it certain that the words in Hebrew were: *ēli, ēli.* In that case, it would be most natural (and in connexion with a biblical phrase also most appropriate) to assume that the whole sentence was uttered in Hebrew, i.e., Ps xxii.2 expressed in the original form" (Gustaf Dalman, *Jesus-Jeshua: Studies in the Gospels,* trans. Paul P. Levertoff [London: 1929], p. 205).

10. E.g., the command to "hate your enemy" in Judaism; cf. Matt. 5:43. Cf. Johann Maier, "Die religiös motivierte Judenfeindschaft. I. Aus Missdeutung des jüdischen Selbstverständnisses," in *Judenfeindschaft: Darstellung und Analysen,* ed. Karl Thieme (Frankfurt: 1963), p. 42.

11. From the wealth of literature on this subject we note only three: Krister Stendahl, *The Scrolls and the New Testament* (New York: 1957); David Flusser, "The Dead Sea Sect and Pre-Pauline Christianity," *ScrHier* 4 (1958): 215–266, 2nd ed. (1965); and "Blessed are the Poor in Spirit . . . ," *IEJ* 10 (1960): 1–13. In the earlier essay Flusser arrives at the following conclusion on the basis of twenty-one striking semantic parallelisms between the New Testament and Qumran: "The(se) terms . . . were evidently coined in the Hebrew language and passed in a Hebrew literary medium into Christianity. They passed as true meaningful theological terms, not as empty or vague locutions" (pp. 263–64).

12. *EH* iii.39.16 (Loeb ed. 1:296–97). Scholars consider that "Hebrew" refers here to Aramaic, but since no Semitic sources have been discovered this theory remains hypothetical.

13. *EH* v.8.2 (Loeb ed. 1:454–55).
14. *Contra Rufinum* vii.77.
15. Cf. *Panarion* 1.29.7, 9.
16. *EH* v.10.3 (Loeb ed. 1:462–65).

17. *Eine Uebersetzungsarbeit von 52 Jahren.* SIJL 27 (1891): 26.

18. *The Jewish Christians of the Early Centuries According to a New Source.* Proceedings of the Israel Academy of Sciences and Humanities 2/13 (1966).

19. *Ibid.*, p. 16.

20. *Ibid.*, pp. 16–17.

21. *Ibid.*, p. 17.

22. Edwyn Robert Bevan and Charles Singer, eds., *The Legacy of Israel* (Oxford: 1927), p. 312.

23. *Ains Juden Buechleins Verlegung* (Ingolstadt: 1541), pp. 4–5.

24. *Uebersetzungsarbeit*, p. 19.

25. *A Hebrew Translation of the Gospel of Mark: Greek-Hebrew Diglot* (Jerusalem: 1969), p. 9.

26. *Ibid.*, pp. 12–13.

27. Johann Maier, "Die religiös motivierte Judenfeindschaft," pp. 38ff.; Jules Isaac, *Jesus and Israel*, trans. Sally Gran, ed. Claire Hutchet Bishop (New York: 1971), pp. 235–244.

28. Isaac, *Jesus and Israel*, pp. 215–16.

29. Marie-Thérèse D'Alverny, "Survivance de la magie antique," in *Antike und Orient im Mittelalter*, ed. Paul Wilpert. MiscMed 1 (1962): 155.

30. Joshua Kettilby, *The Collection of Testimonies Concerning the Excellency and Great Importance of the Hebrew Sacred Language* (London: 1762), pp. 8ff.

31. *PL* 22:508; 28:603.

32. R. Davidson, *Geschichte der Stadt Florenz vom 12. bis zum 16. Jahrhundert* 4/3 (Berlin: 1896–1927): 71.

33. *Ibid.*, p. 73.

34. "In the earthly paradise these books pass by in procession in the form of twenty-four old men" (*Purg.* xxix.82–87).

35. Hans Rheinfelder demonstrates that this does not reflect any knowledge of the Hebrew language; "Dante und die hebräische Sprache," in *Judentum im Mittelalter*, ed. Paul Wilpert. MiscMed 4 (1966), pp. 442–457.

36. "Fuit ergo Hebraicum ydioma illud quod primi loquentis labia fabricarunt" (*De Vulg. El.* i.4.18–29; vi.1–5, 16–40).

37. Cited in Ludwig Geiger, *Das Studium der hebräischen Sprache in Deutschland vom Ende des XV. bis zur Mitte des XVI. Jahrhunderts* (Wroclaw: 1870), p. 40.

38. Bevan and Singer, *The Legacy of Israel*, p. 313; cf. Roger Bacon: "Doctores (linguae Hebraicae) autem non desunt, quia ubique sunt Hebraei" ("Instructors [of the Hebrew language] likewise are not wanting, because everywhere there are Jews") (*Opus Maius*, ed. J. H. Bridges [Oxford: 1900] 3, ch. 13).

39. *Die Judenmission im Mittelalter und die Päpste.* MHP 6, coll. 8 (Rome: 1942): 267.

40. *Ibid.*, p. 268.

41. Joseph M. Canivez, *Statuta capitolorum generalium Ordinis Cisterciansis ad annum 1786* 1 (Louvain: 1933): 227.

42. Johannes de Oxenedes, *Chronica*, ed. Henry Ellis (London: 1859), p. 247.

43. Bartolomo and Giuseppe Lagumina, *Codice Diplomatico dei Giudei di Sicilia* (Palermo: 1884–1895) 2:609.

44. Lists of Christian hebraists prior to the Age of Humanism may be found in the following resources: B. Altaner, "Zur Kenntnis des Hebräischen im Mittelalter," *BZ* 21 (1933): 288–308; Browe, *Die Judenmission im Mittelalter und die Päpste;* Geiger, *Das Studium der hebräischen Sprache in Deutschland;* Samuel A. Hirsch, "Early English Hebraists: Roger Bacon and His Predecessors," *JQR* 12 (1900): 34–88; Geddes MacGregor, *A Literary History of the Bible* (Nashville: 1968), pp. 32–40; James Parkes, "Early Christian Hebraists," *Studies in Bibliography and Booklore* 4 (1959): 51–58; 6 (1962): 11–28; Jehuda M. Rosenthal, *Meḥqarim u-Meqorot* [*Studies and Sources in Jewish History*] (Jerusalem: 1967)1:214–233; Erwin Isak Jakob Rosenthal, "Jüdische Antwort," in *Kirche und Synagogue,* ed. Karl Heinrich Rengstorf and Siegfried von Kortzfleisch, 1 (Stuttgart: 1968): 307–362; Simon Federbusch, *Ha-Lashon ha-ʿIbrit be-Yiśraʾel ube-ʿAmmin* [*The Hebrew Language in Israel and the Nations*] (Jerusalem: 1967); Bevan and Singer, *The Legacy of Israel,* pp. 283–314; Beryl Smalley, *The Study of the Bible in the Middle Ages,* 2nd ed. (New York: 1952); Jules Auguste Soury, *Des études Hebraiques et exégétiques au Moyen Age chez les chrétiens d'Occident* (Paris: 1867); Bernhard Walde, *Christliche Hebraisten Deutschlands am Ausgang des Mittelalters* (Münster: 1916).

45. *De insolentia Judaeorum,* PL 104:69–76.

46. "Quotidie paene . . . cum iudaeis loqui" ("almost daily . . . to speak with Jews") (Samuel Berger, *Quam notitiam linguae Hebraicae habuerint christiani medii aevi temporibus in Gallia* [Nancy: 1893], p. 4).

47. Bevan and Singer, *The Legacy of Israel,* pp. 313–14.

48. *Literary History,* pp. 36–40.

49. *Meḥqarim u-Meqorot* 1:214–233.

50. Charles Marie Gabriel Bréchillet Jourdain, "De l'enseignement de l'hébreu dans l'Université de Paris au XVe siécle [*sic*]," in *Excursions historiques et philosophiques à travers le Moyen Age* (Paris: 1888), p. 236.

51. Sham debates were often staged, Talmud burnings instigated, and coercive sermons frequently preached by clergy who were familiar with Hebrew.

52. "Et ideo pereunt iudaei inter nos infiniti, quia nullus eis scit praedicare, nec scripturas interpretari in lingua eorum" ("And this is why countless Jews among us are lost: no one knows how to preach to them, or to interpret the scriptures in their language") (Roger Bacon, *Opus Maius* 3, ch. 3).

II. Medieval Christian Hebraica

1. Georg Graf, *Geschichte der christlichen arabischen Literatur* 1 (Vatican: 1944): 142ff.

2. Jehuda M. Rosenthal, *Ḥiwi al-Balkhi: A Comparative Study* (Philadelphia: 1949), pp. 4ff.

3. Jehuda M. Rosenthal, *Meḥqarim u-Meqorot* 1: 214–233.

4. "Neuere Ansichten über 'Toldoth Jeschu,'" *MGWJ* 76 (1932): 600.

5. *A Short History of the Jewish People,* rev. ed. (London: 1953), p. 167.

6. *PL* 116:141–184.

7. "R. Meir called it ʾ*wn glywn* ('the false scroll'); R. Yoḥanan called it ʿ*wn glywn* ('the wicked scroll')" (*Sabb.* 116a).

8. Joseph Schulte, "Ein hebräisches Paternoster in einem Missale des 9. Jahrhunderts," *BZ* 6 (1948): 48; Jean Carmignac, "Hebrew Translations of the Lord's Prayer: An Historical Survey," in *Biblical and Near Eastern Studies: Essays in Honor of William Sanford LaSor,* ed. Gary A. Tuttle (Grand Rapids: 1978), p. 21.

9. Cf. Georg Herlitz and Bruno Kirschner, eds., *Jüdisches Lexicon* 5 (Berlin: 1930): 153.

10. *De insolentia Iudaeorum,* PL 104:75A.

11. Bernhard Walde, *Christliche Hebraisten Deutschlands am Ausgang des Mittelalters,* p. 203, appended note to 3.

12. "De triplice psalterio Cusano," in *Realgymnasium des Johanneums zu Hamburg: Berichte über das 57. Schuljahr* (Hamburg: 1891), pp. 5ff.; cf. Xavier Kraus, "Die Handschriften-Sammlung des Cardinals Nicolaus v. Cusa," *Serapeum* 25 (1864): 358; Jakob Marx, *Verzeichnis der Handschriften-Sammlung des Hospitals zu Cues bei Bernkastel a/Mosel* (Trier: 1905), pp. 6–7.

13. "Cotidianum" is found at Matt. 6:11 in the ninth-century Latin manuscripts Cavensis and Sangermanensis.—TRANS.

14. *Toladot ha-Lashon* [*History of the Language*] (Jerusalem: 1968), p. 51.

15. Ms. no. 9152, fol. 15, Bibliothèque Nationale, Paris.

16. Ms. no. 1111, fol. 9, Bibliothèque Nationale, Paris.

17. Ms. no. 971, fol. 20, Bibliothèque Nationale, Paris.

18. "Une ancienne tradition allemande du Notre Père en Hébreu," *MIO* 15 (1969): 215; "Hebrew Translations of the Lord's Prayer," pp. 32–33 [Carmignac attributes this version to the Swiss scholar Theodor Buchmann (or Bibliander; 1504–1564)].

19. "Une ancienne tradition," p. 211.

20. To be read *ha-Shem,* representing the ineffable name of God.—TRANS.

21. Gustaf Dalman, *Aramäisch-Neuhebräisches Handwörterbuch zu Targum, Talmud, und Midrasch* (1897–1901; reprint ed., Hildesheim: 1967), p. 437.

22. For details, cf. Yitzhak Fritz Baer, *A History of the Jews in Christian Spain,* trans. Louis Schoffman 1 (Philadelphia: 1966): 150–59; Roth, *Short History,* p. 140; Adolf Neubauer, "Jewish Controversy and the 'Pugio Fidei,'" *Exp* 7, ser. 3 (1888): 81–105, 179–197.

23. Heinrich Denifle cites Peter Marsilio's description of him: "Erat frater iste . . . Magnus Rabinus et Magister in Hebraico" ("The same brother was . . . a great rabbi and instructor in Hebrew") (*Die Entstehung der Universitäten des Mittelalters bis 1400* [Berlin: 1855] 1:496).

24. André Berthier, "Un Maître orientaliste du XIIIe siecle: Raymond Martin, O.P.," *Archivum Fratrum Praedicatorum* 66 (Rome: 1936): 268.

25. "The Polemical Manuscripts in the Library of the Jewish Theological Seminary of America," in *Studies in Jewish Bibliography and Related Subjects* (New York: 1929), p. 271.

26. "Targum shel ha-Beśorah al-pi-Matthai le-Yaʿqob ben Re'uben [The Hebrew Translation of Matthew by Jakob ben Reuben]: Early Hebrew Translations of the Gospels," *Tarbiz* 32 (1962): 49.

27. "Jewish Controversy and the 'Pugio Fidei,'" p. 100.

28. "Polemical Manuscripts," p. 271.

29. *Die Gottesdienstlichen Vorträge der Juden* (Berlin: 1832), pp. 287ff.

30. *Geschichte der Juden* (Leipzig: 1864), cited in Neubauer, "Jewish Controversy and the 'Pugio Fidei,'" p. 189.

31. "Jewish Controversy and the 'Pugio Fidei,'" p. 189.
32. *Ibid.*, p. 102; Salomon Marcus Schiller-Szinessy is cited: "Raymundus Martin, owing to his ignorance of Rabbinic and even Biblical Hebrew. . ."
33. Walde, *Christliche Hebraisten Deutschlands,* pp. 70–152. Cf. Eberhard Nestle, *Nigri, Böhm und Pellican: Ein Beitrag zur Anfangsgeschichte des hebräischen Sprachstudiums in Deutschland.* Marginalia und Materialen (Tübingen: 1893).
34. Cf. Carmignac, "Hebrew Translations of the Lord's Prayer," pp. 25–26.
35. *Ibid.*, pp. 22–23.

III. Medieval Jewish New Testament Hebraica

1. Edward H. Flannery, *The Anguish of the Jews: Twenty-three Centuries of Anti-Semitism* (New York: 1965), p. 26.
2. Robert Travers Herford, *Christianity in Talmud and Midrash* (1913; reprint ed., Clifton, N.J.: 1966), pp. 35–96; Morris Goldstein, *Jesus in the Jewish Tradition* (New York: 1950), pp. 23–56.
3. Karl Thieme, "Die religiös motivierte Judenfeindschaft: II. Aus christlicher und mohammedanischer Sicht," in *Judenfeindschaft,* pp. 56–57.
4. Samuel Sandmel, *A Jewish Understanding of the New Testament,* rev. ed. (New York: 1974), pp. 127ff., 133, 142, 160ff., 180, 183–84, 187–88, 258–59, 269, 277.
5. Friedrich Heer, *God's First Love: Christians and Jews over Two Thousand Years,* trans. Geoffrey Skelton (New York: 1970), p. 26.
6. Samuel Krauss, ed., *Das Leben Jesu nach jüdischen Quellen* (Berlin: 1902); Gösta Lindeskog, *Die Jesusfrage im neuzeitlichen Judentum* (Leipzig and Uppsala: 1938), pp. 18–57.
7. *History of the Jews,* trans. Bella Löwy et al. (Philadelphia: 1891–1898) 5:185 and index.
8. *Jesus of Nazareth,* trans. Herbert Danby (1925; reprint ed., New York: 1956), pp. 48–54, esp. p. 51.
9. Justin Martyr, *Dialogus cum Judaeo Trypho,* PG 6:471–800; cf. Crispinius Gislebertus, *Disputatio Judaei cum Christiano,* PL 159:1009–1036. For details and similar "dialogues," see Arthur Lukyn Williams, *Adversus Judaeos: A Bird's-eye View of Christian Apologiae until the Renaissance* (Cambridge: 1935).
10. Such collections may be derived in part from Saadia Gaon, *'Emunot we-De'ot* [*Beliefs and Opinions*], ch. 8, "Ma'amar ha-Ge'ulah [Word of the Redeemed]." Cf. Saadia Gaon, *The Book of Beliefs and Opinions,* trans. Samuel Rosenblatt. Yale Judaica Series 1 (New Haven: 1948).
11. Cf. Jehuda M. Rosenthal, *Meḥqarim u-Meqorot* 1:203–213.
12. "Jewish Controversy and the 'Pugio Fidei,'" p. 95.
13. Jacob Mann, "An Early Theologico-Polemical Work," *HUCA* 12–13 (1937–1938): 411–459.
14. Abraham Zifroni, ed., *Hobot ha-Lebabot,* by Baḥya ben Joseph ibn Paquda (Jerusalem: 1949), p. 490.
15. Cf. Jehuda M. Rosenthal, "Defense and Attack in Medieval Polemical Literature," *Proceedings of the Fifth World Congress of Jewish Studies* (Jerusalem: 1969) 2:349.

16. Mss. Vat. Ebr. nos. 80, 171; photocopies in the Hebrew University Library, Jerusalem; cf. Nehemya Allony and D. S. Loewinger, *Roshimat taṣlume Kitbe-ha-yad me-ʿIbriyim be-Makhon* [*Catalog of Photocopies in the Institute of Hebrew Manuscripts*], vol. 3, *Hebrew Manuscripts in the Vatican* (Jerusalem: 1968).

17. Trans. Jehuda M. Rosenthal (Jerusalem: 1963), pp. 154–55.

18. Isidore Loeb, "Polémistes chrétiens et juifs en France et en Espagne," *RÉJ* 18 (1889): 63–70.

19. 1 (Hamburg: 1715): 916.

20. (Parma: 1800), nos. 114–15.

21. *I Manoscritti Palatini Ebraici della Biblioteca apostolica Vaticana e la loro storia.* Studi e testi 66 (Vatican: 1935), p. 137.

22. "Siphrut Hokoḥ ha-'Anṭi-Noṣerit ʿad Sop ha-Me'ah ha-Shemunah-ʿesreh [Literature of Anti-Christian Reproof until the End of the Eighteenth Century]," *'Aresheth* 2 (1960): 173.

23. Krauss, *Das Leben Jesu nach jüdischen Quellen,* p. 232 (Appendix III).

24. Cf. *ibid.* for further details.

25. Shlomo Pines, *The Jewish Christians of the Early Centuries of Christianity According to a New Source,* p. 43.

26. I have discussed this with both Shlomo Pines and David Flusser, but neither could explain the absence of the promised preface.

27. *'Oṣar Hokoḥim* [*Anthology of Proofs*] (New York: 1928), pp. 310–15.

28. E.g., *wmy šybqw lʿśwt lw 'nrgyyh myl lk ʿmw šny mylyn* (lit. "and whoever impresses you to produce for him a mile, go with him two miles") at Matt. 5:41.

29. I hope to devote a separate monograph to the historical and linguistic analysis of this long neglected text.

30. In his critical edition, Rosenthal demonstrates that the reference here is not to another contemporary Karaite of the same name; *Milḥamot ha-Shem,* pp. vii–viii.

31. The two participants in the dialogue are the Christian who "denies" or "corrupts" and the Jew who "affirms" the unity of God.

32. E.g., *Sepher Hokoḥim* [*Book of Reproofs*] and *Sepher Teshubot le-Kopherim* [*Book of Answers for Unbelievers*].

33. Evidently the Spain of the fanatical Almohades, which also saw the flight of the Kimḥi (Kimchi) family and the Tibbonim to southern France.

34. The manuscripts read not only *gśyqwyy'* but also *gśqwny'* and *gsqwny'*. Most scholars, however, such as Moritz Steinschneider (*Die hebraeischen Uebersetzungen des Mittelalters und die Juden als Dolmetscher* [Berlin: 1893], p. 40) and Graetz (*Geschichte der Juden* 7:448), believe that Gascoigne in southern France is intended.

35. Rosenthal, *Milḥamot ha-Shem,* p. 5.

36. Evidently Pope Gregory I (540–604) is intended, whose *Concordia quorumdam testimoniorum S. Scripturae* (PL 79:659–678) was also known to other medieval Jewish authors. Why Gregorian music is mentioned here is puzzling.

37. Rosenthal, *Milḥamot ha-Shem,* pp. 5–6.

38. Christian polemicists also divided their works into twelve chapters—the number of the apostles.

39. Cf. Arno Borst, *Die Katharer* (Stuttgart: 1953), pp. 94, 103; Semen Markovich Dubnov, *Weltgeschichte des jüdischen Volkes* (Berlin: 1927) 4:297.

40. From his magnum opus *'Emunot we-Deʿot,* although not from the well-

known Hebrew translation by Ibn Tibbon but from a version which differs from the Arabic original. Cf. Loeb, "Polémistes chrétiens et juifs," p. 48.

41. Rosenthal, *Milḥamot ha-Shem,* p. 156.

42. *Ibid.,* pp. 156–57.

43. This statement is not in the apocryphal Acts of Peter; cf. Rosenthal, *Milḥamot ha-Shem,* p. 156.

44. Rosenthal, "Siphrut Hokoḥ ha-'Anṭi-Noṣerit," p. 156.

45. *Ibid.,* p. 141.

46. Cf. Saadia Gaon, *'Emunot we-De'ot,* ch. 8.

47. George H. Händler, "Lexikon der Abbreviaturen," appendix to *Aramäisch-Neuhebräisches Handwörterbuch,* ed. Gustaf Dalman, p. 53.

48. Klausner, *Jesus of Nazareth,* p. 232.

49. Goldstein, *Jesus in the Jewish Tradition,* p. 155.

50. "Neither in the Old Testament nor in the rabbinic literature is such a statement to be found" (Johann Maier, "Die religiös motivierte Judenfeindschaft," p. 42). [This statement may now need to be qualified in the light of the Dead Sea Scrolls, e.g., 1QS 1:9–11 and related passages.—TRANS.]

51. E.g., in *'Abod. Zar.* 6b; *b.* 17a.

52. "Polémistes chrétiens et juifs," p. 64.

53. Cf. the preface to *'Eben-Boḥan* [*The Touchstone*] in the Vatican Ms. Neophiti no. 17, fol. 72.

54. See below, pp. 46–47.

55. Cf. Williams, *Adversus Judaeos,* pp. 412ff.

56. Rosenthal, *Milḥamot ha-Shem,* pp. 143–154.

57. Goldstein, *Jesus in the Jewish Tradition,* p. 206; Graetz, *Geschichte der Juden* 7:445; Loeb, "Polémistes chrétiens et juifs," p. 52.

58. Rosenthal, "Defense and Attack," p. 10.

59. Hans-Joachim Schoeps, *Jüdisch-christliche Religionsgespräche in neunzehn Jahrhunderten* (Berlin: 1937), pp. 63–86.

60. Their name indicates that they occupied official positions.

61. Rosenthal, "Siphrut Hokoḥ ha-'Anṭi-Noṣerit," pp. 142ff.

62. This is the view of Rosenthal, but Efraim Elimelech Urbach believes that ms. no. 53 of the National Library in Rome was written before 1269; "Études sur la littérature polémique au Moyen-Age," *RÉJ* 100 (1935): 49. On the date of the compilation of this work, cf. also Erwin Isak Jakob Rosenthal, "Jüdische Antwort," pp. 361–62, n. 64.

63. Ms. no. 712, Bibliothèque Nationale, Paris; cf. Hermann Zotenberg, *Manuscrits orientaux: Catalogues des manuscrits syriaques et sabéens (mandaïtes) de la Bibliothèque Nationale* (Paris: 1874), p. 115.

64. The quotations are given here in their order of occurrence in the manuscript, to show the sequence of the author's argument.

65. The original version underlying this simplification is: "Pater a nullo est factus, nec creatus nec genitus. Filius a Patre solo est, non factus, nec creatus, sed genitus. Spiritus sanctus a Patre et filio non factus, nec creatus nec genitus, sed procedens" ("The Father has come into being from nothing, neither created nor born. The Son is from the Father alone, not made nor created but born. The Holy Spirit is not made from the Father and Son, neither created nor born, but proceeding"). Cf. Heinrik Joseph Dominik Denzinger, *Enchiridion Symbolorum et Definitionum* (Freiberg: 1937), p. 18.

66. I.e., "malady" or "epidemic." Cf. *b. Neg.* iii.3, etc.

67. This corresponds to the Latin "abominatio" ("abomination") of the Vulgate.

68. Cf. Urbach, "Études sur la littérature polémique," pp. 49ff.

69. It is possible that this edition dates from 1269, as Urbach assumes, but the colophon could not have been composed before the year 1410.

70. These are chs. 2 and 6 in Jehuda M. Rosenthal's recent critical edition ("Siphrut Hokoḥ ha-'Anṭi-Noṣerit").

71. The author erroneously attributes this passage also to John, introducing it with the words, "In the book of Yoḥanan it is written for them . . ."

72. "Raka" may be derived either from Greek "hraká," or "racha" from "hráchos," meaning "cad," or from the Aramaic *rêqā'*, meaning "blockhead." Cf. Gustaf Dalman, *Jesus-Jeshua,* pp. 75–76.

73. The text states: "We found that according to their doctrine baptism may be received only once, and that anyone receiving it twice is called a heretic."

74. *Geschichte der Juden* 6:366.

75. Cf. *JA* 1 (1862): 214.

76. Judah Hadassi in his work *'Eshkol ha-Kephar* [*Sage of the Village*] (1836), par. 104; also Adolf Neubauer, *Aus der Petersburger Bibliothek* (Leipzig: 1866), p. 59.

77. Cf. *'Emunot we-De'ot,* ch. 8.

78. Cf. *Kuzari,* ch. 3.

79. Cf. *Mishneh Torah, Melakim* 11:4.

80. Adolf Neubauer, *The Book of Tobit: A Chaldee Text from a Unique Ms. in the Bodleian Library* (Oxford: 1878), pp. ix–xii.

81. It is mentioned several times in the glosses to the *Genesis Rabbah* of Gedaliah ibn Yahya (Salonika: 1594).

82. "Jewish Controversy and the 'Pugio Fidei,'" p. 90.

83. De Rossi (*Bibliotheca Judaica Antichristiana*) cites and describes about 130 works of this category.

84. E.g., Rabbi David Kimḥi in his *Milḥamot Ḥobah* [*Wars of Duty*], first printed in Constantinople in 1710; also Eisenstein, *'Oṣar Hokoḥim,* pp. 66–78.

85. Cf. Justin Martyr, *Dialogus cum Judaeo Trypho.*

86. Peter Browe, *Die Judenmission im Mittelalter und die Päpste,* p. 118.

87. For a similar three-part analysis of history, cf. the triptych of the Verdun altar of 1181 at Klosterneuberg ("ante legem" ["before the law"], "sub lege" ["under the law"], and "sub gratia" ["under grace"], where "gratia" corresponds precisely to the *twrt-ḥn* "law of grace" of Rabbi Joseph ben Isaac Kimḥi). Joachim of Flora also speaks of the three stages of human history; cf. Cipriano Baraut, "Un tratado inédito de Joaquin de Fiore: De vita sancti Benedicti et de Officio divino secundum eius doctrinam," *AST* 24 (1951): 42–118; Beatrice Hirsch-Reich, "Joachim von Fiore und das Judentum," in *Judentum im Mittelalter,* ed. Paul Wilpert, pp. 228–263; and also *Seder Eliyahu Rabba* 2 (beginning).

88. Cf. the *Commentary on the Prophets* cited by de Rossi (*Bibliotheca Judaica Antichristiana,* no. 2) and by A. Marmorstein ("David Kimḥi Apologiste: Un fragment perdu dans son commentaire des Psaumes," *RÉJ* 66 [1913]: 246–251).

89. Marmorstein, "David Kimḥi, Apologiste," pp. 247–48.

90. E.g., *La concordia de los leyes* and *Libro de las gracias.*

91. Edited in Jehuda M. Rosenthal, *Meḥqarim u-Meqorot* 1:324–367.

92. This notion had already appeared in the Talmud (cf. *b. B. Bat.* 91a). Rabbi Joseph the Zealous' book was originally so titled, and Rashi (Rabbi Shelomoh Yitzhaki) appends to many of his comments the note, "by its literal meaning and as an answer to the heretics."

93. *Meḥqarim u-Meqorot* 1:369–372.

94. In Rosenthal's edition it occupies only four pages.

95. Alias Salomon Levy, who was appointed archbishop of Burgos after his baptism.

96. Abraham Geiger, *Judaism and Its History,* trans. Charles Newburgh (New York: 1911).

97. David Gustav Flusser, "Die konsequente Philologie," in *Almanach auf das Jahr 1963* (Hamburg: 1963), pp. 19–20.

98. Eisenstein, *'Oṣar Hokoḥim,* pp. 111ff.

99. Steinschneider shows that in the medieval period the word *nṣḥwn* was actually a synonym for *wkwḥ,* meaning "debate, polemic" (*Jewish Literature from the Eighth to the Eighteenth Century,* trans. William Spottiswoode [1857; reprint ed., New York: 1970], p. 317, n. 25). Thus Jehuda ibn Tibbon, for example, used the expression *bdrk hnṣḥwn* with the meaning "dialectically" in his Hebrew version of Judah Halevy, *Kuzari* (v. 1). Gustav Karpeles (*Geschichte der jüdischen Literatur* [Berlin: 1866] 2:166) translates *nṣḥwn* as "Wettstreit" ("controversy"); Schoeps (*Jüdisch-christliches Religionsgespräch in neunzehn Jahrhunderten,* p. 79) translates the same term as "Widerlegung" ("refutation").

100. David Berger, *The Jewish-Christian Debate in the High Middle Ages: A Critical Edition of the Nizzaḥon Vetus.* Judaica: Texts and Translations 4 (Philadelphia: 1979). The others are *Sepher Niṣṣaḥon* by Rabbi Yomtob ben Solomon Lipmann of Mühlhausen (*ca.* 1405); an anonymous *Altercatio cum Iudaeo;* the *Disputatio* of Rabbi Yeḥiel at Paris (1240) and of Rabbi Moses Nachmanides at Barcelona (1263); the *Ḥizzuq 'Emunah: Liber Munimen Fidei* of the Karaite Rabbi Isaac ben Abraham de Troki (*ca.* 1593; reprint ed., New York: 1970); a later version of the *Toledot Yeshu;* and an exchange of letters between a convert named Johann Stephen Rittangel and an Amsterdam Jew (*ca.* 1642) entitled *Rittangeli cum Iudaeo altercatio.*

101. E.g., the prayer *'Alenu* composed by the Amora Rab (third century) contains the statement, "they bow down and worship the god who cannot save." Peter claimed that this was used in reference to Jesus, although the words are taken verbatim from Isa. 45:20.

102. Cf. Bernhard Walde, *Christliche Hebraisten Deutschlands,* pp. 51–63. Lipmann's book evidently prompted the bishop to seek Jewish instructors to improve his knowledge of Hebrew, and moved other Christians to follow his example.

103. Cf. Wagenseil, *Tela ignea Satanea,* where R. Lipmann's work is given the place of honor and accorded the weightiest "refutatio."

104. The other work was the anonymous *Toledot Yeshu.*

105. Konrad Schilling, ed., *Monumenta Judaica Handbuch* (Cologne: 1963), p. 182.

106. Wagenseil does indeed claim in his preface to the Hebrew-Latin edition that the manuscript he found in the archives of Sebastian Münster was from the pen of a certain Rabbi Mattathia ("cuiusdam R. Mattathia autoris") who is said to have lived in the twelfth century. And yet it seems quite certain that the work was written toward the end of the fifteenth or in the early sixteenth century. Cf. Urbach, "Études sur la littérature polémique," pp. 72–77. Its composition before 1490 is precluded not only by references to several rabbis who began to teach at this time, but also by numerous New High German words which appear in the Hebrew text (e.g., "Taufe," "Kreuz," "Kirche," "Krippe," "Glocke"). Another work with basically the same title is the *Zikkaron Sepher*

Niṣṣaḥon [Memory of Victory Book] of Lipmann, written in poetical verses, and apparently composed by one of Lipmann's disciples on the basis of his original work. The first four verses suggest by an acrostic that his name was *Mslm*. Wagenseil refers to it in *Tela ignea Satanae* as "carmen memoriale libri Nitzachon a R. Lipmann compositi" ("the poetical memorial book *Niṣṣaḥon* composed by Rabbi Lipmann").

107. Wagenseil (*Tela ignea Satanae*) refers to it as *Liber Nitzachon vetus*.

108. Cf. Urbach, "Études sur la littérature polémique," p. 73.

109. Wagenseil, *Tela ignea Satanae*, p. 82.

110. *Ibid.*, p. 51.

111. *Ibid.*, p. 71.

112. *Ibid.*, p. 140.

113. *Ibid.*, pp. 148–49.

114. This name has been variously garbled by scholars and bibliographers, e.g., "Sprot" (Wolf, *Bibliotheca Hebraea* 1:695, 1127); "Schiphruth" (Jacques Basnàge de Beauval, *Histoire des Juifs* [Rotterdam: 1716] 5:1789); "Scipruth" (Giulio Bartolocci, *Bibliotheca Magna Rabbinica* [Rome: 1675] 4:358); and also "Schephart," "Schephert," etc. (e.g., Moritz Steinschneider, *Catalogus librorum hebraeorum in bibliotheca Bodleiana* [1852–1860; reprint ed., Berlin: 1931], p. 2551).

115. *Geschichte der Juden* 8:24–25.

116. A detailed discussion of the variants, corrections, and expansions by the author is found in Alexander Marx, "Polemical Manuscripts," pp. 265–273.

117. Ibn Shaprut is in error. *Sepher Milḥamot ha-Shem* was written by Jakob ben Reuben. See above, pp. 25ff.

118. E.g., Allony and Loewinger, *Roshimat taṣlume*, nos. 311, 472, 519, 530, 707.

119. *Ibid.*, p. 22, no. 100.

120. For this information I am indebted to Dr. Colette Sirat, secretary of the Hebrew Paleography Committee in Paris, who graciously examined this manuscript while in Jerusalem at the Fifth World Congress for Judaic Studies in August 1969.

121. Händler, "Lexikon der Abbreviaturen," p. 82.

122. *Ibid.*, p. 105.

123. "Vorlesungen über die Kunde hebräischer Handschriften, deren Sammlungen und Verzeichnisse," *Beiheft zum Zentralblatt für Bibliothekwesen* 7/19 (Leipzig: 1897): 70ff.

124. Exod. 32:4, 8; Deut. 9:16; Neh. 9:18; Ps. 106:19.

125. Exod. 34:29, 30, 35 in the Latin Vulgate version of the Old Testament.

126. The title page of Jean Du Tillet's edition reads: "Evangelium Hebraicum Matthaei recens e Judaeorum penetralibus erutum, cum interpretatione Latina, ad vulgatam, quoad fieri potuit, accommodata—Parisiis, apud Martinum Iuuenem, sub insigni D. Christophori, e regione gymnasii Cameracensium, 1555" (*Evangelium Hebraicum Matthaei recens e Judaeorum penetralibus erutum, cum interpretatione latina* [Paris: 1555]). See below, pp. 58ff.

127. In the foreword of the Latin-Hebrew edition by Giovanni Battista Jona, "*'rbʿ bśwrwt mhtwrh hḥdšh 'qr nʿtqw mlšwn ʿbry ʿl ydy ywḥnn hṭwbl ywnh* [*Four Gospels of the New Testament literally translated from the Hebrew language by John the Baptist Jona*], Roma S. Congreg. Propaganda Fidei 1668."

128. *Histoire critique du texte du Nouveau Testament* (Rotterdam: 1689), pp. 232–33.

IV. Modern Christian Hebraica

1. *Diqduq de-Lishan arami 'O ha-Kasda'aḥ: Chaldaica Grammatica* (Basel: 1527).

2. *Sepher ha-Diqduq weha-Kol ha-Tebot shinmeṣaw be-Lashon ha-Qadosh* [*Book of the Grammar and All the Words Found in the Sacred Language*]: *Grammatica Eliae Levitae* (Basel: 1537).

3. *Shilush Leshonot—Dictionarium trilingue* (Basel: 1530).

4. For further works by Sebastian Münster, his biography, and other matters, cf. Ludwig Geiger, *Das Studium in der hebräischen Sprache in Deutschland,* pp. 74–88; Karl Heinz Burmeister, *Sebastian Münster Bibliographie* (Wiesbaden: 1964).

5. In the dedication of his translation of Levita's *Sepher ha-Ṭa'amim, Accentum Hebraicorum liber unus* (Basel: 1539). Cf. Geiger, *Das Studium der hebräischen Sprache in Deutschland,* p. 75.

6. Paul Leonhard Ganz, *Die Miniaturen der Baseler Universitätsmatrikel* (Basel: 1960), p. 139 and fig. 53.

7. Cf. *DD. Ioannis Œcolampadii Et Huldrichi Zwinglii Epistolarum Libri Quatuor,* ed. Theodor Bibliander (Basel: 1536), p. 3.

8. Eck's position is cited in the original by Geiger, *Das Studium der hebräischen Sprache in Deutschland,* p. 77, n. 1.

9. K. H. Burmeister, *Sebastian Münster: Versuch eines biographischen Gesamtbildes.* BBG 91 (1963); Martin Luther, *Tischreden* (Weimar ed.) 4, no. 5001.

10. Luther, *Tischreden* 5, nos. 5533, 5521, 5723; 3, no. 503.

11. Martin Luther, *Briefwechsel* (Weimar ed.) 8, no. 3205, 20ff.

12. See the preface to Münster's translation of R. Abraham bar Ḥiyya, ha-Nasi, *Sphaera Mundi* (Basel: 1546), cited in Josef Prijs, *Die Baseler Hebräischen Drucke, 1492–1866,* ed. Bernhard Prijs (Olten: 1964), p. 509. Cf. Münster, *Evangelium secundum Matthaeum in lingua Hebraica, cum versione Latina atque succinctis annotationibus* (Basel: 1537); *Messias Christianorum et Iudaeorum, Hebraice et Latine* (Basel: 1539); Adolf Herbst, *Über die von Sebastian Münster und Jean du Tillet herausgegebene hebraeischen Übersetzungen des Evangeliums Matthaei* (Göttingen: 1879).

13. Geiger, *Das Studium der hebräischen Sprache in Deutschland,* p. 88.

14. Sebastian Münster, *Epitome Hebraicae Grammaticae* [*Mishley Shelomah Proverbia Solomonis*] (Basel: 1520). I am indebted to Jean Carmignac for a photocopy of this work.

15. In the introduction: "Non qualiter apud Hebraeorum vulgus lacerum inveni, sed a me reintegratum et in unum corpus redactum emittimus" ["We publish this not in fragments, as I found it among the Jewish people, but restored to its wholeness as I have reconstructed it"].

16. *Histoire critique,* p. 234.

17. E.g., Johann Christoph Wolf, *Bibliotheca Hebraea* 3:1135; Giulio Bartolocci, *Bibliotheca Magna Rabbinica* 2:52; Moritz Steinschneider, *Catalogus librorum hebraeorum in bibliotheca Bodleiana,* p. 2555; "Le Livre de la Foi: Paul Fagius et Sébastien Munster," *RÉJ* 5 (1882): 58; Thomas Herbert Darlow and Horace Frederick Moule, *Historical Catalogue of the Printed Editions of*

Holy Scripture (London: 1911), vol. 2, *Polyglots and Languages Other Than English*, p. 706.

18. *Über die Münster-du Tillet Übersetzungen*, p. 9, citing Antonio Maria Biscioni, *Bibliothecae ebraicae graecae florentinae* (Florence: 1757), and Giovanni Bernardo de Rossi, *Bibliotheca Judaica Antichristiana*.

19. Moritz Steinschneider rightly observes: "The editor (A. Herbst) had traced the sources given in the Bodleian Catalogue and reproduced them in the German introduction, and yet he made no use of any of the manuscripts listed on p. 10. The Catalogue . . . 'was not to be found' at the University in Göttingen—whatever that may mean!" (*Ha-mazkir: Hebräische Bibliographie* 20 [Berlin: 1880]: 2).

20. So Johann Christoph Wagenseil in his foreword to *Sepher Niṣṣaḥon Yashan:* "Habuit eundem librum Sebastianus Münster . . ." ["Sebastian Münster had the same book . . ."] (*Tela ignea Satanae*).

21. *Critica sacra, sive Animadversiones in loca quaedam difficiliora Veteris et Novi Testamenti* (Amsterdam: 1693), p. 9.

22. *Bibliotheca Sacra* (Paris: 1723), p. 81.

23. Simon, *Histoire critique*, p. 232.

24. *De Interpretatione* (Paris: 1661), p. 181.

25. *Die Baseler Hebräischen Drucke, 1492–1866*. Here again I must express my gratitude for technical assistance at the University Library in Basel.

26. In the introduction of his back-translation of the Gospel into Hebrew Jean Mercier speaks of the "Matthaeum hebraicum nuper a Judaeis Romanis extortum" ("Hebrew Matthew recently wrested from the Roman Jews") (*Evangelium Matthaei ex Hebraeo Fideliter Redditum* [Paris: 1555], p. 2).

27. *Critica sacra*, p. 9.

28. *Ibid.*, pp. 10–11.

29. *Bibliotheca Magna Rabbinica* 4:358, 408.

30. *Annotationes in Libros Evangeliorum* (Amsterdam: 1641), p. 6.

31. *Synopsis Criticorum aliorumque S. Scripturae interpretum et commentatorum* (Frankfurt: 1678) 4:7.

32. *Histoire critique*, p. 232.

33. *Ibid.*, pp. 232–33.

34. E.g., Gen. 2:4; 6:9; 10:1.

35. *Catalogus librorum hebraeorum in bibliotheca Bodleiana*, p. 2555.

36. *Eine Uebersetzungsarbeit von 52 Jahren*, p. 27.

37. Darlow and Moule, *Historical Catalogue* 2:707.

38. *Über die Münster-du Tillet Übersetzungen*, p. 9.

39. "Shemtob ben Shaprut's Hebrew version of the Gospel of Matthew according to the editions by S. Münster and J. du Tillet-Mercier, newly edited by Dr. Adolf Herbst, Göttingen, 1879."

40. Alexander Marx, "Polemical Manuscripts," pp. 272–73.

41. Cf. Gustaf Dalman, *Jesus-Jeshua*, pp. 133–34.

42. Hermann Leberecht Strack and Paul Billerbeck, *Kommentar zum Neuen Testament aus Talmud und Midrasch* 1 (Munich: 1922): 290ff.

43. Dalman, *Jesus-Jeshua*, pp. 14, 75–76.

44. "Rückblick auf die Vorarbeiten," in *Uebersetzungsarbeit*, p. 27.

45. 2nd ed. (Leipzig: 1877–1888), 15–16:3.

46. *The History of Jewish Christianity from the First to the Twentieth Century* (London: 1936), p. 190.

47. First published at Strasbourg in 1554; Jean Carmignac, "Hebrew Translations of the Lord's Prayer," p. 34.

48. E.g., the Berlin edition of 1670, a copy of which is in the Hebrew University Library in Jerusalem. The latest reprint I have found is that by the London Society for Promoting Christianity amongst the Jews, in 1820.

49. William Thomas Gidney, *The History of the London Society for Promoting Christianity amongst the Jews, from 1809 to 1908* (London: 1908), p. 9.

50. Roger Bacon, *Opus Maius,* ch. 13.

51. Geiger, *Das Studium der hebräischen Sprache in Deutschland,* pp. 41–48.

52. *Ibid.*, p. 41, n. 1.

53. Jakób Jocz, *The Jewish People and Jesus Christ* (London: 1949), pp. 257, 406, n. 342.

54. Wilhelm Horning, *Magister Elias Schadäus.* SIJL 31 (1892): 11ff.

55. Delitzsch, *Uebersetzungsarbeit,* p. 27; cf. Wolf, *Bibliotheca Hebraea* 2:416ff.

56. Jocz, *The Jewish People and Jesus Christ,* p. 257; cf. Gerhard Müller, "Protestantische Orthodoxie," in *Kirche und Synagogue,* ed. Karl Heinrich Rengstorf and Siegfried von Kortzfleisch, 1 (1968): 488.

57. Wolf, *Bibliotheca Hebraea* 2:416.

58. *Uebersetzungsarbeit,* pp. 27–28.

59. *The Four Gospels in Hebrew.*

60. Peter Browe, *Die Judenmission im Mittelalter und die Päpste,* p. 277.

61. Mss. Neofiti nos. 32–33; photocopies in the Hebrew University Library, Jerusalem; cf. Franz Julius Delitzsch, *Wissenschaft, Kunst, Judenthum* (Grimma: 1838), pp. 293–94.

62. For further details, cf. F. Vernet, "Juifs (Controversies avec les)," *DTC* 8 (1924): 1899; also Bartolocci, *Bibliotheca Magna Rabbinica* 3:48–52.

63. *Bibliotheca Magna Rabbinica* 4:408.

64. Exod. 4:10.

65. Jona, preface to *Quatuor Evangelia Novi Testamenti.*

66. *Histoire critique,* p. 235.

67. *Uebersetzungsarbeit,* p. 28.

68. *Die Vier Evangelia des Neuen Testaments vor Zeiten Hebräisch und Lateinisch von Joanne Baptista Jona zu Rom Anno 1668 ausgegeben—nun aber zu grössere Ehre Gottes aufs neue in beyden und zugegebenen Teutschen Sprach auch mit Hebräischen Buchstaben* [*The Four Gospels of the New Testament Formerly Granted in Hebrew and Latin by Johannes Baptista Jona at Rome in the Year 1668—But Now to the Greater Glory of God Again in Both and the German Language Added Along with Hebrew Characters*] (Prague: 1746).

69. "The Christian-missionary, the biblical-chiliastic, the utilitarian, the liberal-humanitarian, and the religious type of philosemitism" (*Philosemitismus im Barock: Religions- und geistesgeschichtliche Untersuchungen* [Tübingen: 1952], p. 1).

70. Berthold Altaner, "Die Durchführung des Vienner Konzilbeschlusses über die Errichtung von Lehrstühlen für orientalischen Sprachen," *ZKG* 52 (1933): 227–28.

71. Cecil Roth, *A History of the Jews in England,* 2nd ed. (Oxford: 1949), p. 148.

72. Cf. p. 64.

73. Roth, *A History of the Jews in England,* p. 148.

74. Herbert Schöffler, *Abendland und Altes Testament* (Bochum-Langendreer: 1937), pp. 49–50.

75. H. Schmidt, *Cromwell und das Alte Testament* (Bonn: 1954), pp. 83–84.

76. Schoeps, *Philosemitismus im Barock,* pp. 53ff.

77. *Ibid.*, p. 61.

78. Preface to *Tela ignea Satanae,* p. 5.

79. *Gesang-Buch der Herrnhut* 2, no. 1994.

80. Yiddish or a corrupted Hebrew form for *tlwy* "the crucified one," alluding to Deut. 21:23, "for a hanged man is accursed by God."

81. Heb. *gw'l* "savior."

82. Heb. *brwk hšm* "Praised be the Name" or "Thanks be to God."

83. Heb. *m'myn* "believing."

84. Heb. *bwd'y* "certainly."

85. Evidently a corruption of Heb. *šbry-lb* "deep pain."

86. Heb. *ʿqr* "essential, basic"—one of Maimonides' thirteen articles of faith, which are regarded as comprising the Jewish creed.

87. Heb. *mwdh* "confessing."

88. Heb. *ʿwlm hb'* "the world to come."

89. *Philosemitismus im deutschen evangelischen Kirchenlied des Barock* (Stuttgart: 1963), p. 68.

90. *Ibid.*, p. 66.

91. *Ibid.*, p. 68.

92. A Yiddish expression for Heb. *'wtw 'yš* "that man" in the Herrnhut hymnal of 1731, no. 1996, verse 1.

93. Samuel Krauss, ed., *Das Leben Jesu nach jüdischen Quellen.*

94. Heb. *šbt.*

95. Heb. *qhlh* "community, congregation," thus "church."

96. Heb. *'kl* "eat."

97. Heb. *ʿlh* "whole offering" or "burnt offering," as in Gen. 22:6–8.

98. Herrnhut hymnal, no. 1997.

99. Heb. *bśwrh* "news" or "good news" here probably means the Gospel.

100. Heb. *kprh* "atonement."

101. Heb. *mḥylh* "forgiveness."

102. Heb. *mʿwl* "sin."

103. Herrnhut hymnal, no. 1996, verse 2.

104. *Evangelisches Kirchengesangbuch,* no. 273; cited in Riemer, *Philosemitismus*, p. 71, n. 15.

105. Schoeps, *Philosemitismus im Barock,* pp. 92ff.

106. K. U. Nylander, "Ett unicum fran Upsala Bibliothek," *KT* 1 (1895): 231ff.

107. Schoeps, *Philosemitismus im Barock,* pp. 120ff.

108. *Paulus des Apostels Brief an die Römer* (Leipzig: 1870), p. 105, n. 1.

109. Ms. no. 00 1:32, Cambridge University Library.

110. Ms. no. 00 1:16, Cambridge University Library.

111. "Hebräische Ubersetzungen des Neuen Testaments," in *Real-Encyclopaedie für protestantischen Theologie und Kirche,* 3rd ed., ed. Albert Hauck 3 (Leipzig: 1897): 102–3.

112. Solomon Schechter, "Notes on Hebrew MSS. in the University Library at Cambridge," *JQR* 6 (1894): 144–45.

113. *Uebersetzungsarbeit,* p. 28.

114. Jocz, *The Jewish People and Jesus Christ,* p. 251.

115. (Halle: 1730–1735), pp. 3–5.

116. Johannes Friedrich Alexander de Le Roi, *Geschichte der evangelischen Judenmission seit Entstehung des neueren Judentums,* 2nd ed. (Leipzig: 1899), pp. 126, 153, 173–75.

117. Jocz, *The Jewish People and Jesus Christ,* pp. 250–51.

118. De Le Roi, *Geschichte der evangelischen Judenmission,* p. 10.

119. *Uebersetzungsarbeit,* p. 29.

120. *Christian Researches in Asia* (Boston: 1811), pp. 312ff.

121. The allusion is probably to those known as the *bny yśr'l* ("children of Israel") from Cochin, most of whom have since emigrated to Israel.

122. Buchanan, *Christian Researches in Asia,* p. 316.

123. Schechter, "Notes on Hebrew MSS.," p. 142.

124. Gidney, *History of the London Society,* p. 55.

125. The title page of the complete edition bears the date 1813, but the *Annual Report* of the London Society for Promoting Christianity amongst the Jews indicates that only Matthew appeared at that date.

126. LSPCJ, *New Testament in Hebrew* (London: 1813), p. iv, Dedication to the Bishops.

127. These criticisms were contributed especially by the hebraists Samuel Lee in Cambridge, Heinrich Friedrich Wilhelm Gesenius in Halle, Ernst Friedrich Karl Rosenmüller and Friedrich August Gottreu Tholuck in Berlin, and R. Neumann from Wroclaw.

128. *Uebersetzungsarbeit,* p. 17.

129. Darlow and Moule, *Historical Catalogue* 2:727.

130. The eight were d'Allemand, the Rev. John Henry Brühl, Ezekiel Margoliouth, Neumann, Bishop Alexander, Hoga, Biesenthal, and Reichardt.

131. De Le Roi, *Geschichte der evangelischen Judenmission* 2:15.

132. *Wissenschaft, Kunst, Judenthum,* p. 308.

133. De Le Roi, *Geschichte der evangelischen Judenmission,* pp. 16, 44ff.

134. W. T. Gidney, *Missions to Jews,* rev. ed. (London: 1914), p. 111.

135. *Ibid.*, p. 153.

136. *Wissenschaft, Kunst, Judenthum,* p. 308.

137. *Paulus des Apostels Brief,* p. 29.

138. David Kaufmann, "Franz Delitzsch—ein Palmblatt aus Judah auf sein frisches Grab," in *Gesammelte Schriften* (Frankfurt: 1908) 1:290.

139. *Wissenschaft, Kunst, Judenthum,* pp. 279ff.

140. *Idem.*

141. *Ibid.*, pp. 308–9.

142. Full title: *Paulus des Apostels Brief an die Römer, aus dem griechischen Urtext auf Grund des Sinai-Codex in das Hebräische übersetzt und aus Talmud und Midrasch erläutert* [*Paul the Apostle's Letter to the Romans, Translated into Hebrew from the Greek Original on the Basis of the Sinai Codex and Interpreted from the Talmud and Midrash*].

143. *Ibid.*, pp. 8ff.

144. *Eine neue hebräische Übersetzung des Neuen Testaments* (Leipzig: 1864), p. 1.

145. "Das hebräische Neue Testament," *ThLB* 10/1 (January 4, 1889): 1.

146. *Paulus des Apostels Brief,* p. 26.

147. *Siphre ha-Berit ha-Ḥadashah Neʿtaqim me-Lashon Yon le-Lashon ʿIbrit* [*Books of the New Testament Translated from the Greek Language into the Hebrew Language*], 5th ed. (Leipzig: 1883), Foreword.

148. *Uebersetzungsarbeit,* pp. 30–31.

149. Hans-Joachim Kraus, *Psalmen I. Biblischer Kommentar: Altes Testament* (Neukirchen: 1960), *ad loc.*

150. Eliezer Ben-Yehuda, *Millon ha-Lashon ha-ʿIbrit* [*A Complete Dictionary of Ancient and Modern Hebrew*]: *Thesaurus Totius Hebraitatis* 4:5797.

151. The last of Maimonides' thirteen credal articles.

152. *Briefe*, ed. Edith Rosenzweig (Berlin: 1935), p. 78.

153. Cf. p. 81.

154. Gustaf Dalman, "Das hebräische Neue Testament von Franz Delitzsch in neuer Ausgabe," *ThLB* 12/31 (July 31, 1891): 290–91.

155. Part 1, "The Three Languages of Palestine in the Time of Jesus Christ," esp. pp. 7–8, 16–17.

156. *Wissenschaft, Kunst, Judenthum*, p. 216.

157. *Ha-berit ha-Ḥadashah*, 5th ed., pp. 30–31.

158. *Ibid.*, p. 30.

159. Dalman, "Das hebräische Neue Testament," col. 290.

160. "Studies in the Hebrew Background of the Gospels," *ASTI* 7 (1968–1969): 65.

161. See above, pp. 83–84.

162. Dalman, "Das hebräische Neue Testament," cols. 290–91.

163. *Ibid.*, col. 291.

164. "Franz Delitzsch," pp. 290ff.

165. *The Epistle of Paul the Apostle to the Romans Translated into Hebrew* (Edinburgh: 1855), p. 2.

166. Franz Delitzsch, "Critical Observations on My Hebrew New Testament," *Exp*, 3rd ser. 9 (1889).

167. Kaufmann, "Franz Delitzsch," p. 302.

168. *A Hebrew Translation of the Gospel of Mark* (Jerusalem: 1966), p. 68.

169. "Das hebräische Neue Testament," col. 1.

V. Christian Neo-Hebraica in the State of Israel

1. *Paulus des Apostels Brief*, p. 8.

2. Chaim Rabin, *Toladot ha-Lashon*, pp. 74ff.

3. Chaim Rabin, *Die Renaissance der hebräischen Sprache* (Zurich: 1962), p. 7.

4. "Das hebräische Neue Testament," col. 1.

5. It appeared shortly after Eliezer Ben-Yehuda's first appeal, published in the weekly *Ha-shaḥar* [*The Light*] under the title "She'elah Nikbadah [A Burning Question]" (9 [1879]: 359–369).

6. Eliezer Ben-Yehuda in the weekly *Ha-maggid;* cited in Simon Federbusch, *Ha-lashon ha-ʿIbrit be-Yiśraʾel ube-ʿAmmim*, p. 356.

7. Rabin, *Die Renaissance der hebräischen Sprache*, p. 8.

8. *Ibid.*, p. 10.

9. Federbusch, *Ha-lashon ha-ʿIbrit be-Yiśraʾel ube-ʿAmmim*, p. 386.

10. *Ibid.*, p. 358.

11. *Ibid.*, p. 392.

12. "Das hebräische Neue Testament," col. 290.

13. Naphtali Hertz Tur-Sinai, *The Revival of the Hebrew Language* (Jerusalem: 1960), p. 18.

14. With regard to this theory of Hans Bauer, which has also won Godfrey Rolles Driver's approval, cf. Rabin, *Toladot ha-Lashon*, p. 6.

15. *Die Renaissance der hebräischen Sprache*, p. 14.
16. *The Revival of the Hebrew Language*, p. 18.
17. *Die Renaissance der hebräischen Sprache*, p. 11.
18. Academy of the Hebrew Language, *The Historical Dictionary of the Hebrew Language: Prospectus* (Jerusalem: 1969), pp. 9–10.
19. Tur-Sinai, *The Revival of the Hebrew Language*, pp. 21–22.
20. This quotation, as well as all biographical and bibliographical details with regard to Father Bauchet, is from his letters and writings, which he has most graciously made available to me. Here again I must express my gratitude for his generosity.
21. Medan to the Foreign Ministry in Jerusalem, October 9, 1967.
22. See above, p. 68.
23. Tisserant to Bauchet, April 7, 1965 (photocopy in my possession).
24. Cf. Jakob ben Reuben's use of *prṣwp;* cf. also Jean-Marie Paulus Bauchet, *'Or we-'Osher* (Jerusalem: 1945), p. 41.
25. Cf. p. 26.
26. Cf. p. 42.
27. Abraham Eben-Shoshan, *Ha-millon ha-Ḥadash* [*The New Dictionary*] (Jerusalem: 1958), p. 607.
28. *Ibid.*, p. 382.
29. *Ibid.*, p. 1519.
30. *Ibid.*, pp. 114–15.
31. Giovanni Battista Jona also referred to Pope Clement IX with the title *qdwš hkhn hgdwl* "holy high priest"; see above, p. 68.
32. Eben-Shoshan, *Ha-millon ha-Ḥadash*, p. 136.
33. E.g., Profiat Duran, and Isaac de Troki in *Ḥizzuq 'Emunah*.
34. *'Or we-'Osher*, p. 351.
35. *Millon ʿIbri Shalem* [*The Complete Hebrew Dictionary*], 3 vols. (Ramat-Gan: 1969–1971).
36. Eliezer Ben-Yehuda, *Millon ha-Lashon ha-ʿIbrit* 2:778; Eben-Shoshan, *Ha-millon ha-Ḥadash*, p. 1070.
37. *Gephen Poriyah* (Jerusalem: 1946), p. 45.
38. Rabbi Zolli was baptized in Rome in 1946, receiving his Christian name Eugenio from his godfather, Pope Pius XII, and spent the rest of his life in the Vatican as librarian and hebraist.
39. Dionys Schötz, "Makkabäische Brüder," *LTK*, 2nd ed. 6 (1960): 1319.
40. H. A. R. Gibb and J. H. Kramers, eds., *Shorter Encyclopedia of Islam* (Leiden: 1961), s.v. "Shahid," p. 515.
41. Matthew was also issued in an unpointed edition.—TRANS.
42. Bauchet's revision of the complete New Testament, *Ha-berit ha-Ḥadashah be-ʿIbrit* [*The New Testament in Hebrew*], was published at Rome in 1975, bearing the imprimatur of Victor Guazzelli, V.C., Westminster, Great Britain, dated July 3, 1972.—TRANS.
43. Gustaf Dalman, *Jesus-Jeshua*, p. 134.
44. *The Words of Jesus* (Edinburgh: 1902), pp. 28–29.
45. *Évangile selon Saint Marc*, 5th ed. (Paris: 1929), pp. xviii–xix.
46. "Hebrew Background of the Gospels," pp. 67–68.
47. *The Gospel According to St. Mark* (London: 1902), p. 102.
48. "The Faith of Paul," *JJS* 3 (1952): 103–4.
49. "'In My Name,'" *ASTI* 5 (1966–1967): 101ff.
50. *Jesus*, trans. Ronald Walls (New York: 1969), p. 20.

51. Jacob Levy, *Wörterbuch über die Talmudim und Midraschim* (Berlin: 1924) 3:338.

52. Eben-Shoshan cites several examples in this sense, with some from the works of Shmuel Yosef Agnon; *Ha-millon ha-Ḥadash,* p. 1215.

53. *'Or we-'Osher,* p. 21.

54. Jean-Marie Paulus Bauchet, "Hebrew-English Church Glossary," p. 1338, no. 3371.

55. See above, p. 25.

56. See above, pp. 30–31.

57. David Kaufmann, *Geschichte der Attributenlehre in der jüdischen Religionsphilosophie des Mittelalters von Saadja bis Maimûm* (1877; reprint ed., Amsterdam: 1967), pp. 38ff.

58. *Kuzari* i.4; cf. David Cassel, ed., *Das buch Kusari des Jehudah ha-Levi;* Jehudah ibn Tibbon version (Leipzig: 1853), p. 10.

59. Gustaf Dalman, *Aramäisch-Neuhebräisches Handwörterbuch,* p. 426.

60. Ehud Ben-Yehuda and David Weinstein, eds., *Hebrew-English Dictionary* (New York: 1961), p. 298.

61. See above, n. 23.

62. *Ha-millon ha-Ḥadash* 7:2715.

63. Edward A. Levenston and Reuben Sivan, comps. (Tel-Aviv: 1966), p. 1161.

64. [J. Roussillon], "Les termes hébreux en théologie chrétienne," *RT* 1 (1960): 84.

65. William Oscar Emil Oesterley cites several sources as reliable evidence for his claim that "the ʿAlenu was of pre-Christian origin, and was adopted by the early Christian churches in their worship service" (*The Jewish Background of the Christian Liturgy* [Oxford: 1925], pp. 68, 144).

66. Bauchet repeats the same trite argument in his list of trinitarian proofs in *'Or we-'Osher,* p. 253.

67. E.g., the text of the Passover Haggadah (suggested by David Daube, "He That Cometh" [sermon delivered at St. Paul's Cathedral, London, October 12, 1966], p. 12); the ʿAlenu prayer (Cecil Roth, *Short History,* pp. 214, etc.); and the famous *Birkat hamminim,* the malediction against heretics (Ismar Elbogen, *Der jüdische Gottesdienst in seiner geschichtlichen Entwicklung* [Leipzig: 1913], p. 38; Hermann L. Strack and Paul Billerbeck, *Kommentar zum Neuen Testament* 4:208ff.).

68. The events, data, and details of the present account are drawn largely from personal notes and correspondence with the priests and religious concerned, to whom I must express here my gratitude for their assistance and cooperation. The many documents and provisional texts which they made available to me have been of the greatest value for my research.

69. So Eduard Y. Kutscher, "Aramaic," *EJ* 3 (Jerusalem: 1971): 259–287.

70. *La Liturgie Syrienne—Anaphore des douze apôtres* (Paris: 1950), with an abstract of the apostolic letter of Pope Pius XII, "In Suprema ad Orientales" (1948).

71. Geddes MacGregor, *Literary History,* p. 28.

72. One of the reasons was the trilingual inscription on the Cross, in Hebrew, Latin, and Greek (John 19:20).

73. Herbert Weiner, *The Wild Goats of Ein Gedi* (Cleveland: 1963), p. 47.

74. As it is translated in the Jerusalem Bible (e.g., Exod. 24:5; 32:6) and other versions (e.g., NEB "shared-offerings," TEV "fellowship offerings").

75. "The celebration of the Holy Mass is essentially a community action . . ." (Anselm Schott, *Das vollständige Römische Messbuch*, 8th ed. [Freiburg im Breisgau: 1941], pp. 4–5).

76. Cf. Bauchet and his struggle with the Hebrew word for Trinity; see above, pp. 112–13.

77. For examples from the *Mekilta* and the codices, cf. David Hoffmann, *Der Schulchan-Aruch und die Rabbinen über das Verhältniss der Juden zu Andersgläubigen* (Berlin: 1885), esp. ch. 15, pp. 142ff.

78. E.g., in the weekday morning service, in the blessing immediately following reference to the Torah: *wḥyy ʿwlm btwknw* . . . "and hast planted everlasting life in our midst."

79. Cf. David Hill, *Greek Words and Hebrew Meanings: Studies in the Semantics of Soteriological Terms*. NTSM 5 (Cambridge: 1967), pp. 183ff.

80. Cf. James Barr, *Biblical Words for Time*, 2nd rev. ed. SBT 33 (Naperville, Illinois: 1969), p. 70; also Ernst Jenni, "Das Wort ʿōlām im Alten Testament," *ZAW* 64 (1952): 197–248; 65 (1953): 1–35.

81. Introduction to *Das vollständige Römische Messbuch*, pp. 5–6.

82. "Catholic Life in Israel. II. Comment: Liturgy and Sacred Art in Israel," *CNI* 21/2 (1970): 18.

83. The information in this section is based on personal notes, documents, and liturgical texts most kindly placed at my disposal by the priests and religious concerned.

84. Since the reunification of Jerusalem in June 1967 it has been surpassed by the Greek Orthodox church.

85. Cyrille Charon [Karalevsky], *Histoire des Patriarcats Melkites (Alexandrie, Antíoche, Jérusalem) depuis le schisme monophysite du sixième siècle jusqu'à nos jours* (Rome: 1910) 3:557ff.

86. Kutscher, "Aramaic"; cf. "Das zur Zeit Jesu gesprochene Aramäische," *ZNW* 51 (1960): 46–54.

87. This *sdr hʿbwdh* is still among the additional prayers of the annual Day of Atonement liturgy.

88. Founded in 1950 by the Finnish Missionary Society, the school at first accepted only Jewish orphans, foundlings, and refugee children, but it soon expanded its program to include other categories of Jewish elementary school children with the clear purpose of converting them to Lutheran Christianity.

89. *Evangelisches Gesangbuch*, no. 346.

90. Published in Jerusalem by Šalhebet-YH.

91. According to Rabbi Akiba in *Mek.* Exod. 21:30 (93a) and Rabbi Ishmael ben Yoḥanan ben Baroqa in *B. Qam.* 40a.

92. From the brochure *Beit Abraham* (Jerusalem: 1965).

93. I have been requested to guard the anonymity of the Israeli respondent, and accordingly quote only his words.

94. See above, pp. 80–81.

95. From the group's prospectus, *Nes Ammim—Christliche Siedlung in Israel* (Bonn and Bad Godesberg: 1975).

96. *Idem.*

97. Newsletter, February 1970, p. 5.

98. *Petaḥim,* Hebrew-English bimonthly of Jewish thought, 5 (August 1968): 13.

99. *Neweh-Shalom,* St. Isaiah House Bulletin (Summer 1970).

100. Led in December 1967 by the Swedish diplomat Gunnar V. Jarring

under appointment by Secretary General U Thant as a special representative of the United Nations to promote a peaceful and accepted settlement in the Near East following the war of June 8–15, 1967.

101. Peter Schneider, *Ecumenical Theological Research Fraternity Bulletin* 1 (1969).

102. See above, pp. 101–2.

103. See above, pp. 83–84.

104. Eben-Shoshan, *Ha-millon ha-Ḥadash,* p. 942.

105. *Jesus-Jeshua,* p. 8.

106. E.g., in *Tanḥuma Beḥuqqotai* 8; *Deut. Rab.* 5; cf. Eben-Shoshan, *Ha-millon ha-Ḥadash,* p. 2847.

107. Eben-Shoshan, *Ha-millon ha-Ḥadash,* p. 217.

108. From the prayer of remembrance ʿOd Yizkor; cf. Eben-Shoshan, *Ha-millon ha-Ḥadash, ad loc.*

109. *HE* iii.39, where Matthew's collection of logia is mentioned.

110. *Jesus-Jeshua,* p. 13.

111. Helmut Gollwitzer, "Ausser Christus kein Heil? (Johannes 14,6)," in *Antijudäismus im Neuen Testament? Exegetische und systematische Beiträge,* ed. Willehad Paul Eckert, Nathan Peter Levinson, and Martin Stöhr. ACJD 2 (Munich: 1967), p. 175.

112. Cited in Joel Carmichael, *The Death of Jesus* (New York: 1962), pp. 21–22. Carmichael, Hugh J. Schonfield, and other authors do not regard the act of Judas as an intentional betrayal.

113. *Hebrew Translation of Mark* (Jerusalem: 1966).

114. The following citations and conclusions are from my notes on a lecture by Lindsey on October 19, 1969, or from the introduction to his diglot edition of the Gospel of Mark, pp. 9–65.

115. "A Modified Two-Document Theory of the Synoptic Dependence and Interdependence," *NT* 6 (1963): 239–263.

116. See above, n. 50.

117. Eberhard Nestle, Erwin Nestle, and Kurt Aland, *Novum Testamentum Graece,* 25th ed. (Stuttgart: 1963).

118. E.g., *b. Šabb.* 112b.

119. Eben-Shoshan, *Ha-millon ha-Ḥadash,* p. 269.

120. Cf. Rabin, *Toladot ha-Lashon,* p. 49, with reference to the transcription of Hebrew words in the second column of Origen's *Hexapla.*

121. *Mark: Greek-Hebrew Diglot,* p. 75.

122. See above, pp. 109–10.

123. E.g., *Pesaḥ.* 49b; *Giṭ.* 60a; *Soṭa* vii.8.

124. Although his exact title in Modern Hebrew is *ywšb r'š hknst* (lit. "chairman of the Knesset").

125. *B. Yoma* vii.1.

126. As in *b. Pesaḥ.* iv.5; *Tosepta Yebam.* i.11.

127. Depending on his material, the *ḥrš* may also be called a mason (2 Sam. 5:11), a smith (1 Sam. 13:19), or a carpenter (2 Sam. 5:11).

128. *Sacred Sites and Ways: Studies in the Topography of the Gospels,* trans. Paul P. Levertoff (New York: 1935), p. 201.

129. *Gen. Rab.* liii.8; *j. Ketub.* 25; *b. Yebam.* 113a.

130. *Gen. Rab.* liii.8.

131. Hill, *Greek Words and Hebrew Meanings,* pp. 61ff.

132. *J. Ber.* 5c; *Sanh.* 22b; cf. Eben-Shoshan, *Ha-millon ha-Ḥadash,* p. 2869.

133. *Jesus,* p. 29.

134. "Ο ΥΙΟΣ ΜΟΥ Ο ΑΓΑΠΗΤΟΣ," *JTS* 27 (1926): 113–129; cited also in Walter Bauer, *A Greek-English Lexicon of the New Testament and Other Early Christian Literature,* 2nd ed., trans. and rev. W. F. Arndt and F. W. Danker (Chicago: 1979), p. 6.

135. Shlomo Pines, *Jewish Christians of the Early Centuries,* p. 63.

136. "Israel, My Firstborn—and the Sonship of Jesus, a Theme of Moslem Anti-Christian Polemics," in *Studies in Mysticism and Religion,* ed. Efraim Elimelech Urbach, Raphael Jehudah Zwi Werblowsky, and Chaim Wirszubski (Jerusalem: 1967), pp. 177–190.

137. *Ha-millon ha-Ḥadash,* p. 1365.

138. *Šabb.* 128a–b.

139. *Jesus,* p. 46.

140. *Maʿaś.* iv.5.

141. *Jewish Christians of the Early Centuries,* p. 63.

142. A. Sebastianus Marmardji, ed., *Diatessaron de Tatien* (Beirut: 1935), p. 66.

143. *Die Botschaft Jesu—Damals und Heute* (Bern: 1959), pp. 27ff.

144. *Jesus: Der Mann aus Nazareth und seine Zeit.* Themen der Theologie 1 (Stuttgart: 1969), pp. 79ff.

145. Eben-Shoshan, *Ha-millon ha-Ḥadash,* p. 2156.

146. For a list of quotations from Strabo, Flavius Josephus, etc., cf. George Wesley Buchanan, "Mark 11.15–19: Brigands in the Temple," *HUCA* 30 (1959): 169–177; 31 (1960): 103–5.

147. E.g., *Ber.* 57b; 59a; *Sipre* on Deut. 32:24.

148. Echoing Deut. 33:12.

149. E.g., *Šebu.* iii.1, 5, 8, 10.

150. On scorn for tax collectors, cf. *B. Qam.* x.1; 113a; *Sanh.* 26b.

151. *Gen. Rab.* 46 (29a); *Baraita Ned.* 32a.

152. Hillel says in *Šabb.* 31a: ". . . That is the whole law; the rest is interpretation. Go and learn!"

153. "With confidence in the Rock of Israel . . ." echoing 2 Sam. 23:3.

154. Cf. Lindsey's translation of Mark 8:37, p. 163 above.

155. See above, n. 131.

156. Also Flavius Josephus *Ant.* xviii.3.1.

157. *Ibid.,* 116–19.

158. "Josephus on Jesus," *JHS* 1 (1968): 290.

159. E.g., Deut. 21:13; 24:1; Mal. 2:11.

160. E.g., Gen. 16:3; Num. 30:8, 12.

161. Cf. Bauchet on Matt. 1:18, p. 108 above.

162. *Sipre* Num. 15:30–31; *Para.* 112 (33a); *Sanh.* 99b; *Sukk.* 52a.

163. *Sanh.* vi.4; 46a.

164. Billerbeck admits that there is no element of "blasphemy . . . in Jesus' witness to himself." He accepts the trial of Jesus before the Sanhedrin as a fact and accuses the high court of "perverting justice" (*Kommentar zum Neuen Testament,* pp. 1007–8).

165. *Jesus-Jeshua,* p. 105.

166. Rashi, *Sepher ha-ʾOrah* [*Book of the Light*] i.43.

167. Cf. Joachim Jeremias, *Jerusalem in the Time of Jesus,* trans. F. H. Cave and C. H. Cave, 3rd ed. (Philadelphia: 1969), pp. 77–84. The figure four thousand represents about 0.1 percent of the Jewish population of the period.

168. "Der Prozess Jesu im Religionsunterricht," in *Judenhass—Schuld der*

Christen?!, ed. Willehad Paul Eckert and Ernst Ludwig Ehrlich (Essen: 1964), p. 132.

169. Cf. *'Em* 5 (1970): 220–256; also *FF* 7 (1980): 17–23.

170. Cf. 2 Kgs. 15:10, MT; Eben-Shoshan, *Ha-millon ha-Ḥadash*, p. 2277.

171. *Ned.* 41a.

172. After the first cup of wine is raised and replaced on the table, the words are said: "Go and learn (*ṣ' wlmd*) what Laban the Aramean meant . . ."

173. *Exod. Rab.* xv.4; *Num. Rab.* 8 (149a).

174. The New Testament was published by the United Bible Societies in Jerusalem in 1976. The translators included the Rev. Magne Solheim (a Lutheran and representative of the United Bible Societies), Dr. Robert L. Lindsey (Baptist Convention in Israel), and Fr. Gabriel Grossman, O.P. (Dominican Institute of St. Isaiah); *The Church Herald* (May 13, 1977), p. 5—TRANS.

175. *Die Schrift und Luther* (Berlin: 1926); cited in Rolf Rendtorff, "Martin Bubers Bibelübersetzung," *'Em* 5 (1970): 96.

176. Martin Buber, *Gesammelte Werke* 2:1182.

177. Dizengoff Street is in the center of Tel-Aviv and is the modern Israeli symbol of "high life," hippies, and youthful irresponsibility.

178. "Catholic Life in Israel," p. 19.

179. The Memorial of Pascal, a parchment amulet dated November 23, 1654: ". . . Dieu d'Abraham, Dieu d'Isaac, Dieu de Jacob, Non des philosophes et des savants . . ." (". . . God of Abraham, God of Isaac, God of Jacob, not of the philosophers and the scholars . . .").

180. Markus Barth, "What Can a Jew Believe about Jesus—and Still Remain a Jew?" *JES* 2 (1965): 383 (originally an address at the Tree of Life Synagogue, Pittsburgh, February 24, 1965).

181. From the constitution of the UCCI, published in the pamphlet *The United Christian Council Invites You* (Jerusalem: 1962), p. 1.

182. Weiner, *The Wild Goats of Ein Gedi*, p. 274.

183. *UCCI News* 1/4 (1970): 3.

184. *Ibid.*, p. 17.

185. *Ibid.*, p. 19.

186. *Ibid.*, 1/3 (1970): 10–11.

187. *Ibid.*, 1/4 (1970): 12.

188. Cited in Johann Eck, *Ains Juden Buechleins Verlegung*, p. 46.

189. See above, p. 16.

190. "God Spoke in Hebrew," *EncT* 2 (1968): 89ff.

191. The Ulpan is an intensive Hebrew language course designed especially for new immigrants.

192. Otto Betz, Rudolf Mayer, and P. Schäfer.

193. "Der 5. Weltkongress für Jüdische Studien in Jerusalem," in *Das Institutum Judaicum der Universität Tübingen im Jahre 1968–1970* (Tübingen: 1970).

194. In his magnum opus, *The Life of Jesus*, trans. Charles Edwin Wilbour (1864; reprint ed., New York: 1955).

195. "Kirche als Israel Gottes und das Problem der Judenmission," in *Jüdisches Volk—Gelobtes Land: Die biblischen Landverheissungen als Problem des jüdischen Selbstverständnisses und der christlichen Theologie*, ed. Willehad Paul Eckert, Nathan Peter Levinson, and Martin Stöhr. ACJD 3 (Munich: 1970), pp. 334–35.

196. "Theologisch-politischer Traktat," *Yedi'ot Ḥadashot* (November 28, 1969).

197. From an Israeli government press release issued in Jerusalem on March 1, 1964.

198. From a report of the Israeli Ministry of Religions issued in Jerusalem in late June 1970 and published in the press (e.g., Jerusalem *Post* [June 29, 1970], p. 6).

199. Robert L. Lindsey, "The Ecclesiological-Ecumenical Issue," *UCCI News* 1 (1970): 15.

200. The hapax legomenon "epioúsios" (which occurs also in the Pater Noster in Luke 11:3) has been translated variously as "spiritual bread," "daily bread" ("cotidianum" in the Vulgate of Luke and as a variant reading in some manuscripts of Matthew; also *ywm ywm* "everyday" by Petrus Negri), "bread necessary for being" (which is closest to the literal meaning of "epì ousían"), "regular bread" (represented by *thamia* in the earliest Hebrew version [see above, pp. 7–8]; by *tamid* in the Pater Noster from Cusa [cf. p. 9]; by "thamid" in the "German" Pater Noster [cf. p. 10]; and *tmydy* in Shemtob ibn Shaprut's *Touchstone*), or as *mḥr* "our bread for the morrow" in the lost Hebrew Gospel (according to Jerome). In this last form the fourth petition stands in contradiction to Matt. 6:34 ("do not be anxious about tomorrow").

201. As of August 1975.

202. *Gen. Rab.* 47 (29c); *Pesiq. R.* 42 (178a); *Midr. Lam.* 1:5 (52a).

203. E.g., Athanasius ("Perì tēs enanthrōpēseōs toû lógou"; PG 25:125) and in the Nicene Creed ("enanthrōpēsanta"; Heinrik Joseph Dominik Denzinger, *Enchiridion Symbolorum et Definitionum,* p. 30).

204. Cf. Eben-Shoshan, *Ha-millon ha-Ḥadash,* p. 125.

205. *Šabb.* 116a.

206. *B. Ber.* ix.2.

207. Lindsey, *Mark: Greek-Hebrew Diglot,* p. 71.

208. United Christian Council in Israel, *Christian Terms in Modern Hebrew* (Jerusalem: 1966), p. 15, no. 198.

209. *The Essence of Judaism,* trans. Victor Grubenwieser and Leonard Pearl, ed. Irving Howe (New York: 1961), p. 5.

210. E.g., pp. 198ff. in Herbert Albert Laurens Fisher, *A History of Europe* (Tel-Aviv: 1952), which is among the readings for a required course at the Institute of Medieval Studies at the Hebrew University.

211. (Jerusalem: 1964), p. 11.

212. Rudolf Stählin and Oskar Simmel, *"Sakrament" in christliche Religion* (Frankfurt: 1969), pp. 275–76.

213. UCCI, *Christian Terms in Modern Hebrew,* p. 11.

214. Stählin and Simmel, *"Sakrament" in christliche Religion,* pp. 275–76.

215. UCCI, *Christian Terms in Modern Hebrew,* p. 43.

216. E.g., Ps. 84:12 (Eng. v. 11; Vulg. 83:12); Prov. 3:34; Zech. 12:10.

217. Stählin and Simmel, *"Sakrament" in christliche Religion,* p. 275.

218. *Roš Haš.* iv.5.

219. UCCI, *Christian Terms in Modern Hebrew,* p. 30.

220. [Roussillon], "Les termes hébreux en théologie chrétienne," p. 98.

221. E.g., Colbi, *Ha-naṣrut,* p. 14; Fisher, *A History of Europe,* p. 199.

222. *A Concordance to the Septuagint* (1897; reprint ed., Oxford: 1975).

223. *UCCI News* 1/3 (1970): 15–16.

224. *Analytical Concordance to the Delitzsch Hebrew Translation of the New Testament, Containing 90,000 Entries from the New Testament with Equivalents from the Greek Original,* comp. Samuel Paul Re'emi (Jerusalem). Vols. 1 (א-ה) and 2 (ו-מ) were published in 1973 and vol. 3 (נ-ת) in 1974.—TRANS.

VI. Supplement: Further Developments in Christian Neo-Hebraica

1. Leo Baeck, *Das Evangelium als Urkunde der jüdischen Glaubensgeschichte* (Berlin: 1938).
2. *Paulus des Apostels Briefe,* p. 46.
3. *Idem.*
4. *Ibid.*, p. 121.
5. *Übersetzungsarbeit,* p. 32.
6. *Paulus des Apostels Briefe,* p. 121.
7. See above, p. 183.
8. Cf. pp. 26, 112–14, 184.
9. Cf. pp. 24–25, 39–42, 103, 127–28, 184.
10. Cf. pp. 26, 32, 37, 54–55, 68, 185–86.
11. Cf. pp. 32, 41, 81, 186–87.
12. Cf. pp. 106–7, 187.
13. Cf. pp. 41–42, 125, 187–88.
14. Cf. pp. 24, 102, 188–89.
15. Cf. p. 189.
16. Cf. pp. 189–190.
17. Cf. pp. 32, 104, 117, 119, 130, 190.
18. Cf. pp. 190–91; 227, n. 224.

VII. Conclusion

1. Jürgen Moltmann, "Der Gott der Hoffnung," in *Gott Heute,* ed. Norbert Kutschki (Mainz: 1967), p. 121.
2. Cited in Jules Isaac, *Jesus and Israel,* p. 184.
3. See above, p. 5.
4. Naphtali Hertz Tur-Sinai, *The Revival of the Hebrew Language,* p. 23.
5. "Hebrew Background of the Gospels," p. 91.
6. See above, pp. 158–59.
7. *Mark: Greek-Hebrew Diglot,* pp. 9, 77; see also p. 3 above.
8. "Dead Sea Sect," pp. 263–64.
9. Otto Betz, "Israel bei Jesus und im Neuen Testament," in *Jüdisches Volk—Gelobtes Land,* ed. Willehad Paul Eckert, Nathan Peter Levinson, and Martin Stöhr, p. 275.
10. *Ibid.,* p. 280.
11. See above, pp. 185; 207, n. 7; cf. *Šabb.* 116a, where Rabbi Meir speaks of *'wn glywn* "false scroll" and Rabbi Yoḥanan of *'wn glywn* "wicked scroll."
12. "Die Auseinandersetzung mit dem entstehenden Christentum," in *Die Lehren des Judentums—Nach den Quellen,* ed. Simon Bernfeld 5 (Berlin: 1928): 57.
13. E.g., Heinz Kremers on "Jesus, the Prophet from Nazareth" (Hebrew University, Jerusalem, May 8, 1968) and Kurt Schubert on "The Pharisees, Their History and Their World View" (Bar-Ilan University, Ramat-Gan, February 9, 1971).

Bibliography

Abelard, Peter. *Dialogus inter Philosophum, Judaeum et Christianum.* PL 178:1609–1682.

Abrahams, Israel. "Some Rabbinic Ideas on Prayer." *JQR* 20 (1908): 272–293.

Academy of the Hebrew Language. *Sepher ha-Mekorot: Ha-millon ha-Hisṭori la-Lashon ha-ʿIbrit* [*The Historical Dictionary of the Hebrew Language*]: *Prospectus*. Jerusalem: 1969.

Ackroyd, Peter R. "Two Hebrew Notes." *ASTI* 5 (1966–1967): 82–86.

Agobard of Lyons. *De insolentia Judaeorum.* PL 104:69–76.

Alcalay, Reuben. *Millon ʿIbri Shalem* [*The Complete Hebrew Dictionary*]. 3 vols. Ramat-Gan: 1969–1971.

Algermissen, K. "Juden III. Judenmission." *LTK* 5 (1933): 689–690.

Allony, Nehemya, and Loewinger, D. S. *Roshimat taṣlume Kitbe-ha-yad me-ʿIbriyim be-Makhon* [*Catalog of Photocopies in the Institute of Hebrew Manuscripts*]. Vol. 3: *Hebrew Manuscripts in the Vatican.* Jerusalem: 1968.

Alonso Schökel, Luis. *Sprache Gottes und der Menschen.* Düsseldorf: 1968.

Altaner, Berthold. "Die Durchführung des Vienner Konzilbeschlusses über die Errichtung von Lehrstühlen für orientalischen Sprachen." *ZKG* 52 (1933): 226–236.

———. "Zur Kenntnis des Hebräischen im Mittelalter." *BZ* 21 (1933): 288–308.

Amulo of Lyons. *Liber contra Judaeos.* PL 116:141–184.

Anderson, A. A. "The Use of 'Ruaḥ' in 1QS, 1QH and 1QM." *JSS* 7 (1962): 293–303.

Bacher, Wilhelm. "Die Ausdrücke, mit denen die Tradition bezeichnet wird." *JQR* 20 (1908): 572–596.

———. "Die hebräische Sprachwissenschaft (Vom 10. bis zum 16. Jahrhundert)." In *Die jüdische Literatur seit Abschluss des Kanons,* ed. Jakob Winter and August Wünsche 2 (1894): 133–235.

Bacon, Roger. *Opus Maius.* Ed. J. H. Bridges. 3 vols. 1897–1900. Reprint. 2 vols. Philadelphia: 1928.

Baeck, Leo. *Aus drei Jahrtausenden.* Tübingen: 1958.

———. "Die Auseinandersetzung mit dem entstehenden Christentum." In *Die Lehren des Judentums—Nach den Quellen,* ed. Simon Bernfeld, 5:57ff. Berlin: 1928.

______. *The Essence of Judaism*. Trans. Victor Grubenwieser and Leonard Pearl. Ed. Irving Howe. New York: 1961.

______. *Das Evangelium als Urkunde der jüdischen Glaubensgeschichte*. Berlin: 1938.

______. "The Faith of Paul." *JJS* 3 (1952): 93–110. Reprinted in *Judaism and Christianity*, pp. 139–168.

______. *Judaism and Christianity*. Trans. Walter Kaufmann. Philadelphia: 1958.

______. *Paulus, die Pharisäer und das Neue Testament*. Frankfort: 1961.

Bäck, Samuel. "Die Apologeten vom 14. bis Ende des 18. Jahrhunderts." In *Die jüdische Literatur seit Abschluss des Kanons*, ed. Jakob Winter and August Wünsche 3 (1896): 655–719.

Baer, Yitzhak Fritz. *A History of the Jews in Christian Spain*. Trans. Louis Schoffman. 2 vols. Philadelphia: 1961–1966.

Bahr, Gordon J. "The Seder of Passover and the Eucharistic Words." *NT* 22 (1970): 181–202.

Baraut, Cipriano. "Un tratado inédito de Joaquin de Fiore: De vita sancti Benedicti et de Officio divino secundum eius doctrinam." *AST* 24 (1951): 33–90.

Baron, Salo Wittmayer. *A Social and Religious History of the Jews*. 8 vols. 2nd rev. ed. New York: 1952.

Barr, James. *Biblical Words for Time*. 2nd rev. ed. SBT 33. Naperville, Illinois: 1969.

______. "Hypostatization of Linguistic Phenomena in Modern Theological Interpretation." *JJS* 7 (1962): 85–94.

______. *The Semantics of Biblical Language*. Oxford: 1961.

Barth, Markus. *Israel und die Kirche im Brief des Paulus an die Epheser*. Munich: 1959.

______. "What Can a Jew Believe about Jesus—and Still Remain a Jew?" *JES* 2 (1965): 382–405.

Bartolocci, Giulio. *Bibliotheca Magna Rabbinica*. 5 vols. Rome: 1675–1694.

Basnage de Beauval, Jacques. *Histoire des Juifs*. 9 vols. Rotterdam: 1716.

Bauchet, Jean-Marie Paulus. *Ha-berit ha-Ḥadashah be-ʿIbrit* [*The New Testament in Hebrew*]. Rome: 1975.

______. *Evangelium secundum Marcum: Ha-beśorah ha-Qedoshah Marqos* [*The Gospel of St. Mark*]. Jerusalem: 1950.

______. *Evengelium secundum Matthaeum: Ha-beśorah ha-Qedoshah-Mattay* [*The Gospel of St. Matthew*]. Jerusalem: 1948.

______. *Gephen Poriyah* [*A Fruitful Vine*]. Jerusalem: 1946.

______. *L'Hebreu pour tous*. Baghdad: 1940.

______. "Hebrew-English Church Glossary." Unpublished manuscript. N.d.

______. *'Or we-'Osher* [*Light and Salvation*]. Jerusalem: 1945.

______. *Toledot Nephesh* [*History of a Soul*]. Jerusalem: 1948.

______. *Yalquṭ ha-Beśorah ha-Qedoshah* [*Anthology of the Holy Gospels*]. Rome: 1975.

Bauer, Walter. *A Greek-English Lexicon of the New Testament and Other Early Christian Literature*. 2nd ed. Trans. and rev. W. F. Arndt and F. W. Danker. Chicago: 1979.

Ben Chorin, Shalom. "Theologisch-politischer Traktat." *Yediʿot Ḥadashot,* November 28, 1969.

Ben-Yehuda, Ehud, and Weinstein, David, eds. *Hebrew-English Dictionary.* New York: 1961.

Ben-Yehuda, Eliezer. *Millon ha-Lashon ha-ʿIbrit* [*A Complete Dictionary of Ancient and Modern Hebrew*]: *Thesaurus Totius Hebraitatis.* 16 vols. 1908–1958. Reprint. New York: 1960.

Berger, David. *The Jewish-Christian Debate in the High Middle Ages: A Critical Edition of the Niẓẓaḥon Vetus.* Judaica: Texts and Translations 4. Philadelphia: 1979.

Berger, Samuel. *Quam notitiam linguae Hebraicae habuerint christiani medii aevi temporibus in Gallia.* Nancy: 1893.

Bergmann, Juda. *Jüdische Apologetik im neutestamentlichen Zeitalter.* Berlin: 1908.

Berthier, André. "Un Maître orientaliste du XIIIe siècle: Raymond Martin, O.P.," *Archivum Fratrum Praedicatorum* 6 (Rome: 1936): 267–311.

Betz, Otto. "Israel bei Jesus und im Neuen Testament." In *Jüdisches Volk—Gelobtes Land,* ed. Willehad Paul Eckert, Nathan Peter Levinson, and Martin Stöhr, pp. 275–289.

Bevan, Edwyn Robert, and Singer, Charles, eds. *The Legacy of Israel.* Oxford: 1927.

Beyer, Klaus. *Semitische Syntax im Neuen Testament.* Studien zum Umwelt des Neuen Testaments 1. Göttingen: 1962.

Biscioni, Antonio Maria. *Bibliotheca ebraicae graecae florentinae sive Bibliothecae mediceo-laurentianae catalogus.* Vol. 1: *Bibliothecae hebraicae florentinae catalogus.* Florence: 1757.

Black, Matthew. *An Aramaic Approach to the Gospels and Acts.* 2nd ed. Oxford: 1954.

______. *The Scrolls and Christian Origins.* New York: 1961.

______. "Second Thoughts. IX. The Semitic Elements in the New Testament." *ET* 77 (1965): 20–23.

Blinzler, Josef. *The Trial of Jesus.* Trans. Isabel McHugh and Florence McHugh. Westminster, Maryland: 1959.

Bloch, Peter. "Nachwirkungen des Alten Bundes in der christlichen Kunst." In *Monumenta Judaica,* ed. Konrad Schilling, 2:735–781.

Blum, Joshua. *Ha-beśorah lepi Yoḥanan* [*The Gospel According to John*]. Jerusalem: 1967.

______, and Eliḥai, Yoḥanan. *Beśorat Yeshuʿa ha-Mashiaḥ lepi Matityahu* [*The Gospel of Jesus the Messiah According to Matthew*]. Jerusalem: 1970.

Blumenkranz, Bernard. "Les auteurs chrétiens latins du Moyen Age sur les Juifs et le Judaïsme." *RÉJ* 109 (1948): 3–67; 111 (1951): 5–61; 113 (1954): 5–36; 114 (1955): 37–90; 117 (1958): 5–58.

______. "Das Bilderevangelium des Hasses." In *Judenhass—Schuld der Christen?!,* ed. Willehad Paul Eckert and Ernst Ludwig Ehrlich, pp. 249–256.

______. "Jüdische und christliche Konvertiten im jüdisch-christlichen Religionsgespräch des Mittelalters." In *Judentum im Mittelalter*, ed. Paul Wilpert, pp. 264–282.

Boman, Thorleif. *Hebrew Thought Compared with Greek*. Trans. Jules L. Moreau. New York: 1970.

Bonsirven, Joseph S. *Palestinian Judaism in the Time of Jesus Christ*. Trans. William Wolf. New York: 1964.

Borst, Arno. *Die Katharer*. Stuttgart: 1953.

Braun, Herbert. *Jesus: Der Mann aus Nazareth und seine Zeit*. Themen der Theologie 1. Stuttgart: 1969.

Browe, Peter. *Die Judenmission im Mittelalter und die Päpste*. MHP 6, coll. 8. Rome: 1942.

Bruce, Frederick Fyvie. "The Dead Sea Scrolls and Early Christianity." *BJRL* 49 (1966): 69–90.

Buchanan, Claudius. *Christian Researches in Asia, with Notices of the Translation of the Scriptures into the Oriental Languages*. Boston: 1811.

Buchanan, George Wesley. "Mark 11.15–19: Brigands in the Temple." *HUCA* 30 (1959): 169–177; 31 (1960): 103–5.

Bultmann, Rudolf. *The Theology of the New Testament*. Trans. Kendrick Grobel. 2 vols. New York: 1952–1955.

Burmeister, Karl Heinz. *Sebastian Münster: Versuch eines biographischen Gesamtbildes*. *BBG* 91 (1963).

Burton, Ernest De Witt. *Spirit, Soul, and Flesh*. Chicago: 1918.

Caddick, Richard. *The Four Gospels in Hebrew*. London: 1798.

Callenberg, Johann Heinrich. *Dritte Fortsetzung seines Berichtes von einem Versuch das arme jüdische Volck zur Erkänntnis und Annehmung der christlichen Wahrheit anzuleiten*. 18 vols. in 3. Halle: 1730–1735.

Canivez, Joseph Marie. *Statuta capitulorum generalium Ordinis Cisterciensis ad annum 1786*. Louvain: 1933–1941.

Carmichael, Joel. *The Death of Jesus*. New York: 1962.

Carmignac, Jean. "Une ancienne tradition allemande du Notre Père en Hébreu." *MIO* 15 (1969): 207–216.

______. "Hebrew Translations of the Lord's Prayer: An Historical Survey." In *Biblical and Near Eastern Studies: Essays in Honor of William Sanford LaSor*, ed. Gary A. Tuttle, pp. 18–79. Grand Rapids: 1978.

______. "Studies in the Hebrew Background of the Gospels." *ASTI* 7 (1968–1969): 64–93.

Cassel, David, ed. *Das buch Kusari des Jehudah ha-Levi*. Jehuda ibn Tibbon version. Leipzig: 1853.

Cassuto, Umberto. *I Manoscritti Palatini Ebraici della Biblioteca apostolica Vaticana e la loro storia*. Studi e testi 66. Vatican: 1935.

Charon [Karalevsky], Cyrille. *Histoire des Patriarcats Melkites (Alexandrie, Antíoche, Jérusalem) depuis le schisme monophysite du sixième siècle jusqu'à nos jours*. Rome: 1909–1910.

Chwolson [Khvol'son], Daniel Abramovich. "Der Am Ha-Aretz in der alten rabbinischen Literatur." *BEJ* (Leipzig: 1910), pp. 1–54.

______. *Das letzte Passamahl Christi und der Tag seines Todes*. St. Petersburg: 1892.

Cohn, Ḥaim Hermann. *The Trial and Death of Jesus*. New York: 1971.

Colbi, Saul P. *Ha-naṣrut* [*Christianity*]. Jerusalem: 1964.

______. *A Short History of Christianity in the Holy Land*. Tel-Aviv: 1965.

Cross, Frank Moore. *The Ancient Library of Qumran and Modern Biblical Studies*. Rev. ed., 1958. Reprint. Grand Rapids: 1980.

Cullmann, Oscar. *Baptism in the New Testament*. Trans. John Kelman Sutherland Reid. SBT 1. Chicago: 1950.

______. *Christ and Time*. Trans. Floyd V. Filson. Philadelphia: 1950.

Dalman, Gustaf Hermann. *Aramäisch-Neuhebräisches Handwörterbuch zu Targum, Talmud, und Midrasch*. 1897–1901. Reprint. Hildesheim: 1967.

______. "Das hebräische Neue Testament von Franz Delitzsch in neuer Ausgabe." *ThLB* 12/31 (July 31, 1891): 289–291.

______. *Jesus-Jeshua: Studies in the Gospels*. Trans. Paul P. Levertoff. 1929. Reprint. New York: 1971.

______. *Sacred Sites and Ways: Studies in the Topography of the Gospels*. Trans. Paul P. Levertoff. New York: 1935.

______. *The Words of Jesus*. Trans. D. M. Kay. Edinburgh: 1902.

Danby, Herbert. *The Mishnah*. 1933. Reprint. New York: 1967.

Dantine, Wilhelm. "Kirche als Israel Gottes und das Problem der Judenmission." In *Jüdisches Volk—Gelobtes Land,* ed. Willehad Paul Eckert, Nathan Peter Levinson, and Martin Stöhr, pp. 322–335.

Darlow, Thomas Herbert, and Moule, Horace Frederick. *Historical Catalogue of the Printed Editions of Holy Scripture*. Vol. 2: *Polyglots and Languages Other Than English*. 2 vols. in 4. London: 1903–1911. [Esp. pp. 701–737. Hebrew editions]

Daube, David. "He That Cometh." Sermon delivered at St. Paul's Cathedral, London, October 12, 1966.

______. *The New Testament and Rabbinic Judaism*. London: 1956.

Davidson, R. *Geschichte der Stadt Florenz vom 12, bis zum 16. Jahrhundert*. Berlin: 1896–1927.

Davies, William David. *Paul and Rabbinic Judaism*. 2nd ed. 1958. Reprint. Philadelphia: 1980.

De Dieu, Lodewijk. *Critica sacra, sive Animadversiones in loca quaedam difficiliora Veteris et Novi Testamenti*. Amsterdam: 1693.

De Le Roi, Johannes Friedrich Alexander. *Geschichte der evangelischen Judenmission seit Entstehung des neueren Judentums*. 2nd ed. 2 vols. in 1. Leipzig: 1899.

Delitzsch, Franz Julius. "Critical Observations on My Hebrew New Testament." *Exp,* 3rd ser. 9 (1889): 310–15.

______. *Eine neue hebräische Übersetzung des Neuen Testaments*. Leipzig: 1864.

______. *Eine Uebersetzungsarbeit von 52 Jahren*. SIJL 27 (1891).

______. "Das hebräische Neue Testament." *ThLB* 10/1 (January 4, 1889): 1–2.

______. "Neue Beobachtungen über hebräische Spracheigenthümlichkeiten I-XII." *ThLB* 10–11 (1889–1890).

______. *Paulus des Apostels Brief an die Römer, aus dem griechischen Urtext auf Grund des Sinai-Codex in das Hebräische übersetzt und aus Talmud und Midrasch erläutert*. Leipzig: 1870.

———. *Siphre ha-Berit ha-Ḥadashah Neʿtaqim me-Lashon Yon le-Lashon ʿIbrit* [*Books of the New Testament Translated from the Greek Language into the Hebrew Language*]. Leipzig: 1877. Rev. eds. 1878, 1880, 1882, 1883, 1892, 1899.

———. *Wissenschaft, Kunst, Judenthum*. Grimma: 1838.

Denifle, Heinrich. *Die Entstehung der Universitäten des Mittelalters bis 1400*. Berlin: 1885.

Denzinger, Heinrik Joseph Dominik. *Enchiridion Symbolorum et Definitionum*. 30th ed. Freiburg: 1955.

De Oxenedes, Johannes. *Chronica*. Ed. Henry Ellis. London: 1859.

De Rossi, Giovanni Bernardo. *Bibliotheca Judaica Antichristiana*. Parma: 1800.

De Troki, Isaac ben Abraham. *Liber Munimen Fidei: Ḥizzuq 'Emunah* [*Faith Strengthened*]. Trans. Moses Mocatta. 1851. Reprint. New York: 1970.

Doeve, Jan Willem. *Jewish Hermeneutics in the Synoptic Gospels and Acts*. Assen: 1953.

Driver, Samuel Rolles, and Neubauer, Adolph. *The Fifty-third Chapter of Isaiah According to the Jewish Interpreters*. 2 vols. 1876–1877. Reprint. New York: 1969.

Dubnov, Semen Markovich. *Weltgeschichte des jüdischen Volkes*. 10 vols. Berlin: 1927–1930.

Dubois, J. Marcel. "Catholic Life in Israel. II. Comment: Liturgy and Sacred Art in Israel." *CNI* 21/2 (1970): 18–20.

Dukes, Leopold. *Literaturhistorische Mitteilungen ueber die ältesten hebräischen Exegeten, Grammatiker und Lexikographen*. 2 vols. Stuttgart: 1844.

Dupont-Sommer, André. *The Dead Sea Scrolls*. Trans. E. Margaret Rowley. Oxford: 1952.

Du Tillet, Jean. *Evangelium Hebraicum Matthaei, recens e Judaeorum penetralibus erutum, cum interpretatione Latina* [*Hebrew Gospel of Matthew, newly brought forth from the hiding places of the Jews, with Latin interpretation*]. Paris: 1555.

Ebeling, Gerhard. "The Meaning of 'Biblical Theology.'" *JTS*, n.s. 6 (1955): 210–225.

Eben-Shoshan, Abraham. *Ha-millon ha-Ḥadash* [*The New Dictionary*]. 5 vols. Jerusalem: 1958–1962. Rev. ed. 7 vols. Jerusalem: 1966–1970.

Eck, Johann. *Ains Juden Buechleins Verlegung*. Ingolstadt: 1541.

Eckert, Willehad Paul. "Hoch- und Spätmittelalter—Katholischer Humanismus." In *Kirche und Synagogue*, ed. Karl Heinrich Rengstorf and Siegfried von Kortzfleisch, 1 (1968): 210–306.

———. "Martin Buber—Zwei Glaubensweise: Frage und Versuch einer Antwort." In *Judenhass—Schuld der Christen?!*, pp. 439–456.

———. "Das Verhältnis von Christen und Juden im Mittelalter und Humanismus: Ein Beitrag zur Geistes- und Kulturgeschichte." In *Monumenta Judaica*, ed. Konrad Schilling, 2:131–198.

———, and Ehrlich, Ernst Ludwig, eds. *Judenhass—Schuld der Christen?!* Essen: 1964.

———, Levinson, Nathan Peter, and Stöhr, Martin, eds. *Antijudäismus im*

Neuen Testament? Exegetische und systematische Beiträge. ACJD 2. Munich: 1967.

______. *Jüdisches Volk—Gelobtes Land: Die biblischen Landverheissungen als Problem des jüdischen Selbstverständnisses und der christlichen Theologie*. ACJD 3. Munich: 1970.

Edelmann, Rafael. "Jüdisches Geistesleben am Rhein von den Anfängen bis 1945." In *Monumenta Judaica*, ed. Konrad Schilling, 2:668–712.

Eisenstein, Judah David. *'Oṣar Hokoḥim* [*Anthology of Proofs*]. New York: 1928.

Elbogen, Ismar. *Der jüdische Gottesdienst in seiner geschichtlichen Entwicklung*. 4th ed. Hildesheim: 1962.

Eliḥai, Yoḥanan [J. Roussillon]. "Les termes hébreux en théologie chrétienne." *RT* 1 (1960): 80–99.

Epstein, Isidore. *The Babylonian Talmud*. 35 vols. 1935–1948. Reprint. 18 vols. London: 1961.

Eusebius. *The Ecclesiastical History*. Trans. Kirsopp Lake, John Ernest Leonard Oulton, and Hugh Jackson Lawlor. 2 vols. Loeb Classical Library. New York: 1926–1932.

Fahlgren, Karl Hjalmar. *Ṣᵉdāḳā: Nahestehende und entgegengesetzte Begriffe im Alten Testament*. Uppsala: 1932.

Farmer, William Reuben. *The Synoptic Problem: A Critical Analysis*. New York: 1964.

Federbusch, Simon. *Ha-lashon ha-ʿIbrit be-Yiśra'el ube-ʿAmmim* [*The Hebrew Language in Israel and the Nations*]. Jerusalem: 1967. [Esp. ch. 18, "Ha-ʿibrit be-ʿOlam ha-Noṣeri" ("Hebrew in the Christian World"), pp. 134–185]

Fisher, Herbert Albert Laurens. *A History of Europe*. Tel-Aviv: 1952. [Hebrew]

Flannery, Edward H. *The Anguish of the Jews: Twenty-three Centuries of Anti-Semitism*. New York: 1965.

Flusser, David Gustav. "Blessed are the Poor in Spirit . . . ." *IEJ* 10 (1960): 1–13.

______. "The Conclusion of Matthew in a New Jewish Christian Source," *ASTI* 5 (1967): 110–120.

______. "The Dead Sea Sect and Pre-Pauline Christianity." In *Aspects of the Dead Sea Scrolls*, ed. Chaim Rabin and Yigael Yadin. *ScrHier* 4:215–266. 2nd ed. Jerusalem: 1965.

______. *Jesus*. Trans. Ronald Walls. New York: 1969.

______. "Jewish Roots of the Liturgical Trishagion." *Immanuel* 3 (1973–1974): 37–43.

______. "Die konsequente Philologie." In *Almanach auf das Jahr 1963*, pp. 19ff. Hamburg: 1963.

Foerster, Werner. "Der Heilige Geist im Spätjudentum." *NTS* 8 (1962): 117–134.

Friedrich, Gerhard. "Die Problematik eines Theologischen Wörterbuchs zum Neuen Testament." In *Studia Evangelica*, ed. Kurt Aland et al., pp. 481–86. Texte und Untersuchungen zur Geschichte der altchristlichen Literatur 73. Berlin: 1959.

Fritsch, Theodor. *Antisemiten-Katechismus*. 25th ed. Leipzig: 1893.

Funk, Robert W. *A Greek Grammar of the New Testament and Other Early Christian Literature*. Chicago: 1961. [Translation and revision of Friedrich Blass and Albert Debrunner, *Grammatik der neutestamentlichen Griechisch*, 10th ed. (Göttingen: 1959)]

Ganz, Paul Leonhard. *Die Miniaturen der Baseler Universitätsmatrikel*. Basel: 1960.

Gehman, Henry Snyder. "The Hebraic Character of Septuagint Greek." *VT* 1 (1951): 81–90.

Geiger, Abraham. *Judaism and Its History*. Trans. Charles Newburgh. New York: 1911.

Geiger, Ludwig. *Johann Reuchlin: Sein Leben und seine Werk*. Leipzig: 1871.

______. *Das Studium der hebräischen Sprache in Deutschland vom Ende des XV. bis zur Mitte des XVI. Jahrhunderts*. Wroclaw: 1870.

Gesenius, Heinrich Friedrich Wilhelm. *Geschichte der hebräischen Sprache und Schrift*. Leipzig: 1815.

Gibb, Hamilton Alexander Rosskeen, and Kramers, Johannes Hendrik, eds. *Shorter Encyclopaedia of Islam*. Leiden: 1961.

Gidney, William Thomas. *The History of the London Society for Promoting Christianity amongst the Jews, from 1809 to 1908*. London: 1908.

______. *Missions to Jews*. Rev. ed. London: 1914.

Gislebertus, Crispinius. *Disputatio Judaei cum Christiano*. PL 159:1009–1036.

Goldstein, Morris. *Jesus in the Jewish Tradition*. New York: 1950.

Gollwitzer, Helmut. "Ausser Christus kein Heil? (Johannes 14, 6)." In *Antijudäismus im Neuen Testament?"* ed. Willehad Paul Eckert, Nathan Peter Levinson, and Martin Stöhr, pp. 171–194.

Graetz, Heinrich Hirsch. *Geschichte der Juden*. 9 vols. Leipzig: 1864.

______. *History of the Jews*. Ed. and trans. Bella Löwy et al. 6 vols. Philadelphia: 1891–1898.

Graf, Georg. *Geschichte der christlichen arabischen Literatur*. 5 vols. Vatican: 1944–1953.

Gregory I. *Concordia quorumdam testimoniorum S. Scripturae*. PL 79:659–678.

Gross, Henri. *Gallia Judaica*. 1897. Reprint. Amsterdam: 1969.

Grotius, Hugo. *Annotationes in Libros Evangeliorum*. Amsterdam: 1641.

Güdemann, Moritz. "Johannes-Evangelium und der Rabbinismus." *MGWJ* 37 (1893): 249–257, 297–303, 345–356.

Guttmann, Jakob. "Über einige Theologen des Franziskanerordens und ihre Beziehungen zum Judentum." *MGWJ* 40 (1896): 314–329.

Hadas, Moses. *Hellenistic Culture: Fusion and Diffusion*. New York: 1959.

Händler, George H. "Lexikon der Abbreviaturen." Appendix to *Aramäisch-Neuhebräisches Handwörterbuch*, ed. Gustaf Dalman.

Hamann, Karl Ludwig Friedrich. "De triplice psalterio Cusano." In *Realgymnasium des Johanneums zu Hamburg: Bericht über das 57. Schuljahr*, pp. 5ff. Hamburg: 1891.

Harnack, Adolf von. *Sprüche und Reden Jesu: Die zweite Quelle des Matthäus und Lukas*. Leipzig: 1907.

Hatch, Edwin. *Essays in Biblical Greek*. Oxford: 1889.

———, and Redpath, Henry Adeney. *A Concordance to the Septuagint*. 1897. Reprint. Oxford: 1975.

Heer, Friedrich. *God's First Love: Christians and Jews over Two Thousand Years*. Trans. Geoffrey Skelton. New York: 1970.

Heinemann, Joseph. *Prayer in the Talmud: Forms and Patterns*. Studia Judaica 9. New York: 1977.

Henle, Paul, ed. *Language, Thought and Culture*. Ann Arbor: 1958.

Herbst, Adolf. *Über die von Sebastian Münster und Jean du Tillet herausgegebene hebraeischen Übersetzungen des Evangeliums Matthaei*. Göttingen: 1879.

Herford, Robert Travers. *Christianity in Talmud and Midrash*. 1903. Reprint. Clifton, New Jersey: 1966.

Herlitz, Georg, and Kirschner, Bruno, eds. *Jüdisches Lexicon*. 4 vols. in 5. Berlin: 1927–1930.

Hill, David. *Greek Words and Hebrew Meanings: Studies in the Semantics of Soteriological Terms*. NTSM 5. Cambridge: 1967.

Hirsch, Samuel Abraham. "Early English Hebraists: Roger Bacon and His Predecessors." *JQR* 12 (1900): 34–88.

Hirsch-Reich, Beatrice. "Joachim von Fiore und das Judentum." In *Judentum im Mittelalter,* ed. Paul Wilpert, pp. 228–263.

Hoffmann, David. *Der Schulchan-Aruch und die Rabbinen über das Verhältniss der Juden zu Andersgläubigen*. Berlin: 1885.

Hoijer, H., ed. *Language in Culture*. Chicago: 1954.

Holtz, Traugott. *Untersuchungen über die alttestamentliche-Zitate bei Lukas*. Texte und Untersuchungen 104. Berlin: 1968.

Horning, Wilhelm. *Magister Elias Schadäus*. SIJL 31 (1892).

Huet, Pierre Daniel. *De Interpretatione*. Paris: 1661.

Hutter, Elias. *Polyglot New Testament*. Nuremberg: 1599.

Imbonati, Carlo Giuseppe. *Bibliotheca Latino-Hebraica sive De scriptoribus latinis, qui ex diuersis nationibus contra Iudaeos, vel de re Hebraica vtcumque scripsere*. Rome: 1694.

Isaac, Jules. *Genèse de l'Antisémitisme*. Paris: 1956.

———. *Jesus and Israel*. Trans. Sally Gran. Ed. Claire Hutchet Bishop. New York: 1971.

Jastrow, Marcus. *A Dictionary of the Targumim, the Talmud Babli and Yerushalmi, and the Midrashic Literature*. 2 vols. in 1. 1903. Reprint. Brooklyn: 1975.

Jenni, Ernst. "Das Wort ʿōlām im Alten Testament." *ZAW* 64 (1952): 197–248; 65 (1953): 1–35.

Jeremias, Joachim. *Jerusalem in the Time of Jesus*. Trans. F. H. Cave and C. H. Cave. 3rd ed. Philadelphia: 1969.

———. *Unknown Sayings of Jesus*. Trans. Reginald H. Fuller. 2nd ed. London: 1964.

Jocz, Jakób. *The Jewish People and Jesus Christ*. London: 1949.

———. "The Son of God." *Judaica* 13 (1957): 129–142.

Jona, Giovanni Battista [Rabbi Jona of Safed]. *Quattuor Evangelia Novi Testamenti ex Latino in Hebraicum sermonem versa* [*Four Gospels of the New Testament Translated from Latin into the Hebrew Language*]. Rome: 1668.

Jones, G. Lloyd. *The Discovery of Hebrew in Tudor England: A Third Language*. Manchester: 1983.

Jourdain, Charles Marie Gabriel Bréchillet. "De l'enseignement de l'hébreu dans l'Université de Paris au XVe siécle." In *Excursions historiques et philosophiques à travers le Moyen Age,* pp. 233–245. Paris: 1888.

Justin Martyr. *Dialogus cum Judaeo Trypho.* PG 6:471–800.

Käsemann, Ernst. "God's Righteousness in Paul." Trans. Wilfred F. Bunge. In *The Bultmann School of Biblical Interpretation: New Directions?,* ed. James M. Robinson et al. *Journal of Theology and Church* 1 (1965): 100–110.

Karpeles, Gustav. *Geschichte der jüdischen Literatur.* 2 vols. Berlin: 1886.

Kaufmann, David. "Ein Übersetzungsfehler bei den Synoptikern." *MGWJ* 37 (1893): 393–95.

______. "Franz Delitzsch—ein Palmblatt aus Judah auf sein frisches Grab." In *Gesammelte Schriften* 1:290ff. Frankfurt: 1908.

______. *Geschichte der Attributenlehre in der jüdischen Religionsphilosophie des Mittelalters von Saadja bis Maimûn.* 1877. Reprint. Amsterdam: 1967.

Kayserling, Meyer. *Biblioteca Española—Portugueza—Judaica.* Strasbourg: 1890.

Kedar-Kopfstein, Benjamin. "The Vulgate as a Translation." Ph.D. dissertation, Hebrew University, Jerusalem, 1968.

Kettilby, Joshua. *The Collection of Testimonies Concerning the Excellency and Great Importance of the Hebrew Sacred Language.* London: 1762.

Kilpatrick, George Dunbar. *The Origins of the Gospel According to St. Matthew.* Oxford: 1946.

Kittel, Gerhard, and Friedrich, Gerhard. *Theological Dictionary of the New Testament.* 10 vols. Trans. Geoffrey W. Bromiley. Grand Rapids: 1964–1976.

Klausner, Joseph. *Jesus of Nazareth.* Trans. Herbert Danby. 1925. Reprint. New York: 1956.

Klostermann, Erich. *Das Markusevangelium.* 4th ed. Tübingen: 1950.

Kosmala, Hans. " 'At the End of the Days.' " *ASTI* 2 (1963): 27–37.

______. "The Conclusion of Matthew." *ASTI* 4 (1965): 132–147.

______. " 'In My Name.' " *ASTI* 5 (1966–1967): 87–109.

Kraus, Hans-Joachim. *Psalmen.* 2 vols. Biblischer Kommentar: *Altes Testament.* Neukirchen: 1960.

Kraus, Xavier. "Die Handschriften-Sammlung des Cardinals Nicolaus v. Cusa." *Serapeum* 25 (1864): 353–365.

Krauss, Samuel. "Neuere Ansichten über 'Toldoth Jeschu.' " *MGWJ* 76 (1932): 586–603; 77 (1933): 44–61.

______, ed. *Das Leben Jesu nach jüdischen Quellen.* Berlin: 1902.

Kuhn, Karl Georg. *Achtzehngebet und Vaterunser und der Reim.* Wissenschaftliche Untersuchungen zum Neuen Testament 1. Tübingen: 1950.

Kutscher, Eduard Y. "Aramaic." *EJ* 3 (Jerusalem: 1971): 259–287.

______. "Das zur Zeit Jesu gesprochene Aramäisch." *ZNW* 51 (1960): 46–54.

Lagrange, Marie-Joseph. *Évangile selon Saint Marc.* 5th ed. Paris: 1929.

Lagumina, Bartolomo, and Lagumina, Giuseppe. *Codice Diplomatico dei Giudei di Sicilia.* 3 vols. Palermo: 1884–1895.

Laible, Heinrich. *Jesus Christ in the Talmud, Midrash, Zohar, and the Liturgy of the Synagogue.* Trans. A. W. Streane. Cambridge: 1893.

Legrain, Maroussia. *'Ashirah le-YH [I Will Sing to the Lord].* Jerusalem: 1969.

Le Long, Jacques. *Bibliotheca Sacra.* Paris: 1723.

Levenston, Edward A., and Sivan, Reuben, comps. *Millon Megiddo he-Ḥadish [The Megiddo Modern Dictionary]: English-Hebrew.* Tel-Aviv: 1966.

Levita, Elias. *Accentum Hebraicorum liber unus.* Trans. Sebastian Münster, Basel: 1539.

______. *Massoreth ha-Massoreth [Tradition of the Masorah].* Ed. Christian D. Ginsburg. 1867. Reprint. 2 vols. in 1. New York: 1968.

Levy, Jacob. *Wörterbuch über die Talmudim und Midraschim.* 4 vols. Berlin: 1924.

Lindeskog, Gösta. *Die Jesusfrage im neuzeitlichen Judentum.* Leipzig and Uppsala: 1938.

Lindsey, Robert Lisle. "The Ecclesiological-Ecumenical Issue." *UCCI News* 1 (1970).

______. *A Hebrew Translation of the Gospel of Mark.* Jerusalem: 1966.

______. *A Hebrew Translation of the Gospel of Mark [Sepher ha-Beśorah ʿal pi Marqus]: Greek-Hebrew Diglot.* Jerusalem: 1969.

______. "A Modified Two-Document Theory of the Synoptic Dependence and Interdependence." *NT* 6 (1963): 239–263.

Loeb, Isidore. "Polémistes chrétiens et juifs en France et en Espagne." *RÉJ* 18 (1889): 43–70, 219–242.

London Society for Promoting Christianity amongst the Jews. *The Liturgy of the Church of England.* London: 1837.

______. *New Testament in Hebrew.* London: 1813. Rev. eds. 1815, 1816, 1817, 1837, 1852.

Luther, Martin. *Sho'el u-Meshib Qaṭon [Shorter Catechism].* Trans. Aimo Murtonen. Jerusalem: 1960.

MacGregor, Geddes. *A Literary History of the Bible.* Nashville: 1968.

Maier, Johann. "Kontinuität und Diskontinuität: Jüdisches Erbe im christlichen Glauben." In *Judentum im christlichen Religionsunterricht,* pp. 7–45. Schriften der Evangelischen Akademie in Hessen und Nassau 93. Frankfurt: 1972.

______. "Die religiös motivierte Judenfeindschaft: I. Aus Missdeutung des jüdischen Selbstverständnisses." In *Judenfeindschaft,* ed. Karl Thieme, pp. 22–47.

______, ed. *Die Texte vom Toten Meer.* Munich and Basel: 1960.

Maigret, J. "God Spoke in Hebrew." *EncT* 2 (1968): 89ff.

Mandelkern, Saloman. *Veteris Testamenti Concordantiae hebraicae.* 2 vols. 1895. Reprint. New York: 1955.

Mann, Jacob. "An Early Theologico-Polemical Work." *HUCA* 12–13 (1937–1938): 411–459.

______. "Rabbinic Studies in the Synoptic Gospels." *HUCA* 1 (1924): 323–355.

Manson, Thomas Walter. *The Sayings of Jesus*. 1949. Reprint. Grand Rapids: 1979.

Marmardji, A. Sebastianus, ed. *Diatessaron de Tatien*. Beirut: 1935.

Marmorstein, A. "David Kimḥi Apologiste: Un fragment perdu dans son commentaire des Psaumes." *RÉJ* 66 (1913): 246–251.

Martini, Raymundus. *Pugio Fidei adversus Mauros et Judaeos*. Paris: 1651.

Marx, Alexander. "The Polemical Manuscripts in the Library of the Jewish Theological Seminary of America." In *Studies in Jewish Bibliography and Related Subjects: Studies in Memory of Abraham Solomon Friedus (1867–1923)*, pp. 265–278. New York: 1929. [Esp. Appendix I, "The Different Versions of ibn Shaprut's Even Bohan," pp. 265–278]

Marx, Jakob. *Verzeichnis der Handschriften-Sammlung des Hospitals zu Cues bei Bernkastel a/Mosel*. Trier: 1905.

Mercier, Jean. *Evangelium Matthaei ex Hebraeo Fideliter Redditum*. Paris: 1555.

Metzger, Bruce M. "The Language of the New Testament." In *The Interpreter's Bible*, ed. George Arthur Buttrick, 7:43–59. Nashville: 1951.

Migne, Jacques Paul, ed. *Patrologia: Series Graeca*. 168 vols. Paris: 1857–1868.

———. *Patrologia: Series Latina*. 222 vols. Paris: 1844–1855.

Miller, Madeleine Sweeny, and Miller, John Lane. *Harper's Bible Dictionary*. 8th rev. ed. New York: 1973.

Miskotte, Kornelis Heiko. *Das Judentum als Frage an die Kirche*. Wuppertal: 1970.

Moltmann, Jürgen. "Der Gott der Hoffnung." In *Gott Heute*, ed. Norbert Kutschki, pp. 116–126. Mainz: 1967.

Mowinckel, Sigmund. *He That Cometh*. Trans. George W. Anderson. Nashville: 1956.

Münster, Sebastian. *Diqduq de-Lishan arami 'O ha-Kasda'aḥ: Chaldaica Grammatica*. Basel: 1527.

———. *Epitome Hebraicae Grammaticae* [Mishley Shelomah Proverbia Solomonis]. Basel: 1520.

———. *Evangelium secundum Matthaeum in lingua Hebraica, cum versione Latina atque succinctis annotationibus*. Basel: 1537.

———. *Messias Christianorum et Iudaeorum, Hebraicae et Latine*. Basel: 1539.

———. *Sepher ha-Diqduq weha-Kol ha-Tebot Shinmeṣaw be-Lashon ha-Qadosh* [*Book of the Grammar and All the Words Found in the Sacred Language*]: *Grammatica Eliae Levitae*. Basel: 1537.

———. *Shilush Leshonot—Dictionarium trilingue*. Basel: 1530.

Néhèr, André. *L'Exil de la Parole: Du silence biblique au silence d'Auschwitz*. Paris: 1970.

Nes Ammim Verein Deutschland. *Nes Ammim—christliche Siedlung in Israel*. Bonn and Bad Godesberg: 1975.

Nestle, Eberhard. *Nigri, Böhm und Pellican: Ein Beitrag zur Anfangsgeschichte des hebräischen Sprachstudiums in Deutschland*. Marginalia und Materialen. Tübingen: 1893.

———, Nestle, Erwin, and Aland, Kurt. *Novum Testamentum Graece*. 25th ed. Stuttgart: 1963.

Neubauer, Adolf. *Aus der Petersburger Bibliothek.* Leipzig: 1866.
______. *The Book of Tobit: A Chaldee Text from a Unique Ms. in the Bodleian Library.* Oxford: 1878.
______. "Jewish Controversy and the 'Pugio Fidei'" *Exp* 7, ser. 3 (1888): 81–105, 179–197.
Nötscher, Friedrich. *Zur theologischen Terminologie der Qumran-Texte.* BBB 10. Bonn: 1956.
Nylander, K. U. "Ett unicum fran Upsala Bibliothek." *KT* 1 (1895): 231ff.
Oecolampadius, Johann. *DD. Ioannis Œcolampadii Et Huldrichi Zwinglii Epistolarum Libri Quatuor.* Ed. Theodor Bibliander. Basel: 1536.
Öhman, Suzanne. "Theories of the 'Linguistic Field,'" *Word* 9 (1953): 123–134.
Oesterley, William Oscar Emil. *The Jewish Background of the Christian Liturgy.* Oxford: 1925.
Oesterreicher, John M. *Der Baum und die Wurzel: Israels Erbe, Anspruch an die Christen.* Freiburg im Breisgau: 1968.
Orlinsky, Harry Meyer. *The So-called "Suffering Servant" in Isaiah 53.* Cincinnati: 1964.
Otto, Rudolf. *The Kingdom of God and the Son of Man: A Study in the History of Religion.* Trans. Floyd Vivian Filson and Bertram Lee Woolf. Boston: 1957.
Parkes, James. *Conflict of the Church and Synagogue.* Cleveland: 1961.
______. "Early Christian Hebraists." *Studies in Bibliography and Booklore* 4 (1959): 51–58; 6 (1962): 11–28.
Perrin, Norman. "The Son of Man in Ancient Judaism and Primitive Christianity: A Suggestion." *BR* 2 (1966): 17–28.
Petuchowski, Jakob J., and Brocke, Michael, eds. *The Lord's Prayer and Jewish Liturgy.* New York: 1978.
Pines, Shlomo [Salomon]. "Israel, My Firstborn—and the Sonship of Jesus, a Theme of Moslem Anti-Christian Polemics." In *Studies in Mysticism and Religion,* ed. Efraim Elimelech Urbach, Raphael Jehudah Zwi Werblowsky, and Chaim Wirszubski, pp. 177–190. Jerusalem: 1967.
______. *The Jewish Christians of the Early Centuries of Christianity According to a New Source.* Proceedings of the Israel Academy of Sciences and Humanities 2/13 (1966).
Polus, Matthaeus (Matthew Poole). *Synopsis Criticorum aliorumque S. Scripturae interpretum et commentatorum.* 5 vols. Frankfurt: 1678–1679.
Porzig, Walter. *Das Wunder der Sprache.* 5th ed. Bern: 1975.
Posnanski, Adolf. *Schiloh: Ein Beitrag zur Geschichte der Messiaslehre.* Leipzig: 1904.
Prijs, Josef. *Die Baseler Hebräischen Drucke, 1492–1866.* Ed. Bernhard Prijs. Olten: 1964.
Rabin, Chaim. "Noṣerim." *Textus* 5 (1966): 44–52.
______. *Die Renaissance der hebräischen Sprache.* Zurich: 1962.
______. *Toladot ha-Lashon* [*History of the Language*]. Jerusalem: 1968.
Re'emi, Samuel Paul, comp. *Analytical Concordance to the Delitzsch Hebrew Translation of the New Testament, Containing 90,000 Entries from the New Testament with Equivalents from the Greek Original.* 3 vols. Jerusalem: 1973–1974.

Renan, Joseph Ernest. *The Life of Jesus*. Trans. Charles Edwin Wilbour. 1864. Reprint. New York: 1955.

Rendtorff, Rolf. "Martin Bubers Bibelübersetzung." *'Em* 5 (1970).

Rengstorf, Karl Heinrich, and von Kortzfleisch, Siegfried, eds. *Kirche und Synagogue*. 2 vols. Stuttgart: 1968–1970.

Rheinfelder, Hans. "Dante und die hebräische Sprache." In *Judentum im Mittelalter*, ed. Paul Wilpert, pp. 442–457.

Richardson, Alan. *An Introduction to the Theology of the New Testament*. New York: 1959.

Riemer, Siegfried. *Philosemitismus im deutschen evangelischen Kirchenlied des Barock*. Stuttgart: 1963.

Robertson, William G. *The New Testament in Hebrew*. London: 1661.

Robinson, John Arthur Thomas. *Twelve New Testament Studies*. SBT 34. Naperville, Illinois: 1962.

Rosenthal, Erwin Isak Jakob. "Jüdische Antwort." In *Kirche und Synagogue*, ed. Karl Heinrich Rengstorf and Siegfried von Kortzfleisch, 1 (1968): 307–362.

Rosenthal, Jehuda M. "Defense and Attack in Medieval Polemical Literature." *Proceedings of the Fifth World Congress of Jewish Studies* 2:345–358. Jerusalem: 1969. [Hebrew]

______. *Ḥiwi al-Balkhi: A Comparative Study*. Philadelphia: 1949.

______. *Meḥqarim u-Meqorot* [*Studies and Sources in Jewish History*]. 2 vols. Jerusalem: 1967.

______. *Milḥamot ha-Shem* [*Wars of the Lord*], by Jakob ben Reuben. Jerusalem: 1963.

______. "Siphrut Hokoḥ ha-'Anti-Noṣerit ʿad Sop ha-Me'ah ha-Shemunah-ʿesreh [Literature of Anti-Christian Reproof until the End of the Eighteenth Century]." *'Aresheth* 2 (1960): 130–179.

______. "Targum shel ha-Beśorah al-pi-Matthai le-Yaʿqob ben Re'uben [The Hebrew Translation of Matthew by Jakob ben Reuben]: Early Hebrew Translations of the Gospels." *Tarbiz* 32 (1962): 48–66, III–IV. [Hebrew with English summary]

Rosenzweig, Franz. *Briefe*. Ed. Edith Rosenzweig. Berlin: 1935.

______. *Die Schrift und Luther*. Berlin: 1926.

Roth, Cecil. "The Disputation of Barcelona (1293)." *HTR* 43 (1950): 117–144.

______. *A History of the Jews in England*. 2nd ed. Oxford: 1949.

______. *A Short History of the Jewish People*. Rev. ed. London: 1953.

Saadia Gaon. *The Book of Beliefs and Opinions*. Trans. Samuel Rosenblatt. Yale Judaica Series 1. New Haven: 1948.

Salkinson, Isaac Edward. *The Epistle of Paul the Apostle to the Romans Translated into Hebrew*. Edinburgh: 1855.

______. *Ha-berit ha-Ḥadashah* [*The New Testament in Hebrew*]. London: 1885. [Reprinted 15 times 1886–1961]

Sandmel, Samuel. *A Jewish Understanding of the New Testament*. Rev. ed. New York: 1974.

Schechter, Solomon. "Notes on Hebrew MSS. in the University Library at Cambridge." *JQR* 6 (1894): 136–145.

Schilling, Konrad, ed. *Monumenta Judaica: 2000 Jahre Geschichte und Kultur der Juden am Rhein*. Vol. 2. *Handbuch*. Cologne: 1963.

Schirmann, Jefim. "Hebrew Liturgical Poetry and Christian Hymnology." *JQR* 44 (1953): 123–161.

Schmidt, H. *Cromwell und das Alte Testament*. Bonn: 1954.

Schneider, Peter. *Some Explanatory Notes to Dr. Levertoff's Liturgy: The Meal of the Holy King*. Jerusalem: 1966.

Schöffler, Herbert. *Abendland und Altes Testament*. Bochum-Langendreer: 1937.

Schoeps, Hans-Joachim. *Jüdisch-christliches Religionsgespräche in neunzehn Jahrhunderten*. 2nd ed. Frankfurt: 1949.

______. *Philosemitismus im Barock: Religions- und geistesgeschichtliche Untersuchungen*. Tübingen: 1952.

Scholem, Gershom Gerhard. *On the Kabbalah and Its Symbolism*. Trans. Ralph Manheim. New York: 1965.

______. *Von der mystischen Gestalt der Gottheit*. Zurich: 1962.

Schonfield, Hugh J. *The History of Jewish Christianity from the First to the Twentieth Century*. London: 1936.

Schott, Anselm. *Das vollständige Römische Messbuch*. 8th ed. Freiburg im Breisgau: 1941.

Schulte, Joseph. "Ein hebräisches Paternoster in einem Missale des 9. Jahrhunderts." *BZ* 6 (1908): 48.

Schweitzer, Albert. *The Mysticism of Paul the Apostle*. Trans. William Montgomery. 1931. Reprint. New York: 1955.

Segal, Moses H. "Mišnaic Hebrew and Its Relation to Biblical Hebrew and to Aramaic." *JQR* 20 (1908): 647–737.

Simon, Marcel. *Versus Israel: Étude sur les relations entre chrétiens et juifs dans l'Empire romain, 135–425*. Paris: 1948.

Simon, Richard. *Histoire critique du texte du Nouveau Testament*. Rotterdam: 1689.

Simpson, Edmund Kidley. *Words Worth Weighing in the Greek New Testament*. London: 1946.

Smalley, Beryl. *The Study of the Bible in the Middle Ages*. 2nd ed. New York: 1952.

Soury, Jules Auguste. *Des études Hébraiques et exégétiques au Moyen Age, chez les chrétiens d'Occident*. Paris: 1867.

Stählin, Rudolf, and Simmel, Oskar. *"Sakrament" in christliche Religion*. Frankfurt: 1969.

Stauffer, Ethelbert. *Die Botschaft Jesu—Damals und Heute*. Bern: 1959.

Steinschneider, Moritz. *Catalogus librorum hebraeorum in bibliotheca Bodleiana*. 1852–1860. Reprint. Berlin: 1931.

______. "Christliche Hebraïsten." *ZHB* 1 (1896–1897): 86–90; 2 (1897): 147–151.

______. *Die hebraeischen Uebersetzungen des Mittelalters und die Juden als Dolmetscher*. 2 vols. Berlin: 1893.

______. *Jewish Literature from the Eighth to the Eighteenth Century*. Trans. William Spottiswoode. 1857. Reprint. New York: 1970.

______. "Le Livre de la Foi: Paul Fagius et Sébastien Munster." *RÉJ* 5 (1882): 57–67.

______. *Ha-mazkir: Hebräische Bibliographie*. 21 vols. in 5. Berlin: 1858–1882.

______. "Vorlesungen über die Kunde hebräischer Handschriften, deren Sammlungen und Verzeichnisse." *Beiheft zum Zentralblatt für Bibliothekwesen* 7/19. Leipzig: 1897.

Stendahl, Krister. *The Scrolls and the New Testament*. New York: 1957.

Stern, Gustaf. *Meaning and Change of Meaning*. Göteborg: 1931.

Storosum, Ch. "Der jüdische Keim des sakralen Kirchengesanges." *Areopag* 1 (1966): 46–68.

Strack, Hermann Leberecht. *Jesus, die Häretiker und die Christen nach den ältesten jüdischen Angaben*. Leipzig: 1910.

______, and Billerbeck, Paul. *Kommentar zum Neuen Testament aus Talmud und Midrasch*. 6 vols. Munich: 1922–1961.

Strecker, Georg. *Der Weg der Gerechtigkeit*. Göttingen: 1962.

Suhl, Alfred. *Die Funktion der alttest. Zitate und Anspielungen im Markusevangelium*. Gütersloh: 1965.

Swete, Henry Barclay. *The Gospel According to St. Mark*. London: 1902.

Thieme, Karl. "Die religiös motivierte Judenfeindschaft: II. Aus christlicher und mohammedanischer Sicht." In *Judenfeindschaft*, pp. 48–79.

______, ed. *Judenfeindschaft: Darstellung und Analysen*. Frankfurt: 1963.

Thoma, Clemens. *Kirche als Juden und Heiden*. Vienna: 1970.

______. "Der Prozess Jesu im Religionsunterricht." In *Judenhass—Schuld der Christen?!*, ed. Willehad Paul Eckert and Ernst Ludwig Ehrlich, pp. 111–138.

Tremellius, Emmanuel. *Sepher Ḥaynuk Beḥirey-YH* [*The Book for the Instruction of God's Elect*, or *Catechism for Enquiring Jews*]. Strasbourg: 1554.

Turner, C. H. "Ο ΥΙΟΣ ΜΟΥ Ο ΑΓΑΠΗΤΟΣ." *JTS* 27 (1926): 113–129.

Tur-Sinai, Naphtali Hertz. *The Revival of the Hebrew Language*. Jerusalem: 1960. [Hebrew]

United Bible Societies. *Scriptures of the World*. Stuttgart: 1982.

United Christian Council in Israel. *Christian Terms in Modern Hebrew*. Jerusalem: 1966.

______. *Glossary of Christian Terms in Modern Hebrew*. Jerusalem: 1976.

Urbach, Efraim Elimelech. "Études sur la littérature polémique au Moyen-Age." *RÉJ* 100 (1935): 49–77.

Villanueva, Joaquin Lorenzo. *De la leccion de la Sagrada Escritura en lenguas vulgares*. Valencia: 1791.

Wagenseil, Johann Christoph, ed. *Tela ignea Satanae*. Altdorf: 1681.

Walde, Bernhard. *Christliche Hebraisten Deutschlands am Ausgang des Mittelalters*. Münster: 1916.

Weiner, Herbert. *The Wild Goats of Ein Gedi*. Cleveland: 1963.

Werblowsky, Raphael Jehudah Zwi. "On the Baptismal Rite According to St. Hippolytus." *StPatr* 2 (1957): 93–105.

Whorf, Benjamin Lee. *Collected Papers on Metalinguistics*. Washington: 1952.

Wilcox, Max. *The Semitisms of Acts*. Oxford: 1965.

Williams, Arthur Lukyn. *Adversus Judaeos: A Bird's-eye View of Christian Apologiae until the Renaissance*. Cambridge: 1935.

Wilpert, Paul, ed. *Antike und Orient im Mittelalter*. MiscMed 1. Berlin: 1962.

———. *Judentum im Mittelalter: Beiträge zum christlich-jüdischen Gespräch*. MiscMed 4. Berlin: 1966.

Winter, Jakob, and Wünsche, August, eds. *Die jüdische Literatur seit Abschluss des Kanons*. 3 vols. 1894–1896. Reprint. Hildesheim: 1965.

Winter, Paul. "Josephus on Jesus." *JHS* 1 (1968): 289–302.

———. *On the Trial of Jesus*. Studia Judaica. Forschungen zur Wissenschaft des Judentums 1. 2nd ed. Berlin: 1974.

———. "Zum Prozess Jesu." In *Judenhass—Schuld der Christen?!*, ed. Willehad Paul Eckert and Ernst Ludwig Ehrlich, pp. 93–101.

Wolf, Johann Christoph. *Bibliotheca Hebraea*. 4 vols. Hamburg: 1715–1731.

Zeitlin, Solomon. "The Halaka in the Gospels and Its Relation to the Jewish Law at the Time of Jesus." *HUCA* 1 (1924): 357–373.

Zifroni, Abraham, ed. *Hobot ha-Lebabot*, by Baḥya ben Joseph ibn Paquda. Jerusalem: 1949.

Zotenberg, Hermann. *Manuscrits orientaux: Catalogues des manuscrits syriaques et sabéens (mandaïtes) de la Bibliothèque Nationale*. Paris: 1874.

Zunz, Leopold. *Die Gottesdienstlichen Vorträge der Juden*. 2nd ed. Frankfurt: 1892.

Abbreviations

ACJD	*Abhandlungen zum christlich-jüdischen Dialog*
AST	*Analecta Sacra Tarraconensia*
ASTI	*Annual of the Swedish Theological Institute in Jerusalem*
BBB	*Bonner Biblische Beiträge*
BBG	*Baseler Beiträge zur Geschichtswissenschaft*
BEJ	*Beiträge zur Entwicklungsgeschichte des Judentums*
BJRL	*Bulletin of the John Rylands Library*
BR	*Biblical Research*
BZ	*Biblische Zeitschrift*
CD	Damascus Document
CNI	*Christian News from Israel*
DTC	Alfred Vacant, Eugène Mangenot, and Émile Amann, eds., *Dictionnaire de Théologie Catholique*
EJ	*Encyclopaedia Judaica*
'Em	*'Emunah*
EncT	*Encounter Today*
ET	*Expository Times*
Exp	*Expositor*
FF	*Face To Face*
HE	Eusebius *Historia Ecclesiastica*
HTR	*Harvard Theological Review*
HUCA	*Hebrew Union College Annual*
IEJ	*Israel Exploration Journal*
JA	*Journal Asiatique*
JES	*Journal of Ecumenical Studies*
JHS	*Journal of Historical Studies*
JJS	*Journal of Jewish Studies*
JQR	*Jewish Quarterly Review*
JSS	*Journal of Semitic Studies*
JTS	*Journal of Theological Studies*
KT	*Kyrklig Tidskrift*
LSPCJ	London Society for Promoting Christianity amongst the Jews
LTK	*Lexikon für Theologie und Kirche*
MGWJ	*Monatschrift für Geschichte und Wissenschaft des Judentums*

MHP	*Miscellanea Historiae Pontificiae*
MIO	*Mitteilungen des Instituts für Orientforschung*
MiscMed	*Miscellanea Mediaevalia*
MT	Masoretic Text
NEB	New English Bible
NT	*Novum Testamentum*
NTS	*New Testament Studies*
NTSM	*New Testament Studies.* Monograph Series
PG	Jacques Paul Migne, ed., *Patrologia: Series Graeca*
PL	Jacques Paul Migne, ed., *Patrologia: Series Latina*
RÉJ	*Revue des Études Juives*
RSV	Revised Standard Version
RT	*Revue Thomiste*
SBT	*Studies in Biblical Theology*
ScrHier	*Scripta Hierosolymitana*
SIJL	*Schriften des Instituts Judaicum in Leipzig*
StPatr	*Studia Patristica*
TEV	Today's English Version (Good News Bible)
ThLB	*Theologisches Literaturblatt*
UCCI	United Christian Council in Israel
VT	*Vetus Testamentum*
Vulg.	Vulgate
ZAW	*Zeitschrift für die alttestamentliche Wissenschaft*
ZHB	*Zeitschrift für hebräische Bibliographie*
ZKG	*Zeitschrift für Kirchengeschichte*
ZNW	*Zeitschrift für die neutestamentliche Wissenschaft*
ZTK	*Zeitschrift für Theologie und Kirche*

Index

Index of References

1. Biblical Writings

C. *APOCRYPHA*

2. RABBINIC AND RELATED WRITINGS

3. THE KORAN

Index of Hebrew Terms